PRAISE FOR 'SEVEN SUMMERS'

"Welch's background as a journalist is clear here, as he engagingly relates his experiences ('The High Sierra was the stuff of Michelangelo') … . [He] acknowledges that Cheryl Strayed's book Wild *brought many hikers to the trail. But this account, exploring how people connect along the way and how two older men can push themselves to walk over 2,000 miles, never feels derivative—it's refreshing and authentic. A spirited, honest, and funny memoir, perfect for nature lovers."*

—Kirkus Reviews

"After reading scores of accounts of walking the Pacific Crest Trail that begin in the desert south and proceed linearly and predictably, Bob Welch's account of completing the PCT with his brother-in-law, Glenn, is refreshingly bumpy. Written with self-deprecating humor, Seven Summers *seems part Bill Bryson's* A Walk in the Woods, *part Barney Mann's* Journeys North, *but all uniquely The Oregon*

Boys. The book is accessible for those who have never set foot on the trail and enjoyable reading for seasoned veterans. I appreciate the quality of Welch's prose and the deeply personal nature of the journey—and, of course, the setting is the magnificent PCT."

—**Rees Hughes,** Co-Editor, *Crossing Paths: A Pacific Crest Trailside Reader (2022), A Pacific Crest Trailside Reader: California (2011),* and *A Pacific Crest Trailside Reader: Oregon and Washington (2011)*

"Seven Summers *is pure trail magic. Bob Welch is a relatable and humorous storyteller, and his decade-long Pacific Crest Trail quest—with its many twists and turns—is genuinely moving, as much about embracing relationships and 'hiking your own hike' as about reaching the Canadian border. I devoured this book like a fresh stack of pancakes, as will any reader who loves a grand adventure."*

—Noah Strycker, PCT thru-hiker who reached Canada in 2011 and author, *Birding Without Borders: An Obsession, a Quest, and the Biggest Year in the World*

"Bob Welch's Seven Summers *is a 2,650-mile, can't-put-it-down trek along America's western backbone. With every footsore step of the way, Welch brings us endless thrills, nail-biting suspense, and his trademark deadpan humor. He is the master of metaphor and the silly simile. He toggles from reverence to irreverence, taking us to spiritual heights on lofty peaks, then hurtling us back to earth with 'toilet paper stuck to the back of your sandal' scenes. You're going to love this book!"*

—A. Lynn Ash, author, *Vagabonda: Solo Camper Out West*

"With Twain-like humor and humility, Welch reveals life on one of America's greatest trails. Follow him along the annual human-powered conveyor belt of extremes in nature, the daily nitty-gritty, the surprise encounters, and the many triumphs of endurance. This is a book that makes you laugh out loud—and sometimes cringe in sympathy. A walk, and a read, well worth the trip."

—**James Meacham,** co-editor, *The Atlas of Oregon* and *The Atlas of Yellowstone*

"Seven Summers *is not a map of the PCT trail, but a guide to what true friendship means and the steep, winding path that leads there. Nearly every chapter includes loving, quirky portraits of 'strangers who became friends': Cisco and Roadrunner, Hot Dog, Malto, Eagle Eye, and others. At the center are the lifelong bonds between The Oregon Boys, Bob and Glenn—and between Bob and his wife Sally, who leaves loving notes in his backpack and picks up her smelly husband at trail's end. Kindness abounds: A restaurant reopens to feed starving hikers. A friend of Bob's, Geoff, drives a thousand miles to take Bob and Glenn to dinner. That*

Bob's friends returned his love wasn't 'trail magic,' but affirmation that unselfish acts of kindness get paid forward. Faith is the wind at Bob's back, lifting spirits, softening grief, and healing blisters."

—Brent Northup, veteran film critic and head of the Communication Department at Carroll College, Helena, Montana

"Seven Summers *is part perspiration and part inspiration, a splendid tale of American can-do-ism delivered by a master storyteller. Welch is, once again, at his best in this robust and humorous account of hiking the Pacific Crest Trail. The book places us alongside Bob and Glenn, right down to the climbs, heat, trail dust, and 'cat holes.' We also get an honest and highly personal look at The Oregon Boys, flaws and all. Upon reaching journey's end—after Bob and Glenn's hard-to-conceive 2,650 miles on the trail—I found myself savoring what must have been their profound satisfaction in this enormous accomplishment, even if Welch doesn't trumpet it himself. The account is enhanced still further by Don White's pen and ink drawings that deepen both the human and nature scope of the story.*

"One needn't be a long-distance hiker to be captivated by this remarkably crafted story of friendship, teamwork, and commitment!"

—Stuart McDowell, author, *The Last Lighthouse Keeper*

"Bob Welch is the king of similes and specifics, and his magic touch continues in Seven Summers, *beginning with 'feeling less energetic than a smoked salmon.' Reading this book, you'll experience the terrain, the challenge, the elevation changes, and the incredible landscapes right along with Bob and his hiking partner. Most of us will never hike the PCT, but, reading* Seven Summers, *we are grateful that Bob did it for us."*

—Dorcas Smucker, author, *Coming Home to Roost*

"In Seven Summers, *Bob Welch draws on his journalism background to weave a clear and compelling story of hardship, beauty and personal growth. As he juxtaposes the discomforts of long-distance hiking with the stunning landscapes he encounters, Welch transforms from goal-oriented hiker to lover of nature, which he describes as poetically as John Muir."*

—Dave Imus, creator of award-winning maps of Oregon and the United States.

Other books by Bob Welch

Cross Purposes
Saving My Enemy
The Wizard of Foz
52 Little Lessons from A Christmas Story
Lessons on the Way to Heaven
My Oregon III
52 Little Lessons from Les Misérables
Cascade Summer
Resolve
52 Little Lessons from It's a Wonderful Life
My Oregon II
Pebble in the Water
My Oregon
American Nightingale
The Things That Matter Most
My Seasons
Where Roots Grow Deep
A Father for All Seasons
More to Life Than Having It All

Collaborative efforts

1972 (with Steve Bence)
Leave No Man Behind (with Dr. Tony Brooks)
Boy in the Mirror (with Jim Bartko)
Healing Wounds (with Diane Carlson Evans)
Letters from Dachau (with Clarice Wilsey)
i am n (with The Voice of the Martyrs)
Easy Company Soldier (with Don Malarkey)

Children's books

The Keyboard Kitten (Illustrated by Tom Penix)
The Keyboard Kitten Gets Oregonized (Illustrated by Tom Penix)

To Sally and Ann,
without whom this adventure would not have been possible.

To my hiking partner, Glenn,
whose commitment to our journey and to me never wavered.

And to the memory of my brother-in-law, Greg,
with us in spirit.

PCT hikers breaking camp below Washington's 12,280-foot Mount Adams at 6:50 A.M. August 31, 2016.

SEVEN SUMMERS
(AND A FEW BUMMERS)

BOB WELCH

With pen and ink drawings by Don White

Ragamuffin Books
New York London Paris Yachats

Front cover pen and ink drawing by Don White.

Back cover photo by Glenn Petersen of Welch at Mica Lake near Glacier Peak in Northern Washington, August 2021.

Cover design, maps, and graphics by Bob Welch.

All photos in book by Bob Welch unless otherwise noted.

Mileage for places along the trail, and for elevation, is based on the *Pacific Crest Trail Data Book,* sixth edition, 2022.

The total mileage for the trail is based on the Pacific Crest Trail Association's common use of 2,650 miles. The trail expands and shrinks each year, depending on fire re-routes, trail modifications, etc., but the PCTA's distance is generally accepted.

Ragamuffin Books
New York London Paris Yachats

ISBN: 9798398476705

Printing 100123.1000a

Also available as an e-book and audio book, read by the author, on amazon.com

To contact the author:

Email: bobwelch@bobwelchwriter.com

Web: bobwelchwriter.com

Snail mail: PO Box 70785, Springfield, OR 97475

Twitter: @bob_welch23

Call him not old whose visionary brain
Holds o'er the past its undivided reign,
For him in vain the envious seasons roll
Who bears eternal summer in his soul.

—Oliver Wendell Holmes Sr.

MAP OF THE BOOK: 2011–18

MAP OF THE BOOK: 2019–22

2019: NORTH FROM MEXICO & SOUTH FROM LAKE TAHOE

2021: CALIFORNIA DESERT, HIGH SIERRA, & NORTHERN WASHINGTON

2022: CALIFORNIA DESERT & NORTHERN WASHINGTON

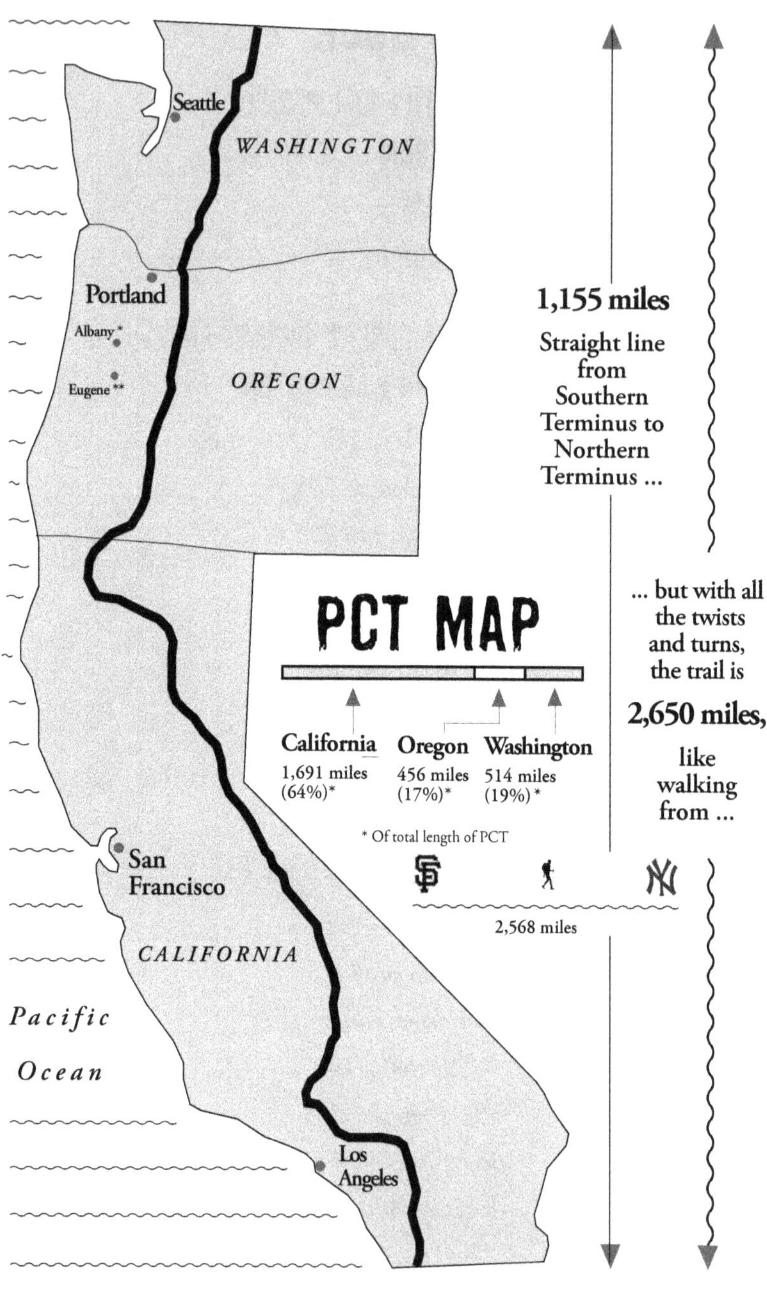

* Home of Glenn Petersen
** Home of Bob Welch

PCT ELEVATION

Mount Everest = 29,035'

Trail ascends 489,418 feet and descends 488,411 feet. The nearly one million-foot elevation change is equal to hiking up and down 16 Mount Everests—from sea level.

FIRST PART OF THE TRAIL

Side view of mountains, looking west

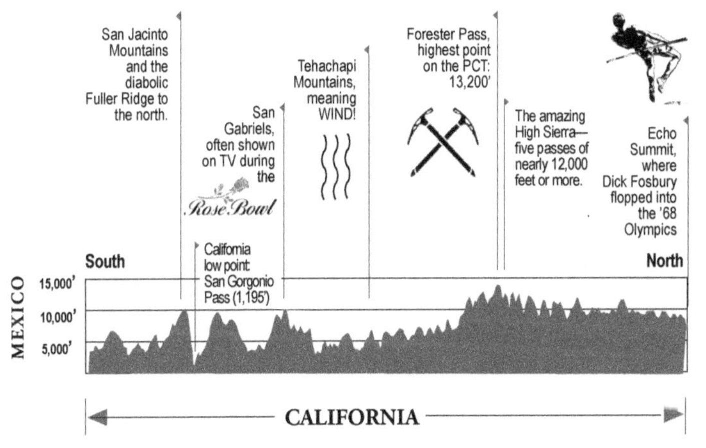

SECOND PART OF THE TRAIL

Side view of mountains, looking west

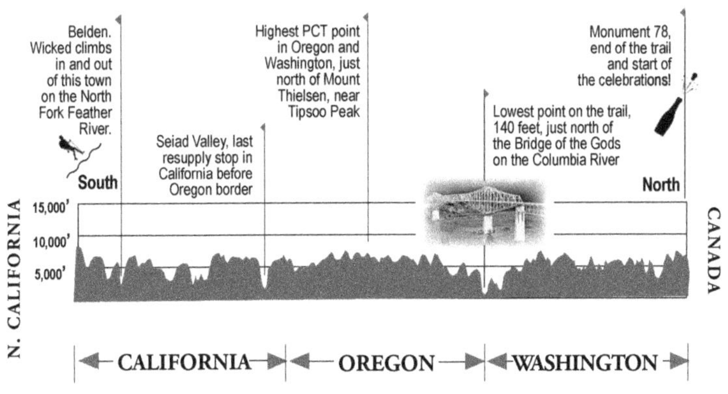

PACIFIC CREST TRAIL
NATIONAL SCENIC TRAIL

TRAILHEAD IN

THE LURE OF THE PCT

Without trails, we would be lost.
—Robert Moor, *On Trails: An Exploration*

It was July 2013, and after a fifteen-mile hike near Oregon's North Sister, I was lying outside my tent with all the energy of a smoked salmon. "I'm dead," I said to my brother-in-law Glenn.

In 2011, we'd hiked more than ninety percent of the Oregon portion of the Pacific Crest Trail before being thwarted by the Dollar Lake Fire on Mount Hood. A year later, we completed the 456-mile trail.

Now, after the second of a three-day, forty-five-mile loop around the Three Sisters, we were waiting for the sun to set so we could justify going to sleep feeling only partly wimpy instead of totally wimpy. Our fifteen miles had felt like thirty—on broken glass. My feet were toast. My body spent. My mind parched.

"Why do we do this long-distance hiking?" I asked. "Why can't we be like normal hikers? Why can't we hike eight miles, arrive midafternoon, read, nap, cook a hot meal, watch a sunset, make s'mores, contemplate the meaning of life in the stillness of dusk, then fall asleep beneath a starry sky? Maybe even brush our teeth at some point?"

"So, you mean, why be normal when we can end a day like this—too tired to untie our shoes?" asked Glenn.

"Exactly."

I thought of how in 2010, after Glenn accepted my offer to hike the

Oregon PCT with me, I had challenged him with ten reasons why I thought it was a horrible idea. My motive was simple: to see whether he really wanted to do it or simply liked *the idea* of doing it. His response?

"I am in."

He was. And I was. But that was then, and this was now.

"I'm done," I said. "No more of this for me."

Glenn did not respond. I assumed he didn't want to go there, couldn't hear me—we both had hearing challenges—or had fallen asleep, perhaps all three. But, hey, we had accomplished our original goal—to hike the Oregon PCT. I had written a book, *Cascade Summer,* about the experience. It was time to move on.

Months later, Glenn emailed me. No small talk. No clearing of his throat. No acknowledgment that I had made it clear I was not taking another step on the trail, in fact, had stated in Eugene's newspaper where I worked, *The Register-Guard,* that "the PCT is an itch I've scratched." Instead, just: "How about hiking the 211-mile John Muir Trail in California this summer? It overlaps the PCT."

Without hesitation, I replied, "I am in."

My reversal seemed rooted in the same inexorable pull reflected in John Muir's iconic words: "I hear the mountains calling; I must go." Or, more contemporarily, Richard Dryfuss's character in *Close Encounters of the Third Kind* being drawn to the Devils Tower. It made no sense; he just knew he had to be there. And so did I.

My decision defied logic. I mean, really: The trail was for young people who had time, trim bodies, and a sense of immortality. On those counts, I was 0-for-3: busy, bulky, and turning sixty in February 2014. But, strangely, I never considered saying no to Glenn's offer.

Hiking the John Muir Trail would prove to be a gateway drug to highs I'd never imagined—and to lows that would bring me to tears. The summer of 2014 and those that followed would prove to be among the richest seasons of my life, beckoning me to write a second hiking book, the one you're now holding in your hands or listening to in your ear buds. Not to say: *Wow, look what I did!* But to say: *Hey, look what any of us can do, even if, at first, our idea might have seemed outlandish.*

BEFORE WE HIT the literary trailhead, some context: In speaking to audiences about *Cascade Summer*, I found most people had only a cursory understanding of the PCT, as did I before embarking on the trail. Many saw the Mexico-to-Canada journey as little more than a pine-needled Interstate 5.

Uh, not so much.

▲ First, finding flat stretches on the PCT is like finding unbroken sand dollars on the beach; only about ten percent of the trail resembles anything level. It climbs nearly sixty mountain passes and descends into nineteen major canyons. The trail ascends 489,418 feet and descends 488,411 feet, its nearly one million feet in elevation change the equivalent of hiking from sea level to the summit of Mount Everest and back down sixteen times. It dips as low as 140 feet at the Columbia River in Washington and climbs as high as 13,200 feet at Forester Pass in California. "The PCT has only four directions," a fellow hiker once told me. "Up and upper, and down and downer."

▲ Second, it twists like a snake, dives like a seahawk, and soars like an eagle for a distance farther than San Francisco is from New York. Though 2,650 miles in length, it would, if stretched straight, be only 1,155 miles long. The PCT is carved into two of the most rugged mountain ranges in North America and, thus, must travel the often-diabolical twists and turns of the terrain.

▲ Third, while mostly benign, in places the PCT requires hikers to cross streams that pound downward in violent torrents, to endure triple-digit temperatures, and to navigate knife-edge trails flanked by dual drop-offs of a thousand feet or more. Some PCTers have finished their hikes not in Canada but in rescue choppers. Some have gone missing. Some have perished.

▲ Fourth, the trail is incredibly diverse, a patchwork quilt of wilderness wonder that passes through seven national parks and twenty-five national forests. Southern California's desert brings the threat of rattlesnakes and heat exhaustion. The snowy Sierra Nevada, a 400-mile-long block of sculpted granite, sometimes requires micro spikes and ice axes. After months of experiencing above-the-timberline views, hikers entering Oregon's Cascades can sink into claustrophobic depression at what some call "The Green Jungle." And in Washington, September rains have rusted the spirits of countless PCT hikers, sometimes soaking them into submissions of defeat.

▲ And, finally, yes, at times the trail *is* covered with pine needles. But you also might find yourself walking on ice, snow, slush, sand, scree, shale, cinder, stream bottoms, sawdust, rocks, roots, boulders, lava, logs, bogs, grass, granite, gravel, plants, dirt, pine cones, fir cones, animal bones, plank bridges, log bridges, suspension bridges, jagged ridges, dirt roads, gravel roads, paved roads, and horse manure. And, at times, over logs, under logs, and around logs.

All of which helps explain why of the more than 100,000 people who have attempted to hike the entire PCT, not many more than 10,000 are estimated to have completed it, only about twice the number of those who have summited Mount Everest. The highest completion rate in a single year (2014) has been thirty-four percent, according to the annual PCT Survey.

So, what was an old guy like me doing on the trail in the first place? The median age of PCT hikers is thirty-three and only eight percent are sixty or older. In 2015, when I committed to doing the whole thing, I was sixty-one.

My purpose in hiking the PCT wasn't to "win one for the Q-Tips," the seniors who should be rocking away over a good Sudoku challenge. To prove I could do it. To escape something. Or to find myself.

Instead, I was simply intrigued by the possibilities. The unknown. The adventure the trail offered. Curiosity had driven my forty-year career in journalism, and I was now intrigued by a few delicious questions: *Could I do this? Could I survive? And if I did, what would I discover in the process?*

The trail, because of smart phones, GPS devices, and lightweight equipment, has never been easier to hike—no, wait, *less hard* to hike—than it is now. In 1970, eighteen-year-old Eric Ryback of Michigan completed a north-to-south PCT trip using an aluminum-frame pack and paper maps. Unlike today, he had no PCT-specific app on which he could see where water, campsites, and resupply points were—or trade helpful info with hiking friends along the trail. But on May 1, 2000, when the U.S. Air Force Space Command outside Colorado Springs pressed a button to inaugurate something called the Global Positioning System (GPS), following a trail became far easier. That said, any hikers who think such relative luxuries will get them to Canada are like young baseball players who think a $500 bat is going to get them to the big leagues. Nope, you still must swing the thing and meet the ball. Likewise, those who complete the entire PCT still must take the same number of steps Ryback took—six million.

FINALLY, a few housekeeping chores:

▲ First, while I partnered with my brother-in-law on this trip, the observations, opinions, and analysis are strictly mine. I'm not speaking for the both of us. In other words, blame me, not him.

▲ Second, because some will have read *Cascade Summer* about my 2011 Oregon adventure and others will have not, I've condensed that book into the first five chapters of *Seven Summers*—without the historical Judge John Waldo side story. I'm hoping that's enough to refresh the memories of those who have read it and enough to bring up to speed those who have not. That said, if you're interested only in the post-Oregon story, feel free to skip ahead to Chapter 6 on page 83.

▲ Third, to help hikers orient themselves to the trail, the PCT is numbered by miles, starting south from the U.S.-Mexico border near Campo, California, and going north to Monument 78 at the U.S.-Canada border.

Discrepancies exist on exactly how long the trail is. I go with 2,650 miles because that's what the Pacific Crest Trail Association goes with. However, for my on-trail numbers, I use the *Pacific Crest Trail Data Book,* even though it measures the trail at 2,652.6. The trail changes in length every year when sections are rebuilt. What's more, fires and other unforeseen factors can force "workabouts"—Plan Bs—that change the length. Bottom line: At times, there will be some inconsistencies in the numbers, but that's inevitable—and OK.

▲ Finally, this is a book of creative nonfiction. Much of it can be documented by notes I kept; emails, text messages, blog posts, and satellite communication reports of mine that I saved; photographs I took; books, articles, and maps I read; and people I interviewed, most notably the partner with whom I shared the journey, Dr. Glenn Petersen. Conversations are offered from the best of my memory with the intent of capturing the spirit of an exchange, if not a word-for-word replay. And when I've used hyperbole it's usually in splashes of humor involving true incidents that, like fish stories, get larger with the telling. As Mark Twain wrote in *The Adventures of Huckleberry Finn*: "There was things which he stretched, but mainly he told the truth."

Here, then, is my truth, my story, my adventure of hiking the Pacific Crest Trail.

Bob Welch
Eugene, Oregon
August 2023

1 MAIN PACK

Loads from top

Turn page to see specific items stowed inside

*
Used foam pad 2011-18; stored on top, outside

Items 2 and 3 below not drawn to scale in relation to main pack

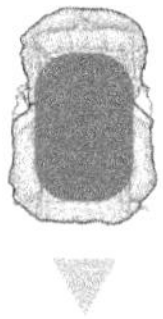

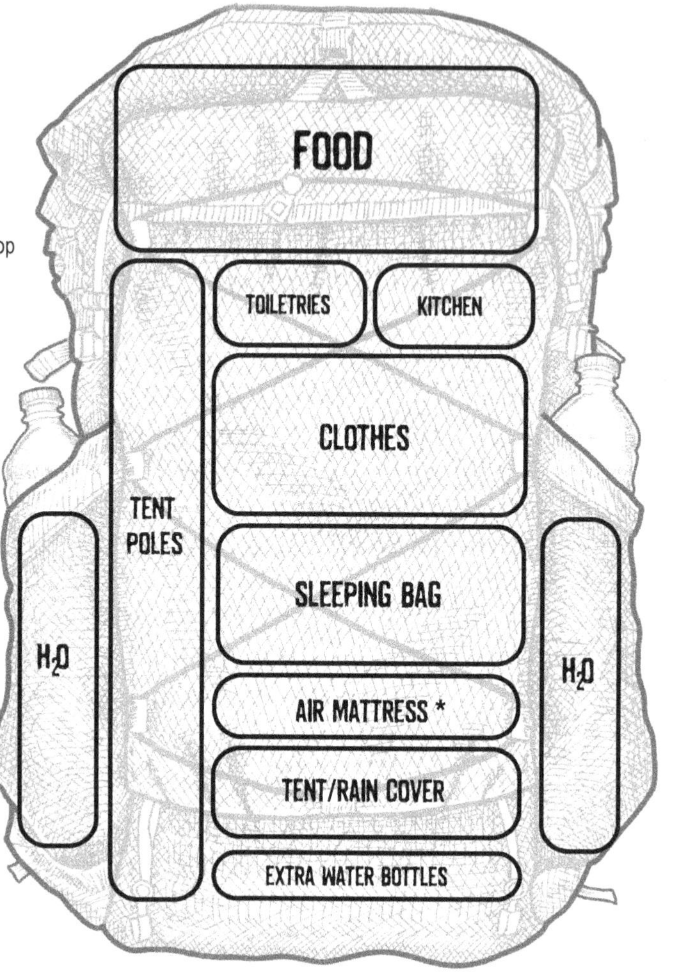

FOOD

TOILETRIES

KITCHEN

CLOTHES

TENT POLES

SLEEPING BAG

H_2O

H_2O

AIR MATTRESS *

TENT/RAIN COVER

EXTRA WATER BOTTLES

2 OUTER NETTING ON MAIN PACK

(Back of pack: loads from top into netting)

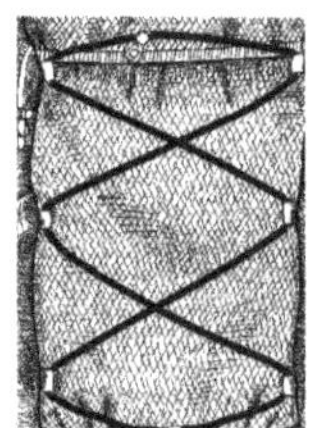

Headlamp
Water filter
Foot-care bag
Emergency kit
Extra sunglasses
Rain wear/pack cover

Clipped to front right shoulder strap of main pack: GPS device (Spot Connect, 2011-18), Garmin InReach Mini Explorer (2019-22)

3 HIP BELT STORAGE

(Front: zippered pockets)

POCKET ABOVE

IPhone/ear buds
Sunblock
Knife

On zipper pull tab:
Rope from my Dad's 1980s pack

POCKET ABOVE

Beef jerky
Trail mix
Misc. candy

On zipper pull tab:
Small, plastic REI thermometer

AGE 57

2011

OREGON

1 INSIDE BACKPACK *

SLEEP: Tent—Six Moon Designs Lunar Solo (2011-18), Nemo Hornet 1-Person Ultralight (2019-22). **Pad**—Therm-a-Rest Z-Lite accordion (2011-18), blow-up mattresses (2018-22). **Bag**—Mountain Hardwear Phantom 32 down. **Pillow**—Exped (2011-18; misc. after that.)

WATER: 100-ounce CamelBack bladder (2011-14). Two 1 L. Smart Water plastic bottles (2015-22), filled, with two to four empties, depending on water availability on each stretch.

FOOD: **Utensil**—One plastic spork. **Stove**—Glenn packed a Jetboil (2011-18) and I took spare fuel canister, then went "cold" (2018-2022). **Breakfast**—Svenhard's Danish variety pack (2012-16), Quaker Chewy Dipps (Chocolate Chip) (2016-19), Hostess Baby Bundts (2021-22). **Lunch**—Mission Street Tacos with Jack Links Beef & Cheese Sticks, potato chips, full-size candy bar. **Dinner**—Freeze-dried meals (2011-17), Mission Street Tacos with various packaged tuna flavors (2018-22). **Snacks**—Jack Links jerky, orange slices, Cinnamon Bears, licorice, trail mix, nuts, and miscellaneous candy, heavy on the chocolate.

CLOTHES (TO WEAR WHILE NOT HIKING): Sleep socks, sleep boxers, nylon long-sleeve shirt, long johns (upper and lower), down jacket, stocking cap, gloves, and Buff bandana; one spare pair hiking underwear and socks to wear on alternate days.

TOILETRIES: Toothbrush, handle sawed by half; toothpaste squeezed into 2x2-inch plastic bag; floss stick; Wet Ones (one tissue per day); Anti Monkey Butt (for chaffing); meds; Tums; ear plugs; toilet paper (one roll, cardboard core removed, of course!).

MISC.: IPhone, Anker backup battery, book, card-sized notebook, cash, credit card, driver's license, permits.

* **Backpack itself:** ULA Ohm, 2011-18; ULA Catalyst, 2019-22.

2 OUTER NETTING ON MAIN PACK

Water filter: Katadyn Hiker Pro (2011-2014), Katadyn BeFree 1.0 L (2015-22).

Foot care: Duct tape (2011, which was really dumb), Kinesio Tape, Second Skin, and metatarsal pads (2018-22), needle (for popping blisters).

Wet weather: REI rain jacket (2011-16), Frogg Togs rain suit (2017-22). Pack cover.

Emergency kit: Three extra headlamp batteries, space blanket, first-aid kit, whistle, 15 feet of tent line, Bic lighter, matches, insect repellent, mosquito head cover, EpiPen (for a malady I had called mastocytosis), safety pins, spare main pack waist buckle.

3 HIP BELT POCKETS

See previous page for detailed list of items.

4 WEARING WHILE HIKING

Clothes—Dri-fit shortsleeve t-shirts, Columbia six-pocket detachable pants, Under Armor Boxer Jock Johns (2012-18), Deluth Trading Co. Armachillo Cooling Boxer Briefs, thigh length (2019-22), wide-brimmed sun hat. **Shoes**—Merrill Moab Ventilators (2011-15), Asic trail shoes (2016-17), various Altras (2018-22). **Socks**—Darn Tough (2012-18), Liners and Wrightsock (2019-21), just Wrightsock (2022). **Gaiters**—REI and Dirty Girl.

Trekking poles: Eight different pairs over the years: REI, Leika, and Black Diamond.

1

COMMITMENT

The trails of the world be countless, and
Most of the trails be tried;
You tread on the heels of the many, till you
Come where the ways divide;
And one lies safe in the sunlight, and the
Other is dreary and wan,
Yet you look aslant at the Lone Trail, and
The Lone Trail lures you on

—Robert Service

I heard her footsteps before I actually saw her. It was August 1999 and, amid the hardened black lava that gives Oregon's Old McKenzie Pass a lunar landscape look, I had just reached the main north-south trail after a short hike to the top of 6,872-foot Little Belknap Crater. I was sitting on a rock, waiting for my brother-in-law, Glenn Petersen, who wasn't far behind on a trail so easy that some do it in flip-flops.

"Morning," I said.

"Hello," said a northbound young woman perhaps half my age, well-tanned, shouldering a good-sized pack, and not panting like the forty-five-year-old guy greeting her.

"Where'd you start?" I asked, wiping the sweat from my nose with a backhand.

"You mean today or in the beginning?"

"The beginning, I guess."

"Mexico."

I nearly fell off the rock.

"And you're finishing where?"

"Canada."

Obviously, this wasn't time for me to boast about bagging Little Belknap. Instead, I fished out a pen and a pad of sticky notes from my day pack.

"I'm starting soon as a columnist at *The Register-Guard* in Eugene, about sixty miles west of here," I said. "I'd love to write about you after your trip is over. Would you mind if I got your email address and contacted you?"

"Hey, I live in Eugene, too," she said. "I'm a student at the University of Oregon."

"No way," I said, extending a hand. "Bob Welch."

"Laura Buhl," she said, accepting the shake.

She was, I soon learned, twenty-six. Had been on the trail for nearly five months. Was hiking on her own, averaging twenty-one miles per day. And hoped to finish September 25, celebrate with friends in Seattle, then start classes at UO the next day.

"What's your first class?" I asked.

"Jog-Run."

THE DAY I met Laura Buhl was the day I discovered the Pacific Crest Trail. Until then, I'd never heard of it, even though my father, who had died three years before I'd met Buhl, had hiked portions of the PCT's precursor in Oregon, the Skyline Trail.

In my interview with Buhl two months later—she reached Canada on the exact date she hoped to—I learned that the PCT stretched from Mexico to Canada, mainly near the crest, or mountain tops, of the Sierra Nevada Range in California and the Cascade Range in Oregon and Washington.

"I've always been intrigued by the romance of the border-to-border trip," Buhl told me for my column. "Two borders. One trail. It's perfect."

Perfect, yes. But perfect for young folks such as Buhl who had the time, unencumbered lives, and bones, tissues, and muscles of youth. Not perfect, however, for old folks like me with full-time jobs, a handful of book deadlines, and more body fat than free time.

But even if the idea of hiking a PCT section wouldn't germinate for more than a decade, the seed had been planted. Slowly, the possibilities took root. In 2009, at age fifty-five, I enlisted Glenn and my son Ryan, then thirty, to see if we could do something that I'd insisted to my *Register-Guard* column readers was possible: in Lane County, where I lived, to watch a sunrise from the lowest point (sea level at Florence) and a sunset at the highest point (the 10,363-foot South Sister) in a single day.

We did it. We started at the Pacific Ocean at 6:11 A.M., ate breakfast in Eugene, fly-fished the McKenzie River, played nine holes of golf at Tokatee Golf Club, drove to Devils Lake west of Bend, and climbed 5,000 feet to see a wisp of sunset atop the South Sister at 6:26 P.M.

That experience got me thinking back to Buhl and the PCT. Hiking the entire trail was out of the question. I had a job in which readers expected three columns a week. I had a wife (Sally), two sons (Ryan and Jason), two daughters-in-law (Susan and Deena) and two grandchildren (Cade and Avin, children of Ryan and Susan) whom I didn't want to be away from for five months. That said, I began listening to a still, small voice: *Oregon. Just do Oregon.*

IT WAS a call to return to something that once had been part of my life but had been put on the shelf now for twenty-five years: hiking high-mountain trails.

The back country had long been in the Welch blood. In a 1905 journal about his neighborhood baseball team in Portland, my father's father, Will Adams, drew sketches revealing his love for the outdoors even as a teenager. "Season's over," said one. "Now for camping." In another: "Back to the woods."

Decades later, he camped with his son, Warren—my father—at Sparks Lake near the South Sister. As a teenager, Dad would hitchhike with his buddies from Portland to the Eagle Creek Trailhead on the Columbia Gorge. Backpacks on, they'd fish the creek while hiking to Wahtum Lake, fish the lake while there, and fish the creek en route back.

In 1946, at twenty-two, he married a woman, Marolyn Schumacher, who loved to camp, even if she never forgave the man for taking them fishing to Three Creek Lake on their honeymoon.

In the 1960s, Dad, a professional photographer, made a movie called *Trout in the High Country*, whose final words were a poignant plea that the wilderness would still be as available, and as untamed, for his son as it had been for him. I inherited the man's woodsy wanderlust.

I was raised in Tuffy boots that I wore on family backpack trips to places such as Breitenbush and Bagby Hot Springs. And became the teenager whose room was literally wallpapered in *Sports Illustrated* photos except for a poster of a hallowed forest, upon which John Muir's words whispered: "In God's wildness lies the hope of the world—the great fresh unblighted, unredeemed wilderness."

Physical challenges of all types intrigued me. As a teenager, I was enamored by the story of sixteen-year-old Californian Robin Graham sailing around the world, as chronicled in his book *Dove*. As a college student, with my buddies John Woodman, Jay Locey, and "Dandy" Dan Roberts, I began hiking deeper into the woods, higher into the sky, and longer into the summer. Over the years I became the only known person wacky enough to travel the seven miles on the beach from Oregon's Yachats to Waldport by walking, running, bicycling, skim boarding, and hitting a golf ball on a 12,320-yard, par-72 hole I designed myself. (I shot a four-under-par 68.)

In my nearly six decades, I had run cross-country in high school, two marathons, the Hood-to-Coast Relay, and dozens of 10Ks. But in my mid-fifties, pain in the metatarsal region of my feet forced me to stop running. So, instead, I began walking, which morphed into hiking.

My two sons played baseball. Welch summers had been devoted to following maps to ballparks, not to high-mountain lakes. Now, however, those boys were men and that season of my life was over. Time was ticking. And I had deep respect for poet Dylan Thomas's view that we should "not go gentle into that good night," but instead "rage against the dying of the light." So, in the spring of 2010 I made the decision: I would hike the Oregon portion of the Pacific Crest Trail.

The announcement prompted raucous protest from my well-worn second metatarsal joint on my right foot. But I had a good orthopedic doc, Don Jones; I would find a way.

Sally offered her blessing, though we agreed it wouldn't be wise for me to hike alone. The two of us were different in many ways. She was quilter to my writer, patience to my impetuousness, and reason to my risk. But she saw, and appreciated, my passion for this journey, for which I would forever be grateful.

The question was: Who was going to be my plus-one?

If I had been writing an old-time classified ad for such a partner, I would have said something like this:

> Me: Fifty-six-year-old Adventure Lite guy seeking male buddy to hike Oregon portion of PCT. I like rain, fog, snow, sailing, used-bookstores, and quiet walks on the beach followed by night-putting with glow-in-the-dark golf balls. Contemplative. Curious. Complicated. And zany. (Once read a pocket-sized dictionary on a backpack trip.). High energy, low organization. Love fast food and most chocolates, especially Milk Duds. Addictions: beyond the aforementioned, reading, writing, Pepsi, and sports. Four strangers I'd choose to have dinner with if I could: writer/storyteller Garrison Keillor; writers David French and Ann Voskamp; and, if you could

bring one back from the dead, World War II nurse Frances Slanger.

You: Can hike 456 miles and withstand pain, boredom, and—most significantly—*me.*

I needed someone with a zest for hiking and the outdoors. Someone who had the flexibility to get the time off. And someone who could stay committed for a month on the trail. But as the ad suggested, most of all I needed someone who could put up with a sometimes quirky partner, which was concerning for the same reason W.C. Fields famously said, "I don't want to belong to any club that will accept me as a member."

As a sailor, I knew the maritime rule: Each day you spend on a small boat with someone else shrinks the vessel by a foot. And being with someone 24/7 on a taxing trail seemed like a land-locked sailboat experience. So, who could I get to round out this two-person team?

"I know," said She Who Knows All. "Glenn."

When Sally suggested her sister Ann's husband, my reaction was like an NFL fan hearing his team's No. 1 draft pick was not a skill position player but an offensive guard. A guy who blocks. *Wha, wha.*

Glenn, after all, gave Ann Pyrex one Valentine's Day. Did a triathlon using a bicycle that had upright handlebars and a plastic child's seat on back. And after going to Hawaii for a medical convention told me, "I don't *get* that place." His favorite Disneyland attraction had long been the Tiki Room—*seriously.* For Christmas, I once gave him a signed copy of a book that seemed to speak to his life: *Dare to Be Dull,* personally autographed to Glenn by the author, Joseph L. Troise, whom I'd interviewed in Seattle. He loved it, of course, quietly proud of his independent nature.

And yet this was the guy who I might be with for thirty days and 456 miles?

"Don't you see?" said She Who, "he's *exactly* what you need. He's not someone who's going to drive you crazy by talking all the time; you can do that to him. Plus, he's a doctor. And an Eagle Scout."

Hey, that *was* a pretty good combination, considering I hated the sight of blood and, as a fourth-grader, had been kicked out of a Cub Scout meeting by Kenny Clark's mom for acting up. I later quit Scouts altogether, a freckle-faced rebel not only without a cause, but without a Tenderfoot Badge.

In terms of personality, Glenn was like the human embodiment of the Hippocratic Oath: "At first, do no harm." He wasn't going to get on my nerves or be yapping all the time. And in terms of skills, he knew how to treat a sprained ankle and tie a clove hitch, which might come in handy.

IRONICALLY, GLENN and I had first gotten to know each other while backpacking on Eagle Creek, a trail that had been approved as a PCT alternative. On Memorial Weekend 1974, Sally and I—soon to be engaged—joined Glenn and Ann, whom Glenn was dating, for a backpacking trip in the Columbia River Gorge. At the time, Glenn looked like a young John Denver, complete with the granny glasses, and drove a 1952 Chevrolet. While at a side creek to get water, the two of us got into a good-natured water fight to impress our respective girlfriends. I won. He says he won. We had been competing ever since, most passionately at golf and Scrabble, both of which he usually won, but just barely.

In many ways, Glenn and I were opposites, in TV's "Odd Couple" terms my Oscar Madison (sportswriter slob) to his Felix Unger (fastidiously organized). He had grown up in Eugene, home of the more liberal University of Oregon, and attended Oregon State University, for whom he now rooted. I had grown up in Corvallis, home of the more conservative OSU, and attended UO, for whom I now rooted. I was a columnist at *The Register-Guard* in Eugene; Glenn was a family practice doctor in Albany, forty miles north. I was more socially outgoing; he, at best, let others carry a conversation and, at worst, dozed off at family gatherings. I wore my feelings on my sleeve; he could be facing total calamity and be less animated than the Mount Rushmore presidents.

In many ways, however, we were similar. Same ages, essentially, Glenn just eighteen months older: my fifty-six to his fifty-seven in spring 2010. Married to two best-friend sisters. Independent. And a common Christian faith.

We were bound by a birthday card we'd ping-ponged back-and-forth for more than thirty years. And by a certain trust in each other that cut deep—literally; after a round of golf in the mid-1980s, he'd done my vasectomy back at his doctor's office. (With him in an obvious power position and me not wanting to risk retaliation, I had purposely let him win the golf match. And it all worked out: Sally and I, with two great sons, had no more children.)

But here's what made us most compatible: beneath all the joking, we respected each other deeply. Though he was a prime target for my comedy—something, I think, he enjoyed, at least most of the time—he knew, deep down, that I held him in high esteem. He was all those Boy Scout things—brave, honest, loyal, etc., as if he'd just walked out of the organization's 1964 handbook—but more: A great husband. A caring father. A committed believer whose faith played out in the real world without hypocrisy.

I remember exactly when I realized his true character. By his mid-thirties, Glenn, along with Ann, was deeply involved in Christian medical teams volunteering in Haiti, the poorest country in the Western Hemisphere. In 1988, he talked me into joining the team for a fifteen-day trip. One afternoon, a "tap-tap," a Haitian bus that carried about five times as many people as it was designed for, flipped. Half a dozen people had been injured, some seriously.

While serving as a gopher, I watched as Glenn and the medical staff calmly stopped what they were doing and treated the injured. As I watched him tend to those in need, his gloved hands covered in blood, I saw my brother-in-law more clearly than ever before. Later, after the clinic had closed, our team gathered for dinner, but Glenn wasn't there. I wandered over to the church. There he was, quietly setting up the sound system for our evening service.

That was Glenn Petersen. He was as earnest as Jefferson Smith, played by Jimmy Stewart, in *Mr. Smith Goes to Washington*. And kind to a fault. He didn't rub it in when his Beavers beat my Ducks, nor did I when my Ducks beat his Beavers. He could beat me at golf and not gloat. I could beat him at Scrabble and only gloat for a short time—unless it was a decisive win in which further humiliation seemed justified, like if I'd won with a triple-word doozy like "squeeze."

All in all, although Glenn wasn't the "let's-go-deep" guy I'd rush to if my world were crumbling, I decided She Who was right: he would make a great long-distance hiking partner. But was he even mildly interested? I asked.

"Sounds fun," he said. "Let's do it!"

That wasn't good enough for me. I remembered advice I'd read from a PCT book called *The Cactus Eaters* by Dan White about not quitting when conditions were at their worst. If you really think you must quit, a hiker suggested, quit when conditions were at their best. That will prove that your decision was based on well-considered logic instead of knee-jerk emotion—after, say, hiking twenty miles with blisters in a cold downpour.

So, in the spirit of "conditions at their worst," I sent Glenn an email with ten reasons why hiking the Oregon PCT was a really bad idea, ranging from "sixteen to twenty-one miles per day" to "a long time away from our families" to "dehydration, starvation, snake bites, mosquitoes, etc."

On July 1, 2010, he sent a three-word email reply: "I am in."

I WAS STOKED.

"Let's do a shakedown cruise," I wrote to him. "See if this is realistic."

On August 13, 2010, we stuffed ourselves at the Vida Cafe east of Eugene and headed an hour to the Willamette National Forest to hike on the PCT near the 10,085-foot North Sister. I wanted to learn what, if any, of our existing equipment could be used. (Only a little, I learned). What changes we might need to make regarding what to bring. (Less of everything.) And what thirty to forty miles in a weekend actually felt like. (Ouch.)

We hiked eight miles Friday night and fifteen Saturday, returning to the trailhead in the late afternoon with plans to get in a few more miles before dark. The schedule then had us climbing to the top of Scott Mountain Sunday. But I was mentally shot. Sitting with my back to a tree, I had no desire to take another step. So I cast my verbal fly rod to see if Glenn would bite.

"Let's just grab a burger at the Vida Cafe and call it good."

It was a euphemistic smokescreen for what I was really saying: "Let's quit. I'm in over my head. The PCT is a pipe dream." I wasn't at all proud of the suggestion, but pride evaporates fast when you're too tired to even reach for your water bottle.

Glenn's response may have been the most critical line spoken in our entire hiking experience together. He didn't berate me. He didn't guilt me. But he also didn't acquiesce to me. Instead, he got me a second bottle of water and said: "Rest a little more, then we'll get going. We got this, Bob!"

And he was right. We made it to the top of Scott Mountain and reached our goal: thirty-four miles between Friday night and noon Sunday. Had Glenn given in to my whim, it's possible we would have bagged the whole PCT idea. But he didn't give in and we didn't quit.

If that was *the* pivotal moment, two others that weekend inspired me: first, meeting a PCT hiker whose advice was "hike your own hike" and, second, meeting Helen Chou, an eighty-year-old Korean woman who had hiked the 1,692-mile California portion of the trail and was now doing Oregon. Her pack was only slightly smaller than a refrigerator, but her perseverance equally large.

I came home, wrote "Chou" on a sticky note for inspiration, and vowed that Glenn and I would hike the 456-mile Oregon portion of the PCT in midsummer 2011.

I BEGAN TRAINING a full year in advance: Hikes to the top of nearby Spencer Butte and Mount Pisgah with a backpack carrying a ten-pound wrestling trophy I'd received as a white-elephant Christmas present. Stadium stairs at Sheldon High. P90X CrossFit workouts. The works.

If I was in an airport and had a spare half hour, I'd find stairs to go up and down. Nearly a third of PCT hikers don't train at all before starting the trail, according to a 2022 PCT Survey. As an Old Guy, I believed I had to.

Soon after my column on the trial hike was published in *The Register-Guard*, a reader invited me to lunch. A tad younger than I, Craig Mayne had hiked the Oregon section of the PCT the previous summer, ironically, with his brother-in-law—at least to start. (His brother-in-law got bad blisters, and quit. That, I figured, would be me.)

When Craig and I met, he already had a three-page list of suggestions for me. Nonetheless, between bites, I peppered him with question after question. What kind of water filter did he take? What didn't he take that he wished he had? What *did* he take that he wished he hadn't?

"Splurge on one item," he said. His was a 3.4-ounce blow-up pillow. "Made all the difference. Slept like a baby." I bought a pillow just like Mayne's. Glenn planned to carry a solar battery pack to power his GPS and our iPhones, mine of which would be used first, for maps; second, as a way to communicate home; and third, as a way to post updates on my *Register-Guard* blog.

The stereotype suggests hiking is about simplifying your life, but the deeper I got into planning, the more complex I realized this journey would be. Preparing required hundreds of decisions over the smallest of details. Though my life would need to fit into a thirty-to-forty pound pack, I still needed most of the same basic "systems" of my non-trail life, only in miniature: food, water, shelter, clothes, emergency supplies, entertainment, even sanitation, meaning an ultra-light six-inch aluminum shovel to dig "cat holes" so I could bury the solid waste six inches in the ground—and plastic doggy bags to store my used toilet paper, which in wilderness areas had to be packed out.

Every what-to-bring decision pitted one concept against the other: comfort vs. hardship, safety vs. danger, and emotion vs. function. Oranges and apples were fun to eat and would give me an emotional boost. But would they be worth it? No. Too much weight for too little benefit. But the pillow was only a little more weight for a lot of benefit. *Bring it!*

Choosing what to pack was an exercise in compromise, a puzzle with no perfect solution. You can eye-roll the fifty-pound limit airlines impose on passengers for checked bags, but the experts know the end game: If everyone brings just a little bit extra, the plane won't get off the ground. As the Spanish proverb says: "On a long journey, even a straw weighs heavy."

Deciding on food was particularly challenging. If I'd need 5,000 to 6,000 calories a day to compensate for the energy required to walk fifteen to twenty miles, I would need a lot of bang for my buck with each bite. A key consideration, then, was calories per ounce. Tortilla wraps come in at 100 calories per ounce, breakfast pastries 120, trail mix 130, Snickers bars 150, and peanut butter 170.

While I loosely set a minimum standard of items with at least 100 calories per ounce, I also wanted to enjoy my food. To me, food was one of the rewards for hard miles hiked. At 240 calories per ounce, olive oil is as efficient as you can get, but who wants to bathe everything they eat in it?

To save weight, I got creative. I would take a college football magazine, but only after ripping out all advertising and stories I knew I wouldn't read. I would take a novel, but only a small, skinny book, ripped into thirds. (It brought a whole new concept to the idea of "light reading.") I'd take the first section and have the other two sent to me at resupply points.

My imagination became friend and foe. I could conjure creative ways to pack light, but I could also imagine tragic endings, often accompanied by headlines like:

Eugene Man Lost on PCT;
'Should Have Brought Whistle,'
Says Eagle Scout Brother-in-Law

A safety whistle, though light, was likely to never be blown, but if you were lost, it could save your life. I would bring one. On the other hand, swimming trunks would come in handy at lakes, but nylon, quick-dry underwear would function just as well. I would not bring trunks. To find multiple uses for a single item was like a triple-word Scrabble play: underwear for swim trunks, trekking poles to prop up your tent, socks for emergency gloves.

You could, I realized, overthink the weight stuff. I'd heard of hikers being chided by purists for not removing the label from their plastic water bottles. That said, ounces could quickly become pounds—and, yes, I "de-cored" the cardboard tube from within my roll of toilet paper.

Long-distance hiking, I came to realize, meant preparing to live like a minimalist even as I maximized my Visa card. The Eugene REI store became my home away from home. I lay awake nights, wondering whether I could, say, get by with a plastic trash bag or should take an actual poncho. Or whether I should use safety pins or straw-size bungee cords to affix the previous day's socks and underwear to my pack to dry them out . By the day we left, I would easily have more than $1,000 into my preparation.

Since our shakedown, I had cut 5.14 pounds of gear by upgrading only four items. I replaced a 4-pound backpack with a 1.38-pound ULA Ohm; a 4.19-pound tent with a 1.71-pound Six Moon Designs Lunar Solo; a 2.25-pound sleeping bag with a 1.44-pound Mountain Hardwear Phantom 32; and a 2.5-pound blow-up sleeping pad with a 0.61-pound Therm-a-Rest Z-Lite sleep mat.

At the same time, I'd added what some would call extraneous, but I would call essential: a small segment of one-eighth-inch rope taken from my father's old aluminum-frame backpack and tied to mine. Just to honor the man who introduced me to the wilderness.

THE LAST month before our departure I was locked into my usual hurly-burly schedule. I had a book deadline. Glenn had just returned from Haiti. He was working three jobs, not only at his family practice but at an urgent care facility and at a juvenile detention center, then running the streets of Albany as late as 11 P.M. every night.

"What are your three biggest fears?" I asked him.

"That's easy," he said. "Snow, snow, and snow."

The winter had produced near-record snowfalls in West Coast mountains, making trails slippery, slow to travel, and hard to find. The challenge wasn't just the extra time snow required or the difficulty of following the trail, but the danger it puts hikers in when they would be on steep slopes.

Two weeks before departure, we gathered at the Welch abode in Eugene for a four-person summit: Glenn, Ann, Sally, and me. As our official navigator, Glenn had mapped our camping, water, and resupply stops—five of the latter—for all thirty days.

Because neither of us could be off work for a whole month, we would break the trip into a couple of two-week sections. Our first stretch, July 22 to August 5, 2011, would be from the California border to Central Oregon's Elk Lake, 57 percent of the trip; the next section, August 16 to August 26, from Elk Lake to the Bridge of the Gods on the Columbia River.

In our backyard, we pored over maps that I'd tacked to the side of the house. And Glenn demonstrated his full-body mosquito netting.

"Whataya think?" he said.

"I think I would rather be eaten alive by mosquitoes than be seen in that."

More seriously, we discussed a topic we'd just as soon avoid. The protocol if one of us, for any reason, had to leave the trail. An illness. A sprained ankle. Something else unforeseen. Was this "both in/both out?" Or should the "other guy" feel free to proceed, assuming, of course, that the person with the illness or ailment was safely en route home? Our decision: If he so desired, the healthy hiker should feel free to continue on his way to the Columbia.

Not, of course, that we expected to face such a decision.

Welch family collection

Welch family collection

Top: In a 1905 sketch book based on his Portland youth baseball team, my grandfather, Will Adams, suggested that he pined for the outdoors even as a teenager. Above: That's him (white hat) camping in the 1930s at Sparks Lake in Central Oregon with his wife Fay and their fish-on-finger teenage son, Warren, who would become my father.

Welch family collection

Welch family collection

Top: That kid holding the fish on the previous page grew up and married Marolyn Schumacher, who shared his love for the trees and trails of Oregon's Cascade Range. Above: Me eating camp breakfast with sister, Linda, and father, Warren, at Breitenbush Hot Springs, circa 1960, just a few miles from what would become the PCT. Note Beaver sweatshirt long before my interest in journalism nudged me to the University of Oregon.

Welch family collection

Petersen family collection

Petersen family collection

Top: Back to nature in my longhair twenties. Above left: The book I gave Glenn to commemorate his independent approach to life. Above: Glenn and me in 1979, looking about fifteen. Actually, I was twenty-five and he was nearly twenty-seven.

Welch family collection

Courtesy of Laura Buhl

Above: In 1996, two days before he would die of congestive heart failure at seventy-two, my father and I were together with the family celebrating his and Mom's fiftieth anniversary at Black Butte Ranch in Central Oregon. I was forty-two. He'd always said when it was his time to go he wanted to hike into a favorite high Cascades lake and "let winter take me home." Noting that he died at a plush resort snug to the mountains, I told Mom, "I guess he just took the deluxe route." Left: Three years after my father died, a stranger, Laura Buhl, introduced me to the PCT when I met her near Little Belknap Crater in 1999.

FIRST SUMMER

START: JULY 22, 2011

GOAL: NORTH 456 MILES
FROM CAL.-ORE. BORDER
TO ORE.-WASH. BORDER

Section shown on map, below

Elevation this section (feet)

Start	6,068
End	219
High	7,572 (North of Mt. Thielsen)
Low	219 (Bridge of the Gods)

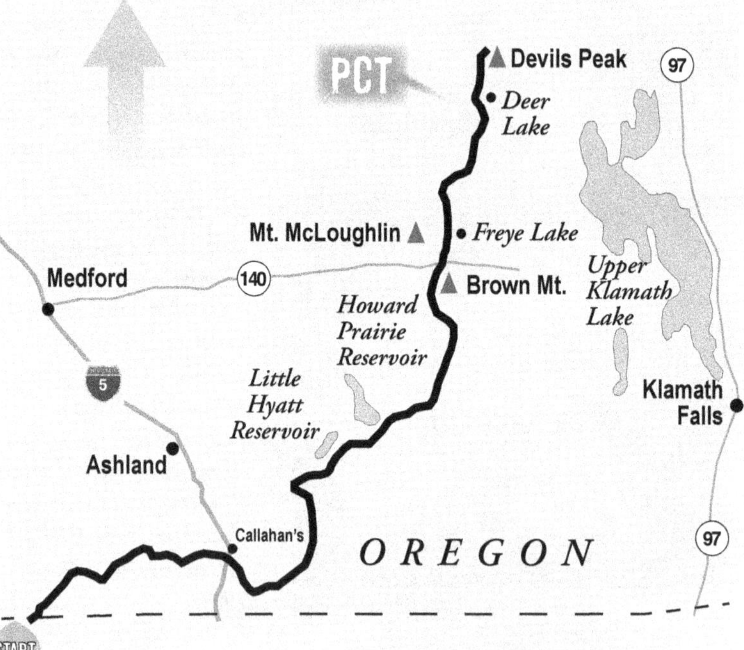

2

BAPTISM

No first step can be really great; it must of necessity possess more of prophecy than of achievement; nevertheless, it is by the first step that a man marks the value, not only of his cause, but of himself.

—Katherine Cecil Thurston

After navigating a maze of U.S. Forest Service roads for more than an hour, the Welches and Petersens arrived at a place I'd imagined for more than a year: the Oregon-California border. It was thick with trees and, I presumed, memories for thousands of PCT hikers over the years, who, after 1,692 miles of California, had finally reached a new state.

We had barely stepped out of the Petersens' Isuzu Trooper when we saw two backpackers heading north toward us: both thirtyish, both slim, and both clearly trail-hardened. The biggest difference was his dark, Brillo-pad beard contrasted with her blonde ponytail.

"Are you guys actual PCT hikers?" I asked.

"That's us, mate," said the man.

"Welcome to Oregon," I said.

"Thanks, I'm Ben [Dyer]," he said, extending a hand, "and this is my partner, Kate [Manning]."

Australians, they had started at the Mexican border in April and, among "thru-hikers"—technically, Glenn and I were "section hikers"—believed themselves to be behind only a guy they called Marcus, a hiker from Germany.

Ann fetched the couple apples, pop, and red licorice—"thank you so much," they said as they shed their packs—and we talked for about twenty minutes. About their journey thus far. About the trail ahead. And about the seemingly unending snow in the Sierra Nevada; "at one point, I fashioned myself some crampons out of trail shoes and roofing nails," said Ben.

He was, we would come to learn, a do-it-yourself guy who used walking sticks he'd made from tree branches instead of conventional trekking poles. Glenn, who'd fiddled with his own DIY projects ranging from tarp tents to pop-can stoves, was enthralled with Ben. In the record snow, Ben and Kate made it through the High Sierra with no GPS, just a map and compass. *Wow.*

"Where you headed?" Ben asked

"Just doing Oregon," I said. "Weirdly, you caught us right at our departure."

"Great! Maybe we'll see you at Callahan's," he said, referring to the hiker-friendly lodge on Interstate 5 just south of Ashland, a two-day walk for us.

They left. After posing for photos at the sign on a tree indicating the Oregon-California border, I looked at Glenn.

"Time out?"

He looked at his Casio, whose face, weirdly, was always on the inside, not outside, of his wrist.

"One-twenty-three," he said.

"Copy that."

With that we took the first of what we'd expected to be one million steps, the amount, we'd read, that Oregon required.

That night, after twelve miles, some in foreboding patches of deep snow and the last six with an aggravating blister, I had just wiggled into my bag when I smelled something inside my tent.

"Ahhhhhhh!"

"What?" Glenn said from his neighboring tent. "Cramp?"

"No, *cat.*"

"Huh?"

"I hung my tent on the boys' old basketball hoop in the carport a couple of nights ago after spraying it with mosquito repellent. A neighborhood cat obviously sprayed on it."

The laughter from Glenn's tent erupted like a Yellowstone geyser.

AS A REPORTER, I had long ago learned the wisdom of asking questions. So, when we met a threesome trail-named the Colorado Boys the next morning, Saturday, July 23, 2011, I asked what advice they'd offer a couple of newbies.

"Ten by ten," one told us.

"Meaning?"

"We try to get ten miles in by 10 A.M. Get a good, early start."

I quickly did the math. "Are you kidding?"

"Nope. Dead serious."

I looked at Glenn. "How 'bout we just try to be the two-by-fours?"

Later, when we reached Callahan's Mountain Lodge, it seemed like an undeserved blessing: the "PCT Special." Hikers got a shower, dinner, breakfast, and a place on the back lawn to throw a sleeping bag for only $40. All juxtaposed against a soon-to-start wedding, for which guests were wearing formal wear.

"With the wedding out back, if you wouldn't mind pitching your tents until a bit later that would be appreciated," an affable young man at the desk told me.

"Sure, no problem."

As trail-worn hikers arrived, so did guilt—at least for me. Given that these folks had been on the PCT for more than three months and we had been on it for less than three *days*, I couldn't help but feel a bit like Rosie Ruiz. She was the marathoner who appeared to have won the women's division of the 1980 Boston Marathon, only to be stripped of the title when it was learned she had joined the race only half a mile from the finish line.

But if we were rookies, Ben and Kate didn't treat us that way. When we bumped into them while waiting for a shower in the corner of a maintenance building, they welcomed us into the conversation like old friends.

"Good to see you, mates," said Ben.

With a pair of tin snips, he was fashioning a metal wind break for his stove. We started sharing a bit about ourselves. Ben, thirty-one, was interested in hearing about the life of a newspaper columnist and, after learning I did a little sailing, about boats.

"I'd like to sail," he said. "First, I'd like to kayak the Amazon River, then I've been thinking about sailing around the world. What kind of boat do you think I'd need to build? I'd like to build my own boat."

It was like asking for investment advice from a kid counting Chuck E. Cheese tokens.

"You don't want me telling you what kind of boat to build to sail around the world in," I said. "I sail a twenty-two-foot Catalina on a lake near Eugene that averages fourteen feet in depth and feels like bath water. Much different than sailing around the world."

He laughed. His partner, Kate, grimaced. Twenty-nine, she was deep in conversation with Doc Petersen about what he believed could be a stress fracture in her foot, certainly not surprising considering how far she'd come.

Both were schoolteachers on sabbaticals. They were mellow, affable, and loved the trail.

"People help each other out," Ben told me. "Like in the High Sierra. Marcus, the German guy, lost his sunglasses. We fixed him up with a makeshift pair."

From a shopping trip after a hitch into Ashland, Ben tucked a twenty-four-ounce can of Foster's Premium Ale into his pack.

"I've got this little tradition," he said. "I get down the trail a bit, then leave one of these for a PCT hiker behind me."

When the July sky started fading blue to black, we rolled out our bags on the lodge's back lawn—no tent tonight—as Ben and Kate set up a homemade tarp tent with a speed and precision suggesting this wasn't their first rodeo. Nineties music blared from the deck, but I was too enamored by the sky to notice; I saw two shooting stars that night, a sort of celestial "welcome to the trail," I surmised.

An hour after finally falling asleep, I was awakened by a thrashing around of something. A wedding guest, presumably a touch tipsy, had tripped on Ben and Kate's tarp lines and nearly fallen on top of me. We'd now experienced it: our first wildlife on the trail.

On Sunday morning, Glenn and I climbed east into the lower reaches of the southern Cascades, through a pine-oak woodland, the two of us fueled by stacks of Callahan's pancakes and a desire to put the sound of the freeway behind us. We hiked with Ben and Kate. Good conversation. Nice views of Pilot Rock. And a short chat with three PCT section hikers, one of whom introduced herself as "Dream Dancer."

"And your trail names?" she asked.

"Bob and Glenn," said Glenn.

I'd been toying with "QuackPacker," to reflect a backpacker whose alma mater was the University of Oregon Ducks, but didn't offer it.

"No, no, no," Ben interjected. "You're 'The Oregon Boys.'"

It was like being blessed by the Pope himself.

AT HYATT LAKE Resort the next morning—ours was a slow withdrawal from civilization—we spread dew-soaked sleeping bags on picnic tables to dry, one of the downsides of "cowboy camping" without tents. Inside the restaurant, with permission, I recharged my iPhone. We would not see an electrical outlet for another eighty miles, at Crater Lake.

Beyond us, only two parties were eating: three locals who obviously knew the chef and waitress, and a man and woman roughly our ages. They were clean and tidy. In other words, not the kind of folks who had slept in horse dung the previous night, as Glenn and I discovered we had. After introducing ourselves, we learned they were Californians, married, and heading north to Canada on the PCT, having started in Sierra City, California, seven weeks and 400 miles ago.

"Roadrunner," the woman said with a slight accent. *Swiss? German?*

"Cisco," said the man, holding out a hand to shake as a smile creased beneath a salt-and-pepper beard.

The moment of truth had arrived. Did I dare introduce myself as Quack-Packer or the two of us as "The Oregon Boys?"

"Uh, I'm Bob," I said. "And this is my brother-in-law, Glenn." (Rookie fear.)

The couple, we learned, had spent the previous night in a cabin next door. Given their fresh-looking appearances, I wouldn't have been surprised had they stayed at a Four Seasons.

"We're hoping to make Canada by mid-September," said Cisco.

OK, so maybe they were out of our league in more than just the dress/cleanliness category.

"Goot luck to you," said Roadrunner, who, we learned, had been born and raised in Germany. "Maybe vee will zee you on zee trail."

"And to you guys," I said. "Take care."

We next saw them on our mile-long walk back to the trail—on road asphalt that was escalating my blisters from bad to worse. The two zinged past us, facing backward in a pickup truck, waving with broad smiles. That was strange; a ride would have been nice.

At a water stop a few miles beyond Howard Prairie Reservoir, I saw something on a stump just off the trail.

"Hey, Glenny," I said. "Ben and Kate were here."

"How do you know?"

I nodded to the twenty-four-ounce Foster's Premium Ale sitting beside a small pile of "look-here!" rocks, beneath which a note said:

"Take it, fellow PCT hiker. Enjoy it. And somewhere up the trail, pass on a favor to another PCT hiker."

I loved Ben's spirit, which I learned had its own name on the PCT: Trail Magic. Before my journey was over, I would be blessed by plenty of it—and would give some of my own away.

BY NOW, Glenn and I had the water thing down. If you knew you had "for-sure" water at certain points, you didn't have to carry as much on your back, which made hiking easier. For the same reason, we always tried to "camel-up"—drink as much as possible—at each stop.

Glenn drank sparingly; he was like the Bionic Man. I drank often, mainly because of a condition I had called mastocytosis—my body overproduced "mast" cells—whose meds made me thirstier than before the ailment hit.

Because neither of us was particularly flexible, we couldn't reach the water in our packs' lower side pouches and, unlike many hikers, didn't like carrying our plastic bottles attached to our chest straps. Thus, we got into the rhythm of stopping and getting each other's bottles from the pouches. It worked great—unless we were hiking alone, which we would do at times.

After sixty-four mindless switchbacks on a cinder trail near Brown Mountain, we arrived at Cascade Canal. It was a well-shaded oasis that intersected the trail at Highway 140, the road from Medford to Klamath Falls. I filtered my water, using a Katadyn Hiker pump. To not do so was to risk getting giardia, whose symptoms of diarrhea, nausea, and stomach pain could ruin a trip in a hurry. I soaked my feet in the water, then laid back with my aching nubs propped on a log.

"Face it," said Glenn. "At any given moment, some part of our body will be aching."

"Yeah, but so far, no mosquitoes," I said, trying to be positive.

The reality? After four hot days on the trail, certain parts of my body were interacting with other parts of my body; if you're looking for a literary metaphor, think dangling participles. At first, the friction was just a casual "hello, how are you?" But as the miles passed and the temperature rose and the legs churned, the two grew closer, leaving me only one choice to curb the chafing: Anti Monkey Butt: Like Gold Bond only with a cute monkey mascot.

No sooner had I hidden myself in the trees to make an application then I saw them: Cisco and Roadrunner, bounding across the highway and on up the trail with all the zeal of Julie Andrews twirling on an Austrian hillside in *Sound of Music.*

Who were these people?

If the sight of the two Californians brought a tinge of regret regarding the past—leaving us in their dust at Hyatt Lake—the Messenger of Doom, whom I was about to encounter, brought fear regarding the future. I saw the Portland hiker just after crossing Cascade Canal, coming south toward us with warnings of deep snow on the steep pitches of Devils Peak, twenty-six miles ahead.

"We nearly died."

The words slammed me like an icy snowball to the ear.

"Do you have ice axes?" she asked.

"No."

"Micro spikes?"

"No."

"Neither did we. That's why we turned around."

She and her husband, Rob, had been so shaken by what they'd encountered that they'd aborted their Oregon PCT trip.

The news changed everything. My gut roiled. In a single conversation, I realized the trip we'd planned for a year was already in jeopardy.

Ann Petersen

Aussies Kate Manning and Ben Dyer, left and second from right, respectively, had been hiking for nearly 1,700 miles when we saw them after our arrival at the Oregon-California border in July 2011.

FIRST SUMMER

START: JULY 25, 2011

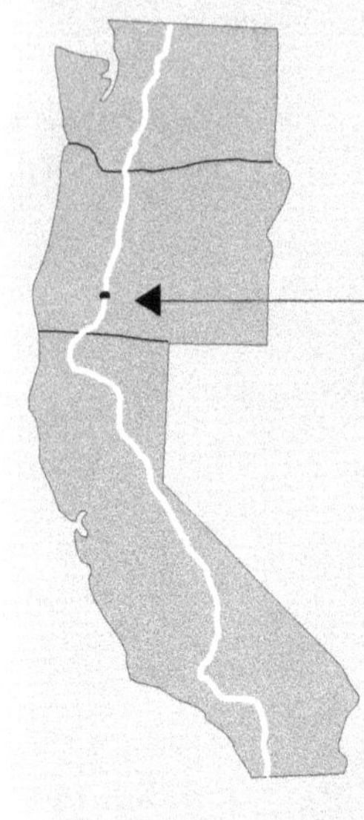

NORTH 23 MILES
FROM FREYE LAKE
TO DEVILS PEAK

Section shown on map, below

Elevation this section (feet)

Start	6,190
End	7,320
High	7,320 (Devils Peak)
Low	6,035 (Red Lake Trail Jct.)

OREGON

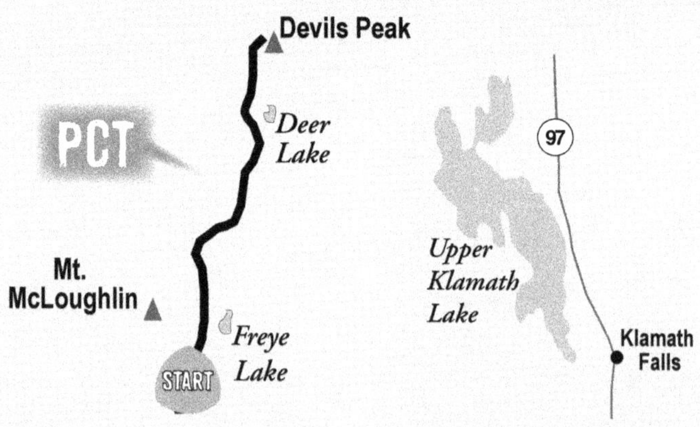

FEAR

If a man will begin with certainties, he shall end in doubts; but if he will be content to begin with doubts, he shall end in certainties.

—Francis Bacon

Things only got worse when, two hours later, we realized we had overshot Freye Lake, our scheduled camping spot, by at least half a mile. We had already put in twenty-two miles; we had been on the trail for more than thirteen hours. And darkness was suggesting it was closing time.

To reach the off-trail lake, our near-marathon suddenly became a near-marathon with steeplechase barriers. Over blowdown. Under blowdown. Fighting through tangles of fir limbs. Pushing through bitterbrush. My shirt was soaked, my legs squishy tired. Like a madman, I stretched ahead of Glenn, my iPhone with GPS app in one hand, my two trekking poles in the other. I increased my pace, fueled by weariness and a desperation to find this lake. We needed food and sleep.

A huge old-growth tree lay on its side, chest-high, crossing my path. I planted a boot on a branch and, with whatever energy I had left, leveraged myself to the top. I walked atop the fallen tree with the psychotic resolve of an Old West bandit atop a hijacked train, looking for the right place to jump off with the bags of stolen gold. My eyes darted from the blue dot on the iPhone map—the dot signified us getting closer to the lake—to the forest, with hopes water would soon appear through the trees.

My boot hit a snag. I tripped and fell forward off the log, landing on my chest, fortunately without injury. But the moment seemed to unleash another threat. Mosquitoes were suddenly dive-bombing me like Kamikaze pilots. The reason we hadn't seen any to this point was apparently that they'd all gathered here for a delayed "Welcome to Oregon" party. We were the guests of honor for hosts who, with snow-clogged trails dissuading hikers, hadn't seen much in the way of fresh meat this summer.

Though we soon found Freye Lake, I slunk into frustration, donned my mosquito-net hat, and pumped some lake water through my already-balky filter. When a mosquito slipped between my neck and the mesh and flew into my mouth, I made the mistake of spitting. Bad idea with a mosquito net covering your face.

I was not a happy camper. And Glenn, beat to the bone, had lost his Mr. Rogers optimism.

The lake sat in a bowl. Unless we wanted to fight through more blowdown to the flatter far side, our only choices for tent spots, in old Sears catalog terms, were "steep," "steeper," or "steepest."

"How's this spot for the tents?" Glenn asked, pointing to a "steeper" spot.

"Yeah, whatever," I said, hardly looking up.

I slid toward the lake all night, hardly sleeping. At one point I thought: *I wish I were home.*

Only later would I realize, or admit, that what really was eating at me had nothing to do with missed lakes, mosquitoes, or slippery slopes. Instead, it was a latent fear: having to face Devils Peak.

"WONDER WHAT happened to the Californians," I said the next morning after we'd bushwhacked our way up a hill in the dark—lighting our way with headlamps—and caught our breaths when rejoining the PCT.

"Yeah," said Glenn. "Not like there's a lot of water up here. Freye Lake is about it. Thought they'd be camping there, too."

After a couple of hours, we were hiking above Fourmile Lake when I heard footsteps behind me. I turned. There was a young man in shorts, T-shirt, and a pack that couldn't have weighed more than twenty pounds.

"Scared me," I said.

"Sorry," he said. "Blood Bath's the name."

Scared me more. A serial murderer with a strong cardiovascular system? No, a thru-hiker from Maine, the first Mexico-to-Canada hiker we'd seen since Ben and Kate at the border some eighty-eight miles and six days before. He had already hiked thirteen miles. It was 9:30 A.M., meaning he had shattered the "ten-by-ten" pace.

"And how did you get the name Blood Bath?" I asked.

"At the PCT Kickoff Party at Lake Morena* in May. They had this relay where you had to carry bear canisters. I cut my hand on one. It was a mess." Fortunately, bear-resistant food storage containers weren't required in Oregon as they were in California's High Sierra.

As we chatted he kept glancing up the trail.

"Sorry, I need to roll," he said. "I told myself I'd try to get in at least one fifty-miler on this trip. Today's the day."

Glenn and I watched as he stretched north with race walker strides, then looked at each other. *Fifty miles in one day?*

"Hey," I said, "how many nearly sixty-year-old guys are out here like us?"

"Not many, Bob," said Glenn. "Because unlike us, they've got brains." He then burst into his customary "aren't-I-funny?" laugh.

We pressed on. When we would hit a whale's-back of snow, I was glad we'd brought trekking poles. Though a few hikers didn't use them, I couldn't imagine *not.*

After the Blood Bath encounter, we'd barely regained our stride when we noticed a couple of hikers sitting trailside, a man in a neat blue shirt and a woman in a neat mauve shirt. It was *them.*

"Goot morning," said Roadrunner, who, with Cisco's help, appeared to be preparing an exotic brunch. "Vee meets again."

They had a small tablecloth spread on a log. *Who does this on the PCT?* Goodness, the previous night, amid my slipping and sliding, I'd awakened to feel lumps beneath my back and realized I'd *slept* on my breakfast: a couple of Svenhard's pastries. No wonder my breakfast tasted flat.

Cisco was stirring dried mushrooms into a dish they were concocting. In our short time on the trail, we had never made anything more exotic than freeze-dried dinners, created by pouring hot water into a foil pouch, shaking it, and letting it set for eight minutes.

"How did we miss seeing you last night?" I asked. "Freye Lake is about the only place up here with water. Where'd you guys camp?"

"About two hundred feet north of Highway 140, just off the trail, near where we saw you," said Cisco.

Far behind us, meaning they were making amazing time today.

We learned a little more about them. That they were from the San Francisco area. That Roadrunner (Baerbel Steffestun), fifty-two, got her trail name because of her speed. And that Cisco (Rich Combs), sixty, got his nickname because his father, a surgeon, had been called that, based on the movie *The*

* Lake Morena, California, is a day's hike north of the U.S.-Mexico border from Campo, the latter where northbound thru-hikers start their journeys.

Cisco Kid.

The two learned a little more about us. That we were brothers-in-law. That I was a newspaper columnist and Glenn a family-practice physician, albeit one who, with the bill of his hat flipped skyward, now looked a bit like Elmer Fudd of 1960s cartoon fame. And that we were a tad concerned about getting over Devils Peak.

"The problem, as with most mountains, is the north face," said Cisco. "With the sun in the southern sky, it's shaded much of the day. It's steep and melts slowly. If it's icy, could be trouble."

"Normally you vould have switchbacks on zee face," said Roadrunner. "But zee switchbacks vill be buried in snow. Instead, you'll have a sheer vall zat falls into a glaciated bowl."

She laced the phrase with a sense of trepidation, not as if she feared it herself but that other, less experienced types, might. *Glaciated bowl.* It sounded like something you'd read in *Into Thin Air*, the best-selling book by my 1972 Corvallis High classmate Jon Krakauer about the eight climbers who died on Mount Everest in 1996.

It sounded like a repository for bodies, a final stopping place for those who either didn't have ice axes or those who didn't know how to use one to stop a slide. The stakes, I realized, were about to rise.

"Bon appetit," I said, masking my fear. And we headed on.

"SHE'S A BOOK editor," I told Glenn on up the trail. "He works for some sort of environmental agency. No kids. Second marriages for them both. And total outdoor nuts."

"What?" asked Glenn.

"I'm just guessing about Cisco and Roadrunner," I said. "What do you think?"

"I don't think, Bob," he said. "I just hike."

Yes. That's what we did, wasn't it? We hiked. More than 200,000 steps thus far, I figured, such calculations one more way, with my sportswriter's background, of keeping my mind off blisters and fatigue. I could come up with PCT "box scores" at the drop of a hiker's hat.

When we reached our off-trail camping spot, Deer Lake, in the midafternoon heat, I plunged into the lake for a swim. I hadn't showered in four days. At 6,200 feet the water was ice cold but cleansing. The smell of lake water brought back childhood memories of our family's annual camping trips to Cultus Lake in Central Oregon.

At dusk, Glenn got a fire going, our first of the trip. For the first time, the experience felt like actual camping. After our freeze-dried dinners—Beef

Teriyaki and Rice for me—we leaned against logs and talked, our heads propped against the softness of our Z-pads. There was a long pause while the fire occasionally spit a spark. I looked into a night sky splashed with stars, which triggered a thought.

"You ever see that 'Twilight Zone' episode about the hitchhiker?" I asked Glenny.

"Nope."

Not surprising. Glenn had the pop-culture IQ of a monk, which was probably more honorable than shameful. Entire fads—bellbottoms, Pet Rocks, Sony Walkmans—had come and gone without him noticing.

"So, this woman is driving across the country, right, and sees this old guy hitchhiking. No big deal; she doesn't stop. But on ahead, there he is again. Strange, but possible; she'd made a stop for gas so maybe he'd gotten a ride with someone else, and they'd dropped him up ahead. But then it happens again and again. He's always there, out in front of her as she drives by, holding out his thumb with this innocent yet slightly sinister look on his face. And she's going crazy."

No response.

"Glenny, don't you get it? Cisco and Roadrunner are the 'Twilight Zone' hitchhikers of the PCT! They just pop up out of nowhere, ahead of us. It took us two hours to slog up that mountain last night, and yet there they were, ahead of us by midmorning but telling us they stayed down near the highway. What did they do, start hiking at 3 A.M.? I mean, did they really leave from Sierra City like they said, or did they just morph out of nothingness behind their breakfast menus at Hyatt Lake?"

He didn't answer.

"Glenny?"

The forest was quiet, save for a chorus of bullfrogs. And Glenn's soft snoring.

THE NEXT DAY, at 7,000 feet on the west flank of Luther Mountain, we reached the highest point since the trip started. What impressed me, besides a sprinkling of red, purple, and yellow wildflowers, was the sheer vastness of the land beyond: massive mountains splashed with sheer walls of shale. Craggy peaks interspersed with rolling buttes of timber speckled with snags bleached white by time. Geographic features that were small potatoes compared to, say, the Three Sisters, and yet were scattered 360 degrees around us in a display so large as to humble me amid God's sprawling grandeur.

"Mornin'."

I mentally lurched. The guy, tin coffee cup in hand, was standing like a statue just off the trail to my right, flanking a couple of tents.

"Hello," I said.

"Acorn," he said, extending a hand. At first, I thought he was offering me a nut. Oh, wait, Acorn was his trail name and he just wanted to shake. He was, I realized, a PCT hiker; we hadn't seen many.

"I'm Bob," I said. "That's my brother-in-law, Glenn. You thru-hiking?"

"No, doing a section with my daughter, from Ashland to Crater Lake. Got turned back by Devils Peak. Too tough. Too much snow. So far, four have made it past. Four have turned around."

Exactly what I didn't want to hear. I wanted something definitive one way or the other. When Glenn arrived the three of us chatted.

"We didn't have ice axes or crampons so decided to hang out here for a while," Acorn said. "See if it gets better."

"You see a couple named Cisco and Roadrunner?" I asked.

"Yeah, they were by here a little earlier."

I turned to Glenn and whispered, "How did they get past us again?"

"Must have gone up ahead of us after we'd peeled off for Deer Lake."

Said Acorn: "I think they camped at the Snow Lakes Trail junction."

That was six miles above where we'd stayed. If so, they'd done twenty-four miles to our fourteen the previous day. *Man, these guys were fast!*

Glenn and I moved on, Devils Peak looming ahead. Partially melted tracks creased the snow ever so faintly, probably Cisco and Roadrunner's.

Trekking poles firmly anchored, Glenn planted each foot in the snow with caution, then moved forward. I followed suit, willing myself to look ahead, to focus on each step, and to not look down. I'd already calculated that a fall wouldn't mean death—this wasn't Mount Everest's Khumbu Icefall—but some broken bones and scrapes on a shale outcropping a few hundred feet down the slope. OK, *maybe* death.

Focus, I told myself. Not on the danger, but on the process necessary to avoid the danger. It was the only thing that had gotten me through a scary experience when, for a two-part *Register-Guard* column series in 2002, I'd climbed a 180-foot crane being used to help build the University of Oregon's new south grandstands at Autzen Stadium. What enabled me to make it to the top was focusing on what I could control—gripping each wrung with my hand and stepping up each rung with my feet—and ignoring what I could not.

DEVILS PEAK TOWERED above us, a remnant of some eons-old volcano. The trail snaked through crumbly crag from the south side of the ridge to the north on the Devils Peak/Lee Peak Saddle. After two days of stewing about what lay beyond, it was time for us to peer over the edge and find out.

The ridge fell dramatically off into a quarter-mile slope of white that ended with a peninsula of trees and a snow-fed lake—Roadrunner's "glaciated bowl," or half bowl. My spirits soared when I saw we didn't have ice. The early afternoon snow appeared to be sun softened. The marks left by others suggested a few had simply post-holed their way down with deep steps into the snow; others had thrown caution to the wind and glissaded on their butts or backs down the cirque. Some, it appeared, had skied on their shoes.

"Wow," said Glenn, a view suddenly opening to distant peaks to the north, where we were headed.

It looked like a portal of sorts, like the closet through which the Pevensie children found Narnia in *The Lion, the Witch and the Wardrobe.* For the first time we were seeing the story we had climbed into.

"This isn't bad, is it?" I said, looking for some assurance. "I mean people clearly got down this thing."

"Sure did," said Glenn. "Looks like good sledding."

"The question is: Can we stop once we get going?"

I was already thinking about technique: whether we should drag our trekking poles to slow us down and prevent us from getting out of control. And how we had one shot to get down and, if we underestimated our speed, we might crash into the trees or the small lake that had formed from runoff.

"We need to be careful about this," I said. "Should we take our hands out of our pole straps? Should we dig in our—"

Glenn wasn't around to listen. In a total un-Petersen-like move, he'd already plunged down the slope, using his boots as skis in a sort of semi-controlled slide/ski. Within a few moments, I saw he was already home free, having stopped on a less steep part of the slope.

"Hey, come on down!" he yelled. "I'll get some video of you!"

Until now, I realized, I'd worried so much about the dangers of Devils Peak that I hadn't been able to let go of the fear even when the empirical evidence screamed, "All safe!" But Glenn's gutsy descent alleviated that fear.

I launched forward, leaned back, and slalomed left and right, partly out of control but knowing the worst I could do was face plant in soft snow. When the two of us reached the bottom, I surged with unbridled joy.

"Is that all you got?" I turned and yelled at Devils Peak. It was as if two days of fear had melted into a lake of relief as large as the greenish pool beyond.

What could stop us now?

FIRST SUMMER

START: JULY 25, 2011

GOAL: NORTH 154 MILES FROM DEVILS PEAK TO ELK LAKE

Elevation this section (feet)

Start	7,320
End	5,250
High	7,572 (near Tipsoo Peak.)
Low	5,250 (Shelter Cove)

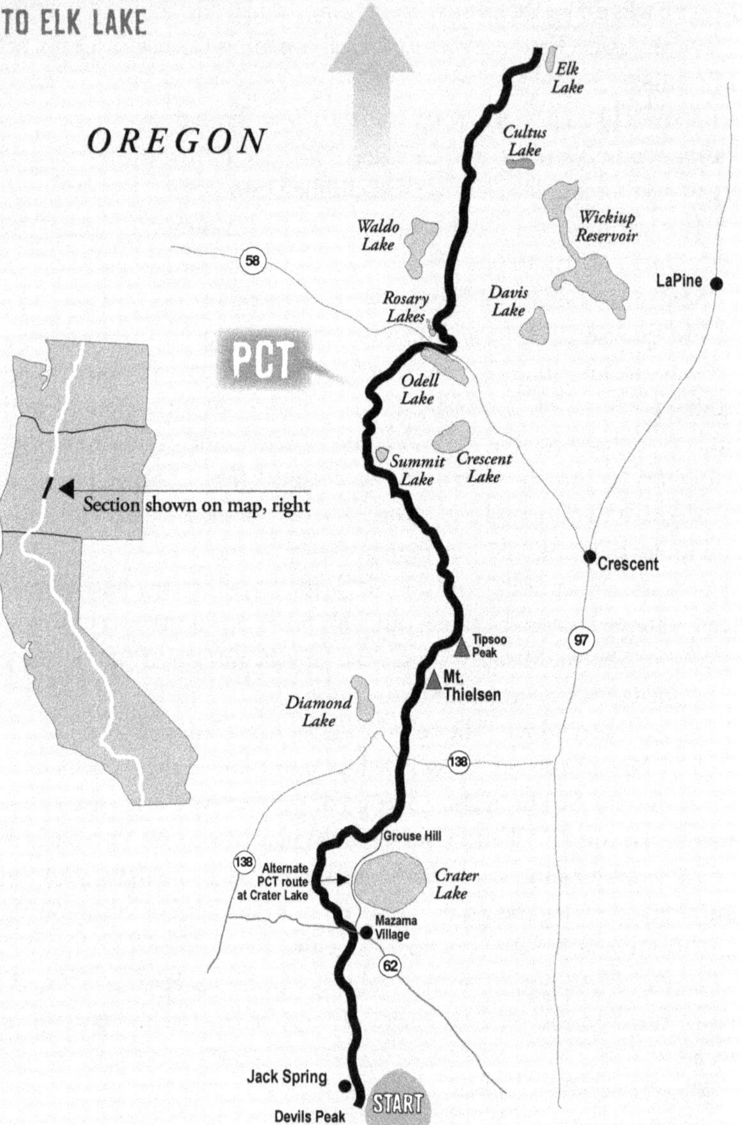

SNOW

It is far better to know where one is, and realize that one does not know, than to be certain one is in a place where one is not.

—Lieutenant Barral,
From *Digressions su la Navigation du Cap Horn*, 1827

LIKE TWO blind mice with trekking poles, Glenn and I bounced left and right through the white carpeted woods. There's a bumper sticker that says, *Not all who wander are lost,* but we certainly were—at least some of the time. Not many footprints had been punched to follow because at this point in the PCT season, July 28, the trail had been only lightly traveled. Based on Ben and Kate's belief that they were behind only a German hiker and my belief that we'd been passed by only Bloodbath, Cisco, and Roadrunner, we surmised we were among the first ten PCT hikers through these parts. The PCT "bubble" was likely many weeks back, in northern California.

The snow had changed everything. Every mile was a hard-fought mile. At times, I'd be walking on a dirt trail and come face to face with a mass of snow higher than my head. (Chisel my way up and move forward.) At times, I'd slip into a tree well. (Pick myself up and move forward, even after a fall had broken my sunglasses.) At times, I'd be striding across the snow "sun cups" and, *whoops,* feel a leg plummet deep in the snow. (Wonder whose idea this trip was.)

I trudged on in my lostness. Then came that voice again.

"Well, if it isn't zee doctor and zee newspaper man."

Roadrunner—again? She and Cisco were sitting on a log, of course, much like we'd seen them three days before. Glenn and I exchanged quick glances, brows furrowed in common suspicion; the couple came and went like mist.

"Vee took zee cutoff and stayed zee night near Stuart Falls," said Roadrunner. "It vas beautiful."

I dared not describe our night in the fire-charred, mosquito-thick reaches of Jack Spring. I'd had a midnight meltdown trying to transition from cowboy-camping to putting up my tent. And Glenn was wobbling off the tracks, too.

"Yeah, we're having a little trouble keeping on the trail," I said. "Low batteries on the GPS you know. Snow's tough."

Cisco glanced at Roadrunner, then back at us.

"Hey," he said. "Wanna join us?"

Every ounce of my pride shouted no.

"You bet!" I said. "Sounds good! Thanks!"

By now, I had a twig splint on my sunglasses and Glenn was still rocking the Elmer Fudd look. True, this was *our* state and we certainly didn't need outsiders telling us how to navigate it. But beneath such muted bravado was a growing sense of desperation. My blistered little toes were screaming in pain. The snow wasn't going away. And finding our way through it was costing us serious time. These two knew what they were doing; they'd been hiking for hundreds of miles. So, we humbled ourselves and happily followed the Californians into the boundaries of Crater Lake National Park.

Cisco had a GPS superior to those that Glenn and I were using. And he and Roadrunner had experience, instincts, and the minds of engineers, which, professionally, both were.

"The trail has a mind of its own," Cisco said. "It goes where it wants to go. Think like the trail would think. *Where would I go now*?"

Amid the snow, they taught us to look for cut logs; in wilderness areas where logging was prohibited, that's the only reason you'd see a clean-cut log—made by a bucksaw clearing a trail. They taught us to look for water drainage from snow masses; the rivulets tended to follow the confines of a trail in the same way a river stays in its banks. They taught us to spread out laterally; when looking for the trail, four sets of eyes looking at the same narrow swath was, as Cisco said, a "waste of visual resources."

"Vhere you staying zonight?" asked Roadrunner.

"We have reservations at the Mazama campground," said Glenn. "And you?"

"Same place," she said, "but no reservations. Ve hope zee rangers vill take pity on us."

BY MIDAFTERNOON we hit Highway 62 and, across the road, dipped into Mazama Village, tucked nine trail miles below Crater Lake's rim. We hadn't been there five minutes when a young PCT hiker in a skirt arrived, ripped off her pack, and said, "That's it! I'm done with this friggin' state! Oregon is one green tunnel. Nothin' but trees, trees, trees!" I last saw her thumbing a ride on Highway 62, presumably headed for the Medford Airport.

I was sorry she was stopping just when Oregon's lake-and-volcanic-peak beauty was starting but remembered the advice a PCT hiker had offered us on our shakedown cruise: "hike your own hike." To each his or her own.

Me? I found arriving at Crater Lake both terrific and terrible. Terrific because there was a store, a restaurant, a shower, and a campsite we had reserved, complete with a picnic table at which to sit. (I really missed sitting on something softer than dirt, rocks, and logs.) Terrible because it represented civilization, which, frankly, I hadn't missed much, especially the TV news back at Hyatt Lake's restaurant, which had led with a mass shooting.

I felt like a scuba diver surfacing too fast and suffering from the bends—in my case, emotional bends. I had gone five days while seeing only trees, mountains, lakes, and a trail; no cell coverage to link me to reality. Suddenly, I was in a place with recreational vehicles, gift shops, and fresh-off-the-bus sightseers in Hard Rock Cafe shirts. All I wanted to do was scarf down an all-you-can eat lunch buffet, grab a shower, and nap at our reserved—and, presumably, flat—campsite.

As I walked toward the store, I remembered something Craig Mayne, the guy who had done the Oregon PCT the previous year, had written about his arrival at Crater Lake.

> You hike into a place filled with tourists. You've been on the trail for days. You're dirty, ragged, and tired. Your face and legs are covered with dust. Your diet has consisted of freeze-dried food, Clif Bars, and filtered lake water. People look at you as they go by in their cars, as they walk around in their expensive clothes—clean, spotless, and pressed and holding their cameras and eating their ice cream. You stand out like a sore thumb. But as they pass, you can see it in their eyes, that touch of envy, that … desire to feel what you are experiencing. You feel the exhaustion that comes from hiking for days on the trail. You look down at your wrinkled clothes, your dirty pack, and boots, and you feel a sense of pride.

To some degree, I could relate. No offense to the tourists; they made their choices and lived accordingly; couldn't fault them for that. Hike your own hike, and all that. But I was content to be on the trail, not on the air-conditioned bus.

At the campground's kiosk, Glenn was checking in on one side of the hut while Roadrunner was seeking mercy on the other. Told by the ranger that she needed to have a reservation, Roadrunner responded, "But ve're hiking zee PCT. Isn't there someplace vee could—."

"Sorry."

Glenn didn't miss a beat. "Can they stay at our site, as our guests?"

The ranger shrugged. "Works for us."

In sum, Cisco and Roadrunner saved our Oregon PCT trip and we saved them—*Glenn* saved them—from having to be homeless for a night. That afternoon, the four of us enjoyed the first of two festive meals we would share at a Mazama restaurant, Annie Creek.

I raised a glass. "To Canada for Cisco and Roadrunner!" I said.

Clink. Clink. Clink.

"And to the Columbia River for Bob and Glenn!" said Roadrunner.

IN THE MORNING we went our separate ways. As Glenn and I waited for Ann and Sally at Crater Lake, I took my knife and cut holes in the side of each of my boots so my little toes could get some wiggle room; one had ballooned up with a blister the size of a salmon egg. I then wrapped the boot in duct tape, but not before placing empty plastic jam containers—procured from the restaurant—over each hole to allow my little toes to breathe but to also keep out the dirt. Glenn just shook his head, trying to stifle a laugh.

"What?" I said. "This will work. Wait and see."

Ann and Sally arrived with our resupplies and dropped off my two nieces, Molly, twenty-six, and Carrie, thirty, who would be hiking with us for four days. As we headed north, we were afforded off-and-on views of Crater Lake, with Wizard Island rising like a castle within its watery kingdom. Few lakes offer the massive and majestic beauty of Crater, whose turquoise waters enchant. No lake in the U.S. is as deep (1,949 feet).

As we left it and headed north on a plateau, the snow, to our dismay, showed no signs of going way. Meanwhile, we saw two hikers a half mile in front of us.

"Is that who I think it is?" asked Glenn.

"Who else could it be?" I said, then started whistling the four-note "Twilight Zone" music.

As we post-holed our ways further north, we realized Cisco and Roadrunner were marking trail for us with tiny snowmen, an incredible act of kindness. We trudged on, an effort that felt less like hiking than cross-country skiing. Glenn's daughters, Molly and Carrie, were good sports, but this wasn't what they'd signed up for. And their father noticed.

"They'd have more fun going lower and finding actual dirt," he said to me later. "There's a trail after Grouse Hill to Diamond Lake. I'm thinking tomorrow I take the girls down there to hike for a few days. Our original plan was to have Ann meet us at Summit Lake in three days to resupply us. Instead, she'll pick me and the girls up at Diamond Lake and drop me off at Summit to rejoin you."

"And I'm *where* during all this?"

"Going over Mount Thielsen with Cisco and Roadrunner," he said. "Assuming they'll take you!" He laughed. "Seriously, this only works if you go with them, Bob; not a good idea to be going it alone in snow."

"What about you?"

"I'll come back and do this section some other time. I'm still hiking the whole thing."

Initially, I didn't like the idea of Glenn and I going our separate ways. But by the time we arrived at Grouse Hill, where Cisco and Roadrunner were camping, I'd warmed to it. After dinner, the six of us had a sort of "Survivor" Tribal Council at which Glenn unveiled his plan.

"So, zee idea is for us to 'adopt' Bob?" Roadrunner asked.

I felt a little like the kid nobody wanted to choose for their kickball team, but slowly a smile creased Roadrunner's face.

"Well, of course vee vill take Bob!" she said. "But trust me; I am an engineer. Ziss idea with the duct tape and jam containers on your boots vill not vork, my friend!"

THE NEXT DAY, Sunday July 31, the three of us completed a challenging 17.6-mile hike around the snow-thick—and sometimes scary—west shoulder of 9,184-foot Mount Thielsen.* Near camp, I gingerly made my way over a snow bridge spanning Thielsen Creek. Had it collapsed, I would have fallen into a dark tube of icy water, a thought that only occurred to me *after* I was safely across and pitching my tent on one of the few patches of dirt amid the snow.

Cisco clicked a photo of me standing in front of my tent, my arms raised to the heavens, a huge smile on my face. I was sky-high: relieved, relaxed, and refocused. It had been a great day sprinkled with laughter. Roadrunner made fun of the patch job on my boots; I made fun of her inability to pronounce words starting with the letter "T," joking that we were on Mount *Zeelsun*.

Two days later, as planned, Cisco, Roadrunner, and I met up with Glenn at Summit Lake, where Ann, who'd returned from Albany, treated us to a

---

* Pronounced "TEEL-SEN."

stunning taco salad before bidding us farewell.

En route to Summit, Cisco had taught me about the stars and Roadrunner about the challenge of leaving one's country to assimilate in another. And both about the importance of post-lunch naps. They insisted I lead from time to time, even if I had initially demurred because of my inexperience in snow.

Once reunited with Glenn, the four of us hiked together for two days, leaving the snow behind. Among the highlights was meeting Malto, an eccentric hiker crushing the trail with twenty-five- to thirty-mile days. He wore a golf visor, under which he had a white towel, making him look like an Arabian sheik. He told us he survived almost entirely on a power drink he'd concocted himself, the base of which was maltodextrin—thus his trail name—with added electrolytes.

My daily menu looked something like this: two Svenhard's Danishes upon waking; beef jerky and trail mix during a midmorning break; potato chips and beef and cheese sticks for lunch; and a freeze-dried meal for dinner, with candy bars and soft candy mixed in for power boosts during the day.

"Good luck," Malto said and, like a race car among Ramblers, pushed onward to Canada. Surprisingly, however, we had not seen the last of him.

ROADRUNNER was right. The idea with the duct tape and jam containers ultimately flopped; by the time we reached Odell Lake, the tape on my boots was flapping like the sideboards of the burned-out car John Candy was driving in *Planes, Trains & Automobiles*. At the Shelter Cove store, as we sipped cold drinks and licked even colder ice cream, an affable fishing guide named Mike Jones took matters—and a roll of duct tape—into his own hands. With great pride, he upgraded my wrap job—without the jam cups.

"Thanks, Mike," I said. "OK, so we know you can tape boots, now let's test your assessment of PCT hikers."

"I'm all in," he said from behind a white, horseshoe-shaped mustache. "Whataya got, sport?"

"One of the four of us is a doctor. Mike, who would you say is most likely, and least likely, to *be that* doctor?"

His head swept left to right like an old Rainbird sprinkler.

"Well," he said, eyeing Roadrunner. "She's your doctor. And the least likely?" He nodded toward Glenn. "Elmer Fudd over there."

I nearly spit out my Mountain Dew.

TWO DAYS later—Friday, August 5—I experienced my first "hiker's high" whereby I felt I could walk forever. The irony is I'd gone it alone on the 18.4-mile stretch from Jezebel Lake to Elk Lake because my feet were so blistered the previous day I feared I'd slow down the others. But on this day I felt ageless, my connection to the woods so engaged that my body seemed to transcend pain.

Part of what kept me going strong was the evocative smell of the Central Oregon of my youth: pine needles, pitch, and sandy trails. It was near here where my father and I would, after swimming and water skiing with family and friends, hike from Cultus Lake to the Teddy Lakes and Muskrat Lake in the late afternoons to fish. Here where Woody, Loce, and Roberts and I had hiked from Elk Lake to Cultus, stopping for a skinny dip in Mac Lake. With my mind lost in memories, the miles ticked by with me barely noticing.

After waiting for the others at the turnoff to Elk Lake, we gathered with Sally and Ann on the resort's deck for a celebratory dinner. Cisco insisted the meal was on them, though it hardly seemed fair. We hadn't saved their trip, they'd saved ours. We laughed. Compared mosquito stories. And talked of people, places, and, of course, the Tribal Summit at Grouse Hill.

Fresh clothes. Good food. Family. New friends. I looked up from my cheeseburger and fries and scanned the lake, beyond which Mount Bachelor rose, and thought: *I am a fortunate man.* Soon, the sun that had infused Bachelor with a pinkish hue began to fade; we'd need to head for home soon.

"We couldn't have done it without you," I said. "Thank you, guys."

"It vas nice having you for our adopted son, Bob," Roadrunner said. "Zank *you*. Ve'd been hiking together for 400 miles vhen ve came across you."

"And drove right past us as I recall," I said. "Not that I'm still bitter."

Laughter

"You lightened us up, made us laugh," said Cisco. "We needed that."

"You taught us how to follow a trail in the snow," I said. "Modeled how to hike and never get dirty. And how to put on a good trail brunch featuring nutritious foods. But, folks, let the record show that at Windigo Pass, Cisco took a quick glance to make sure you weren't looking, Roadrunner, and said to me, 'Got anymore of those Good & Plenties?'"

More laughter

"And let zee record also show," said Roadrunner, "zat your duct-taped boots did *not* vork."

Howling.

I shook Cisco's hand and hugged Roadrunner. We said our goodbyes.

As Glenn, Ann, Sally and I drove south on Cascade Lakes Highway, I wondered if we might see Cisco and Roadrunner again: say, off to the side of the road later that night, beneath a sky splashed in "Twilight Zone" stars, both hanging out hitchhikers' thumbs.

Top: Glenn celebrated the unparalleled beauty of Crater Lake. Above: Cisco and Roadrunner led the way on a steep, snowy shoulder of Mount Thielsen.

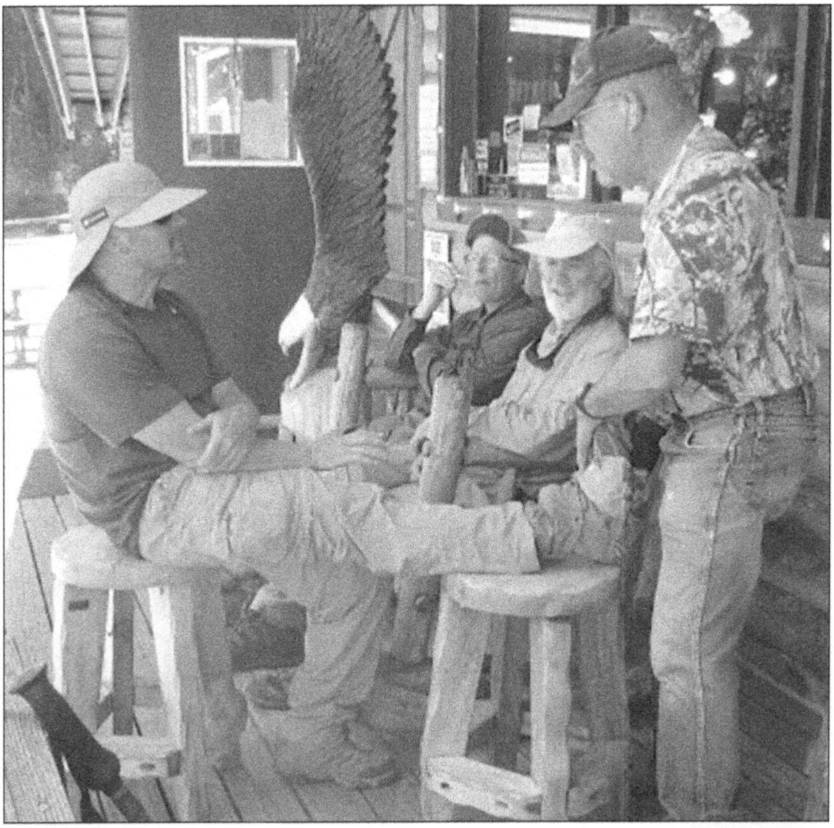

Roadrunner (Baerbel Steffestun)

Glenn Petersen

Top: At Odell Lake, fishing guide Mike Jones re-wrapped my boots. Above left: Me with the almost mythical Malto, near Waldo Lake. Above right: Glenn's Beverly Hillbillies look, with empty water jugs. Lower right: my twig-splinted sunglasses.

Cisco (Rich Combs)

After a 17.6-mile slog through snow around the west shoulder of Mount Thielsen (behind me), I was more stoked than at any point since clearing Devils Peak.

Glenn Petersen

Top: After "adopting" me, Cisco and Roadrunner became great hiking friends. Above: At Summit Lake, Glenn, right, rejoined us after hiking a few days with daughters Carrie and Molly.

FIRST SUMMER

START: AUGUST 27, 2011

GOAL: NORTH 204 MILES FROM ELK LAKE TO BRIDGE OF THE GODS

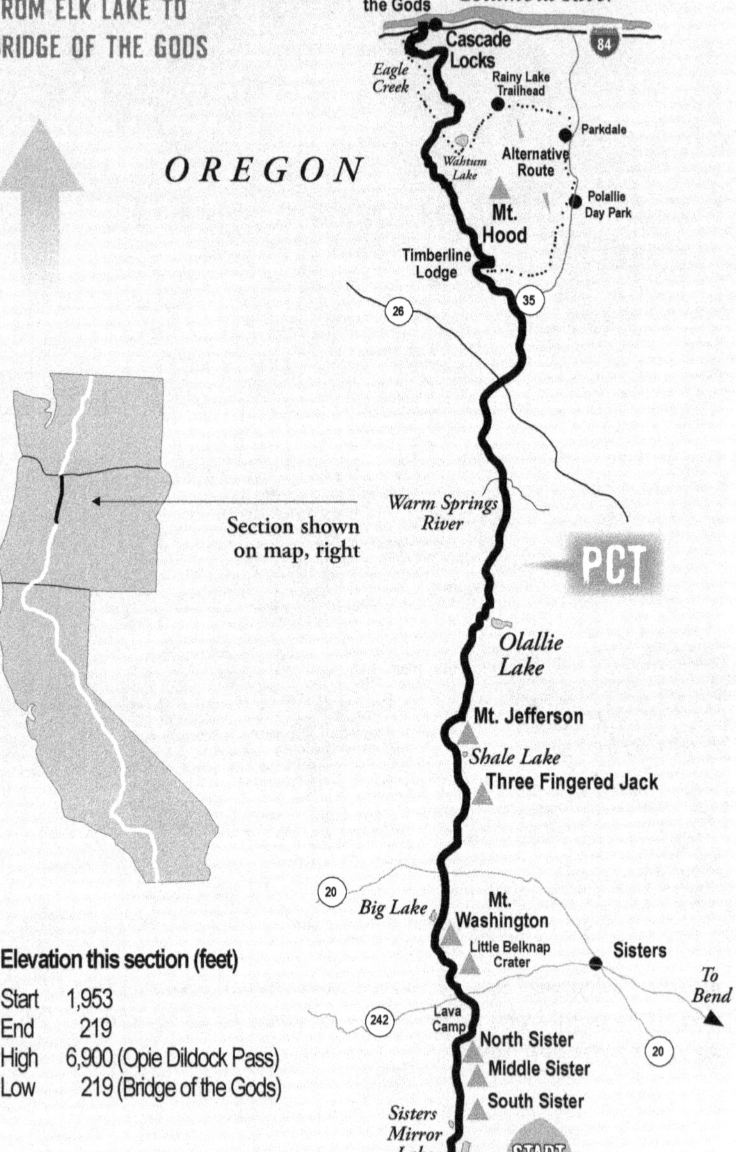

Elevation this section (feet)

Start	1,953
End	219
High	6,900 (Opie Dildock Pass)
Low	219 (Bridge of the Gods)

5

SEPARATION

We find after years of struggle
that we do not take a trip; a trip takes us.

—John Steinbeck

Just as we were getting assimilated back to the real world, it was time to return to the trail. After being home for three weeks, we bid farewell to our fill-in "Uber team," Glenn's eighty-something parents, Paul and Pauline, at Elk Lake. Ann and Sally were at a Youngberg family reunion on the coast that we'd just left, where our third grandchild, Keaton (Jason and Deena's first child), had made his all-family debut.

Meanwhile, Glenn and Ann's daughter, Katie, and husband David, were due any day with the Petersen's first grandchild. In fact, after Glenn and I skirted the alluring Three Sisters and arrived at Lava Camp the next night, the first thing Glenn did was find cell coverage for an update. No baby yet. We scarfed down a few s'mores at a campfire hosted by Lost & Found, a former PCT-hiker-turned-Trail-Angel, then turned in.

The next morning, August 28, as we made our way around a twisting trail through the lava beds on the Old McKenzie Pass, Glenn's phone buzzed.

"All right!" he said. "Jeremiah Walker Black has arrived!"

"Woo hoo! Congrats, Grandpa Glenn!"

A less significant, but still cool, milestone, followed: crossing the Little Belknap Crater junction where Laura Buhl had introduced the PCT to me twelve years earlier. A few miles ahead we saw rocks lined up on the trail to show the 2,000-mile mark for the PCT's thru-hikers en route to Canada. We had 156 miles left to finish Oregon.

The next day, Monday, August 29, I was nearing Rockpile Lake when I realized that late in the morning was my favorite time to hike: deep enough into the daily adventure to have some miles under your belt, the temperature still reasonable, and the prospect of stopping for lunch giving you something to look forward to: semi-immediate gratification.

Midafternoon, approaching Mount Jefferson, a guy passed me going south. He was on a horse with a rifle in his scabbard, the reins in one hand and a Bud Lite in the other. For the first time on the trail, a touch of fear flared within. Later that night, at Shale Lake, Glenn and I were huddled around a small fire—the weather had turned cool—when we saw two headlamp lights gyrating toward us in the darkness. *Is one of them Bud Lite?*

No. In a moment two hikers emerged from the darkness: a young man and woman. Both slim. And both spent. He had a dark brown beard, a black earring in his left ear. Her light hair was pulled back. A handsome pair.

"Hello, I am Bugs," said the man with a pronounced foreign accent. "And this is Bunny. May we camp with you?"

"Of course," Glenn said.

"Welcome to the Shale Lake Sheraton," I said. "Where you from?"

"Israel," he said.

Like us, they were "NoBos"—northbound PCT hikers, as opposed to SoBos, those who were southbound. As we chatted, we learned more about them, how, for example, they both had completed mandatory military stints in their homeland, then traveled here to hike the trail they'd heard so much about. They were hoping to make Canada.

"Wow," I said. "You're the real deal."

While they set up their tents and made dinner, Glenn and I warmed our hands by the fire. I was pumped because we had guests and because we'd created an extra sense of purpose for the next day: Rather than hike twenty miles, I'd figured out that if we went three additional miles we could reach Olallie Lake, whose grocery store, I surmised, might sell hot dogs.

"Can you imagine feasting on that tomorrow night?" I asked. "Hot dogs! The filet mignon of the PCT!"

Glenn was an easy sell; we were going for it. Only in our third week of hiking the PCT, we'd already tired of the same old food.

A lot of hikers, I had found, basically folded their eating habits into a daylong snack; some went so far as to eat while they hiked. Me? I liked the definition of breakfast, lunch, and dinner. Emotionally, I needed things to look forward to.

We said goodnight to Bugs and Bunny, and slipped into our respective tents. Outside, the couple huddled around the fire, talking softly. It would be our coldest night of the trip, by far. As I lay there, listening to the two, it was with a sense of wonder at moments like these that would arrive out of nowhere: chatting with Ben, the Aussie, about sailing around the world or with Cisco about star patterns in the sky.

"Every journey has a secret destination of which the traveler is unaware," said Martin Buber, an Austrian-born Jewish philosopher. I had assumed I knew where this trail was taking me: to the Oregon-Washington border. But perhaps I was being too narrow in my expectations. Perhaps it was leading to destinations that had not yet been revealed.

For now, I drifted toward sleep, thinking how wonderful it was to be snug in a small tent high in the Cascade Range, listening to the sound of an Israeli couple around a campfire speaking softly in Hebrew.

THE NEXT DAY, Thursday, September 1, we tramped through Jefferson Park, a lake-sprinkled meadow just north of 10,497-foot Mount Jefferson. It is, on a clear day, majestic; on this day, however, less so because of low clouds that shrouded much of the mountain.

As we climbed out of the park, I recognized a SoBo coming down from higher reaches. Theresa O'Brien had been in the audience at Central Presbyterian Church in Eugene when I'd spoken on *American Nightingale,* a book I'd written about the first nurse to die after the landings at Normandy in World War II. She was hiking with her twenty-something daughter.

"Where you guys headed?" I asked.

"Lana's doing Cascade Locks to Crater Lake, with various friends and family members joining her on different stretches."

"Nice. You left from where we're headed: Cascade Locks."

"Careful climbing out of here," she said. "It's really cold up there. Ice pellets falling from the trees. Snowfields."

"Yikes, I thought we'd left the snow behind us near Thielsen."

"Nope, 'fraid not."

We donned our gloves and stocking hats. Theresa hadn't overstated the weather shift. Soon, we were entering Mount Hood National Forest on a rocky plateau pocked with snow, a lonely, foreboding patch of trail that did not speak of summer or even whisper autumn, but chattered winter.

The good news: Despite some tough sledding, literally, over 23.6 miles we made it to the Olallie Lake store before it closed at 7 P.M. The bad: The store didn't carry hot dogs. I brooded for about five minutes, then drowned my sorrows in a family-sized bag of Lay's barbecue potato chips.

The next night we camped on the Warm Springs River—seemed more *creekish* to me—where, soon after arrival, a young man set up his tent near us. He proceeded to build a huge fire, surprising since the woods were already shrouded in light smoke from a wildfire somewhere east of us, near Warm Springs, and extra caution would seem to be in order. *Was he afraid of something?* Rick was thirtyish, and a civilian accountant for the Coast Guard.* He was section-hiking a chunk of the PCT to Timberline Lodge.

Glenn went over to say hello. As I set up my tent I half-listened to Rick.

"So, last night, I came through Jeff Park and it's cold and windy, but I decided to go on. I climbed up, crossing that snowfield in the dark and then came to all that shale. Pitch black. I was dead tired; thirty miles on the tires. Wind blowin' like crazy. I realized I couldn't make it to Olallie, I was going to have to camp right there."

I took a few steps closer, Rick gesturing behind the flickering flames.

"I'm in my tent, right, and I hear this noise, something scratching around out on the rocks, so I pull out my hunting knife."

I stepped closer. "Then what?"

"And I wait. And the noise continues. It's like whatever's out there is stalking me, circling me."

"Bear?" I asked, by now having joined the two around the fire.

"That's what I'm thinking," he said. "I put on my headlamp, zip open the flap and"—my eyes widened, the fire sparked—"there was nothing there."

The story collapsed like a crumpled ultralight falling from the sky. Still, I'd enjoyed it. I had spent a few hundred nights in the woods and had never seen a bear or cougar. Then again, I had interviewed dozens of people convinced that they had seen Bigfoot. The fact that one such sighting came at a Burger King parking lot in suburban Bellevue, Washington, didn't do much to raise the believability of their reports. And yet, I had to admit, I loved a good wild animal story, even if surmising such tales tended to exaggerate the teller's courage.

At night around a campfire, I'd never heard the story told by a guy who heard a noise outside his tent, imagined a bear, and promptly cowered into the fetal position while peeing his pants—which may well have been closer to the truth.

The morning after Coast Guard Rick's bear tale, we hiked a record 25.1 miles, saw Mount Hood looming in front of us—a big emotional boost—and dry-camped just above State Route 26. The end was near.

---

* Not his real name.

BLUEBERRY WAFFLES. Sausage. Scrambled eggs. Doughnuts. Orange juice. Fruit. As I finished my all-you-can-eat brunch in rustic Timberline Lodge's upstairs dining room Saturday, September 3, the only question was what to eat in Rounds II and III. The answer was pancakes, bacon, more orange juice, and more fruit, whereupon I fast-forwarded to lunch: rice, gravy, salmon, dinner salad with blue-cheese dressing, and a roll. Oh, and then dessert: vanilla ice cream with fudge topping crowned by a dollop of whip cream, and chocolate-chip cookies.

I had never packed more calories into a single meal—nor done so amid such a clash of cultures: the lodge's food was lavishly heaped on silver trays and was being consumed by me, a guy who was dirty, sweaty, smelly, and unshaven. Around us, a few well-coiffed tourists dabbed the corners of their mouths with their white cloth napkins.

"It's caddy day at the country club pool!" I told Glenn. "I feel like we don't belong."

"I feel like getting more pancakes," said Glenn, and pushed back his chair.

"Hey, look, it's that hiker from Japan," I said.

I introduced myself. Mij had left the Mexican border May 5 so obviously was making good time on his quest for Canada. Thirty-one, he was a wood stove salesman. We talked a bit despite the language barrier, and posed for a quick photo, the kind of picture you think is cheesy but later you're glad you took.

Outside, on a second-floor deck, I later looked south with amazement: mountain after mountain, ridge after ridge, all which we'd somehow crossed.

"Where you headed?" asked a thru-hiker, a bearded young man whose body was trim and tan.

"Bridge of the Gods," I said. "We're just doing Oregon."

He shook his head sideways. "Hey, man, never say 'just.' *You're doing Oregon.* Dude, that's a fair amount of trail. Don't minimize it."

"Thanks." I never forgot his affirmation.

THE ONLY DOWNERS of the day were that our two football teams—Oregon and Oregon State—had lost, the Ducks to LSU, the Beavers to Sacramento State. But frankly we were focused on something else: the Oregon-Washington border. Two hard days and we'd be done.

We awoke to see a touch of pink bleeding through the black of the eastern horizon. We left at 5:30 A.M., our earliest departure so far, and headed up the trail to skirt the western flank of Hood. The quiet cadence of boots on trail … the feel of bones and muscles awakening to the challenge ahead … the look of the trail, only a small swath of it awash in the light from my headlamp—the headlamp that now brought into view a wooden Pacific Crest Trail sign, the kind we'd seen many of but not like this one. It was flagged with pink "notice-me!" tape.

"Glenny, hold on!" I bent over and shined my light on the red sign:

PACIFIC CREST TRAIL CLOSED
FROM RUSHING WATER CREEK
SOUTH OF RAMONA FALLS TO
WAHTUM LAKE DUE TO WILDFIRE.
A PCT WALK AROUND ROUTE
WILL BE POSTED SUNDAY,
SEPT. 4TH.
THANK YOU FOR YOUR COOPERATION!

My heart sank. A quick call to a local ranger station only made the situation seem bleaker. The ranger described the PCT fire danger as extreme, and the alternative route iffy at best.

"It could be three or four days before we come up with some sort of alternative route for PCT hikers," he said, contradicting the sign.

Conversation over. It was Sunday of Labor Day weekend. Glenn and I needed to be back at work Wednesday; we couldn't be waiting around days for a detour route. It felt like a cruel blow.

"Doesn't look good," said Glenn.

What could I say? Ninety percent of the trail done; ten percent left. I was bummed. I called Sally to ask for a ride home, doing a poor job of trying to hide my disappointment.

"I'm so sorry, babe," she said.

"Thanks. But it is what it is."

I leaned against my pack and, while quietly brooding, scanned my iPhone for a rabbit-out-of-the-hat update. None came. However, two hours later, a ranger arrived with a stack of fresh-from-the-copy-machine maps in her arms.

"PCT hikers, we've got workaround for you!" said MaryEllen Fitzgerald. "We're sending you around the east side of the mountain instead of the west."

The dozen hikers whooped and hollered, Glenn and I among them.

"And you'll be happy to know there are three major water crossings. Have fun, you guys!"

I called Sally and Ann, who turned their drive north into a Portland shopping trip instead of a Bob-Glenn pickup. *We once were lost but now were found.*

In early afternoon, Glenn and I started around the east side of the mountain with a group of "Young Ones." They not only had little apparent fear of crossing a narrow log over the pounding White River, which was running fast and gray from the glacial silt, but later invited us to go "night drunk-walking" with them when we reached Highway 35.*

"Thanks, but no thanks," I said after hearing their idea to have someone hitchhike into Hood River for a case of beer at the highway, then return.

"Hey," I said to Glenn, who couldn't stifle his laughter. "It was nice to have been invited, right? A weird sort of, 'You're welcome around our campfire.'"

Instead, we pitched our tents at a day camp whose "no overnight camping" edict the Forest Service had waived because of the fire. After what seemed like hours of lying awake while listening to the unfamiliar sound of highway traffic, I drifted off to sleep.

I awoke at the sound of a snapping twig. I tensed, the fear magnified by little sense of time or place. *Where am I? What time is it? What's going on?*

When that lens focused—Polallie Day Park and, after a glance at my watch, 4:58 A.M.—I relaxed. Just a deer, I assumed. But I heard more crunching, as if someone, or some*thing,* was walking. A groan of sorts, like a man who'd been kicked in the gut.

I unzipped my tent flap and poked my head out. In the distance: a single light shined in the darkness. *A motorcycle idling up on the highway? Something closer?* Of course, I figured: Glenn's headlamp. *He must be taking a leak. Mystery solved.*

But the light started gyrating like a firefly, up, down, sideways. Unusual.

"Glenny?"

No response. Another soft groan, a guttural heave. Was someone throwing up?

"Glenn, is that you?"

A weak, "Yeah."

I slipped on my headlamp and walked out of the tent in my long johns. In the headlamp's beam there was Glenn: on all fours, some twenty feet beyond his tent, puking.

"You OK?" I asked.

"No," he said. "I have vertigo."

The ailment has nothing to do with heights; ironically, we were at the lowest point, 2,880 feet, of the entire trip thus far. Instead, vertigo is an inner-ear problem that causes severe dizziness; I'd had a small episode of it when I was twenty-three. Everything spins around you—and can lead to nausea. After

* The workaround had hikers walking nearly ten miles along Oregon Highway 35 between Government Camp near Mount Hood and Hood River, then taking a side road to re-enter the forest at the Rainy Lake Trailhead. Once back on an actual trail, hikers were to swing past Wahtum Lake and down Eagle Creek to the Columbia River.

an hour of "just-give-me-a-minute" bravado, Glenn shook his head sideways.

"Bobby, I hate to do this but I better call it quits."

This wasn't supposed to happen. If anyone got sick, it was supposed to be me. Glenn was a doctor. Doctors don't get sick. They make people well. Especially my invincible brother-in-law, my Haiti hero. If anyone was going to falter, it was going to be me. But here we were.

At first, I couldn't find any cell coverage and I had no clear shot to the southern sky to use my Spot GPS satellite device. Was I going to have to leave Glenn and hitchhike into Hood River just to call Ann?

Finally, I found two bars of cell service and connected with her. She arrived four hours later. Between bouts of barfing, Glenn handed me a crude trail map he'd sketched.

"What's this?"

"The route ... you need to take ... to finish," he said weakly.

The guy was puking his guts out and yet his priority was me getting to Cascade Locks. That, in a nutshell, was Glenn Petersen. More than a year of planning and nearly a month together on the trail was now all for naught in terms of us finishing together. I turned my back so Ann and Glenn couldn't see my eyes getting misty.

"Finish ... strong ... Bob," said Glenn.

IN RETROSPECT, we were fortunate in one way. Without the fire closure, we would have taken the PCT west around the rugged shoulder of Mount Hood. Had Glenn gotten sick there, instead of on a main highway, we would have been far from even a Forest Service road, in a more remote area where communication with Ann would have been virtually impossible.

As it was, after dropping off Glenn in Parkdale to rest, Ann took me to the Rainy Lake Trailhead, jumping me ahead about eight miles on this alternative route. She wished me well, we hugged, and I headed on, alone, the sky tinged with smoke.

When I got to Wahtum Lake, thoughts of my father having fished here as a teenager fled when fear suddenly gripped me. There wasn't a soul in sight. It was Labor Day and the lake could be accessed from a road; the place should have been packed. But I hadn't seen another person all day.

It felt eerie. I saw a lone car with a sign on its windshield: "Evacuate! Because of nearby fires ... "

With a pit in my stomach, I headed north, down into the Eagle Creek Basin and away from the Dollar Lake Fire. Along Eagle Creek, I camped by myself for the first time. Again, not another hiker around.

It was only 11.4 miles to the Bridge of the Gods, most of it along one of the most beautiful stretches PCT hikers will encounter: Eagle Creek stair-stepped its way down to the Columbia River through pounding chutes, deep pools, and waterfalls, one of which—Tunnel Falls—you actually walk *behind.*[*] At Punch Bowl Falls, I scrambled down to water's edge to get a photograph because seventy years ago my father had taken a shot from the same spot.

John Muir, after his visit here, wrote of such falls, " … how delightful the water music … the clashing, ringing spray."

Heading on, I started encountering a different breed of hiker: day-hikers, people in flip-flops, one man pushing a baby stroller. One such laid-back hiker, a kid maybe twenty, asked how far I'd hiked.

"Today or from the start?" I asked. My words took me back to 1999 at Little Belknap when Laura Buhl had asked the same thing after I'd asked her the same question; I'd come full circle.

"Well, how about from the start?" he asked.

"I started in California. I'm just doin' Ore—uh, I'm hiking the whole state of Oregon. Finishing today, in fact."

His eyes widened and he offered what I took as a cross-generational compliment of the highest order.

"Dude!"

LATER, AFTER twenty-six days, nearly 450 miles, snow, fire, and far too much trail mix, I reached the "Entering Washington" sign on the Bridge of the Gods at Cascade Locks. It was Tuesday afternoon, September 6, 2011.

Most of the emotion, frankly, had ebbed, having already been played out in my mind over the last few miles. There was none left.

Sally arrived to take me home. She took a photo of me with my arm around nobody; I was pondering Photoshopping Glenn in, but later nixed the idea, realizing he'd want the real thing. As it was, the moment had all the celebratory pizazz of a one-handed clap, the irony that what I expected to be the happiest moment of my grand PCT adventure was the saddest.

Hours later, just as we were passing Glenn's hometown of Albany on Interstate 5, I called him.

"Way to go, Bobby, you made it!" he said, sounding far more chipper than the day before.

"Yeah, thanks. How are you?"

"Much better."

"Good," I said. "I missed your navigational skills."

---

[*] Though technically not part of the PCT, the Eagle Creek trail is an alternate trail approved by the Pacific Crest Trail Association. Most PCT hikers take it.

I told him how I'd nearly become lost. How Wahtum Lake was posted for evacuation. And how I hadn't seen another hiker until I almost got to the Eagle Creek Trailhead.

He was his usual understated, unemotional self.

"I haven't puked since Parkdale."

"Proud of you, man."

A pause ensued. "Bob," he said, "I just wanna—."

Then nothing. Dead air.

"Glenny, you there? I think we lost cell service."

"Wanna thank you," he said.

Another pause.

"Glenn?"

We hadn't lost connection, I realized. He had broken down.

" ... for inviting me."

The words weren't coming easily for him. This from a guy whose emotions ran like Thielsen Creek, swift and deep, but, for the most part, hidden deep beneath the snow of stoicism.

"It was," he said, "the trip—the trip of a lifetime."

Now it was my words that were log-jammed.

"You're ... right," I finally managed. "The trip ... of a lifetime."

As a touch of fall cooled the air and fog snaked through the valleys below, Glenn took in the view near Three Fingered Jack.

Glenn Petersen

Top: With Mount Washington awaiting us up the trail, I stopped on August 29 to show Glenn the spot where I'd met Laura Buhl in 1999 and first heard about the PCT. Above: As we headed toward Mount Jefferson, Black Butte rose in dawn's early light.

Top: On the Mount Hood workaround, Glenn tightrope-walked across a silty creek on Mount Hood's eastern side. Above: The result of more than 400 soul- and sole-stretching miles.

Sally Welch

Glenn Petersen

Top: At the end of the trail, the Bridge of the Gods at Cascade Locks, Glenn was conspicuously absent. Left: After camping with Bugs and Bunny, of Israel, at Shale Lake, we ran into them again on State Route 26 near Mount Hood. Above: Mij, a hiker from Japan, shared the wonder of a Timberline Lodge brunch with us.

As we talked over our dilemma, Nina and Dennis apparently overheard us. "Hey, have a bunch of our homemade pepper jack jerky," said Dennis. "We're only up here for a long weekend and we have tons. Help yourself!"

AGE 60

2014

THE HIGH SIERRA

THIRD SUMMER *

START: JULY 28, 2014

GOAL: SOUTH 160 MILES FROM RUSH CREEK JCT TO CRABTREE MEADOW, PLUS SUMMIT OF MT. WHITNEY**

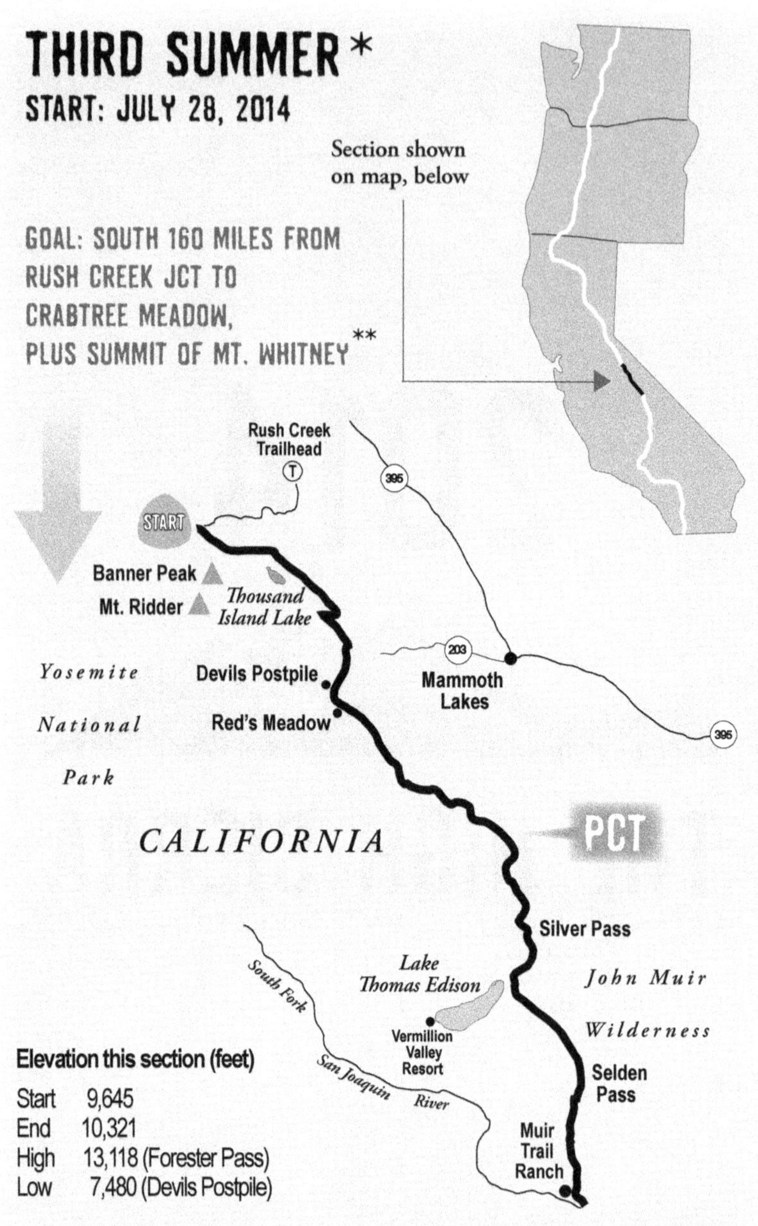

Elevation this section (feet)

Start	9,645
End	10,321
High	13,118 (Forester Pass)
Low	7,480 (Devils Postpile)

* The second summer (2012) was a fifty-mile "makeup" hike to do the stretch from Timberline Lodge to Bridge of the Gods that we missed in 2011 because of fire. Since nothing notable happened other than our survival, I didn't write about it. Other than hitting part of the trail on our Three Sisters Loop, we did not hike the PCT in 2013, which makes 2014 our "Third Summer."

** Not part of the Pacific Crest Trail.

6

REKINDLED

Life begins at the end of your comfort zone.
—Neale Donald Walsch

Glenn guided the Petersen's Trooper on Interstate 5 through the barrenness of Northern California. Destination: Yosemite National Park, six hours south of where we were now, near Redding.

I was fired up. The decision to attempt the 211-mile John Muir Trail had blunted any disappointment I had felt for Glenn and I not finishing Oregon together three years earlier. And I had gotten over my "poor me" lament from our Three Sisters trip in 2013 that had temporarily convinced me to never again step foot on the PCT.

Now, here we were, positioning ourselves to do the crown jewel of the 2,650-mile PCT. "The John Muir Trail is the highest, remotest, and most grueling segment of the Pacific Crest Trail," wrote Eric Blehm in *The Last Season.*

We would be hiking south from Yosemite National Park—specifically the Happy Isles Trailhead, marking the JMT's Northern Terminus—to Mount Whitney. Though the 14,505-foot mountain wasn't on the PCT, it wasn't a technical climb and was so tantalizing close that, as the highest point in the continental U.S., most hikers couldn't resist.

We would be summiting five passes of more than 11,900 feet and experiencing a trail considered one of the most scenic in the world. Most of it lay above 8,000 feet of elevation, offering a smorgasbord of views: jagged mountains, see-through streams, centuries-old trees, and lakes scattered like blue diamonds across the white-granite wilderness.

IN FEBRUARY I had turned sixty. It had been two years since Glenn and I had returned to Mount Hood in August 2012 to do the fifty-mile stretch to the Columbia River that the Dollar Fire had closed the year before. Besides doing the Mount Hood stretch we'd missed, Glenn had teamed up with a buddy, Quinton, to do the Grouse-Hill-to-Summit-Lake section that he'd passed up in 2011. In short, we were all caught up.

Courtesy of Jason and Deena, Sally and I had added two more grandchildren: Lincoln, born in 2012, and McCoy, who arrived just two months before we'd left for Yosemite, giving us five total. Meanwhile, the Petersens had welcomed a second grandson, Silas, born to Katie and David.

Sadly, however, Glenn had lost his eighty-five-year-old father, Paul, six week ago. I last saw him when he and Pauline had dropped us off at the Elk Lake Trailhead for Part II of our 2011 Oregon adventure. Paul, like Glenn, was a quiet, big-hearted man, a carpenter teeming with integrity and goodwill.

Meanwhile, that same year, 2012, I had joined another brother-in-law, Greg Scandrett, for an epic weekend fishing trip on the McKenzie River. What made it particularly special was that Greg and I had had a falling out a few years before and, after working hard to repair our relationship, this had been something of a celebration of our reconciliation. It was the first time the two of us had ever done something like this, just us. And it was satisfying to feel the reconnection.

Professionally, in December 2013 I had left *The Register-Guard* to concentrate on book writing, lead writers' workshops, and teach at University of Oregon's School of Journalism and Communication. Leaving the *Guard* wasn't a transition into retirement, but a way to allow me more flexibility for watching grandkids' games and for adventures, the PCT among them.

NOW, HERE we were en route to Yosemite. Glenn had worked for weeks to try and secure the hard-to-come-by permits, ultimately concluding that our best bet was to show up early and hope for one of the handful they offer each day. We hoped to go 211 miles in sixteen days.

"Looking forward to an In-N-Out burger in Redding," I said.

"Oh yeah, baby!"

"But I'm telling you, the last few times I've eaten at one I've been disappointed in their fries. They—."

Glenn's phone buzzed. It was Ann, whom Glenn punched onto speaker phone.

"Sorry, guys, but I have news," she said. "Just saw this on the Web: 'Saturday, July 26, 2014. Mariposa County, California. A fire burning in Yosemite National Park . . . .'"

I instinctively drew my hands to my face, just as I had three years before with news of the fire on Mount Hood.

" . . . has forced evacuations and road closures.' Let's see, 'has burned 500 acres, according to fire officials.'"

Glenn and I reacted differently to bad news. I processed everything through an emotional filter, feeling the need to grieve, lament, and, if necessary, gnash my teeth. He accepted glitches as if they were nothing but pesky flies, quickly defaulting to an overcoming-the-obstacle mode. He was a doctor/Eagle Scout/Lutheran; he had to stay unemotional. I wrote a personal column where I sometimes bared my soul; I had to analyze, process, feel, and, if warranted, lament.

Now, as we headed south, Ann enlisted help from daughter Carrie, an outdoorsy attorney in San Diego who knew California better than any of us. Fifteen minutes later, Carrie called with an update she read to us: "Yosemite National Park service has issued a mandatory evacuation order. You are being asked to evacuate the area due to extreme fire danger. Red Cross shelters are being set up . . . ."

Clearly, Yosemite as a starting point wasn't going to work. As our navigator, Glenn knew the lay of the PCT land far better than I did; if there was a workaround, he'd find it. And he did.

"I got us a backup permit for Rush Creek, a couple of hiking days south of Yosemite. But the trailhead is in the middle of nowhere, and not someplace I want to leave the car. So, I was thinking we could cut through the mountains at Sacramento, drive south to the closest town to Whitney Portal, a place called Lone Pine. We spend whatever's left of tonight there"—dusk was already settling in—"and, in the morning, find a ride back north to Rush Creek. The car will be waiting for us in Lone Pine when we exit the portal in two weeks."

How could I say no? Though it was already almost 9 P.M., I got on my phone and booked us a $79 room in a Lone Pine motel called the Dow Villa.

"The Web says a lot of Hollywood stars used to stay there when they were filming westerns back in the day, folks like Gene Autry and Gary Cooper."

"That's nice."

"Yeah, I think when you're sleeping in a motel for—what?—four hours, you definitely want that Old Hollywood ambiance."

Later, the scrawled notes from my two-inch-by-three-inch journal said we checked into the Dow Villa at 3:58 A.M.—after thirteen hours and nearly

700 miles on the road. The sun came up soon after my head hit the pillow in a room that had one double bed and no bathroom. *Down the hall to your left.*

WHEN THE INYO National Forest office opened at 8 A.M on Sunday, July 27, we were there, having gotten about three hours of sleep. After asking, we were given the number of a guy named Paul who was known to shuttle hikers to trailheads. And we were issued our "wag bags," thick plastic bags into which we had to deposit any solid waste while going up Mount Whitney.

"Man, these are huge," I said to Glenn. "The size of leaf bags. They'd work for Godzilla if he ever tried hiking Whitney and had the urge to purge."

As we headed back to the motel, the serrated peaks of the Sierra Nevada rose straight up to our west like the teeth of an old-time bucksaw. Unlike Oregon's handful of mountains above 9,000 feet, the largest of which rise in glorious, stage-to-themselves grandeur, California's are packed together, making it hard to hard to tell where one ends and the other begins. The Sierra Nevada has more than 500 peaks of 12,000 feet or higher, Oregon none.

When realizing we'd be hiking south beneath those hallowed spires the next day, the effect on my psyche was profound: part privilege, the idea that I was being allowed to hike these revered mountains; part excitement, the idea that I was heading into the Great Unknown; and part fear, the idea that the mountains' infinite vastness accentuated my relative smallness and inexperience.

For all such humility, after breakfast and a quick pit-stop in the restaurant's bathroom I walked down Lone Pine's sidewalk flush with excitement, as if I were a real PCT hiker. As if I were going to roll up my sleeves and step to the major-league plate in the morning.

A woman approached me, recognizing me as PCT hiker and wanting to talk trail with me, I surmised.

"Excuse me," she whispered, "I don't mean to intrude but it looks like you have some toilet paper stuck on the back of your sandal."

PAUL AGREED to take us to the Rush Creek Trailhead, about 120 miles north, for $220. The next morning, Monday, July 28, we zigzagged up a rocky trail next to an old miner's track. After ten miles, we reached the PCT not far from where we would spend the night: Thousand Island Lake, named not for the salad dressing but for the many tiny islands sprinkled across the multi-fingered lake.

We were here, in the High Sierra, a 400-mile long, thirty-five-to-sixty-mile wide blend of beauty and the beast. A place John Muir once described as "reposing like a smooth, cumulus cloud in the sunny sky, and so gloriously colored, and so luminous, it seems to be not clothed with life, but wholly composed of it, like the wall of some celestial city."

That said, we were greeted by slate skies and rain. Considering this was California, it sure felt like Oregon. But we awoke to clear skies, which revealed wilderness beauty like I'd never seen. The High Sierra was the stuff of Michelangelo. Every bend in the trail seemed to bring some jaw-dropping scene.

Under the watchful eyes of 12,942-foot Banner Peak and 13,149-foot Mount Ritter, we hiked south past Garnet Lake, Shadow Lake, and Rosalie Lake. We hiked across wooden bridges chiseled out of logs. We hiked past the Devils Postpile, vertical stacks of basalt that almost look like trees, "spookily geometric" as *Hiking the Pacific Crest Trail* put it.

Not a single road crossed this swath of remote beauty for 140 miles, from Tioga Pass in the north to Sherman Pass in the south, the longest such roadless stretch of the PCT. We spent the night at Red's Meadow, a store, restaurant, and camping ground that exited to Mammoth Lakes.*

We resupplied. Plastic bear vaults were required on the JMT and so all our food—and anything else that smelled, like sunblock or toothpaste—had to be stuffed into the blue translucent containers. At thirteen inches tall and nine inches wide, they looked like mini beer kegs. Black lids, with a tricky safety lock so bears couldn't unscrew them, sealed in the smell. Hikers generally loathed the things. They weighed 2.5 pounds and were cumbersome to pack.

WE MOVED ON, disciplining ourselves to get up at 4:05 A.M. every morning, be on the trail by 5 A.M., and hike until around 5 P.M. We'd then eat and go to sleep, often next to some crystal-clear stream on whose bottom an array of trout lazily wagged their tails in the current: rainbow, golden, brooks, and browns. My father the fly fisherman would have loved the High Sierra.

I often thought of him as we hiked using headlamps as the forest came to light before sunup. He was a photographer and the dark-to-light mornings in the woods reminded me of the first time, in our basement darkroom, he showed me an exposed print coming to life in a tray of developer: slowly, some parts of the photograph visible before others, and, finally, the picture in all its fullness. Like magic.

On Thursday afternoon, July 31, we stopped for water at Silver Pass Creek. Traditionally, the Young One would swoop in as if the endeavor were

* In 1972, a trans-Sierra road was proposed to transect Red's Meadow from Fresno to Mammoth Lakes but the unlikely duo of President Richard Nixon and California Governor Ronald Reagan put the kibosh on it.

a NASCAR pit stop, dip their Sawyer Minis, then be gone. We took our time, happy to use our frumpy Katadyn Hiker Pro Pumps.

"Hey, mate, haven't seen one of those in a long time," said an Aussie next to me. "Actually, since I was crewing on Noah's Ark."

He guffawed. I laughed, too. It was a great line—and I was flattered he'd taken the time to engage me at all.

Across the creek, a man in an orange shirt was filtering water. He stood out for two reasons: first, on what I'd already noticed as a young person's trail, he was of our vintage—Early Pleistocene. And his shirt represented a color less likely to be found on PCT hikers than on fans of Corvallis-based Oregon State, whose school colors are orange and black.

"Well," he said, "if it isn't the author of *Cascade Summer.*"

"Wait. You've read my hiking book?" I asked, knowing it was self-published and had sold about thirty-one copies, most to friends and relatives.

"Not only that, I heard you speak at the community center at Chintimini Park. I live in Corvallis. Barney Watson."

Watson had been an enology extension specialist—think wine—at OSU for nearly three decades. He was also co-founder of Tyee Wine Cellars southwest of Corvallis. He and a buddy were making a loop of sorts over a few days' time. *What were the chances of running into him in one of the most remote parts of the PCT?*

In the last few hours of daylight, a tinge of smoke from the Yosemite fire infused the forest with a soft hue of bronze; the translucent waters of North Fork Mono Creek splashed and swirled in the delicious light. To honor the beauty—and to cleanse my body for the first time in nearly a week—I lowered myself into a crystal-clear pool for a dip. *Brrrr ... ahhhh!*

ON FRIDAY, AUGUST 1, I was pumped as we descended a series of steep switchbacks to Muir Trail Ranch, where we were to pick up food we'd sent ahead in five-pound plastic buckets. When it came to food and weight, I'd learned long-distance hiking was about trying to find the balance between needs and wants, between what will fuel your body and what will feed your soul, between too much and not enough. Overstuff your pack and you overburdened your body; don't take enough and you don't have the energy to hike. It was a fine line between right and wrong.

"Most hikers," wrote Elizabeth Wenk in *John Muir Trail* regarding this section, "pick up three or four food drops." Glenn and I were attempting to do it with only two: Red's Meadow (east side of the Sierra crest) and Muir Trail Ranch (west). Because we had jobs back home and could afford only so many days off, we wanted, if possible, to avoid time-consuming resupplies off trail.

"Fresh food!" I said to Glenny, who was ahead of me.

"Yeah, instead of Snickers bars," said Glenn, "I'm going to be eating *fresh* Snickers bars!"

"I'm hoping to buy some batteries from someone," I said. "My headlamp was getting pretty dim this morning and I forgot to—."

In an instant, my left shoe hit a roundish rock that rolled me forward with a jolt. To regain my balance, I leapt like a lunging triple-jumper with my right, the steep downhill and weight of my pack propelling dangerously forward. Coming down, my right ankle folded.

"Ahhhhhhhhhhhh!"

I fell face first, the weight of the pack grinding me into the rocky trail. Glenn spun around.

"Knee? Ankle? What?" he asked as he peeled off his pack.

"Right ankle," I said, grimacing.

I struggled out of my shoe, rolled my sock down and cringed to see what looked like a third of a fleshy tennis ball protruding from my outside ankle.

"Looks like a bad sprain," he said.

We were two miles above the ranch and still needed to drop more than a thousand feet.

"Rate the pain, one to ten," said Glenn.

"Maybe five, six."

"Can you put any weight on it?"

I stood. Pain stabbed when I did so but what choice did I have? It was a slow two miles but with trekking poles to ease the pressure, I hobbled into the gathering of other hikers at MTR midafternoon.

The mood was up but I was down. I got my bucket, bought three AAA batteries from a young woman who refused payment until I insisted, then perused the tubs of grub and gear that hikers had off-loaded. "Take what you need," a sign said. "Need what you take."

"Hey, check this out," said Glenn, who hadn't noticed my battery transaction. "You're in luck!" He pointed to a bucket with hundreds of AAA batteries, looking like silver smelt without all the wriggling—and free for the taking.

"Not my day," I said.

"Huh?"

"I just paid a hiker twenty bucks for three."

At a picnic table, I did a bit of food-swapping with other hikers. I had an overabundance of just about everything, which was fine with a kid who happily accepted one of those cinema-sized boxes of Mike & Ikes and promptly tipped it into his mouth as if it were a four-ounce box of raisins. When I raised an unopened bag of soft tortilla shells in the air, a young woman, "Firefly," snapped it up like a trout to a caddisfly.

If we were going on—and that was yet to be determined—we needed to stuff eight days' worth of food in our respective bear vaults. Forget trying to create an organized system; the best you could do was stuff and cram and hope the lid didn't spring off like a Jack-in-a-Box when you opened it. I'd seen hikers so intent on filling every square centimeter that they wedged individual M&Ms into remaining spaces. But here was the worst thing about the bear-vault setup: except for your used toilet paper—thank goodness for small favors—anything that smelled had to go in the vault.

"Jerky, Milky Ways, trail mix, Fritos—it doesn't matter what I eat," I told Glenn. "It all tastes like Anti Monkey Butt smells."

Now, a few hundred feet from MTR, I limped down to the South Fork San Joaquin River, pulled off my shoe and socks, and did two things that I hoped would help me be able to continue: soaked my foot in the icy waters and prayed. Meanwhile, Glenn found us a place to camp, then joined me.

"Bobby, how's it feeling?"

"A little better."

Glenn exhaled. "So, we've got a big decision to make. We're just below 8,000 feet. Our schedule for tomorrow calls for sixteen miles and 3,000 feet of elevation gain. Then five major passes leading up to Whitney, which you know is more than 14,000 feet. That's a lot of steps, a lot of climbing."

I nodded, overwhelmed by it all.

"Bottom line: If we're not going on, this is the easiest place to get off. And, frankly, one of the few places to get off between here and Whitney. There's a rugged road into the ranch and they use a giant-wheeled truck to bring in the hikers' resupply buckets. We could probably go out on that truck."

"Do we have to decide now or can we wait until morning," I asked, "and see if my ankle's gotten better?"

"Morning's fine," he said. "But I need you to know a few things: Only you can make the call. Only you know whether you should keep going. And if you decide the answer's no, don't think you've somehow ruined the trip or disappointed me. I'm honestly good with whatever you decide. Really."

My eyes grew misty. I'd trained hard for six months, driven 700 miles, and hiked eighty miles since Rush Creek. I was physically tired, emotionally spent, and feeling the angst of a situation out of my control, which I hated. I also hated that I could ruin the trip for Glenn. And that the accident had happened on a trail so hallowed that hikers came from all over the world to experience it.

"And what about you?" I asked. "When you went down with vertigo at

Mt. Hood, you had me go on. I think you need that same opportunity if I can't make it. I've got a credit card and a thumb. I can get home."

"Nope. I'm going where you're going. My car. My keys. My choice."

"Yeah, a car that's on the opposite side of a giant mountain range from where we're at now."

"Bob, if you can't make it, we'll go out together west and find a way to get back east to Lone Pine."

I tried to talk but, at first, couldn't. The words stuck.

"I ... appreciate ... that."

At camp that night, lying on my back with my right leg propped atop my bear canister, two things kept my mind off my plight: a giant beef stick and a can of Cheez Whiz. Glenn had traded for them at MTR, the best transaction since the Yankees got Babe Ruth from the Red Sox. I never knew meat and processed cheese could taste so wonderful. After Glenn wrapped my ankle—the doctor dividend was paying off—we ate that entire beef stick as if paupers in the king's court, oozing with appreciation for every bite.

But as I slid gingerly into my bag that night and the sound of the San Joaquin trickled in the distance, my mind kept returning to one question:

Is this my last night on the PCT?

On our first full day in the High Sierra, Glenn paused to soak in the beauty of Thousand Island Lake, with 12,936-foot Banner Peak in the distance.

Beauty unfurled in spectacular views every way we looked, including these two distinctively different trees with Banner Peak in the background.

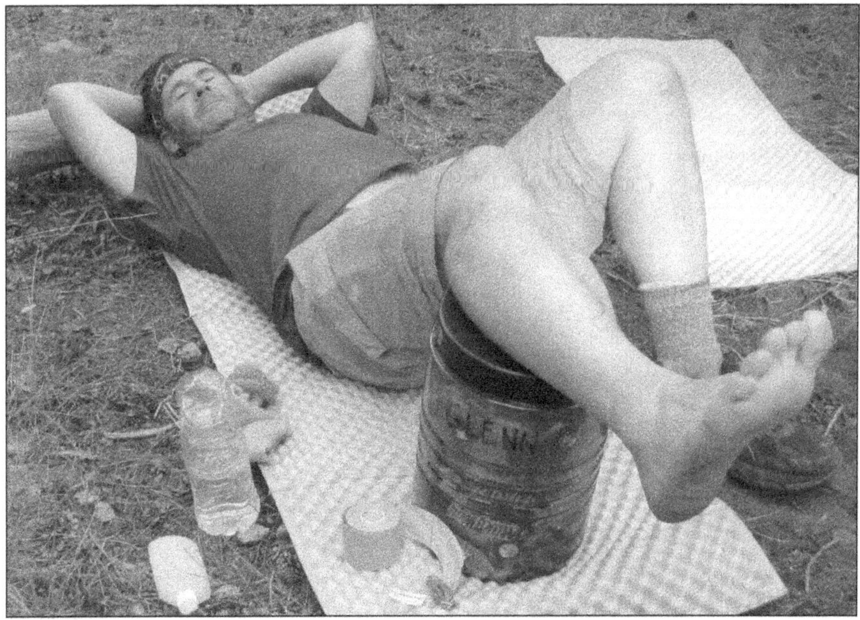

Glenn Petersen

Top: The Devil's Postpile features a rare collection of "columnar basalt" that resembles vertically stacked timber—and marked the first, and last, time on the trip we'd see tourists. Above: On August 1 my sprained ankle put our trip in jeopardy.

THIRD SUMMER
START: AUGUST 2, 2014
SOUTH 28 MILES FROM
MUIR TRAIL RANCH
TO LE CONTE CANYON
Section shown on map, below
CALIFORNIA
START
Muir Trail Ranch
S. Fork San Joaquin River
McClure Ranger Station
Evolution Valley
McClure Meadows
Evolution Creek
PCT
Evolution Lake
Sierra National Forest
Sapphire Lake
Evolution Basin
Bishop Pass Trail (East to Hwy. 395)
Helen Lake
Wanda Lake
Muir Pass
Le Conte Canyon
LeConte Ranger Station
Kings Canyon National Park
Elevation this section (feet)
Start 7,889
End 8,733
High 11,974 (Muir Pass)
Low 7,889 (Muir Trail Ranch)

EDGE

Now faith is the assurance that what we hope for will come about and the certainty that what we cannot see exists.

—Hebrews 1:1

FAITH WOULDN'T be faith if we could explain it. Was the reason I hiked more than sixteen miles and climbed more than 3,000 feet with little pain the next day because I had prayed? Because I had soaked my ankle in the icy Joaquin? Both? Neither?

I couldn't say for sure, even if I was inclined to go with "both." I see no inconsistency between faith and pragmatism, the idea that trusting in God and rolling up your sleeves to help your cause could go hand in hand. As a sign on our family sailboat said: "Pray to God but row for shore!"

What I did know was that when I awoke at 4:05 A.M. on Saturday, August 2, 2014, the swelling was down, the pain had abated, and the light from my head lamp—powered by the most expensive batteries on the PCT—shone brightly. By midmorning, I realized that my ankle was withstanding a pack at maximum weight because of the resupply stop, just over forty pounds, and a trail that seemed to only go "up and upper."

"Unbelievable," I told Glenn as we hiked on a trail high about the San Joaquin. "Thank you, God!"

"Long live The Oregon Boys!"

We passed from the John Muir Wilderness to Kings Canyon National Park. This was remoteness at its purest. Since 98 percent of Kings Canyon's nearly half-million acres were bona fide wilderness, you never sensed you were even on the fringe of civilization; instead, you were literally deep in the woods—the forests, rivers, lakes, and mountains wrapping you in an exquisite cocoon of back-country privilege.

We saw Evolution Creek Falls, which not only signaled beauty but danger. Above it, Evolution Creek was among the more notoriously dangerous early-season PCT water crossings; in Yosemite alone, a dozen or so people drowned each year. But it was late July and the crossing for me was easy, requiring only trading out my Asics trail-running shoes for Crocs.

At a lunch stop along the creek, I couldn't resist; I lay on my stomach on a flat rock, leaned forward and dipped my head into the cold, clear waters—just because I could.

WHEN I first saw the "Entering Kings Canyon" sign, I immediately thought of the book. A few years earlier, I had read *The Last Season,* a fascinating nonfiction story by Eric Blehm about Randy Morgenson, a legendary back country forest ranger in these parts who'd saved countless hikers over the decades then gone missing himself in 1995.* Blehm's book braided the equally interesting strands of the great outdoors and the inner struggles of a passionate ranger whose personal life had unraveled; just before he disappeared, his wife, feeling he belonged more to the mountains than to her, filed for divorce.

At McClure Meadows, I insisted we go off trail a few hundred feet to see the ranger cabin where Morgenson had spent many a summer. I confess, I had an obsessive interest in *The Last Season*. Glenn had read the book, too, though hadn't been grabbed by it like I had. Part of it, I suppose, was that I read the book not only as a reader but as a writer. Blehm had done a masterful job of researching and writing Morgenson's story, and as we walked the woods near where the ranger had disappeared, my mind was like the ears of a deer at even the slightest sound. I'd see places that had been the backdrop for the book and feel an eerie sense of connection.

"What do you think?" I asked Glenn. "Did Morgenson commit suicide? Was it an accident? Was he 'living recklessly' because he'd lost hope, wasn't being cautious, and slipped off a cliff? Or could he have been murdered?"

"No clue."

"I'm going with suicide—not that you asked. In decades of being a ranger the guy doesn't die or get seriously hurt, then he goes missing—coincidentally, just after he's been served divorce papers. Just after he'd mentioned to

* That was the same year Cheryl Strayed, the celebrated author of the 2012 book *Wild,* walked the PCT, though, because of heavy snow, she skipped the High Sierra.

someone that they wouldn't have to put up with him anymore. Just after he'd told a friend that 'the least these mountains deserve is a body.'"

FROM MCCLURE Meadow we climbed to nearly 11,000 feet, my mind steeled on the delicious dividend that would reward us for this gritty day—a night on the shores of Evolution Lake. But the higher we got the more the cloud cover morphed from dull gray to threatening thunderheads.

"Looks ominous," said Glenn, stopping to grab a raincoat out of his pack.

A light wind turned blustery. Like kettle drums, thunder rumbled low, then loud, cracking in cymbal clashes across the Evolution Valley. A bolt of lightning arced toward the jagged edge of 12,944-foot Mount McGee.

We scuttled off the trail, shed our packs, distanced ourselves from our aluminum poles, grabbed our foam sleeping pads and laid down on the thinly wooded mountain side.

A lull, then more of the same. *C-c-c-c-c-c-crack!* Another bolt. Another quiver of fear in my gut. At this elevation, the equivalent of Oregon's Mount Hood, we couldn't hide, but we could make ourselves less likely targets. In time, the storm moved on, and so did we. It had been an unnerving half hour.

In early evening, we set up our tents on a rocky flank of Evolution Lake, which offered the most stunning view of any place I'd camped in my life. Above the 10,850-foot-high lake, granite spires reached for the sky, creating an amphitheater feel to it all, as if the sky, mountains, and lake were music for the ears and we were the audience privileged to listen. The only disappointment was the cloud cover that hung over our perch, precluding the chance to experience what naturalist John Muir had dubbed the High Sierra "range of light."

We set up camp, ate dinner—Freeze-Dried Lasagna—and were just getting in our tents when it happened: the clouds parted slightly and a shaft of orange-pink light from the west suddenly lit up the granite spires that rose above the lake. I grabbed my iPhone and started shooting photos, my haste proving wise; the light came and went with the brevity of a small child offering a goodnight kiss before trundling off to bed.

THE NEXT MORNING, Sunday, August 3, we awoke to a light rain pattering our tents. It sounded more ominous than refreshing. The physics of weather cared nothing about what seemed seasonally "proper" or "improper." Even if it was early August, we were nearly two miles above sea level and would, today, be tackling the first of five major passes—Muir, at 11,955 feet.

Atmospheric physics weren't about to acquiesce to the "summer-equals-warmth" fallacies of non-discerning hikers. Instead, with no regard for seasons or for hikers walking the thin line between safety and danger, the weather gods would remind us that if, back home, our worlds were relatively safe, secure, and predictable, these mountains were not. As Emerson said: "Nature, as we know it, is no saint." *

We stretched rain covers over our packs and hit the trail in the darkness, headlamps lighting our way. Up we climbed through rocky Evolution Basin. We hopped from rock-to-rock to cross a feeder stream into Wanda Lake, named for one of John Muir's two daughters. At first light, the landscape looked cold, foreboding, and sparse, as if we were on an alien planet. I didn't like the vibe, a place so remote that park rangers were helicoptered into and out of their stations.

As we climbed higher, clouds rolled in, obscuring the remaining views of the granite peaks. The rain fell harder. But when we reached the rock hut atop 11,974-foot Muir Pass, built in 1930 to honor the environmentalist and Sierra Club founder, I noted little concern from the dozen Young Ones huddled inside. Me? I was shrouded in unease.

"Most hypothermia cases develop in air temperatures between 30 degrees and 50 degrees," wrote Jeffry Schaffer and Andy Selters in *Pacific Crest Trail: Oregon and Washington.* "Most [people] simply can't believe such temperatures can be dangerous."

I could. This storm wasn't letting up, might get worse, and we had twelve miles to our targeted camping spot—*downhill,* meaning less physiological bang for the buck to ward off the chill. And few places flat enough or wide enough to make camp if we got into trouble.

"Glenny," I said, "I think we need to get off this mountain. Fast."

"Agreed. Let's go."

We headed down Le Conte Canyon along Middle Fork Kings River, the trail, in places, less foot path than stream. My feet darted left and right, my body fueled by urgency.

By early afternoon, we'd been hiking for almost ten hours in the rain, having had only two breaks. Our one-mile-per-hour pace was about half our usual speed and indicative of the trying conditions—especially since it seemed as if we were going faster than usual. My mind was foggy, my knees wobbly, my hands cold. I wanted to stop, rest, and eat, but feared the cure could be worse than the cold. We were a good day's hike from the nearest exit from the PCT, Bishop Pass.

---

* Which is one of the reasons we chose a cover for *Seven Summers* featuring the drawing of a rainy night near Yosemite—to dispel the notion of the PCT as a pine-needled I-5 hiked only in buttery sunshine.

"When hiking minimally dressed during cold, rainy weather we are operating metabolically," wrote Ray Jardine in *The PCT Hiker's Handbook.* "Consequently, at each of our rest stops we might consider ourselves in a red-alert situation. Hypothermia lurks around the corner."

When a low-flying helicopter screamed through the canyon—*thwock, thwock, thwock*—I shuddered as it passed overhead. *Which one of those dozen hikers we'd seen in the hut had slipped off a ledge and broken a leg, shivered himself into hypothermic shock—or worse?*

"How much farther?" I yelled to Glenny over the sound of stream and wind.

"We camped at milepost 842. We're trying to get to 827, where Palisades Creek meets Middle Fork Kings River. Campsite there."

"Fine, but how much *more*?" I said, my impatience growing—and showing.

Whenever I asked a mileage question of Glenn, I would instinctively imagine a number I could live with—and one I'd be thrilled with. In this case, I could live with two but hoped for one.

"Five," he said.

"Are you kidding me?"

Glenn showed no reaction. Or was he reacting but not just in a way I could discern, like a duck's feet madly paddling below the surface? Now wasn't the time to try to plumb the depths of my stoic brother-in-law's mind or soul. I just wanted to get warm.

For half an hour, as we descended, I stewed and processed, ultimately concluding that pride was no friend but enemy. This wasn't about machismo, but about survival.

"G-g-g-lenny," I said. "I g-g-gotta be blunt. I c-c-can't feel my fingers. And I'm outta g-g-as."

"So, you don't think you can make it another four miles?"

"I don't think I can make it another f-f-four *feet.* I need to g-g-get warm."

Glenn was stubborn but not inflexible. He liked setting goals and meeting them, but wasn't averse to being talked out of them if I could provide him a good reason.

"OK," he said. "Let's find some shelter."

It was about 3 P.M. In the next hour I saw the same Glenn Petersen I'd seen in Haiti when the tap-tap rolled and he and the medical staff were dealing with a truckload of victims. It was as if he'd been waiting a lifetime to utilize a handful of procedures he'd learned as a Scout in the basement of Bethesda Lutheran Church and honed at Camp Melakwa.

He guided me to the dryness beneath a huge tree; helped me get my pack off; found a relatively flat spot for tents between a neighboring tree; hacked dead branches away from the tree's base so our tents would fit; and helped me put up my tent, then put up his own, making sure the two vestibules were facing each other "so I can keep an eye on you."

"Get all your clothes off and get in your bag—stat," he said. "Then give me your wet stuff."

Normally, such a mother-hen approach would have eaten at me like battery acid. But in my state of mind (foggy, disconnected) and state of body (shivering violently), I welcomed it like hot chicken soup. I shivered in my bag, which was rated for thirty-two degrees but had a cotton liner that supposedly gave me another ten degrees of warmth.

Glenn hung up our wet clothes on a line he'd strung, then fired up the Jetboil stove. He rummaged through my bear vault, perhaps the hardest task yet given how difficult the lids were to get off in warm conditions, much less in forty-degree rain with cold, numb fingers.

Uncontrolled shivering, which I was doing, was both a fix and a worry: a fix because that's how your body attempts to maintain its vital temperature, a worry because it also indicates hypothermia could be near. It would take me an hour to stop shivering—and two to rediscover my sense of humor.

"Watch out for that first pass," I said, mocking a line from Needle Nose Ned in *Groundhog Day.* "It's a *doozie.*"

"Yep," said Glenn. "Long day."

"On second thought, the pass wasn't the culprit, the rain was."

"Never stopped. One pass down, four to go. Hey, what kind of freeze-dried dinner can I fix you, Bob?"

"Whatever you can find. And it'll probably be at the bottom of the vault, where I keep my OK-to-crush stuff."

He pawed through the vault like a trick-or-treater looking for Skittles. "Looks like Chili Mac, Spaghetti or Chicken and Rice."

"Chicken and Rice. Thanks."

We ate, then fell asleep. In the middle of the night, I was awakened by a scratching sound on the floor of my tent. *What the—?* I soon realized what was happening: a shrew or mouse was skittering between my tent floor and the ground, as if from a PCT version of *Tremors*. I was too tired to care. I went back to sleep.

At the time, I had little perspective on what was happening then and what had happened earlier that day. But later it dawned on me: On August 3, 2014, Dr. Glenn Petersen, my brother-in-law, quite likely saved my life.

Glenn Petersen

Top: Our spot at Evolution Lake afforded the finest view I'd had from a tent. (I wish expense hadn't precluded us from using color inside this book; you'd see the alluring orange light on the mountains and Glenn's barely visible green tent in the lower right.) Above: Slogging while drenched, I wasn't a happy camper.

THIRD SUMMER

START: AUGUST 4, 2014

GOAL: SOUTH 63 MILES FROM LE CONTE CANYON TO CRABTREE MEADOW

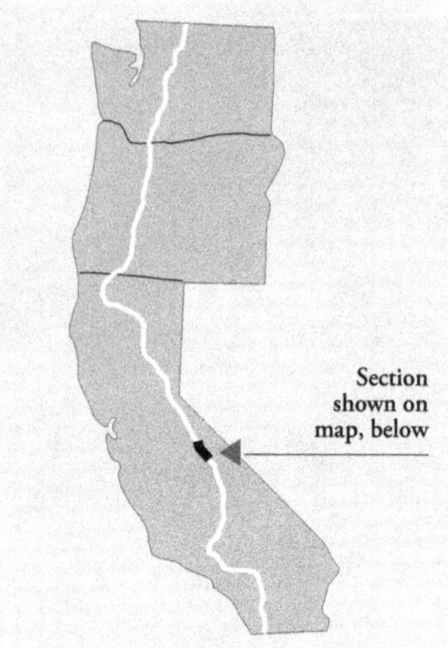

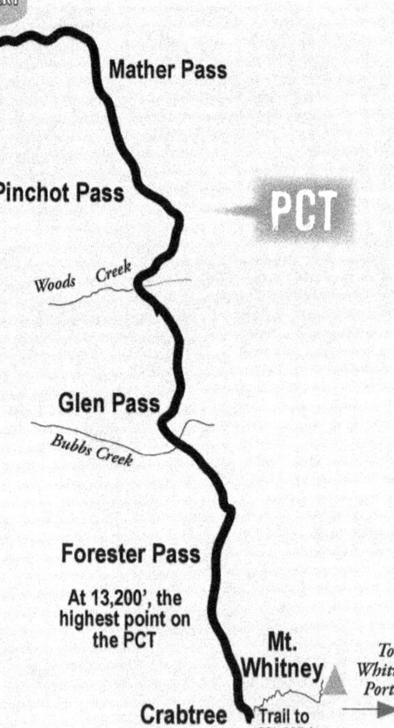

Elevation this section (feet)

Start	8,733
End	10,321
High	13,118 (Forester Pass)
Low	8,356 (Mono Lake Trail Jct.)

8

REVIVAL

Nothing puts things in perspective as quickly as a mountain.

—Josephine Tey

FOR ME, the two worst times during the daily PCT rhythm were the hour after eating lunch—you still had a long way to go, the heat was often intensifying, and you had to rediscover your trail legs—and the hour after awakening in the darkness to begin another day.

You turn on your headlamp. You take your meds. You put on your damp, cold, smelly hiking clothes. You bend to tie your shoes while sitting like an "L" on its back, reminded that you're getting less limber every year. You go to the bathroom in the chilled darkness of the woods, making sure you keep your eye on your partner's headlamp lest you get lost.* And you stuff your entire life in a seventy-five-liter pack, hoping to have not forgotten something while blurred by the mental fog of 4 A.M. You go from dreams to reality, from warm to cold, from slumber to slogging up the trail once again.

The next morning—Monday, August 4—the transition was harder than usual. We awakened to ice on our tents. And left with packs that had probably gained two or three pounds each in water weight from that and yesterday's

---

* The average lost person will generally not travel farther than one hundred meters from where they began, a study by researcher Jan Souman found in 2009. His point: humans are not predisposed to walk in straight lines. Neither do we naturally circle. We wander like "the random squiggles a toddler makes with a crayon," writes Robert Moor in *On Trails.*

rainstorm. My confidence was low, as if the previous day had not only leveled me physically but emotionally.

The skies were cloudy and threatening. We hadn't had a reliable weather report in days. And an encounter with a Redmond, Oregon, family did nothing to clear my pall of uncertainty.

"We got snowed on last night this side of Mather," said a woman, who, along with her husband, was shepherding their school-age children, the youngest we'd seen on the trail. "We've been in our tents for three days. We're getting out of here, going out Bishop Pass. Didn't expect snow in August. Lots of people leaving."

In the Ecclesiastical world of long-distance hiking, there was a time to press on and a time to turn back. What time was it for The Oregon Boys?

Beyond 12,068-foot Mather Pass we still had to get through—*over*—12,093-foot Pinchot Pass, 11,926-foot Glen Pass, and the granddaddy of them all, 13,153-foot Forester Pass, one granite buttress per day.*

"Crossroads time," I said, hoping for clarity from Glenn. "What think ye?"

Glenn's brain, I assumed, had been churning since last night.

"The junction to Bishop Pass that that family is taking is just back up the trail, less than a mile," he said. "We passed it yesterday. So that's an option if we want to call it quits."

"And that exits to the east, the side of the Sierras we started on, right, where the car is?"

"Correct. It eventually brings you to a road that takes you to 395 and the town of Bishop, about sixty miles north of Lone Pine."

"And if we press on but later decide to exit, what options are there?"

"Not many," he said. "And nothing easy. It'll be nearly a full day's hike just to get to a remote trailhead, east or west, followed by an iffy hitch back to civilization. But, look, we're getting deeper into August; I'm thinking this precipitation is an anomaly that won't last—*can't* last. And it's only partly cloudy today. I'm thinking we press on. You?"

I was glad he asked. Here was my chance to be honest, like I'd been the day before in saying I didn't think it was wise for me to continue.

"Onward through the fog."

"Really?"

* Though to the uninitiated it may sound counter-intuitive, passes are low points—in this case in the otherwise seemingly impenetrable High Sierra. Here, passes allowed passage from one lake-dotted, rocky valley to the next. A pass is a means to an end, something to pass through (over), as opposed to a summit, which is the top of a peak and an end unto itself.

"Whatever it takes."

If the previous day had concerned me, it hadn't defeated me. Maybe at a subconscious level it had taught me that we could survive some tough days. At any rate, I was game to continue.

On steep talus, we soon trudged up something called the Golden Staircase, the last portion of the John Muir Trail to be built. I understood why; it brought to mind Led Zeppelin's "Stairway to Heaven" song. A trail-engineering marvel, it featured switchback after switchback coiling into the sky like a cobra, one granite step after another, each the thickness of a railroad tie. No wonder Joseph Le Conte, when first navigating this terrain in 1908, found this stretch the only part of the trail he couldn't get livestock over. It was so steep and seemingly so infinite that I half-expected to find St. Peter standing up top in a Patagonia puffy.

But as I took a breather halfway up—Glenn was behind—I saw it far above: an American flag, waving in the mist. At first, the red, white, and blue image was such a stark contrast to the dark earth tones of the rocky landscape that I did a double take. Was I relapsing into my fuzziness of the previous day? Nope. It was an American flag, fixed to the pack of a kid—a Boy Scout, I realized.

Oh. My. Gosh.

There I was, huffing and puffing up this mountain, and there they were, a dozen members of the so-called lost generation of youth, climbing with far more vigor than I had. In that moment, I vowed two things: I would honor their resolve by doubling down on my own. And I would never again assume that everyone under the age of eighteen is only playing video games and punching iPhones. In fact, I stopped and took some notes to that effect—on my, uh, iPhone.

THE SKIES were thick with clouds, but none leaking precipitation. Around me: a 360-degree view of granite mountains and glacial troughs, the spines going every which way like waves in a choppy sea.

As we hiked past Palisade Lakes we saw young hikers who were only now crawling out of bed and drying their tents. We'd probably made ten miles by then—it was late morning—and it infused me with confidence and just a touch of "Take that, Young Ones" pride.

Near the top of Mather, at nearly 12,000 feet, we came upon a handful of young people who were part of a trail crew. They were, like mountain goats, dug into the side of a nearly forty-five-degree slope amid rocks the size of cars, hotel refrigerators, you name it. They were using Pulaskis and steel pry bars to fix parts of a trail that dated back to 1938.

"No … pun … intended," I said, so tired I could hardly talk. "But … you … guys … rock."

"Thanks," said a young man, part of a group of five, two of whom were women.

"So where … do you … stay … at night?"

He pointed to a lake a good thousand feet below us.

"Heck of … a commute," I said. "Thanks … for the effort."

"Happy to be here."

We reached the top of Mather Pass at 2:30 P.M. The celebratory photograph of us showed something that had been missing lately: smiles. We were the only ones on top. We scarfed down some food, sent a Spot satellite message home—one-way communication only—and started down Mather's steeper south side, the victory fueling our emotional tanks.

Muir had been only a 1,105-foot climb up from Evolution Lake—it was the "down" that almost killed us—and Mather 3,500. For perspective, I had begun measuring our daily climbs in (Mount) "Pisgahs," my thousand-foot training butte back home with which Glenn, too, was familiar.

"We just did three-and-a-half Pisgahs," I told Glenn atop Mather.

The next day we bagged Pinchot, a two-Pisgah pass. Compared to these giants, Oregon's passes were low, few, wide, and obscure. The JMT's were like a succession of gun sights in massive walls of granite.

But once you were atop one, you earned a rare and thrilling bonus: the ability to see, with a single swivel of the head, where you'd been, where you were, and where you were going. The phenomenon was the geographic equivalent of my mother's reminder that we enjoy a life experience in three ways: by looking forward to it, immersing ourselves in it, and looking back on it.

As we descended south, I was reminded that we were closing in on an area where searches looked hard for Randy Morgenson. Earlier in the day, I'd seen a sign for Bench Lake Ranger Station, which *The Last Season* pointed out, was the last known place the ranger had been before having gone missing.

At 5:30 P.M., we crossed a jiggly suspension bridge at Woods Creek that some call "the Golden Gate of the Sierra." It was a shaky experience, like something from *Indiana Jones,* but because you could hold on to cables above the crossway wooden slats, far less scary than if we'd had to wade through the swift waters below.

As per our routine, Glenn and I made camp, filtered water for the next morning's hike over Glen Pass, ate dinner, and went to bed.

I was within two miles of where searchers found Randy Morgenson's remains, only a few hundred feet off the PCT. No wonder it was a restless night of sleep.

WEDNESDAY, August 6 dawned crisp and clear, as if the weather gods had shaken the meteorological Etch-a-Sketch and said: *Time to start over.* This, finally, was the Sierra Nevada Range that I'd expected and, after eight days of mainly clouds, had arrived.

Fin Dome rose dramatically from beyond Dollar Lake to 11,673 feet, its whitish peak contrasting sharply with the UCLA blue sky and reflecting brilliantly in the stillness of the water in front of us.

At Rae Lakes, where Morgenson had staffed the ranger station for many a summer, we met a young couple from Santa Cruz, Nina and Dennis Murphy, who were on a four-day trip. They were affable, outgoing, and encouraging, not necessarily the default format on the PCT thus far. Not that we were finding people rude, self-centered, and dishonoring to the trail and others, but most hikers politely kept to themselves.*

After a fifteen-minute trail mix break with the couple, we pressed upward and onward to Glen Pass. At the top, we had a sort of "we-won-the-Rose-Bowl" giddiness to us. It was extra fun because Nina and Dennis had arrived just before us, and we were reveling in each other's triumphs. It felt as if we were on top of the world.

Looking south, we could see our future: Forester Pass, at 13,153 feet the highest point on the PCT.

Alas, we could also see how empty our bear canisters had become. It happened atop the pass, the realization that we were running dangerously low on food; until then, I couldn't recall a single conversation, or concern, about our rations. At Muir Trail Ranch, we'd crammed the containers with eight days' worth of food; we still had three days left on the trail. But in the bottom of my canister, I now had only two freeze-dried dinners, a handful of candy bars, three tortilla shells, and a couple of Svenhard's pastries so smashed they weren't much thicker than autumn leaves.

"Man, I can't help but think of all that food I gave away at both Red's Meadow and MTR," I said. "An entire sack of tortilla shells."

"Me too."

It seemed that in our pursuit of Whitney, two things were happening: We were burning unusually large amounts of calories because of the steep ups and downs. And we weren't disciplining ourselves on our intake. Between fretting about weather the first few days and turning into slap-happy pass

---

* In terms of the "leave no trace" philosophy, I rarely found trash or unburied toilet paper on the PCT. Generally speaking, if you found a beer can or candy bar wrapper, it suggested you were nearing a town or some other place where the trail offered easy public access. Yes, some hikers cut a few switchback corners, but that was the exception, not the rule. Generally, hikers respected the no-trace edict.

baggers the last few, we'd been scarfing down food like offensive linemen at an all-you-can-eat buffet.

On the Oregon stretch in 2011, I'd organized my food in sandwich bags marked "Monday, Tuesday," etc., which made it easier to stay on pace. With a bear canister, however, I found that was impossible. You had to keep your go-to stuff near the top. And even if you'd had the canister nominally organized in the early days, it took only one deep dive to create a discombobulated mess. Maybe these canisters were keeping bears away each night; all I knew was that they were giant pains in the keister, their most obvious benefit giving you something to sit on.

Our "mountain high" was suddenly being served with a side of "what-were-we-thinking?" low. As we talked over our dilemma, Nina and Dennis apparently overheard us.

"Hey, have a bunch of our homemade pepper jack jerky," said Dennis. "We're only up here for a long weekend and we have tons. Help yourself!"

I didn't need to be asked twice. It was the finest jerky I'd ever tasted.

"Here, have some mozzarella cheese to go with it," said Nina, handing me a cube.

The generosity of this young couple helped save our trip—or at least kept us from standing alongside the trail with "Will Hike for Food" signs.

THAT NIGHT, we camped in a thinly treed swath along Bubbs Creek. I had just stretched out for a nap when Glenny whispered, "Bob, look, over there: a bear." We hadn't seen one yet and I was eager to—at a distance.

I sat up. "Where?"

"Down at that creek, just left of the trail."

I squinted hard, then furrowed my brow. "Uh, Glenn, it's only a bear if this one is wearing a red towel around its neck."

"Huh?"

I got up and took a dozen steps forward.

"Your 'bear' looks a lot like a dark llama with a red towel around its neck."

That's exactly what it was—a red-toweled llama, belonging to the people camped next to us, who were getting water for their pack animal.

By the time we headed up the fifth and final pass, Forester, I had a theory about why these mighty climbs seemed less difficult than I'd expected. Honestly, I could remember afternoons in Oregon—a twenty-three miler to Olallie Lake came to mind—when I was thinking: *I can't go another step. I'm never going to make it. Too tired. Too painful.* But not on this stretch.

So, why had the final four passes in the Sierra not seemed as daunting, despite the thin air, the steep terrain, and the trail consisting mainly of rocks that were harder on the feet than dirt?

▲ First, I'm convinced Diamox—a prescription med Glenny recommended we take to prevent altitude sickness—was doing its job. On the JMT, I never felt any effects of hiking at such high altitudes, even though, as a college student, I'd gotten dizzy atop the South Sister, which is some 1,500 to 3,000 feet lower than these giants.

▲ Second, the five passes were neatly spaced out, so you didn't have to bite off huge chunks of mileage to get them done. We did about fifteen miles each day, twenty percent less than our usual per-day mileage.

▲ Third, the in-your-face nature of these giants fueled my adrenalin. Because I was almost always above the timberline, I knew from first light what my objective was because I was already heading up it. I could look each pass in the eye and sense that each one was looking into my soul, as if to say: *Are you tough enough to get past me?* I liked the challenge.

▲ Finally, because we were almost always above the timberline, the sweeping views distracted me—anesthetized me—from whatever pain I might have otherwise been feeling.

I was awed not only by the 360-degree beauty but by the courage and persistence of those around me, including a guy on a horse leading four pack mules over the top of Forester's steep, three-foot-wide trail chiseled in the rocks.

"Wow," I said. "Can't believe you can get those animals over these narrow, twisting trails."

"Hell, this is nothin'," he said, tipping back his wide-brimmed hat. "I've brought pack trains over this in the moonlight." I didn't doubt it.

The trail descending from Forester's summit had been blasted from a wall of sheer granite. Because it was a narrow, switch-backing ledge, you couldn't afford to relax. It had the feel of a roller coaster ride on which your car stopped at a summit, and, in the stillness, you saw, up close, the eerie context: how high you were and how precarious your position was. With snow, Forester's south-facing avalanche chute was among the trail's most frightening stretches, sloping sixty degrees in some places.

"I can't imagine how the Young Ones, in May or June, get up the south side of this mountain in the snow," I said to Glenn.

"And we thought Devils Peak was scary."

That led to a lively discussion about which was tougher—the PCT or the Appalachian Trail.

"From what I hear, because the PCT was built for both people *and* horses, the grades aren't as severe as the AT," I said. "On the other hand, we're twice as high right now as the highest point on the AT. And this is true wilderness, man; we don't have towns to resupply in every day or so. Give me the PCT, baby!"

THE NEXT DAY, when we reached Sandy Meadow, the views had changed from jagged rocks to smooth-sloping buttes and from granite barrenness to trees. But the landscape we'd left behind was unforgettable. Looking back at the "Big Five" passes, I felt as if I'd accomplished something that made no rational sense, as if my success on 160 miles of the toughest stretch of the PCT, especially after the ankle injury, had some sort of "God wink" to it.

At Crabtree Meadow, our farthest point south, we left the PCT to head east on the trail that would eventually take us to the top of Whitney. For the first time, we caught a glimpse of the mountain—or what we thought was the mountain. Like the trailblazers in the early 1900s, it wasn't easy to differentiate it from the other high points, so nondescript was the peak.

We arrived at Guitar Lake—shaped just like one—on Saturday afternoon, August 9. This would be our base camp for our trip's crescendo climb the next day. I wasted little time plunging into the icy water, knowing that at 11,500 feet this would be the highest lake in which I'd have the privilege of swimming—241 feet higher than the highest point in Oregon, Mount Hood. I took perhaps a dozen strokes and, whooping loudly, U-turned for shore. It felt as cold, or colder, than the Pacific Ocean off Oregon, whose temperatures get down to the high forties.

Sitting on a rock, I marinated in the wonder of this place, feeling peace, privilege and—with a twist of my head toward Whitney—possibility. Later, the wind picked up and clouds scudded in. We camped on a rocky shelf, using good-sized rocks to hold down our tent corners. I was glad we did. The sky blackened. The wind howled. The thunder crackled. As we bedded down for the night, rain began peppering our tents. Remembering what had happened at Muir Pass, I felt more than a little apprehension.

The plan was to close with an eighteen-mile day—eight miles (and about 3,000 feet elevation gain) to the top of Mount Whitney, then a little over ten miles (and 6,606 feet in elevation drop) to Whitney Portal to the east. Before falling asleep, my gut was churning at the challenge ahead. If lacking beauty, Whitney was a formidable block of granite; countless hikers and climbers had died in their pursuit of its summit, which features a rock hut. From the trail—the highest in America—Whitney is not a technical climb, but it can be dangerous, particularly if weather sets in.

In the past year, I'd befriended a climber from Eugene, Mike Hawley, who I'd gotten to know after doing a front-page story on him falling seventy-five feet from near the top of 9,182-foot Mount Thielsen near Oregon's Crater

Lake. Like a rag doll, he'd pinwheeled down on a steep slope of jagged shale. That he survived was amazing.

With my curiosity piqued, in 2013 Glenn and I had attempted to get to Thielsen's "Chicken Ledge," a point far below the top. I didn't come close to reaching even that. We seemed to be climbing straight up. After finding myself on surfboard-sized pieces of rock that teetered, I turned around. Between remembering photographs of Mike's bloody head and interviewing him, his hiking partners, and the search-and-rescue team, my already tepid interest in climbing mountains cooled even more. That said, Whitney had a trail to the top of it. And I pined to see the world from its summit.

At 1 A.M., our predetermined get-up time, we awoke to stars, a good sign considering we'd fallen asleep to the pounding percussion of rain and thunder. We hoped to see a sunrise at the summit about 5:30 A.M.

The climb in the dark was surreal. A few times, I stopped and drank in the utter stillness. Above me, in a wisp of moonlight, I could see the thin outline of trail that would take us to the summit. Behind me, on the switchbacks, I saw only Glenn's headlamp and a sliver of moon that looked perfect, as if hung by a theater prop crew.

We were at 13,450 feet, nearly 3,000 feet higher than I'd ever been before on a trail—Oregon's 10,363-foot South Sister. At 13,000 feet, hikers get only about a third of the oxygen that they get at sea level—and I'd read numerous accounts of people at this point starting to feel altitude sickness. But that's a bullet we dodged; Glenn's heads-up idea to start taking altitude pills from the first day was paying off—and well worth the two side effects I'd felt: tingling in the hands and making soda pop taste terrible.

Although the trail was a sheer drop-off to the west, near the top we were flanked to the east by a huge rock wall that transitioned into spires up top. I could tell because, heading north, I could not see stars to the right as I could to the left. Suddenly, inching forward on a narrow stretch of trail, I realized I *could* see stars to my right, too. Not only that, but I could see lights of civilization far below. Lone Pine, I assumed, where Glenn's car awaited.

Uh-oh. My stomached lurched. I was inching out on a narrow bridge of granite that stretched across one of the handful of windows in the towering spires. Nothing to my left, nothing to my right on a trail like an arena catwalk, perhaps eight feet wide. Fortunately, no wind.

"Narrow," I yelled back to Glenn. "Baby steps."

"Copy that. Baby steps."

We crossed a handful of such gut-grabbers, the only sound the *click-click-click* of our trekking poles and my breathing, which, by now, was getting more pronounced. We swung east to the flat summit, about as wide as a handful of tennis courts. A touch of pink infused the once-dark eastern sky.

We reached the top of Mount Whitney just after 5:30 A.M. on Sunday, August 10—at 14,505 feet the highest point in the contiguous United States. I was breathing hard, but more exuberant than exhausted.

The sky was brightening from pink to orange; sunrise was imminent. A handful of Young Ones whooped it up on the summit's eastern edge, a young woman lying on her stomach, looking over the edge as if atop a skyscraper, a young man dancing just a few feet away. Hikers from Australia, Japan, Tennessee, Utah, and California were celebrating their summiting the peak.

I did not dance, but I was happy enough to. We'd done it. Beyond reaching the top of Whitney, we'd hiked the JMT, or all but the first forty miles that the lightning-caused Meadow Fire at Yosemite had precluded us from doing. We'd survived nearly 47,000 feet of cumulative elevation gain on the most beautiful and beastly trail I'd ever trod. We congratulated a handful of others, one of whom was kind enough to shoot some quick photos of us as, arm in arm, we beamed wide smiles.

I shot photo after photo, knowing the beautiful pink light would fade fast. Soon the sun rose beyond Death Valley to the east, bathing the mountaintop and the rock hut in pink that morphed to gold. Our 360-degree view was spectacular: fresh morning light on dozens of razor-edged ridges and mountains so far below that it seemed as if we were viewing them from a jetliner. Among them: Mount Morgenson, named—unofficially—for the ranger featured in *The Final Season* whose remains were found in 2001, six years after he went missing.*

The temperature was around forty, the wind chill making it feel colder. The wind whipped the navy blue Buff wrapped around my head. We ate some snacks, signed the book—"The Oregon Boys made it!"—and, after about ten more minutes, grabbed our packs to head down.

The biggest irony of the trip was what I'd expected to be the easiest stretch of the Whitney trail—the ten-plus miles down to the portal—turned out to be the hardest. Mentally, I was on a high. The final stretch was akin to marathoners walking to their car after the race, right?

Wrong. The downhill would never end. Switchback after switchback—ninety-nine, in fact—corkscrewed down the steep mountain as seemingly half the population of Southern California passed us going up. It was the closest thing to "treadmill hiking" I'd ever experienced, the sense that we were exerting ourselves but going nowhere.

Finally, late in the afternoon, we made it to the parking lot. Now all we

---

* Spoiler alert, meaning don't read this footnote if you don't want to know the ending: Though I begged to differ, Morgenson's death was officially ruled accidental.

needed was to find a fifteen-mile hitch into Lone Pine. Dr. Dull, a guy so thrifty he had death-bed cars resuscitated rather than buy new ones, proceeded to blow my sweaty socks off.

"Happy to pay for a ride to Lone Pine!" he said, thrusting a $100 bill into the air.

Within minutes, we were in the back of an SUV driven by a guy from Ventura who'd left LA just after midnight, climbed Whitney, and was en route home—with a story to tell about how two brothers-in-law from Oregon had paid for his gas.

As with the Oregon stretch in 2011, fire had diverted, but not stopped, us.

The next morning, as we headed home with Glenn at the wheel, I did the math on my iPhone.

"We now have 610 PCT miles done. Twenty-three percent of the trail."

We didn't talk about it then. But over the winter, I emailed Glenn with a few breakdowns about how in five more summers, averaging 408 miles, we could do the remaining 2,040 miles. The entire 2,650-mile trail. *Canada!*

As usual, Glenn was all in. Two guys who'd originally attempted to do only Oregon were going to try to hike the equivalent of *five* Oregons.

"I've got it all figured out, Glenny," I said. "We can do the whole PCT in what's essentially seven summers. And that's what I'll name the book—*Seven Summers*."

Glenn Petersen

When finding ourselves between a rock and a hard place—essentially every day in the High Sierra—we often looked for humor to get us through. Here, I reminded Glenn, "We're No. 1!" with a rock that said it all.

Top: Celebrating our fourth of the "Big Five," Glen Pass. Above: The next day, we got over the highest point on the PCT, 13,118-foot Forester Pass. While up top, this guy and his mule train casually walked by—on a ledge where a misstep might mean death. Photo doesn't do justice to the dropoffs.

Glenn Petersen

Switchbacks down the south side of Forester were chiseled into the granite, making us imagine what this must be like for thru-hikers coming up this stretch in the snow of late spring. I'm visible, barely, a quarter of the way in from left.

Top: Fin Dome rising beyond Dollar Lake to an elevation of 11,673 feet on a morning when blue skies replaced cloudy skies. Above: Our first glimpse of Mount Whitney, our next day's challenge, from the trail. It's that giant hunk of granite to the left, nearly 3,000 feet higher than Fin.

Top: One of the "Young Ones" danced atop Mount Whitney as the sun rose above the mountains of Death Valley. Above: Glenn and I celebrated atop the 14,505-foot peak, oblivious to what an arduous exit we were about to face. The trip down was a knee buster.

... I sat on a log in numbness, unable to wrap my head around the news. It was too overwhelming. Too discordant with this place—the wilderness, where life teemed and serenity reigned.

AGE 61

2015

SOUTHERN WASHINGTON

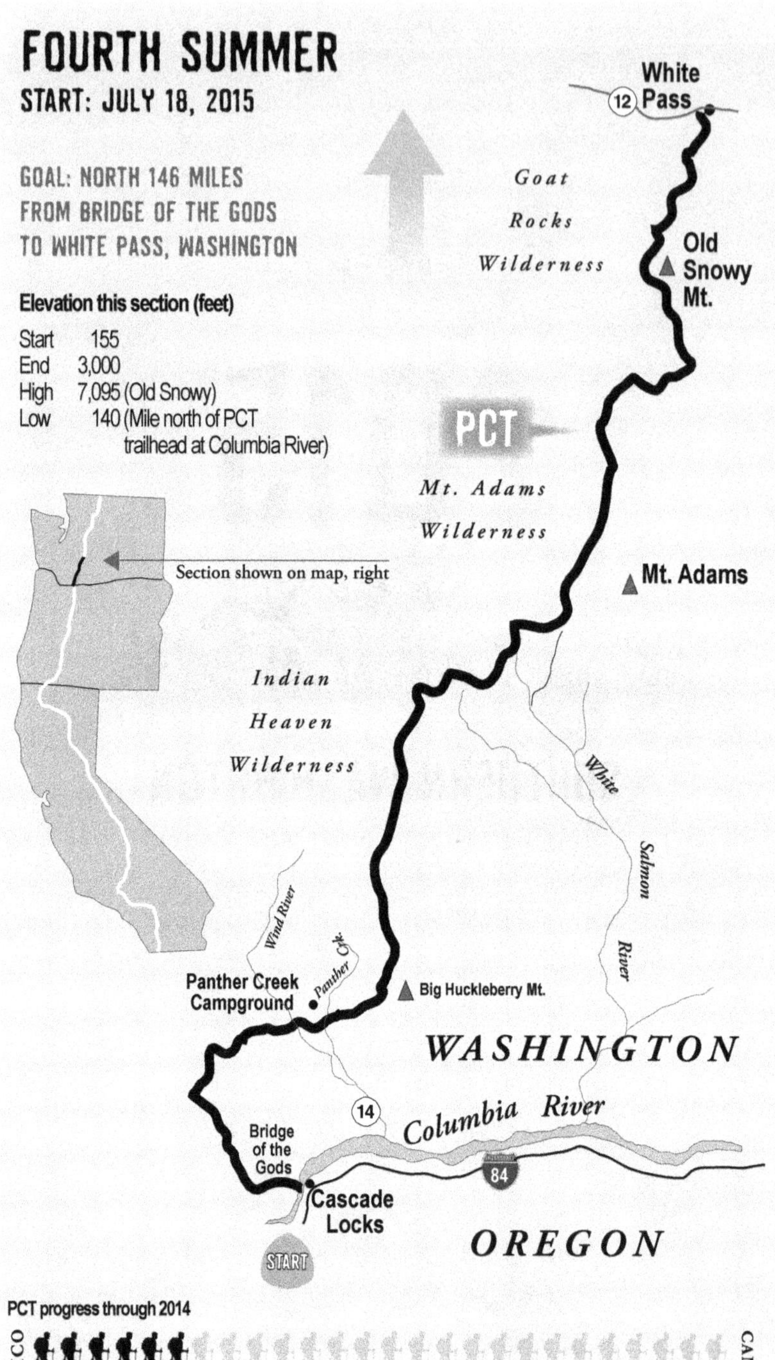

FOURTH SUMMER
START: JULY 18, 2015
GOAL: NORTH 146 MILES
FROM BRIDGE OF THE GODS
TO WHITE PASS, WASHINGTON
Elevation this section (feet)
Start 155
End 3,000
High 7,095 (Old Snowy)
Low 140 (Mile north of PCT trailhead at Columbia River)
Section shown on map, right
12
White Pass
Goat Rocks Wilderness
Old Snowy Mt.
PCT
Mt. Adams Wilderness
Mt. Adams
Indian Heaven Wilderness
White Salmon River
Wind River
Panther Crk.
Panther Creek Campground
Big Huckleberry Mt.
WASHINGTON
14
Columbia River
Bridge of the Gods
84
Cascade Locks
OREGON
START
PCT progress through 2014
MEXICO
CANADA
23% done / 615 miles
77% of PCT left / 2,037 miles to go

9

DESPAIR

Moving on is simple;
it's what you leave behind that makes it difficult.

—Unknown

Only days before our planned 2015 trip was to begin—the southern half of Washington—we were once again vexed by a nemesis from the past: wildfires. "There is a fire southwest of Mount Adams forcing a nineteen-plus-mile workaround," Glenn emailed. "It may be under control and we won't have a problem by the time we reach there early Wednesday A.M. We can try to stay in touch with Ann and Sally for updates."

"Are we jinxed?" I wrote back. "Three years on the PCT. Three fires."

Workarounds, usually created by the U.S. Forest Service in conjunction with the Pacific Crest Trail Association, often involved long hikes off the PCT, substantial road walking, and long returns to the trail. Except for their allowing hikers to continue, most despised them. Adding miles to the PCT was like adding extra pieces to a thousand-piece jigsaw puzzle. Wasn't it challenging enough as it was? Then again, you had to take what the trail gave you—or didn't. The PCT, I was learning, always batted last.

On the weather front, forecasters were calling for temperatures in the nineties for our first few days.

The PCT north out of the Columbia Gorge—at 140 feet elevation, the low point of the trail—was known to be an uninspiring grind through a thick forest canopy that offered few views; in other words, it offered the opposite experience of our previous year's trek on the JMT. The trail arced to the west in a giant "C," meaning at least double the distance to our planned second-night destination, Panther Creek Campground, compared to walking straight north on Highway 14, which some hikers did.

"The first thirty-five miles of the section are often criticized, mostly because they involve an indirect route that gains, then loses, 5,000 feet of elevation," said *The Pacific Crest Trail: A Hiker's Companion.* "Because water can be in scarce supply, you should carry extra. Similarly, there aren't many good campsites, so you may need to use a little ingenuity . . . ."

After being dropped off by Sally and Ann at the Bridge of the Gods where we'd finished our 2012 hike—our "makeup" for fifty miles from Timberline Lodge missed in 2011 after the fire and Glenn's vertigo episode—we started hiking. It was already 9 A.M. We normally liked to be hiking by 5 A.M. to get in as many miles as possible in the cooler hours. In a perfect world, we would have been dropped off the previous night, but Glenn had to work late Friday. The lesson? The PCT didn't exist in some sort of vacuum; it had to be coordinated with our non-trail lives, and the two didn't always mesh.

Having left *The Register-Guard* to write books, I'd tried to get in my training miles but deep into a handful of projects—mine and others for whom I was writing or editing—I'd cut corners. I knew I wasn't in as good of shape as I'd been for the JMT. It had been a busy summer: work deadlines, beach trips, and the privilege of officiating at the June 13, 2015, wedding of Glenn and Ann's youngest daughter, Molly, to Bobby Hodge—at Seattle's Woodland Park Zoo. (Fun, fun, fun!)

I rationalized that this section would be easier than the High Sierra, and that I would find my sea legs once on the trail. But at the time, I was, if not cocky, negligent. Like flossing your teeth the night before going to the dentist after months of not doing so, I'd rationalized that my eleventh-hour training would suffice.

I was wrong. As we headed up the mountain, I was already hot and sweating hard. I felt a twinge of foreboding. It was nothing definite, just a quiet concern that the weather was warm, the two of us huffing more than usual, and the momentum illusive, as if we couldn't find our trail rhythm.

Alas, I'd soon find my anxiety would go far deeper than these concerns.

WE INCHED our way higher and deeper into the woods. I was gassed, Glenn apparently more so. When we'd take a pack-off break, he wouldn't eat or drink much. Instead, he'd flop on the trail as if gut-shot by a sniper.

"I'm just so tired," he'd say, then fall asleep. His dark-gray, long-sleeved hiking shirt was already salt-stained with sweat. I began to worry.

The day's plan had been to hike twenty miles and camp at Rock Creek, but at our sluggish pace I knew that wasn't happening. Rock Creek was our only realistic choice to camp near water, which was always a priority because you were able to drink lots of it without having to carry it. We'd taken a lot of water but were also drinking a lot, me far more than Glenn.

"You're a doctor," I would chide him. "You should be eating more and drinking more."

"I'm *not* a doctor," he'd say, mimicking some age-old commercial. "But I play one on TV."

I just shook my head; at least he still had his sense of humor.

As opposed to my relationship with another brother-in-law, Greg, my connection with Glenn was mortared with fun—golf, Scrabble, hiking, and Christmas present pranks. That said, Glenn wasn't one to share any subterranean feelings, and I reciprocated with stay-safe silence. The result was a consistent relationship, a tight relationship, but not one where we often shared with each other at any depth about feelings, faith, family, politics, whatever.

My relationship with Greg, married to Linda, the oldest of three Youngberg girls, couldn't have been more different: deeper, complicated, and steeled in pain. I'd known Greg a little longer than I'd known Glenn—since starting to date Sally in 1972. He'd married Linda just a month before Sally and I started seeing each other.

In our early years, Greg—four years my senior—emerged as a much-needed spiritual mentor to me. As a student studying to be a pastor, he helped me explore this new forest of Christian faith I'd entered in high school.

Because we never lived close to each other, we mainly saw each other only at family gatherings. But over the years two things deepened our friendship: the advent of email, which made communication fast and easy, and the deepest tragedy imaginable. On the last day of 1994, Greg and Linda's sixteen-year-old son, Paul, fell into an icy river that pounded through a canyon on Washington's Olympic Peninsula. And died.

I grieved his and Linda's loss. Paul was a quiet, good-natured kid with a penchant for mischief and a serious faith in God. Now, just like that, he was gone; initially, search-and-rescue workers had been unable to find his body. The family was racked with pain, none more than Linda, Greg, and their two other children, Traci, twenty-one, and Brad, eighteen.

In the weeks and months to come, I corresponded with Greg like a man inching out on thin ice. I didn't know what to say, how much to say, or when to say it, but gradually realized something: Greg didn't need me to say anything, he just needed me to listen. At the church he pastored, a large Baptist congregation, the elder board had initially surrounded him with support but, in Greg and Linda's eyes, had become impatient with him. After a few months, he felt as if their statute of limitations on his grief had expired; it was time for him to get back to "normal," whatever that could possibly be.

He said it was hard for him to speak from his heart to people in his church, but he could do so with me.

"I really miss Paul," he said in one email message. "And the predominant emotion for me is anger. Anger at God. It is so intense that I fear I will be unable to preach."

He clung to his faith. He continued to preach. He and Linda became huge inspirations for me; put in a similar situation, I wondered if I could have *not* given up on God.

But six years later, our friendship faltered. It was as if one of our relational tires got out of alignment and, suddenly, in 2011—shortly before Glenn and I hiked Oregon—we had a blowout.

The issue didn't matter. What mattered was that we crept back toward each other. I suggested we meet in Portland face to face. We did. It didn't automatically fix things; more than anything, I think the value of the meeting was each of us showing the other that we thought the friendship worth saving.

By spring 2012 we'd rebuilt our trust in each other. I invited Greg to join me for a weekend of camping and fishing, the final day being a guided trip for steelhead on the iconic McKenzie River east of Eugene.

Unlike Glenn and I, Greg and I had never done anything together, just him and me—until this trip. It was magical. We sat around a campfire two nights. We caught fish. We laughed. Best of all, we let down our guards and simply had fun together. For me, it was affirmation that our friendship had been rekindled, perhaps returning stronger than before.

BACK ON the trail, I was feeling less certainty about the Bob-Glenn connection, at least from a hiking standpoint. As noon approached, we wound our way up, past Sacajawea and Proposal Rocks. Glenn's listlessness was getting worse.

I'd never seen him this way. It wasn't uncommon for him to stay silent for long portions of the trail; he was not one to waste words. What concerned me now was that even when we did talk, he wasn't engaging, as if his mind were somewhere else. His leadership presence had waned. His sense of humor had vanished.

"Don't think we're going to make Rock Creek at this pace," I said. "You agree?"

He raised his eyebrows as if in agreement but didn't speak.

"Are you thinking we need to changes our plans on where—."

The buzz of my phone cut me short. I'd thought we left cell service miles ago, back near the river. I walked off the trail and connected. It was Sally. She was sobbing and hard to hear. I turned away from Glenn.

"What is it, babe? What's wrong?"

"It's Greg," she said, sniffling. "He … he ... had a … heart attack."

"What?"

"Bobby, he's … dead. Greg's dead."

Greg couldn't be dead. He was only sixty-five. I'd just talked to him a week ago.

"After dropping you off, Ann and I had just reached Portland when we got the call from Linda."

"How is she?"

"Crushed. But doing as well as could be expected. Holding up. Trying to be strong for the kids."

Glenn wasn't privy to what I was hearing or how wet my eyes were.

Greg and Linda had been married for forty-three years, and, beyond Traci, now forty, and Brad, thirty-eight, had seven grandchildren.

"How did it happen?"

"They were … camping … in Moses Lake," she said. "And … he just felt a tightness in his chest. He said he didn't feel good, then keeled over."

In the discombobulation, we talked about Linda and their now-grown kids and grandkids. How this possibly could have happened. How surreal it all seemed.

"I've talked to Ann and Dad," she said. "Dad says you guys should just keep going; there's nothing you can do. No idea when there might be a service. So, stay on the trail."

My head was swirling, the what's-next-for-Glenn-and-Bob question a minor concern.

"Ann and I are heading up to Moses Lake to be with Linda," she said. "So, we couldn't pick you up today even if you decided to quit. Just keep going. That's what Greg would have wanted you to do."

I wished her safe travels, said goodbye, and turned to Glenn with a lump in my throat.

"Glenny," I finally managed, "I don't know how else to say this."

"What?"

"Greg is dead."

"Scandrett? Wait. What? How?"

"Heart attack. That was Sally. Linda and Greg were camping in Eastern Washington, Moses Lake. Said he didn't feel good, then keeled over."

I didn't expect Glenn to break into sobs, and he didn't. That wasn't from any lack of respect for Greg; that was simply Glenn Petersen being the stoic doctor who'd learned to compartmentalize pain and death so he could do his job. I knew his feelings ran deep but, like a submarine, rarely rose to the surface.

He gently shook his head, eyes misty. I told him what I knew, including Sally's encouragement to keep going. We agreed if we were going to turn around, this was the place to do it—hike seven miles back to Cascade Locks and try to hitchhike, take a bus, or have one of my sons pick us up.

"Whataya think?" I said.

"I feel rotten but it's day one," he said. "If others are good with us going on, I say we do."

"Agreed."

AT OUR FINAL water opportunity until Rock Creek, I sat on a log in numbness, unable to wrap my head around the news. It was too overwhelming. Too discordant with this place—the wilderness, where life teemed and serenity reigned. Too incongruous that a man I pictured in a drift boat, both of us smiling contentedly as the guide photographed us, was suddenly gone.

Glenn and I hiked on in silence, wounded and weary, the news not bringing us together; instead, seemingly driving us deeper into ourselves. We were each processing it, of course, in our own ways, but neither of us was sharing our feelings.

Soon we were each walking alone. To split up like this wasn't unusual, unless we were on a more dangerous section of the trail, in which case we always stuck together. In our 600-plus miles, Glenn would sometimes be far ahead of me; at other times, I'd be far ahead of him. The key, we always said, was to make sure we knew whether the other guy was ahead of us or behind us. If we weren't sure, we could be in trouble. Our two rules were: *Wait for the other guy at any junction—to make sure we both took the same branch of trail.* And, for bathroom stops, *Leave your pack along the trail* so the other guy knew you were off trail, taking care of business.

So, when nature called on this stretch, I did just that. I returned to the trail, sat on a log, and waited for Glenn. Five minutes became ten, ten became fifteen. As the time gap between Glenn and me grew, I began mulling a possibility that roiled my stomach: Could he have not seen my pack and now was ahead of me, not behind me? Conversely, could he be suffering from heat exhaustion or something else and be behind me? Had he fallen, hurt a leg?

I pulled out my cell phone and called him; if Sally's call had come through, wouldn't my call to Glenn do the same? But was his phone even on? And, if so, would he hear it if it were stuffed in a pack pocket or on vibrate? What's more, if he were in trouble, why hadn't he attempted to contact me? Or had he done so but was unable to get through?

I looked at my messages. None. I tried calling Glenn. No connection.

Panic shivered my spine. What was the right play? We'd seen only two other hikers on the trail all morning; there was little chance another NoBo would pass with news about having seen Glenn behind me. And the chance was even slimmer of a SoBo coming by with news of him; only one in ten PCT hikers goes south.

It was a coin-flip decision, but my instincts suggested that Glenn, weary and stunned by the news of Greg's death, had walked past my pack without seeing it. I headed north, up the trail. After about twenty minutes, I rounded a bend beneath Table Mountain, and there he was, awake, pack off, waiting.

I exhaled.

"Wondered where you were," he said. "Good to see you."

"Yeah, had to make a pit stop. Sorry, guess I didn't leave my pack close enough to the trail; my bad. How you doing?"

He took off his hat and ran his hand through his sweat-soaked hair.

"Been better."

"Tough day for our family."

He nodded. "How are you?" he asked.

"Numb. Tired. Discombobulated."

We packed up and moved on. Within half an hour, Glenn was again lying on the trail, napping. During one such siesta a fellow NoBo had to literally step over him.

"Is he OK?" the hiker asked.

"Yeah," I said. "We're fine, just old."

I cajoled Glenn to get up. He grudgingly did so, though he was having a hard time keeping pace. The temperature rose, our water supplies fell. We trudged up and on.

By midafternoon we had climbed 2,400 feet but it seemed like twice that. I was fading, Glenn more so. At a hairpin turn in the trail, he threw off his pack and was again asleep in minutes. Though it wasn't quite 3 P.M., I realized for the first time that I was getting thrust into the leadership role by default. Darkness came early in the woods, even in midsummer.

Two "seasonal streams"—meaning they might have water, depending on the depth of snowpack and the time of year—had proven to be dry. But even if we had eight miles until the sure thing of Rock Creek, water wasn't the immediate issue. Slope was.

Between steep terrain, trees, brush, rocks, and "no-camping" edicts—say, on the slivers of private property or National Park land—most space along the PCT simply wouldn't work for even rolling out a sleeping bag. This was such a place. The challenge wasn't finding a comfortable place, the challenge was finding *any* place where we could lie down and not roll into the bottom of a canyon.

As Glenn slept, I walked around the U-shaped trail in this dense forest that narrowed into a deep ravine. I couldn't see a single place where either of us could sleep, even if wedged to the uphill side of a tree. The map showed a dirt road up top, meaning at least a good chance for at least some flatness, but I wasn't sure Glenn had two uphill miles left in his tank.

Returning, I gently woke him and explained our only option: fight our way to the top and camp there, leaving us six mostly downhill miles to Rock Creek in the morning. He nodded his OK.

It took us a couple of hours, but we wobbled our way to the top and found a flat area to pitch our tents. In previous years, I'd always loved that transition from hiking to eating to sleeping. But not today. We had no shade, I had no appetite, and the heat was stifling. A hiker's purgatory: too gassed to eat, too hot to sleep.

And overriding both was a reality far worse: Greg was gone.

THE NEXT DAY we needed to hike twenty-three miles to Panther Creek to get back on schedule. We managed barely half that. Our bodies were toast, our minds still numbed by the news, our trail-buddy connection waning. For me, you could add a side order of guilt to the assessment order; even if others thought it OK to keep hiking—and, intellectually, I understood—it still seemed disrespectful to Greg's memory.

"We need to talk about whether we keep going," said Glenn, who'd rebounded a bit after food, water, and a night's sleep. "If we get off, Panther Creek is the place to do so."

"That's how far?"

"Eight miles. Next pickup would be White Pass about 200 miles north."

"Yikes," I said. "That's a long ways. How you feeling?"

"Not good. You?"

"Same. Glenny, maybe it's just not meant to be this year."

He nodded his head. "I agree. Let's go home."

I wasn't surprised that we had no cell service. But seeing a ridge where my Spot Connect GPS device looked to have the necessary unobstructed shot to the southern sky, I walked away from Glenn to message Sally and Ann. I couldn't get the device to connect with the satellite. I tried again. Nope. Again. Nope.

Hot, tired, frustrated, and grieving, my anger rose like volcanic lava. This had been the worst two days on the trail ever. I was tempted to throw the hunk-of-junk Spot off the ridge. Instead, I vomited up a few choice words—to whatever chipmunks were listening. And did something I should have done long before. Cried.

It felt good. It felt bad. But it felt *something,* and I suppose that was cathartic.

After a few moments, semi-composed, I tried the connection again. No luck. But for some reason when I tried my cell, I had enough bars to make a call. Sally and Ann would meet us at Panther Creek the next afternoon.

I couldn't wait to be out of this place. It wasn't the trail's fault. It was simply life.

And death.

Greg Hatten

For my other brother-in-law, Greg, and I, our best day together turned out to be among our last days together. Our fishing guide took this photo at the end of a wonderful weekend we spent on the McKenzie River in May 2012.

Beyond its narrowness, what distinguished this section was its seeming endlessness. When I'd reached the top of Old Snowy, I was mentally ready to be done. But the trail snaked down and up like a rocky roller coaster.

AGE 62

2016

SOUTHERN WASHINGTON

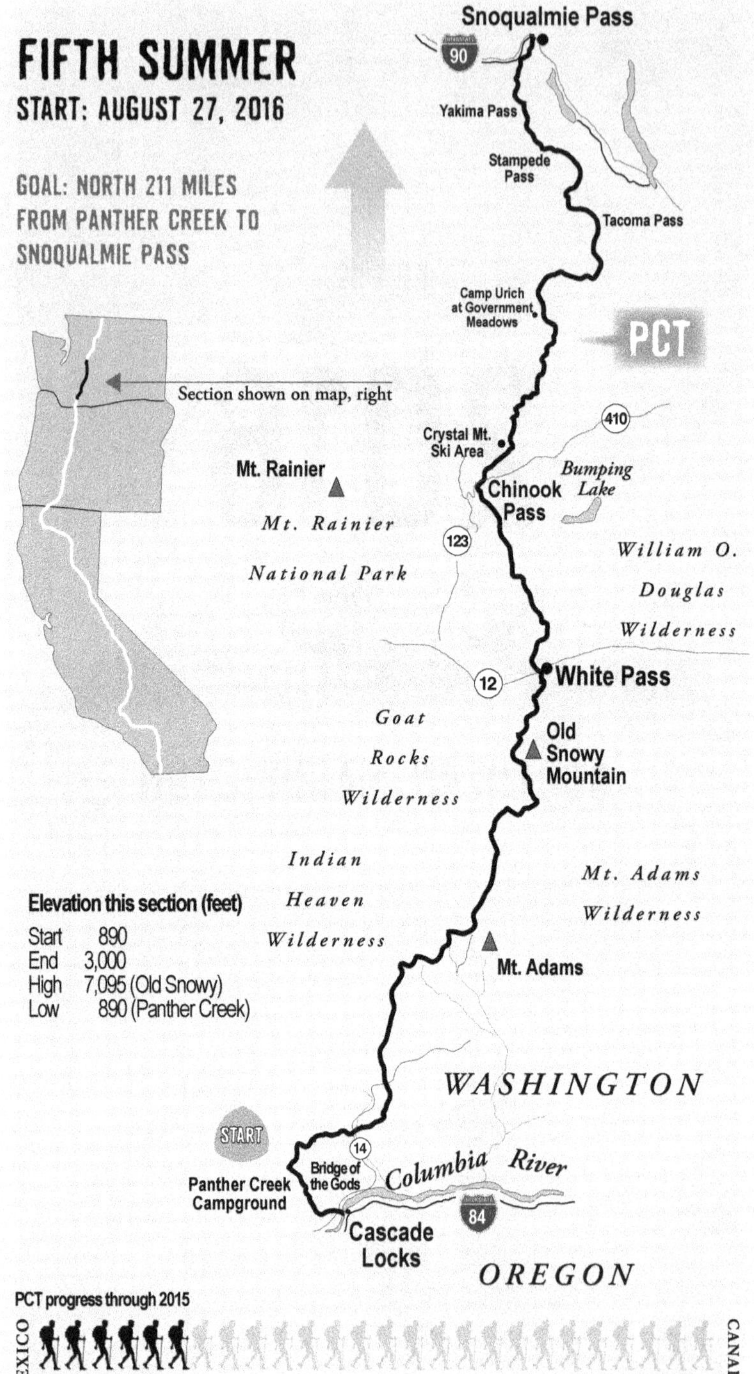

FIFTH SUMMER
START: AUGUST 27, 2016
GOAL: NORTH 211 MILES FROM PANTHER CREEK TO SNOQUALMIE PASS
Section shown on map, right
Snoqualmie Pass
90
Yakima Pass
Stampede Pass
Tacoma Pass
Camp Urich at Government Meadows
PCT
410
Crystal Mt. Ski Area
Mt. Rainier
Chinook Pass
Bumping Lake
Mt. Rainier National Park
123
William O. Douglas Wilderness
White Pass
12
Goat Rocks Wilderness
Old Snowy Mountain
Indian Heaven Wilderness
Mt. Adams Wilderness
Mt. Adams
Elevation this section (feet)
Start 890
End 3,000
High 7,095 (Old Snowy)
Low 890 (Panther Creek)
WASHINGTON
START
14
Bridge of the Gods
Columbia River
Panther Creek Campground
84
Cascade Locks
OREGON
PCT progress through 2015
MEXICO
CANADA
25% done / 650 miles
75% of PCT left / 2,000 miles to go

10

RESOLVE

If ambition doesn't hurt, you haven't got it.

—Kathleen Norris

The months following our failure and Greg's death were difficult. By Christmas 2015 my weight had skyrocketed to a record-high 209 pounds—twenty-five more than what I weighed when starting the JMT in 2014—and my confidence had wilted regarding The Oregon Boys and the PCT.

Greg's death triggered an array of disconcerting feelings, not the least of which was pain for the "time we had wasted on the way," to quote from a song by musician Graham Nash, who'd had a falling out with singing partner David Crosby.

Greg and I had survived years of discordant notes to revive our relationship. Then, suddenly, the song ended. I could not think of Greg without thinking of that time on the McKenzie River, how our best day turned out to be, in essence, our final day.

But good as it was, even that memory—like the hauntingly beautiful song on the soundtrack from *A River Runs Through It*, "The Moment That Could Not Last"—was tinged with a bittersweet reminder: time was precious, and not guaranteed.

That realization, ironically, became part of my impetus for not letting our 2015 experience "beat us twice." Our attempt to get halfway through Washington had failed; we couldn't unring that bell. But the experience would beat us again if we allowed the 2015 disaster to dilute our confidence and hamper our hiking in the future. Greg's days on earth were gone. I was sixty-one. It behooved me to make the most of whatever time I had left.

In a September 2015 email to Glenn, I led off with Buber's quote that "Every journey has a secret destination of which the traveler is unaware," then wrote:

> Just because we didn't reach our goal this time doesn't mean we should wallow in defeat. Because it wasn't a defeat. At least I don't look upon it as such. Did we reach Snoqualmie? No. But did we learn some things that will help us take the next step in our trail journey? Yes. Perhaps that was our "secret destination." Not what we wanted. But perhaps what we *needed.*
>
> This year was just that perfect storm of things that worked against us:
>
> —Lack of time for either of us to properly train.
>
> —Goals that were overly lofty.
>
> —Late start Saturday.
>
> —Uncommon heat.
>
> —Too-heavy packs.
>
> —Out of sync with uphill-in-the-cool-of-the-morning and downhill-in-the-heat-of-the-afternoon rhythm.
>
> —Death of our brother-in-law.
>
> In some ways, it's a wonder we got as far as we did.

For inspiration about bouncing back as a PCT hiker, I needed to only look to a friend of mine, Geoff Tyson, my barber. After reading *Cascade Summer,* he was inspired, in 2013, to hike the Oregon PCT, even though he'd done no backpacking at all. At forty-five, he weighed 254 pounds, smoked heavily, and left the California-Oregon border with a seventy-five-pound pack that included a two-pound, 45-caliber pistol, and extra clips.

He quit after two days. But over the next year, he trained regularly, lost thirty pounds, and cut his pack weight in half. In 2014 he completed the 456-mile Oregon section, weighing 191—he'd lost sixty-three pounds!—by the time he reached the Bridge of the Gods.*

After our setback, I suggested to Glenn that we set goals and hold each other accountable for losing weight. I also suggested we discipline ourselves to carry no more than thirty pounds and create an itinerary that didn't have us hiking more than fifteen miles a day. In other words, I thought the solution

---

* Geoff's trail name was "Doin' Stuff," because a hairdresser who worked in the shop next door to the barber shop said he couldn't get a second task done because he was always "doin' stuff." Now he'd gotten a big task done, hiking Oregon.

to more successful PCT hiking was lowering our body weights, our pack weights, and our expectations.

I also told him I thought we'd forgotten our history. Our story. Our successes.

> We were atop the highest point in the continental U.S. a year ago! We have hiked 456 miles across Oregon. And done the JMT. We are in our early sixties and have run into some hikers who are older than us and doing just great. So, let's not lament what wasn't to be last summer. Let's use it instead as leverage to get back to the PCT legends that we are, baby! The Oregon Boys will ride again!

I loved Glenn's response.

> I need to pick myself up and move on. Starting today. I feel like a lightweight weenie lying on the trail drenched in sweat with the gas gauge below zero. I plan to be back. It's part of being a Beaver, a Lutheran, a Scout, a Dad. Sometimes down, but not out. My motto for all of 2015 and 2016 is: "the weenie will rise again!"

Uh, I'm not sure I would have chosen *that* particular metaphor, but his re-commitment reflected my own. Iron sharpens iron; our individual resolve fueled each other's resolve. As the new year unfolded, Glenn began walking his talk—literally, on the treadmill. And he committed to something called "The Military Diet." Among the diet's go-to allowable foods: toast, grapefruit, cheese, apples, tuna, hard-boiled eggs, hot dogs, and—praise the Lord!—ice cream. In only a month he dropped his weight from 199.5 pounds to 178 pounds. I decided to try it myself. The eating regiment was every bit as bland as it sounded, but it worked. I, too, started losing weight.

In addition, I started considering the idea of supplementing my hikes up Mount Pisgah and Spencer Butte—always with thirty-plus pounds in my pack—by swimming. My right knee was starting to hurt and swell while hiking; swimming wouldn't strain it as severely.

On my sixty-second birthday, February 3, 2016, I wrote to Glenn suggested a modified itinerary for completing the entire PCT in five more summers, which would still mean a total of seven summers on the trail, not counting our "incomplete year" in 2015 (we did only thirty-seven miles) and our "makeup year" in 2012 (I did fifty and Glenn ninety-two):

> How about:
> 2016: Lower Washington.
> 2017: North from Thousand Island Lake to halfway to the Oregon border.

> 2018: North from that halfway point to the Oregon-California border.
>
> 2019: You are retired by now so … 8 weeks. Mexico to Mount Whitney junction.
>
> 2020: Middle of Washington to Canada. Whereupon, I'll write the book "Seven PCT Summers" with an afterword by Glenn Petersen.

Glenn was good with the hiking, but the afterword had him worried; "I'm no writer," he said. And he pointed out he might not be retiring as soon as I thought; he loved being a doctor and his patients loved him. But overall, he was all in. What's more, he pointed out, he had just received a bulk shipment of forty Louis L'Amour paperbacks from ebay for only $39— "with free shipping!" In other words, he had enough reading for many years on the PCT.

By May, he was down to 165 pounds. I stopped considering swimming and started doing it. No pun intended, but from the get-go I was in over my head. On my first day in the pool, I managed four twenty-five-yard lengths. That's all I could do. Four laps. I had no idea swimming was so hard.

There was not only the physical challenge, but the social challenge. Some guys, particularly the younger ones, wore Speedos. I wouldn't think of trying that; if I did, women would mentally *dress* me.

More importantly, everyone else knew what they were doing. Will, Adam, Debbie, Jill, and Jules —all had been regulars for years and left me in their wakes. A guy named Jack Horsley offered me some pointers, which I gladly accepted and implemented; after all, he'd won an Olympic bronze medal in the 200-meter backstroke at the 1968 Olympics. But none of them compared to Vi Peck, an eighty-two-year-old woman who could swim circles around me—despite having had double-knee replacement and two surgeries to replace double-rotator-cuff tears.

I was intimidated, insecure, out of my league. But here's what I learned: You can either humble yourself, learn, and grow—or cower, quit, and stay stuck in your self-consciousness. I chose to learn and grow. Chose to be inspired by others, not to compete with them.

I'd read that short fins worked the legs particularly well, so invested in a pair and went to work. The real advantage was psychological; they made me feel fast even though I wasn't. In three months, I was doing more than a mile in my hour-long workout, nothing for true swimmers but something for a broken-down old backpacker. And, meanwhile, had made a handful of new friends, none of whom cared how fast, or slow, I swam.

By spring, I had dropped seventeen pounds, to 190.

WE HIT THE TRAIL at Panther Creek on August 27, 2016, for what we hoped would be 217 miles to Snoqualmie Pass east of Seattle. (We'd planned to go earlier in the summer but because I had just returned to work part-time at *The Register-Guard*, as an associate editor in the editorial department, late summer was more practical.)

The first week was as easy, beautiful, and confidence-building as the previous year had not been. We lunched in Snowgrass Flats fronting 12,276-foot Mount Adams, and by day five had 14,411-foot Mount Rainier in sight, ahead to our left.

Then, things changed. On September 1, clouds rolled in, temperatures dropped, and rain threatened. We dawned our rain suits, stocking hats, and gloves; in the first half hour one morning, I was drenched after twisting through neck-high, water-soaked brush.

In the Goat Rocks Wilderness, we ascended 7,880-foot Old Snowy, a white-knuckle experience because of what hikers call "The Knife's Edge" part of the northbound descent. But it was the pre-knife stretch that quickened my heartbeat—seeing a trail of footprints punched into the side of the forty-five-degree Packwood Glacier that fronted the mountain.

Sideways stretches on snow could look deceptively easy to cross. "The people ahead [crossed] the slope safely, or so it appears," wrote Jardine in *The PCT Hiker's Handbook*, "but those tracks mean nothing to you. Snow conditions change; maybe the people passed through late in the afternoon when the snow was soft. And now, because the day has not yet warmed, maybe the slope is still frozen. A visual inspection is not the ultimate test … ."

In the gaping basin beneath us, low-hanging clouds swirled upward on the wind, giving the scene an eerie "land before time" feel. I looked back to the footprints across the slope. It was one of those dicey stretches that the Young Ones would take in literal stride. But at sixty-two, I saw one slip and a 1,500-foot slide that was not apt to end well.

As I was pondering as much, words from a male voice intoned as if spoken by God Himself.

"There's an alternative trail that takes you up to the top, around the backside," a fellow "mature" hiker said. "And keeps you on rock instead of glacier."

The trail was up, down, winding, and steep—it probably took an hour longer than the glacier shortcut—but I took every step with a sense of gratitude. On The Knife's Edge section we gingerly worked our way up and down Old Snowy as if on the rock-splayed top of an A-frame roof: narrow with steep drop-offs right and left that were knee-knocking scary.

Beyond its narrowness, what distinguished this section was its seeming endlessness. When I'd reached the top of Old Snowy, I was mentally ready to be done. But the trail snaked down and up like a rocky roller coaster. Light snow began falling, whipped by a cold wind. Finally, in early evening, we came south off the ridge and into the forest cover.

I HAD LONG been fascinated by maps, especially the U.S. Forest Service's slick PCT maps whose four sections of a particular trail legs fold out to almost the size of a sleeping bag. I've twice had the opportunity to ride in hot-air balloons, and looking at a good map is like that: a slow perusal of the world below, offering information, context, and no small amount of wonder.

"A $500 GPS device can tell your position, but a $10 road atlas is still an infinitely more powerful tool for providing context," wrote Ken Jennings in his fascinating book, *Mapheads.*

Alas, for all the context that even the best maps offer, they can't replicate what you see and feel when experiencing the real thing.

"It doesn't matter how many maps I see with the little brown lines squished tightly together," I told Glenn. "I always underestimate how up and down this trail climbs. Why do I keep thinking it might be flat like a map is flat?"

As the wind whipped and rain threatened, we pitched out tents and got our hot freeze-dried dinners cooking. When two SoBos, a young man and woman, arrived, we invited them to join us. They did so, looking beat but apparently not finished for the day.

"We're hoping to get over Old Snowy tonight," the young man said.

"Really?" I said.

"Don't think we should?"

"We came over a couple of hours ago and it was spitting snow. Pretty narrow trail with steep dropoffs. It'll be light in twelve hours."

They stayed. Rain started falling. Glenn and I slid into our sleeping bags.

"Gonna find out if your tent is waterproof!" I all but yelled above the rain-whipped racket.

"And windproof!" he yelled back. "Mine's flapping like crazy!"

"What? I can't hear you! Your tent's flapping like crazy!"

My tent, a simple inverted "V" propped up with a single trekking pole, was facing west on a birdhouse perch. All night long, the rain pelted it as if jet-hosed from a car wash. On the bright side, I stayed dry. On the less bright side, I had to pee about 3 A.M. Venturing out would have soaked me and the inside of my tent, perhaps dangerously so. I strapped on my headlamp, grabbed an empty plastic water bottle, and made do.

THAT AFTERNOON, after a wet 3,000-foot drop beneath the chair-lifts at White Pass Ski Area, we neared Highway 12, which offered a motel and store. Glenn was going strong—downhill was his specialty—but I was coming in like a B-52 with one wing on fire and no landing gear. My feet were barking and one of the fasteners on my adjustable trekking poles had broken, making it inoperable.

Glenn's itinerary had us staying in a state park. Soaked to the bone, I morphed into the most "obstinate Bob" I could muster in thinking we could do better. We trudged on. I knew my quest for relative luxury would be met with Glenn's thriftiness, as if for a church social I was suggesting chicken cordon bleu instead of the usual meatloaf, but so be it.

"Glenny, motel tonight," I said out of the blue.

"But what if there are no rooms available?"

"Too late. When you were peeing back there, I called and got reservations. You owe me seventy bucks."

To my delight, his eyes widened.

"Nice!"

It would be the first time in four years of hiking the PCT that we would sleep in any sort of structure. We arrived at White Pass, a place I remembered from my sports editor days at *The Bulletin* in Bend of the 1970s and '80s as the training slopes for the Mahre brothers, Phil and Steve, who won gobs of Olympic skiing medals.

We picked up our resupply boxes at the Cracker Barrel,* grabbed pizza and pop for dinner, and checked into the motel. We stretched tent line from doorknobs to refrigerator handles to bed posts, hanging our wet clothes as if they were Nepali peace flags. We bridged kitchen counter tops with trekking poles to hang more. We cranked the heater on high, ate pizza, and enjoyed a much more peaceful, and drier, night than the one before—or the one we would have experienced outdoors at a state park.

LIKE BATTERIES, off-trail resupply stops recharged your spirits and your body. Heading out the next morning, we did back-to-back twenties. We shared small talk with a SoBo trail-named Preacher, who had already gone north to Canada and was trying to hike back to Mexico, an undertaking referred to as doing a "yo-yo." At Two Lakes, I soaked feet that by now had a quarter-sized blister on each inner heel.

That night, Saturday, September 3, I wowed Glenny by starting a fire

---

* It was at this same store, five weeks later, that PCT thru-hiker Kris "Sherpa" Fowler was last seen before going missing. Fowler, thirty-four, of Ohio, stopped for a cup of coffee, shut off his cell phone, and was never seen again. Seven years later, his disappearance remains a mystery.

with Fritos, a trick I'd read somewhere. It was, I believe, only the third fire we'd had on the trail. Around it, we laughed about what had happened earlier that day: in the middle of nowhere—and not having seen another hiker all morning—we had come across an outhouse at a rustic picnic area. I zipped in, excited to get to sit on an actual seat! Only seconds after blastoff there was a knock at the door.

"Go away, Petersen!" I said. "I'm on a challenging mission!"

"What?"

It wasn't Glenn's voice.

"Uh, sorry," I said meekly. "Be right out."

It was, I later learned, some kid from Michigan who materialized as if through a Star Trek transporter.

North of Chinook Pass, on Labor Day, September 5, the weather turned cold. We donned gloves for the first time since Goat Rocks Wilderness.

With forty miles left until our Snoqualmie Pass destination, we had started recognizing a few other NoBos and, though Glenn continued to refer to us as "Glenn and Bob," I'd started calling ourselves "The Oregon Boys"—just recently, in fact, to a couple of Young Ones we'd chatted with on a break.

On our second-to-last night, we were scrunched in a small camping spot with a couple other tents as Glenn bemoaned having somehow lost his gloves. On the trail, a young NoBo stopped and looked our way.

"Hey," she said, "aren't you The Oregon Boys?"

It was the first time in four years anyone had referred to us by such and represented some serious "trail cred." Inwardly, I beamed.

"Why, yes, we are!" I said.

"Did one of you lose your gloves back when we stopped to talk?"

OK, so it was short-lived trail cred.

THE MORNING broke damp and dreary. Though I'd fixed my broken trekking pole, my feet were blistered and hurting. It felt as if we were trapped in a rainforest over which the sky no longer existed. The woods were dark, wet, and cold.

With nineteen miles to hike on this next-to-last day, one challenge was physical, the other mental; how could I find a happy place for my mind on a day that looked anything but that?

Over the years, I'd used my imagination to take me away from a pursuit that sometimes could be monotonous. I credited that to two jobs I had as a teenager involving mindless work—raking beans onto a conveyor belt at a cannery and mowing lawns. They forced me to mentally detach. I would put together lists, add numbers, do anything to *not* think about bean-raking or mowing: *Top 10 Crosby, Stills & Nash songs. Quarter-mile splits needed to run a sub-five-minute mile. Number of swaths my mower took to do the Sigma Alpha Epsilon lawn. Etc.*

At times on the trail, our imaginations took our minds off the exhaustion or boredom in another way: One of us would point to meadow in a far-off basin and say something like, "Par 3. Two thousand, five hundred yards. Water left. Canyon right. You're on the tee."

Now, however, my cupboard of mental detachment was bare—until I found a morsel in the far corner of the top shelf.

"Glenny," I said, "I'm going to interview you today about your entire life."

"That'll be good for five minutes. What then?"

"Hey, I'm a journalist. I got paid very average sums of money to draw out people's inner stories. So, what's your earliest memory?"

"A few: Reading comic books and playing football, our neighborhood guys against a bunch of kids down the street. My Uncle George lived next door and taught at South Eugene High and would come home with these castoff football helmets and pads, way too big, but we wore them anyway. We thought we were pretty cool."

Hey, this was working.

"So, what was it like growing up with all your Lutheran cousins, aunts, and uncles on Royal Avenue?"

"Wonderful. I'd walk a block down to my grandmother's house to have her read stories to me; I was probably five or six. Relatives all around the neighborhood. We'd gather often, especially for Christmas. My uncles were always giving one another useless gifts. One year one of them put a couple of chickens in a box, wrapped them up, and put them under the tree."

"Like *live* chickens?"

"Of course! What kind of weirdo gives someone dead chickens for Christmas?"

I rocked the forest with laughter. Alas, all good things must come to an end, and after a few hours of this exchange, Glenn's life had pretty much been reviewed. We both returned to our regularly scheduled mindless hiking.

Click. Click. Click. My trekking poles tapped their way up the trail. *Drip. Drip. Drip.* The rain continued, my blister pain made worse by wet feet, which increased friction. *Don't think about them,* I told myself, which, of course, made me think about them.

Every mile felt like five, every minute like an hour. We'd been on the trail for nearly 200 miles and nine days.

As we crossed a Forest Service road at Tacoma Pass, a voice suddenly startled me to my left.

"Hey, mates, how about a hot dog?"

What? The words came from an Australian thru-hiker with a bushy red beard, a guy who popped out of nowhere like a bridge troll. He nodded to a royal blue canopy about 100 feet down the road, where half a dozen hikers were sitting on—*oh, my gosh!*—lawn chairs. Steam rose from a Coleman stove where a guy our vintage was joyfully grilling dogs and heating water for cocoa. Beyond him: tables of hot coffee, cookies, chips, licorice, breakfast pastries, oranges, apples, pop, orange juice, a virtual smorgasbord of PCT fantasy foods.

"Are you kidding me?" I said, glancing back at Glenn.

"Trail Magic, Bobby!"

We'd encountered a few other people offering similar gestures, among them the Mount Adams Buddhists and a former PCT hiker trail-named Coppertone. But this was the most lavish Trail Magic spread I'd seen.

"Greetings," said the man at the grill, white-haired and white-bearded. "The name's 'Not Phil's Dad.' And you are?"

"The Oregon Boys, Bob and Glenn," I said. "Thanks. This is awesome."

"Happy to do it."

Glenn stayed back, apparently not wanting to appear discourteous in accepting this random act of kindness. Me? Before his pack was off I had downed my first hot dog and was reaching for a second.

"So, what's behind your trail name, 'Not Phil's Dad?'" I asked.

"My son Brian completed the PCT in 2009. Because other hikers said he looked like Phil Collins and he had to keep telling them he *wasn't* the musician, they dubbed him 'Not Phil.' So I decided to be 'Not Phil's Dad.' I do this every year to honor him—to pay forward all the Trail Magic he got along the way."

"That's great. And where's home?"

"Bellevue," he said, referring to a city across Lake Washington from Seattle.

"No kidding. I lived there during the '80s; I was a columnist at *The Journal-American.*"

"Small world. I was an administrator at Highland Middle School then."

"On Bel-Red Road, right? My wife worked at Highland Christian Preschool across the street!"

"Sure! Saw it everyday!"

Glenn soon joined the feast and the fun. Nothing enlivened PCT hikers more than Trail Magic, not only because of its spontaneity but because, deep down, it offered us "undeserved favor." Grace. Goodness. The best of humanity, in this case wrapped in a hot dog bun and served by a heart-of-gold father in honor of his PCT son. What a cool gesture.

In the next half hour, I supplemented the dogs with a Mountain Dew, four Double Stuf Oreos, an orange, and a cup of hot chocolate. The stop energized me for the rest of the day.

BECAUSE OF our need to camp next to water—and you couldn't choose where that was—our final day would need to be a twenty-three miler, longer than we would have liked. On Wednesday, September 7, we left extra early, wanting to make sure we were at the Snoqualmie Pass Ski Area when Sally and Ann arrived for the 4 P.M. pickup.

The first part of the morning was fine. Knowing this was our final day was initially enough to help me overcome the pain of feet that still hadn't found the proper hiking shoes—my Asics weren't cutting it—and had been wet for almost a week. My feet were wrinkled, my blisters deep and wide. But by early afternoon I started to feel my mental wheels coming off, too.

"How much farther?" I asked, expecting "five" but hoping for "three."

"Seven."

"Seven miles? Oh, my gosh. My feet are trashed."

We trudged on, up and down over small passes: Stampede, Dandy, Yakima. Finally, far down to our left, we saw the silver snake of Interstate 90 at Snoqualmie Pass.

"Finally," I said, feeling like an old-time captain who sees a gull and knows land must be near. Alas, an hour later I was still far out to sea—and mentally adrift.

"Why won't this trail go *down*?" I muttered. "Just zigzag us down to the friggin' freeway so we can be done with it already!"

Glenn withheld a snort; he was good about letting me vent. Based on the looks of his feet at the end of some days, I'd come to believe he hurt as much as I did but was better at stuffing his feelings. Me? I could be stoic, sometimes for hours, then mentally flip like a hydroplane catching air at 200 mph.

Glenn was quiet, conscientious, and methodical. I was animated, wacky, and capricious. He never listened to music while he hiked; I often did. He was the tortoise; I was the hare. He was, for now, unwavering in his upbeat pursuit of Snoqualmie; I was unraveling in my despair.

We could still see I-90 but not only were we high on a ridge, perhaps 1,500 feet above the freeway, but starting to climb even higher—on trails that were shifting from dirt to brick-sized shale. Each step felt as if I was stepping on thumb tacks.

"Sorry about your feet, Bob," Glenn said.

His empathy recalled the adage about a true friend being someone who knows all about you, but likes you nonetheless. Frankly, he deserved better.

In the stages of grief, I had hit *denial*, rushed through *anger*, skipped *bargaining* altogether, and gone right to *depression*. Finally, however, came *acceptance*. Perspective. *You're not living in a Third World country in search of a cup of water, pal. You're 99 percent done with this stretch of the PCT. In an hour you're gonna be in a Honda Pilot on your way to a McDonald's. Suck it up, soldier.*

Fifteen minutes later, the trail finally turned downward. I gingerly made my way down a grassy slope beneath the ski area's chairlifts. Far below, I saw two dots: Sally and Ann. Ten minutes later, I fell into Sally's arms and did something I hadn't done in a while, perhaps since Greg's passing: cried.

I sat down, ripped off my shoes and reached for my Crocs. The bottom of my feet looked like wet, white prunes. They ached, but were free at last.

Initially, my meltdown robbed me of any sense of accomplishment. Only later would I learn we had climbed 451 feet more per day than in the High Sierra two years before. Only later would I think back to the dark winter of 2015-16 when Glenn and I were struggling to get our minds and bodies back in the PCT game. Now, we had righted that wrong.

The weenies, indeed, had risen.

A soak in Two Lakes at day's end was sheer bliss. The rain had hastened the development of bad blisters on my feet for the first time since 2011.

Top: Glenn nearing the top of Old Snowy. Above: Celebrating atop the peak.

Top: As we headed down "The Knife's Edge" whose two flanks fell off as if you were hiking atop an A-frame roof, Glenn disappeared in the low clouds (top of photo). Above: In a White Pass motel, we hung wet clothes everywhere, even in the kitchen on a trekking pole.

Glenn Petersen

Top: Trail Magic rocked my soul on the day after Labor Day at Tacoma Pass. Above: The "angel" behind it was Not Phil's Dad (Richard Lee), who, each year, set up and served hikers in honor of his son, Brian, who had been on the receiving end of such generosity when he'd hiked the PCT in 2009.

By midafternoon, I couldn't see Glenn behind me, so I stopped, took off my pack, and lay down on my back beside the trail. Above, the towering trees framed a porthole to the sky, a few birds circling in the center. The forest was silent, the moment timeless, the mood almost sacred.

AGE 63

2017

NORTHERN CALIFORNIA

SIXTH SUMMER

START: AUGUST 23, 2017

GOAL: NORTH 361 MILES FROM CHESTER, CALIFORNIA TO OREGON–CALIFORNIA BORDER

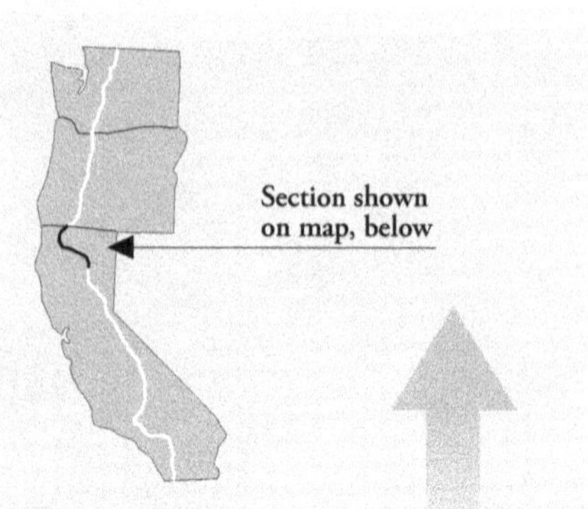

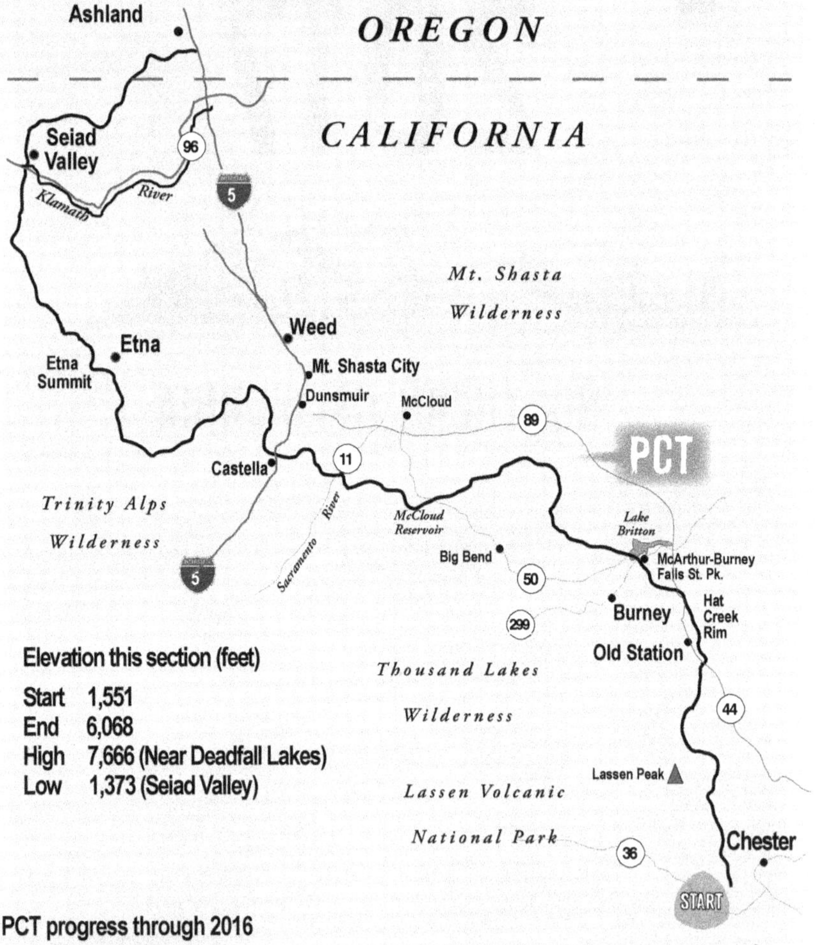

Ashland

OREGON

CALIFORNIA

Seiad Valley

96

Klamath River

5

Mt. Shasta Wilderness

Weed

Etna

Etna Summit

Mt. Shasta City

Dunsmuir

McCloud

89

PCT

Castella

11

Trinity Alps Wilderness

Sacramento River

McCloud Reservoir

Lake Britton

Big Bend

McArthur-Burney Falls St. Pk.

50

5

299

Burney

Hat Creek Rim

Old Station

Thousand Lakes Wilderness

44

Lassen Peak

Lassen Volcanic National Park

Chester

36

START

Elevation this section (feet)

Start	1,551
End	6,068
High	7,666 (Near Deadfall Lakes)
Low	1,373 (Seiad Valley)

PCT progress through 2016

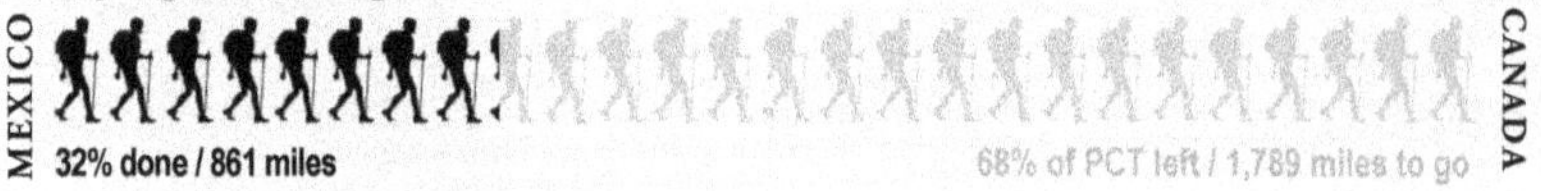

MEXICO

CANADA

32% done / 861 miles

68% of PCT left / 1,789 miles to go

EYES

A good laugh overcomes more difficulties and dissipates more dark clouds than any other one thing.

—Laura Ingalls Wilder

We spent considerable time over the winter putting together our 2017 trip, only to bag our plan in the spring because of near-record snowfalls in the High Sierra. Jack Haskel, spokesman for the PCTA, said the association was hearing stories "every week, if not every day" involving avalanches, falls on slippery slopes, exposure, and near drownings in neck-high creeks.

"I'm worried," he said, "that someone will die."

Glenn and I didn't need any more convincing. From the get-go, our goal had never been to get from Point A to Point B at the end of each day. Our goal was to have a measurable pulse at the end of each day; getting someplace was gravy. So, instead of going from Rush Creek north through Yosemite as planned, we chose to stay at lower elevations in Northern California. We would go 361 miles northwest from Chester, California—seventy miles east of Red Bluff—to the Oregon border.

After Sally and Ann dropped us at the trailhead on August 24, 2017, we were, depending on which geographic expert you trusted, either on the northern reaches of the Sierra Nevada or the southern reaches of the Cascade Range. We didn't much care. We were just happy to be back on the trail again after nearly eleven months.

One of the hardest parts about preparing for the PCT, at least for me, was getting all my non-trail knots tied up before I left. In the last few months before leaving, I'd gone with Sally to the Czech Republic and Poland; signed a contract to write a book on high jumper Dick Fosbury; and helped organize a ninetieth birthday party for my mother, Marolyn. I was ready to hike.

Since our 2016 hike, Glenn and Ann's grandchildren quiver had doubled; Katie and David welcomed twins Margaret and Annaliese in October. However, the health of Glenn's eighty-seven-year-old mother, Pauline, was ebbing. In fact, Glenn considered foregoing the trip so he could be there for her, but his family encouraged him to go hike, saying, "We got this."

Now, on this Thursday morning in late August, we headed north toward Mount Shasta on one of the less mountainous stretches of the PCT we'd faced. The trail was smooth, the temperature cool, and our spirits high. I breathed deep the pine-sweet air.

Glenn led the way with his "thinking-outside-the-pack" idea of storing light items in a self-made net he'd hung on the back.

"You're the only PCT hiker with a homemade crab net on the back of your pack," I said.

"Don't think I don't see the other hikers with their envious stares."

"That's not envy, it's disbelief," I said. "I should trail-name you 'Crab Net.'"

The early going was easy, transitioning from pine to hundreds of perfectly symmetrical noble firs, any of which She Who Loves a Good Noble would have warmly welcomed as our annual Christmas tree.

"Ground control to Major Tom," I began singing, the song a trail favorite of ours reflecting the challenge of hard-of-hearing Glenn staying in contact with hard-of-hearing Bob. "Ground control to Major Tom."

Suddenly, a southbound hiker appeared, chiming in with, "Take your protein pills and put your helmet on!"

I stopped as she neared. "Wait. You know 'Space Oddity?'"

"Of course," said the woman,* appearing to be a fellow Baby Boomer. "David Bowie, right? How you two doing?"

"Great. You?"

"Loving it. Another day in paradise. Enjoy, guys!"*

By midafternoon, I couldn't see Glenn behind me, so I stopped, took off

---

* In 2017, the year we were now hiking, forty-two percent of PCT hikers were female. That was up seven percentage points from the first PCT Survey taken in 2013, an increase certainly fueled by author Cheryl Strayed's PCT-related book *Wild* (2012) and the movie of the same name that followed (2014).

my pack, and lay down on my back beside the trail. Above, the towering trees framed a porthole to the sky, a few hawks circling in the center. The forest was silent, the moment timeless, the mood almost sacred. Not a single mosquito spoiled the serenity.

With exceptions for singing, of course, the sound of the PCT was silence. Yes, I loved the sound of a hoot owl, the trickling of a long-awaited creek, and the yip of a distant coyote. But I never tired of the quiet of the forest.

Since we'd begun six years ago, I'd heard such silence shattered by nature only twice: Once, when a hundred-foot fir cracked, splintered, and thudded to the forest floor near me in Southern Oregon (2011); oddly, at least to hikers, the tree was obscure in its life of silence and only noticed upon its noisy death. And a week later, at the northern base of Mount Thielsen, when I heard a rock slide rip loose a thousand feet above me.

For now, I just closed my eyes and allowed myself to be serenaded by the soothing sounds of the silent woods.

ON DAY THREE, just after passing on a resupply stop called Old Station where many hikers stopped, the walk-in-the-park nature of our hike ended. What was planned as a fifteen-mile day turned into nearly twenty-five, most of it on a shadeless plateau that belonged to neither the Sierra nor the Cascades, but to Central California's Modoc Plateau. Either that, or to the PCT's version of purgatory.

The trail on Hat Creek Rim, a "faulted escarpment" thick with high-desert chaparral, was hot, twisting, and as dry as bleached cattle bones. It was August 26, a Saturday, and the temperature hit ninety by midmorning, based on the tiny REI thermometer affixed to my pack. When taking a break, we did so beneath skinny trees whose shade was so meager we had to shift positions every ten minutes to stay in it as the earth rotated.

Twice we realized places we thought would have water did not. What's more, our one lifeline to sanity—a chance to listen to the Oregon State-Colorado State football game via the Internet—proved fruitless: not only did the broadcast come and go like the reverberation in "Crimson and Clover,"* but the Beavers got throttled by unheralded Colorado State, 56-17.

A canyon that needed skirting forced us to make a mind-numbingly long hairpin turn to the east and then back west.

"What book does this section make you think of?" I asked as we stopped to exchange water bottles.

"I dunno. What?"

* Tommy James and the Shondells, 1968.

"*Lonesome Dove*," I said. "Couldn't you just see Woodrow Call dragging Gus McRae's body through here on his way back to Texas, to fulfill his promise?"

"If you say so," said Glenn, who'd read the book but preferred Louis L'Amour.

"I know you'd do the same for me, right? I mean, if something happened to me, you'd drag my body back to Eugene, right?"

"Sure," said Glenn.

"And I'd get you back to Albany, Glenny, but I wouldn't drag you. That's too hard. I'd take you back to Old Station and, using your credit card, have you FedExed to Ann. That way she could absolutely, positively have you overnight!"

WE SAW only one other hiker on the desolate plateau, a SoBo in his twenties, trail-named "Blue Sky." He was as whipped as we were, maybe more judging by the flushed look on his face.

"Got enough water?" I asked.

"Think so. Liter-and-a-half."

"Go easy on it. There's a nice campground when you fall off this giant rock. Running water. Actual bathrooms."

"Ready for that."

"Better things ahead for you," I said. "Cooler. Easier trail. And there's a Pizza Factory in Chester with killer pepperoni."

We chatted a while, then prepared to head our respective directions.

"Hey, thanks," said Blue Sky. "I needed the encouragement."

By the time we reached a spot to camp, just beyond a tank filled by a trail angel—"Water Cache 22"—I felt like a home-from-work cow in a Far Side cartoon I remembered: A cow opens the front door to see her husband, who is nothing but a carcass. "Tough day at the office, dear?" she asks.

When a young SoBo from the Netherlands made camp near us, I didn't have the heart to tell her what lay ahead—other than to point out there was water 2.8 miles away. We'd hiked just short of a marathon. My body was broken, my spirits dead, my candy bars melted. But I'd met our goal for the day's end: I had a measurable pulse.

Even if it had been a tough day at the office.

NORTH OF Mount Lassen, like a quick-change artist, the trail transitioned into yet another look: foliage featuring oak savanna and poison oak. *Note to self: stay out of the latter, lest you add "itching" to the PCT's four horsemen of the apocalypse: weariness, blisters, aching muscles, and chafing.*

Now in my sixth summer on the PCT, I'd learned that hiking had more movable parts than I'd imagined, many of them involving my own body. When taking more than 40,000 steps a day, chafing, for example, could cause problems. So could a pebble in my shoe or a too-long fingernail on the little finger of my left hand; it could dig into the next finger over when my hands were wrapped around the handle of a trekking pole.

In two days, we had hiked more than forty miles, the distance between my home in Eugene and Glenn's in Albany. The sun was laser-beamed on us as if we were ants and some giant kid with a magnifying glass was trying to see if he could make us spontaneously combust. Judging by how I felt, his chances seemed excellent.

Shortly before McArthur-Burney Falls Memorial State Park, we began looking for that night's stop: something called Burney Mountain Guest Ranch, a private operation that provided dinner, cabins, supplies, and a place to camp. I knew little about it, only that as the afternoon wore on, it couldn't come soon enough. I was drenched in sweat. Glenn's long-sleeve gray shirt was stained with salt marks that looked like beach foam left by outgoing waves. "Angels wings," some PCT hikers called the look.

Finally, in my late-afternoon weariness, I saw a sign wood-burned into the butt of a log: "Burney Mountain Guest Ranch." We headed south up the trail where, in the distance, we soon saw a woman walking toward us from a ranch house. *What was that she was carrying, something in each hand?*

"Welcome," she said with a tone as warm as her smile.

Whereupon she handed each of us two scoops of strawberry ice cream in a cup with a white plastic spoon.

"Oh. My. Gosh."

While long-distance hiking in the heat, it's common, at least for me, to dream of all sorts of stuff like this happening, but this actually *was* happening.

"Thanks so much," said Glenn. "This is great!"

I scooped a spoonful into my mouth. I hadn't had anything feel so good on my lips since, at eighteen, first kissing Sally through the water fountain at Avery Park in Corvallis. The ice cream was cold, creamy, tantalizingly delicious, feeding not just my parched body but my withered soul.

"I'm Linda," she said. "Welcome to the Burney Mountain Guest Ranch."

"Thanks," I said. "I'm Bob, and this is Glenn. We're The Oregon Boys."

Linda Morse told us dinner would be served in a couple of hours, then showed us around.

"There's a little store over there with all sorts of hiker-friendly grub. Just write down what you buy, then, when done, total it and we'll square up. Honor system. Showers are over here; hang your towel on the line afterward if you would. You can pitch a tent over there for $15, but just so you know, we had a cat prowling around here a few nights ago. Or you can rent a cabin for $63. They're real nice. They have air conditioning."

She had me at *cat.*

"Wait, uh, do you mean, like, a *bob*cat?" I asked

"Yeah. Or a mountain lion or cougar. The hikers didn't get a good look at it. They're all common around here."

I nodded confidently, as if to suggest this wasn't my first I-could-be-sleeping-next-to-a-bobcat rodeo. Glenn turned sideways, apparently wanting to whisper to me without offending Linda.

"Cabins are kinda steep," he said. "Maybe just pitch the tents, huh?"

"Are you *kidding* me?" I whispered back with staccato speed. "Did you *not* hear what she said? Air-conditioning and *no* bobcats versus no-air conditioning and *possibly* bobcats. It's ninety degrees out. And thirty-one-fifty each—for the privilege of a wonderful night's sleep and waking up alive. Seems like a great deal to me!"

I didn't even wait for Glenn's reply. Instead, I flashed Linda a smile.

"Uh, we'll take a cabin please."

The evening was a much-needed blend of rest and refreshment. We chatted with a few other PCTers, including Tyler, a kid from Puyallup, Washington, who couldn't show us enough photos of the rattlesnakes he'd encountered.

The heat had sapped Glenn's appetite, but he went through the hole-in-the-wall store as if on a one-minute shopping spree, buying great amounts of two items: chocolate milk and V-8. Despite having just eaten lasagna and Caesar salad, I displayed a bit more epicurean adventure, eating three different kinds of potato chips, all washed down with a full-bodied Mountain Dew—a 2017, I believe. We sat on the porch, as the heat subsided, then retired to our air-conditioned cabin.

"Man," said Glenn. "This is heaven."

"Said the guy who wanted to sleep outside in the heat with the bobcats."

THE STATE PARK at Burney Falls, where we needed to pick up sent-ahead food, was two miles from the ranch but the next day it took us 5.5 miles to get there. That's because we overshot it by 1.75 miles. By now, nearly a thousand miles into the trip, I'd reminded myself that roughing up Navigator Glenn for such mistakes was unjustified—like berating the long-snapper on a football team who delivers 150 perfect hikes, then sails one over the punter's head. I needed to just suck it up and wear my Big Bob panties.

Not, of course, that I did. I just kept all my sulking to myself, thinking about having to walk an extra 3.5 miles to get my resupply box and cram down an early lunch at the park's barebones restaurant. The mistake came with a silver lining, however, because as I ate a hot dog—Glenn was calling Ann to get an update on his mom—I met a young hiker from Eugene.

Jai Ralls was on the caboose of the southbound PCT train for Mexico, a small group but driven. He'd left Canada July 24, just thirty-four days ago, and was hoping to get through the High Sierra and to Mexico before the snow flew. After a great chat and two hot dogs, I bid him farewell and grabbed my pack.

Glenn and I crossed a dam, then zigzagged up a forested mountain whose neatly notched trail—*who builds these amazing things in such rugged terrain?*—made me think of the story I'd known for years about how the Pacific Crest Trail came to be.

On January 13, 1926, Catherine Montgomery of Bellingham, Washington, was among the first to raise the idea. A teacher at Washington State Normal School (eventually, Western Washington University), she was meeting with a textbook salesman, Joseph Hazard. Being an ardent mountaineer and knowing Hazard was too, Montgomery asked him a question, Hazard later recounted in his 1946 book, *Pacific Crest Trails.*

"Why [don't] you Mountaineers do something big for Western America?" she asked.

"Just what have you in mind?"

She placed a copy of *American Forestry* magazine on the table.

"A high, winding trail down the heights of our western mountains with mile markers and shelter huts—like these pictures I'll show you of the 'Long Trail of the Appalachians'—from the Canadian border to the Mexican Boundary Line!"

Hazard was intrigued. Later, he raised the possibilities to the Mount Baker Club. The idea spread to fellow climbers and to other West Coast outdoor clubs. The buzz began. However, it remained as only embers of an idea until 1932, when Clinton Clarke, chairman of the Mountain League of Los Angeles County, blew on them. He proposed to the U.S. Forest Service and National Parks Service that a trail be built "along the summit divides of the mountain ranges of (Washington, Oregon and California), traversing the best scenic areas and maintaining an absolute wilderness character."

After the U.S. Forest Service approved of the idea, volunteers went to work. Each of the states already had significant trail routes going north and south. In 1920, for example, the Forest Service had routed the Oregon Skyline Trail from Mount Hood to Crater Lake, which would become the PCT's first section; my father had hiked sections of it. And the 211-mile John Muir Trail, seventeen years in the making, was completed in 1932. Now, connections needed to go north and south from, and to, such mainstays.

Year after year, soon after spring snow melt, groups of volunteers headed for the mountains to continue their work. Using pickaxes, workers carved a two-foot trail through Oregon's forests; using bucksaws, they sliced paths through blowdown in Washington's windy northern sections; using dynamite, they blasted away granite in California's High Sierra.

In 1968 the National Trails Act created the PCT, though the trail wouldn't be officially declared finished until 1993. From Montgomery's idea to completion had taken *sixty-seven years*—essentially three generations. And yet, because of the vision and sacrifices of her and other long-gone people, backpackers like me were privileged to hike it—for free!

On this hot August day, the thought of such sacrifices got me up the side of a mountain, taking my mind off the day's heat and my weariness. But by the time we got to Peavine Creek, our camping spot for the night, I was so parched that I slid out of my pack and oozed into the water as if more fish than human.

AS WE HEADED into the heavily wooded darkness of 5 A.M. the next day—Tuesday, August 29, our sixth—the air was tinged with a hint of smoke. On our way down from Oregon, we'd seen smoke from a fire near Interstate 5, but the fire was far from where we were now.

I surmised that among Glenn's first thoughts on this day would be of his mother. The report he'd heard from Ann at Burney Falls had a sort of "holding steady" sense to it. Pauline had been in a hospital in Portland, where Glenn's brother, Dave, and Dave's wife Karen, were looking after her, but now had been taken to Albany, where she was staying with Ann.

I said a quick prayer for Pauline and the family, then locked into a certain mindlessness that early morning headlamp-hiking lent itself to. You're hardly awake. The world is a grainy blur of blacks, browns, and grays. The trail is not a long, snaking pathway in front of you, but fifteen feet of dirt and rock that only stretches as far as your diffused light allows you to see. You don't know if, to your left, the mountain gives way to a 500-foot canyon or, to your right, some animal is eying you.

I was ensconced in this unreal reality when I saw them, a jolt to my senses because the scene was so unlike anything I'd witnessed on the trail: orange lights, strung out to my left as if Halloween decorations on someone's back fence. *Weird.* As I often did in the morning, I was leading—just as Glenn often led us in the afternoon when my blisters cried out and my mind turned to mush.

"Check it out," I whispered to Glenn after pausing to let him catch up—as if there was anyone within five miles of us. "Are those decorative orange lights on someone's back fence?"

"Strange," he said.

They looked to be maybe only fifty feet from us.

"No, you know what I think they are," he said in the stillness. "Wind turbines—way off in the distance."

"Really?"

"Yeah. And because they're so tall, I think the FAA requires they be lit."

"Hey, I think you're right. Reds lights looking orange because of the smoke filter."

We hiked on through the orange-studded darkness. I retained the lead position, the forest as dark as a cellar. I seldom felt afraid walking in such early morning blackness, fortified by a totally unjustified sense that our leaving so early gave us a certain privilege, as if the forest honored our early morning commitment and—

Yeeeeeeeooooooowwwwwwwwwwwww.

My heart thumped as the high-pitched sound shattered the silence. I stopped in my tracks, feeling as if I'd been zapped by a stun gun. But as Glenn caught up to me, my brain rode to the rescue with rationalization.

"C-c-crow?" I asked.

Glenn didn't say anything.

"Jaybird?"

"No," he said.

"What?"

A second wail: *Yeeeeeeeooooooowwwwwwwwwwwww.*

"Mountain lion," whispered Glenn.

The words leveled me. I didn't want him to say that. I didn't want to believe that was possible. But my body was belying what my fueled-by-fear mind wanted me to believe; I was panting, my heart pounding.

"Look," whispered Glenn. "*There.*"

He pointed with his trekking pole to perhaps the scariest thing I'd seen in my life beyond something in a movie: two glassy eyes in the blackened distance, lit up by our headlamps, staring directly at us. The animal was about 100 feet away.

Yeeeeeeeooooooowwwwwwwwwwwww.

I loved outdoor adventure—until it was staring me in the face and growling. This lion wasn't going away. This was *his* forest and we were intruders.

"Make noise," Glenn said, then started rapping his trekking poles together. "Hey, hey, hey!" he yelled. Pause. "Hey, hey, hey!"

Glenn took a few steps forward. I did not.

"Here we come," I said with no confidence, clicking my poles. "Coming through!"

Pathetic. If, as they say, mountain lions are more likely to attack if they considered you cowardly, small, and afraid—saw you as *prey*—I had just rung the dinner bell and handed the lion a menu with us as "Today's Special." But asserting myself seemed counter-intuitive. What seemed intuitive was to run like hell.

To our right, the terrain sloped up.

"What if we get up high, sort of give him the trail while still asserting ourselves," I suggested, a nervous compromise cloaked in contradiction.

"Hey, hey, hey!" Glenn continued to bellow, clicking his poles together while pretty much ignoring me, which I totally understood. I would have ignored me, too, if I were him. But I wasn't him. I was *me*, which rhymes with pee, which is about what I was ready to do in my pants.

Instead, I did two things: I prayed silently that the mountain lion would scram. And, triggered by my reporter's instincts, I whipped out my iPhone and recorded some footage of blackness with Glenn yelling "Hey, hey, hey!" I suppose I thought if we were attacked the footage might serve as evidence that we hadn't just made up the mountain lion story.

Slowly, we crept forward. The animal bounced left, then back right, as if it were approaching us, bouncing down a zigzag trail.

"Coming through!" Glenn said, poles still clicking.

We baby-stepped through the darkness. Soon, the eyes disappeared.

"We home free?" I asked.

"For now," said Glenn. "But remember, if that mountain lion comes after us and we start running, I only have to beat one person to survive: *you*!"

He laughed his patented Petersen laugh. Somehow that humor was, for me, the "all clear" assurance I needed. Soon, the forest awoke. Lightness brought the trees and trail to life.

We hiked on for an hour, then stopped for a snack break, whereupon I Googled "sound of a mountain lion" on my iPhone.

Yeeeeeeeoooooowwwwwwwwwwww. Yep. Sounded familiar.

THAT AFTERNOON, the heat was insufferable and the smoke thicker. While hiking, nothing hurt worse than a toe-stinger—in full stride, stubbing the front of a foot on a little "shark-fin" rock or root protruding from the trail. What added insult to injury was that it usually happened when you were already dead tired, which I was when I jammed my toe into a rock just before quitting time.

I limped into camp. Beyond the usual stuff, my right knee, which had been aggravated by the toe-stinger, was more painful and swollen than ever.

"How can a book describe the psychological factors a person must prepare for [on the PCT]," wrote Jim Podlesney in *Pacific Crest Hike Planning Guide.* "The despair, the alienation, the anxiety and especially the pain, both physical and mental, which slices to the very heart of the hiker's volition?"

After getting out of my sweaty hiking clothes, I sat there in my underwear and crunched some numbers on my iPhone calculator to take my mind off my broken body.

"Good news, Glenny. We'll soon hit the thousand-mile mark since we began in 2011. Maybe tomorrow or the next day."

"All right, Bobby. We're rocking."

Glenn grabbed his phone. "Gonna give Ann a call," he said.

Ten minutes later he was back. "Mom was admitted to the hospital in Albany today. Bob, I think I need to get home."

"Totally understand."

He exhaled, then grabbed a map. "We're four days and sixty-four miles from I-5. We're at 5,500 feet. Castella, on I-5, is 2,180, so much of it is downhill."

"What if we do it in three?"

"Exactly what I was thinking. Have Ann and Sally pick us up Friday. Little more than twenty-one miles per day for us."

We'd be cutting a fifteen-day trip to ten, and a 361-mile trip to 170 miles, but both of us knew it was the right call.

GIVEN THE seriousness of Pauline's failing health—and perhaps to take our minds off exactly that—the trip to I-5 was raucous, rambunctious, and flat-out fun. Oh, we were reverent about the underlying purpose, Pauline, and disciplined in meeting our goal; the first morning we were on the trail by 3:45 A.M. But beyond that we let the levity flow.

Knowing that Oregon State would be playing its first home football game Saturday against Portland State, I began mimicking my favorite sports announcer, OSU's Mike Parker. He'd interviewed me a few times and impressed me because, unlike most interviewers, he'd read my books and come prepared. Plus, I liked how detailed his game descriptions were; he helped me see what was happening, making him less announcer than storyteller. And, finally, he continually reset the stage: score, down, distance, time—the basics which far too many announcers neglect.

"Welcome, Beaver Nation," I began. "I'm Mike Parker, having been whisked to the Pacific Crest Trail via the BennyCopter. With me, two hikers: OSU alum Glenn Petersen, Class of '74, and his brother-in-law whose name escapes me and attended that *other* so-called university to the south, are attempting to reach I-5 in only three days instead of the four they had planned. Guys, what are you feeling at this moment?"

"Well, Mike, if I can speak for Glenn—and I *can*, and I think the world will be the better for it—I'd say we're feeling, well, tired. Really, really tired."

You get the idea. The trail had taught me you needed to be flexible. Sure, plan your trip with ideal water and resupply stops. But expect that weather, injuries or things back home might force you to reconfigure everything.

You needed to improvise. Combat the aching bones with funny bones. And, yep, simply laugh.

Linda Morse welcoming us with strawberry ice cream at Burney Mountain Guest Ranch was among the coolest moments of my PCT experience thus far.

One late afternoon as we neared Castella, a deer joined us on and off for about fifteen minutes, teasing us by waiting for us, then prancing forward.

The "lodge" was a simple peaked-roof log cabin with a single room not much larger than a two-car garage. A covered front porch stretched across the front, framed horizontally with wood-peeled log rails. Hanging flower baskets framed the entry way: two on the left, two on the right … .

AGE 64

2018

NORTHERN, CENTRAL CALIFORNIA

START: JULY 10, 2018

GOAL: NORTH 192 MILES FROM CASTELLA ON I-5 TO ORE.-CAL. BORDER

Section shown on map below

Elevation this section (feet)

Start	2,154
End	6,068
High	7,666 (Near Deadfall Lakes)
Low	1,373 (Seiad Valley)

PCT progress through 2017

MEXICO

39% done / 1,032 miles

61% of PCT left / 1,618 miles to go

CANADA

FIRE

There is no education like adversity.

—Benjamin Disraeli

Another summer, our seventh on the trail, arrived. At the end of 2014, when I'd first envisioned us doing the whole thing, I imagined us finishing after seven summers. But we were barely more than a third done.

Not that it deterred my enthusiasm in the least. Weeks before our first trip of 2018—in Northern California—I hustled from store to store buying my food. I then funneled it into my pack and into a box that I would send ahead to pick up at Seiad Valley, two days south of the Oregon border.

As was my custom, I set up two eight-foot tables to turn half our garage into PCT Packing Central. Though I seldom felt I had enough time for it, organizing was among my favorite parts of the yearly ritual. Glenn would tell me how many breakfasts, lunches, and dinners we'd need, and, with a shipping scale and multi-sized sandwich bags at the ready, I would funnel tortilla shells, Starkist Tuna Creations, jerky, candy, candy bars, chips, and more into their respective bags. The idea was to limit myself to 1.5 to 2 pounds of food per day, to give myself somewhere around 5,000 calories per day, and to provide enough variety to keep things interesting. Trail food never stayed interesting, but each summer I convinced myself otherwise.

This was the one area where Glenn and I switched roles; I became the stickler for variety, proper portions, and sufficient calories per ounce. And he, like me with my tent and sleeping bag, just threw it in one giant food bag.

He would bring entire packages of cookies and pistachios, entire plastic jars of peanut butter. Me? I would put six Dots in a credit-card-sized plastic bag, one bag for each of our nine days, making sure I had a variety of different-flavored pieces in each package. (I loved the gum drops but the makers, Tootsie Roll Industries, never included enough greens.)

I would start 2018's seven-day stretch with twelve pounds of food, four pounds of water (two one-liter plastic bottles), and twenty pounds of everything else, a total of thirty-six pounds.

Since ending our shortened hike at Castella the previous summer, much had happened: Pauline had been moved to a retirement community, I'd had arthroscopic knee surgery in December, and my friend, Geoff, had hiked 1,506 miles, or fifty-six percent, of the PCT—half again as much as we had.

At one point, near the South Sister, he met a section-hiker named John Pritchett, who asked Geoff what compelled him to do the PCT. Geoff explained knowing me and having read my book, *Cascade Summer.*

"How about you?" Geoff asked John. "Why are you blistering your feet?"

"I blame Welch, too. Like you, I read his book. And like you, I'm friends with him. Bob hired me as his first part-timer when he was sports editor of *The Bulletin* in Bend back in the late seventies. Known him for decades."

Geoff marveled at the coincidence. "Crazy! Two strangers with you in common," he told me.

When Geoff would hit the trail, the regulars back at the barber shop in Springfield slapped a PCT map on the wall and charted his progress with push pins. The barber shop was part of a cluster of businesses—it included a convenience store, flower shop, and beauty salon—and customers and workers alike were hungry for updates on him.

"Remind me again your plans for this year," I said while he cut my hair in May 2018.

"Castella north to as far as I can get," he said. "Maybe finish the whole enchilada. Taking the train to Dunsmuir to start."

"When?"

"July 9."

"Crazy! We're starting at the same spot just a day later! Might see you on the trail."

By now, Glenn and I had done thirty-nine percent of the PCT. Each winter, he would commemorate our latest accomplishment by gifting me a photo calendar and some woodburn design he'd made.

For 2018, a minor change was in order. We decided to trade our foam rubber Z-pads for light air mattresses to soothe our aching, aging bodies at night. I was now sixty-four, Glenn soon to be sixty-six.

But here's what never changed: Glenn's commitment to me, the trip, and his conditioning. Over the winter, he'd bury himself in planning for the following summer's journey and work hard on the treadmill.

I tried to follow suit, though staying in shape in the off season was never easy. One January morning as I swam outside at Eugene's Amazon Pool in temperatures just above twenty degrees, I saw something strange in the mist of the next lane: a duck, apparently racing me. But as our unofficial motto had become: *Whatever it takes.*

THE STRETCH north from Castella was a slog past Castle Crags and Castle Domes, the less showy cousins of similar granite peaks in the High Sierra. In the distance: the Trinity Alps, and the Russian and Marble Mountain Wilderness. Like the trail north from the Columbia River Gorge, this section arced like a huge letter "C" and snaked wildly. At times, hikers would find themselves walking southward—*away* from Canada—for miles. The driving distance from Castella to Ashland, Oregon, on Interstate 5 was sixty miles. Via the PCT? More than 200.

Three days into the trip, we were drying off after taking our air mattresses for a spin on one of the Deadfall Lakes when we saw a couple arriving to cool off, and camp, at the same lake. Thierno (pronounced *Chee-ar-no)* was about six-foot and 200 pounds; he was finishing up nursing school. Marion was five-feet and 105 pounds, and had just finished medical school. They were French.

Husband and wife, they were linked by two things: matching royal blue North Face t-shirts and the pain of having hiked thirty-five miles and climbed nearly 5,000 feet in three days, a brutal PCT baptism for anyone, much less people who had to overcome jet lag from a 6,000-mile trip.

They were wiped. Thierno helped Marion get her boots off, a procedure that, when finished, revealed badly blistered feet. She winced.

"Here, try this," I said, handing her a tiny folding chair that I'd brought as my "guilty pleasure."

She demurred with a polite shake of the head.

"Please," I said, eyes widening. "It's yours to use if you'd like."

This time she accepted, easing into it with a smile that lifted us all, as if we were experiencing the comfort vicariously through her.

"Merci," she said, leaning back and closing her eyes.

I brought the chair because one of the things I missed most on the trail was the simple luxury of sitting on something soft to rest my aching body. And when coming across one online that weighed only twenty-nine ounces, I couldn't resist. Would it be worth the weight, carrying it for perhaps twelve hours a day to use for perhaps only an hour? I'd tried it in northern Washington the previous year and thought it was.

When I asked Marion what led to their coming all the way from France to Northern California to hike the Pacific Crest Trail, her answer was predictable.

"*Wild*," she said, referring to the 2012 book by Portland author Cheryl Strayed. It's about Strayed's 1995 PCT hike of 1,100 miles that helped her re-center herself after her mother's death from cancer.

AFTER A THOUSAND miles on the PCT, I had, over the winter, finally found a shoe that was preventing my feet from getting terrible blisters. I'd gone four summers with Merrells and one with Asics, but in 2017 I'd discovered the Altra Zero Drop, featuring an expansive toe box. And, for the first time since I'd stepped on the PCT, I was feeling no pain.

Before turning in for the night, I shared with Thierno and Marion how I'd battled blisters for nearly a third of the trail until I found Altras.

"Night and day difference for me," I said. "You might check them out."

They nodded, as if interested. They'd been taping their feet with duct tape, something my orthotics specialist in Eugene, Kathy Sherwood, had talked me out of after I tried it my first year.

"Bob," she said, "what is the one thing duct tape is designed *not* to do?"

"Come off?"

"Exactly. So, why would you want to put that on your feet?"

Glenn offered Marion and Thierno Kinesio Tape, strong but far easier to get off than duct tape—and didn't take skin with it. We headed for our tents.

"Good night," I said after giving them my contact info. "Maybe we'll see you up the trail. And when you're coming through Oregon, feel free to contact me if you need help. I live in Eugene, only two hours from the PCT."

Marion stood up to hand me my chair.

"No, no, no, keep it for tonight. Just leave it by my tent."

The next morning, my headlamp illuminated a note on the chair.

> You are both our second experience of the "Trail Magic." Nice to meet you while discovering your wonderful country. Maybe see you in Eugene! Thanks for the tape, Glenn, and the chair, Bob. Best wishes. Marion & Thierno

The couple included their email on the back. We were five miles up the trail when it hit me: I'd recommended Altras to Thierno and Marion but hadn't told them how they could actually *get* the shoes—and soon. With no cell coverage, I pulled over, got out my notebook, and scrawled a message:

> T&M. Call this Ashland outdoor store when you get cell coverage and order your shoes. They will be there when you arrive. Happy Trails!

A quarter mile later, I asked a passing SoBo if he could deliver the message to Thierno and Marion, who were probably a few miles behind me.

"No problem."

"You can't miss them," I said. "He's twice her size and they are French. Wonderful people!"

I doubted we would see the pair again because it sounded as if they were going into Etna—they wanted to see France play Croatia in the World Cup Soccer Championships—and we were not.

Honestly, I wondered how far they'd get, period. Besides fires, what forces most PCT hikers to quit, say the PCT Surveys, is injuries—specifically "overuse injury (foot)," which includes, of course, blisters. Marion had them bad—after only a few days into her hike.

Etna was a small town, about ten miles below the trail, that most PCT hikers hitched into for resupply. But, for several reasons, we weren't stopping. These young thru-hikers seemed to have unlimited time; their deadline was often a September back-to-college day or visa-expiration day. Many were between jobs. Glenn and I had jobs we needed to get back to—next week. And we weren't big fans of hitchhiking, not because of the fear factor but because of the unpredictability and potential wasted time.

SINCE WE HAD begun hiking the PCT seven years ago, we were usually the first PCTers in our neck of the woods to awaken and hit the trail. That was our only advantage over the Young Ones. We rarely hit the trail later than 5 A.M. and, when we needed big miles, weren't averse to breaking sweat by 4 A.M. or even earlier. Granted, that meant being asleep by 6 P.M., 7 P.M. at the latest, and having to hike with headlamps for a couple hours—but it also meant we'd get lots of cool miles in before sunrise and have a better choice for a good camping spot when we stopped late afternoon. The Young Ones often hiked until dark.

Thus, on Friday, July 13, we found a great tent site when we arrived at a seasonal spring (this one with water) after a nineteen-mile day.

Every hiker has a unique getting-ready and end-of-the-day routine. Once arrived at a camp spot, my friend Geoff would, while munching on Sour Patch Kids candy, take a final look at hard-copy maps of the section he'd just hiked and light them on fire. It was a way to symbolically bid farewell to the past—and, of course, to save weight.

Not surprisingly, Glenn's finished-hiking routine and mine were far different. He kept on his sweaty clothes and shoes, put up his tent (zipped tightly to keep mosquitoes out), organized his food for dinner, filtered his water for dinner and the next morning, stacked his ready-to-go water bottles outside his tent like soldiers prepared for formal inspection, and began poring over maps to plan the next day's trip.

I peeled out of my wet clothes, put on dry clothes, traded my sweaty hiking shoes for Crocs, laid back, and enjoyed a bag of chips and a Crystal-Light-enhanced drink to bask in the day's accomplishment.

We were preparing to eat when Thierno and Marion showed up to camp with us again.

"Thank you for the message that hiker gave us," said Marion.

"Oh, you got it?" I said.

"Yes. He greeted us with a hearty '*Bonjour!*'"

WE WERE NOW in the Trinity Alps Wilderness Area, a collage of jagged mountain peaks, ridge beyond ridge of trees, and small lakes. On Tuesday, July 17, I headed out after lunch while Glenn stayed to nap longer. I promised I would wait at any junction. He offered me a thumbs-up, rolled back onto his back and was asleep, it appeared, in seconds.

At times, I enjoyed hiking by myself, and I think Glenn did, too; changing up the routine could ease the occasional spells of monotony, especially in the afternoon. So, for me, did music. At times, I'd listen to James Taylor, Neil Young, Crosby, Stills & Nash, the score from *A River Runs Through It*, or David Gray, lyrics of whom seemed to fit me well: *Please forgive me if I act a little strange, for I know not what I do . . . .*

I wasn't listening to anything, however, when, in the shadow of the Marble Mountains, I rounded a tree-thick switchback and saw it padding across the trail and scampering into the woods 200 feet in front of me: a bear. My first spotting of one. A black bear, I assumed, but cinnamon colored. And in quite the hurry when seeing me.

After telling Glenn how I'd stared down a ten-foot grizzly, we hiked on together, and made camp at Paradise Lake. When Coyote, a young man from Japan, pitched his tent across from us, Glenn chatted him up.

"What's the word?" I asked when he returned.

"I asked him how he was doing and he consulted his phone's translation app, then showed it to me. It said, 'There's very much deer feces.'"

We invited Coyote, thirty-four, for dinner the next night at a picnic table on Grider Creek. Earlier, I'd taken a cathartic swim in a pool so clear I could see the dirt on my individual toes through the water.

At dusk, a guy wearing the swankiest Lycra leggings I'd seen on the trail walked by: they were turquoise and festooned with images of hot dogs in buns, garnished with mustard. He had already done thirty miles, but even though it was dusk he told us he planned to hike another eight to get to the cafe in Seiad Valley, which opened early the next morning.

"We're The Oregon Boys," I said. "Bob and Glenn."

"Hot Dog," he said.

Who woulda thunk?

I KEPT wondering if we might catch my buddy, Geoff, but, nope. Either he was keeping his one-day lead on us or he'd stopped in Etna and we were ahead of him.

We were up by 3:15 A.M. and, while on a road, passed through a sketchy stretch pocked with ramshackle houses, growling dogs, and "Insured by Remington" signs. The cafe was a welcome sight. The hole-in-the-wall restaurant offered giant pancakes that were free if you could eat so many within a certain time frame.* We didn't make the attempt, but enjoyed a great breakfast nonetheless, sitting with Hot Dog and some kid from Colorado who said, "Yeah, thirty-four miles a day feels right for me." *Ah, youth.*

Glenn was enthralled with Hot Dog, which seemed odd because hot dog leggings on the trail were definitely "out there" and Glenn was not an "out there" sort of guy. When the subject turned to foam-rubber sleeping Z-pads vs. blow-up mattresses, Hot Dog didn't hold back.

"Foam pads are crappy," he said, "but at least they are *reliably* crappy. Nobody in the history of hiking has successfully patched an air mattress. Once they get a leak, you're dead."

Hot Dog was from the Bay Area and worked for a company owned by Elon Musk; what he did we couldn't quite figure out. But before the breakfast was over, Hot Dog had become Glenn's new "trail guru."

"He cold-soaks his food thirty to sixty minutes before a mealtime, while hiking, by mixing it together in a plastic peanut-butter jar and hanging it on his pack," Glenn said. "He also drinks cold coffee. And when he stops at a store, he bungee-cords one of those 'ginormous' bags of potato chips to the outside of his pack."

"So, you have a new Jedi Master," I said. I bowed, hands clasped as if in prayer. "Welcome, Master Hot Dog. Me? As a hiker, I'm crappy, but I'm reliably crappy."

---

* In spring 2003, the Travel Channel chose the cafe as the third-best location in the world to "pig out."

IN SEIAD VALLEY our plan was to get our food boxes—they'd be light, since we had only two days to the Oregon-California border—and do something we hadn't done in our nearly 1,300 miles on the trail: take what's known as a "zero." A day off. Just hang out. Read. Relax. Talk with other hikers. But the RV Park where we planned to stay had little shade and the temperature was near ninety—and it wasn't even noon. Plus, few hikers were around.

"Wanna just move on?" Glenn said.

We both knew what was ahead of us—a 5,000-foot climb in broiling temperatures on a nearly shadeless mountain. At a 544-foot-per-mile rise, it was one of the steepest climbs out of any town on the PCT.

"Sure," I said. "Might as well bake while making progress than while *not*."

We started up the trail, the Hot-Dog-inspired Glenn having strapped a family-sized bag of potato chips in his pack's crab net. We zigzagged out of the valley, eager to get back to our home state that was only thirty-eight miles—and two days of hiking—away. The temperature rose. So did the trail. By midafternoon, after six miles, we stopped at a rare shady spot and were napping on the trail when we heard footsteps behind us.

I awakened to see a hiking shoe near my face. Scanning upward, I saw nothing but hot dog bun after hot dog bun against a turquoise background.

"Hey, Hot Dog," I said. "What's up?"

"Sorry to wake you, but heard a fire broke out last night near the border. The PCTA is recommending people leapfrog around this section to Ashland."

"No workaround?" asked Glenn.

"Nope," he said. "No choice but to go back."

"Hey, thanks for the heads-up," I said.

Glenn phoned Ann. She was out the door in a hurry to pick up Sally and head south to retrieve us; it would be nearly a five-hour drive. Meanwhile, realizing Geoff was probably somewhere between us and the border, I phoned, texted, and emailed him, trying to warn him, though got no response.

After getting specifics from Hot Dog, I texted Marion and Thierno:

> Heard you were near Oregon border, maybe near Geoff Tyson (tall thin guy who is my barber in Eugene!) As of 9 am Friday trail closed at Observation Peak (1695) to Grouse Camp (1708) because of nearby fire. There is a complicated and long (19.5 mile) walkaround that requires numerous maps be downloaded. Only other option is 36 miles south to Seiad, which is daunting but safe.
>
> No ways off trail when you hit 1695 closure because of road closures. Fire is very near PCT. Sorry you have this new obstacle but think of big picture.
>
> My best, Bob

We arrived back at the now-closed cafe about 6 P.M. Hikers lounged at picnic tables, curled up in whatever shade they could find, and talked amongst themselves about what to do now. Some had already fashioned "Yreka," "Ashland," or "Medford" signs out of the flaps of cardboard boxes and were standing on Highway 96, hitching to I-5, which was about an hour's drive east of us.

Some hikers were topping off their water bottles and organizing packs as if they planned to take a chance and head north up the mountain. A young woman from France—not Marion—asked if she thought she should stick with those in her "trail family" who wanted to push forward. I told her it didn't seem like a good idea.

Glenn and I decided we could take four other hikers to Ashland or Medford on our way back. But who? Hot Dog, of course, was our No. 1 draft choice; the guy had saved us from a fire. We quietly offered rides to three others, including a married couple from Brooklyn.

When Sally and Ann arrived at 8:30 P.M., we underwent a mind-boggling logistical challenge to fit eight people, six packs, and a cooler in an eight-seat Honda Pilot.

Sally and Ann had the front two seats. I sat in the middle row next to the couple, the woman of whom was not only hiking the trail but doing sketches for an art book she planned to publish about her experience. Glenn was in the backseat with Hot Dog, of course, and a young woman from Sequim, Washington. All of us had packs in our laps—and stunk to high heaven.

But in the two hours we spent together, there was something uplifting about the experience. The mood was upbeat. We got to know our guests. Our guests got to know us. A cacophony of talk enlivened the atmosphere from stem to stern: *So, I'm, like, that's no deer; that's a frickin' bear ... I haven't shaved my legs in so long I forgot how ... I got halfway through that last pancake and my stomach started rumbling like a freight train ....*

To a person, they graciously thanked Sally and Ann, wanting to give them gas money. "Pay it forward," Glenn said. "Trail Magic."

When they'd all been dropped off—some in Ashland, some in Medford—the car grew quiet. I smiled and shook my head; the trail had a wonderful way of pulling people together despite their differences.

However, I grew more sober when two thoughts came to mind: one a regret, the other a concern.

The regret? That I hadn't thought to offer the young French girl a seat in the car; an hour before Ann and Sally arrived, I'd noted she and that group were pressing forward to the trailhead; the tribe can be a powerful pull.

The concern? That my friend Geoff, without cell coverage, might be walking toward that very fire. Same with Marion and Thierno.

I phoned Geoff again in Medford.

Once again: *Call Failed.*

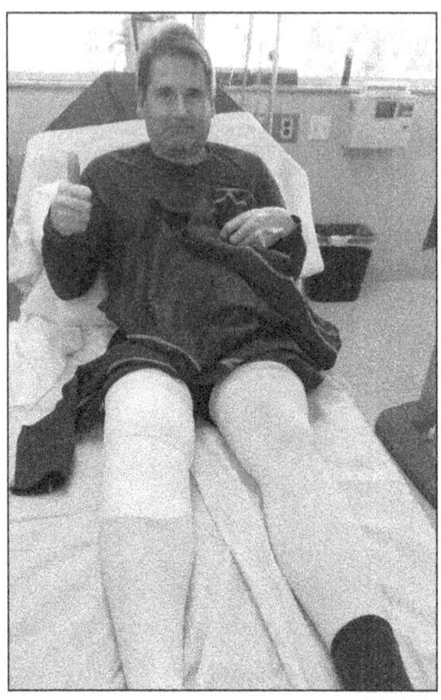

Sally Welch

Left: In December 2017, I had surgery in Eugene to repair a torn medial meniscus in my right knee. Right: Thierno and Marion, of France, camped with us two nights.

This stretch near Etna reminded me of how remote you could feel on the PCT. And yet now and then you'd find a runner or two on the trail doing some forty-mile loop—far from the nearest road.

Top: I never tired of the sky views, including this one near Etna. Above: Glenn broke down his tent after our second night on the Castella-to-Seiad Valley stretch.

The flashy Hot Dog caught us going up a hot mountain to warn us of a fire ahead.

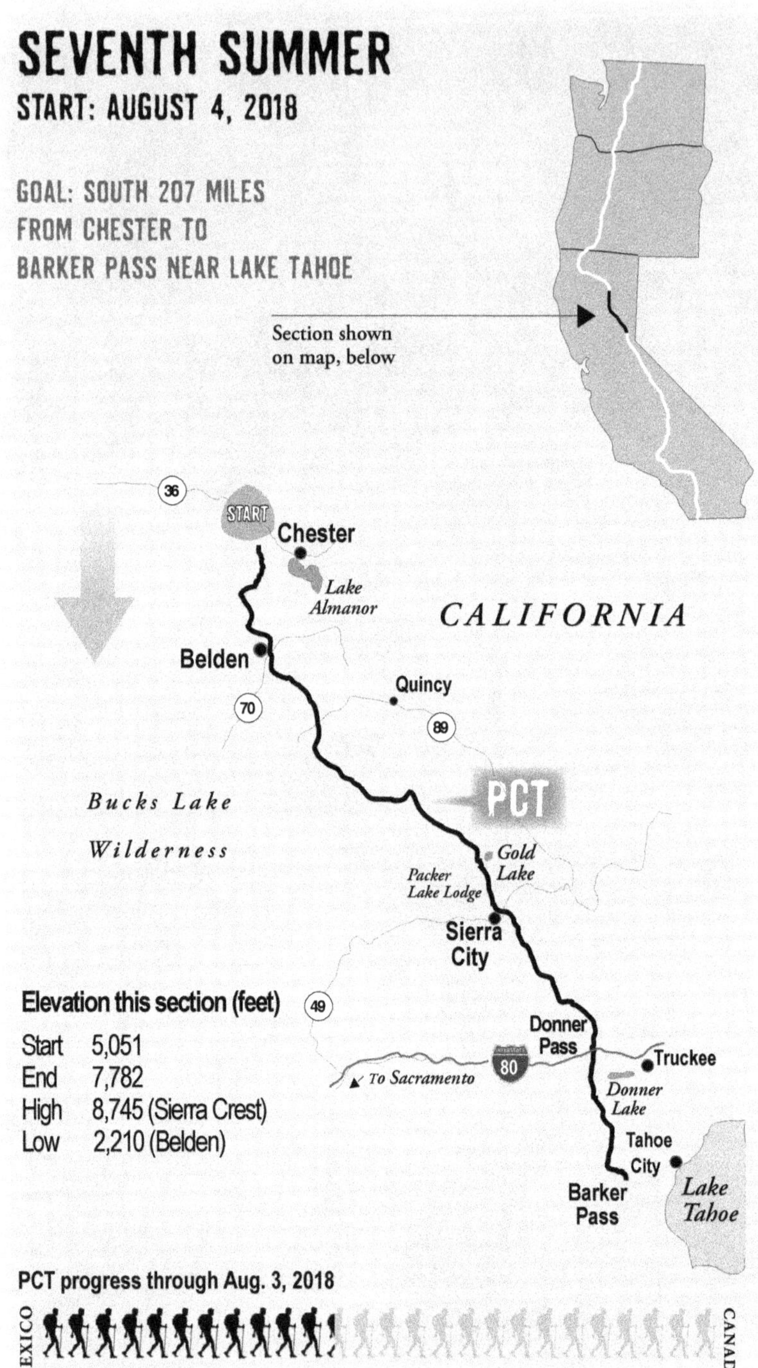
SEVENTH SUMMER
START: AUGUST 4, 2018
GOAL: SOUTH 207 MILES
FROM CHESTER TO
BARKER PASS NEAR LAKE TAHOE
Section shown
on map, below
36
START
Chester
Lake
Almanor
CALIFORNIA
Belden
Quincy
70
89
PCT
Bucks Lake
Wilderness
Gold
Lake
Packer
Lake Lodge
Sierra
City
Elevation this section (feet)
Start 5,051
End 7,782
High 8,745 (Sierra Crest)
Low 2,210 (Belden)
49
Donner
Pass
80
Truckee
To Sacramento
Donner
Lake
Tahoe
City
Barker
Pass
Lake
Tahoe
PCT progress through Aug. 3, 2018
MEXICO
CANADA
45% done / 1,188 miles
55% of PCT left / 1,462 miles to go

13

GRACE

In the woods, too, a man casts off his years, as the snake his slough, and at what period soever of life, is always a child. In the woods, is perpetual youth.

—Ralph Waldo Emerson

My sister-in-law, Ann, could have been an international event planner. Honest. I've seen her organize an eye clinic for medical volunteers in Haiti with utter efficiency. And put on family Christmas Eve parties with more moving parts than a Broadway musical, including a gift-exchange app she commissioned my code-savvy son Jason to develop so nobody drew the same name two years in a row.

Thus, when Glenn and I decided to hike the entire PCT and realized a key part of the effort would be getting us to, and from, trailheads, Ann was the perfect choreographer. She researched good motels to stay at, determined driving distances and—coordinating with Sally—packed coolers with food and drink for all. At season's end, by the time I'd had my sleeping bag dry-cleaned and my gear stowed for the winter, she would have sent me a Drop Box folder of the hundreds of pictures Glenn had shot and politely requested the same from me. (I would reciprocate—about Memorial Day.)

All of which is to say that as we neared smoky Susanville, California, on Friday, August 3, 2018—our base camp before a dumping of Glenn and me at the southbound PCT trailhead at nearby Chester the next morning—there was no reason to worry about where we would stay. Ann undoubtedly had it figured out.

The four of us had been great friends for more than forty years, our first "double date" a two-night backpacking trip in 1974 to Eagle Creek on the Columbia Gorge. Sally and I got married the next year, Ann and Glenn the year after us. We started having kids; they started having kids. We became grandparents; they became grandparents.

And here we were, still crazy after all these years. I mean, really, how many other couples on this Friday afternoon were showing up in some middle-of-nowhere town so the male part of the foursome could go hike 204 miles?

"So, Bob," said Glenn, "explain what happened to Geoff regarding the fire the night we got picked up in Seiad Valley."

It had been only two weeks since our last PCT adventure ended in smoke.

"Well, as you know, Geoff averted the fire," I said.

"Right," said Sally. "And where was he in relation to you guys?"

"Geoff started from Castella at I-5 the day before we did, and we never saw him. Turns out, he did *not* go into Etna, and so on the night you two picked us up in Seiad Valley, he was ahead of us, roughly halfway between there and the Oregon border."

"And is he seeing smoke at this point?" asked Ann.

"A little bit when he goes to bed that night. Waking up, he realizes it's way smokier than the night before. Visibility is only a quarter mile, and he's worried."

"With good reason," said Glenn. "He's heading into a forest fire."

"Exactly. He somehow finds a cell signal and calls a hiker friend who's just gotten over the border before they closed the trail. The guy tells Geoff, 'Man, you gotta go back. It's terrible up here; I can barely see my hands in front of my face.'

"And so as Geoff starts packing up to head back to Seiad Valley a couple of people catch up to him from the south. It's Marion and Thierno."

"Oh, my gosh!" said Ann.

"Yeah, they'd been leapfrogging up the trail a bit; he'd stayed next to them at Seiad Valley. Knew them a bit. And so there's my friend Geoff and the French couple Glenn and I had camped with suddenly partnering up to hike eighteen miles back to Seiad Valley because of a fire."

"But at some point Marion and Thierno realize that you and Geoff know each other, right?" said Sally.

"Yeah, I got an email from them after the incident saying Marion had bought some Altras in Ashland and her feet were feeling great—and they'd hiked with my friend Geoff. When they heard Geoff was from Oregon,

Marion said, 'We camped a couple of days with a couple of guys from Oregon.' And Geoff says, 'Older guys, Bob and Glenn?' And they're like, 'Yes! The Oregon Boys!' And he's like, 'Bob's my friend! I cut his hair!"

That's the strange thing about the PCT: There's no telling what might happen. You had to expect the unexpected—for better or worse.

JUST BEFORE 5 P.M we arrived in Susanville, in the foothills of the eastern Sierra about sixty miles east of Redding. A number of wildfires had sparked to life nearby and everywhere we looked we saw CAL FIRE trucks, firefighters in yellow shirts, and signs saying, "Thank you, firefighters." Our trailhead, thankfully, was thirty-five miles west of Susanville, near Chester.

"What's this place where we're staying?" I asked Ann.

"The Lassen Inn.* Everybody good with checking in first, then grabbing a bite?"

"Sounds good," I said. "Good idea to get reservations in advance, Ann. With all these firefighters in town, bet this place is booked solid."

"They're all in town to see us off," dead-panned Glenn, then, as usual, gave himself a huge guffaw.

"After dinner I'd like to grab a photo of me in front of Lassen High, where a reporter friend of mine graduated," I said. "That OK?"

"Sounds good," said Ann, the pilot of the Pilot.

As we wound through Susanville, I was awash in anticipation of starting a new PCT section the next morning. Ending Part I with the fire had been a definite downer, but now we had the chance to start writing some new PCT history—with our legs. I was jazzed. I sensed we all were.

Then, as if on cue, the chatter died. We had all gotten our first glimpses of the Lassen Inn.

"Uh, is this it?" I asked.

Ann nodded yes.

Well-tattooed people were hanging out here and there. The cars parked in front looked as if from a used-car lot you'd want to avoid. The "Free Wi-Fi" sign might as well have said, "Last remodeled in the days of eight-track tapes."

Ann checked us in. Light luggage in hand, Sally and I headed up the stairs to our second-story room. A woman was sitting on the staircase, bent forward with her elbows on her thighs, smoking a cigarette.

"Good luck," she said.

The inference brought to mind the "Dead Man Tell No Tales" warning you hear just before going down the first plunge on Disneyland's Pirates of

* Not the motel's real name.

the Caribbean ride.

We walked into our room, which smelled of smoke, disinfectant, and time; lots of time. Ratty towels. Little furniture. The bed looked like anywhere you'd want to be but in it.

Sally and I widened our eyes to each other with matching *are-we-really-going-to-stay here?* expressions.

"Let's go eat," said Ann.

"Uh, yeah, sounds good," said Sally, nodding.

Sally and Ann weren't just sisters, they were best friends and respected each other deeply. When we put on our Beachside Writers Workshops, Ann was happy to assist Sally. But in PCT planning, Ann had emerged as the transportation leader and Sally was happy to be her wing woman. That said, Sally wasn't known to question Ann's decisions, one of which was now staring us in the face like Freddy Krueger, though nobody was talking. That is, until I started to.

"Uh, does anyone else—I mean, would you object if . . . "

Sally's eyes widened with a don't-go-there look.

" . . . If we, uh, were to swing by the school for my pic on the way *to* dinner instead of *after*? Gonna lose the light."

"No problem," said Ann.

In the backseat, as we drove, I Googled the motel's reviews. It had a 2.0 rating on 5.0 scale. I showed Sally what I was finding.

"A run-down dump . . . quite noisy, no deadbolt. Most people aren't going to want to stay here!"

"Bathroom shower won't turn off. This place should be leveled with bulldozers. Mental patients on the top floor screaming obscenities."

And just for "a convincer": "Zero Star Motel. The desk person/manager tried to charge $268 a night instead of the $65-a-night, saying we were to stay a week."

We were to stay a week. The line chilled me, conjuring up Stephen King's book *Misery*, in which an author wrecks his car out in the country and a crazed farm woman invites him in, ostensibly to help him recover from his injuries. Ultimately, however, she tells him *he was to have his foot chopped off with an ax* because she didn't like the ending to his latest novel.

Then it happened, the brashest statement I've ever heard anyone in Sally's family make.

"Ann, I love you as my sister," she blurted, "but I *cannot* stay a night in that place!"

A worrisome pause ensued, but vanished in a splash of laughter as if the *ker-thump* of a cannonball jump into a deep pool. Ann shook her head with a sort of seemed-like-a-good-idea-at-the-time resignation. Nobody was challenging Sally's stance.

"Hey," said Ann, "when I saw the place I was thinking the same thing you guys were!"

Glenn and I started Googling alternatives, both of us quickly coming to the same conclusion: the town's motels were, indeed, booked. At dinner, while I swatted flies and tried to scarf down a McDonald's fish sandwich whose slab of cheese was the size of a postage stamp, Ann drilled deeper into the Internet for a room. By the time we'd left the restaurant she had one tentatively secured at a new casino on the outskirts of town.

"Contingent upon us inspecting the room first," said Ann, "and finding it clean."

No arguments from anyone.

AS WE STARTED south from Chester the next day, Glenn and I each had a new twist to our approach: I was adding audio books to music for my afternoon's enlightenment, and Glenn, inspired by Hot Dog, was "going cold" with his food. No Jetboil. Instead, he was mixing freeze-dried meals with water and eating them cold. I was happy to let that be his deal, not mine.

"Time out?" I said.

He looked at his Casio.

"Five-fourteen," he said.

"Copy that."

Other than reaching Milepost 1325, the halfway mark of the PCT—and about a hundred miles farther than the average PCT thru-hiker reaches before quitting, according to the PCT Survey—our opening day was uneventful. Not the case on day two when the idea hit me as we were taking a 9 A.M. break.

"Glenny, we already have ten miles under our belts," I said. "Forget two-by-fours, we are now 'ten-by-nines!' And the restaurant in Belden closes at eight. We'd need to do another sixteen from here, but if we really hammer the downhill stretch we can earn ourselves cheeseburgers and fries."

True, it wasn't as if we'd been living on huckleberries for a month; we'd only left the previous day. But chances to eat restaurant food on the PCT were rare and treasured—and helped focus your mind on the reward, not the weariness.

"Let's do it," said Glenn.

We increased our pace, limited lunch to fifteen minutes, and by late afternoon had spotted the North Fork Feather River, along which Belden rests.

"I can taste those fries!" I said. "Almost there!"

We still had six miles to go—and because this was only day two of an eight-day stretch before resupply, we had near-maximum weight on our backs in food. I was parched, my legs getting the wobble of a marathoner who'd hit the wall. Glenn was weary, too.

"Distance?" I asked.

He pulled out his phone, swiped, tapped.

"Two-point-four miles."

"Should arrive just about seven," I said.

"And the restaurant closes at eight?"

"Yep."

Two hours later, we arrived.

"Good work, partner," I said, offering him a fist bump.

He dropped his pack on a bench, and bent over, head in hands.

"You OK?"

He nodded "yes," which I knew meant "no." Otherwise, he would have said it.

"Let's get you some food."

I pulled on the restaurant front-door handle. It was locked.

"What?"

I looked at the sign: "Open 7 to 7."

"The Internet said *eight*. What time is it, Glenny?"

"Seven-oh-five."

"Are you kidding me? Are you *kidding* me?"

I glanced left, then right, which revealed a screen door. I heard pots and pans clanging, suggesting kitchen.

"Excuse me," I said, knocking on the wood-framed door, behind which a couple of guys were washing dishes.

"Hey, sorry to interrupt you, but my brother-in-law and I are PCT hikers who got up at 4:05 A.M. and went twenty-six miles just so we could eat one of your delicious cheeseburgers."

"Sorry, we close at seven."

"Do you think there's any chance you could make an excep—."

"Sorry, but—."

Looking beyond me, the guy saw Glenn down the way, bent over on the bench. He cocked his head sideways, as if reconsidering, then exhaled.

"OK, get your butts out on the back deck, overlooking the river," he said. "Katie'll be out in a sec. I can fix ya up with some chili-cheese fries, salads, and drinks. But, sorry, no burgers. Grill's been cleaned."

"Oh, no, no, no, that's perfect. Great. Love chili-cheese fries. Thanks. Really appreciate it!"

I went back to tell the good news to Glenn, who, by now, had started to shiver. It was eighty-five degrees.

"You OK? They're gonna fix us a little something on the back deck!"

His eyes widened and his head nodded, but he proved to be so run down that as we sat with a hiker from the Netherlands, Glenn couldn't enjoy the salad or chili fries. He downed two giant orange juices and three glasses of water. He poked at his salad, nibbled a few fries, but the blank look on his face reminded me of the farmer in that "American Gothic" pitchfork painting.

"Here, maybe you could use these," the waitress said, handing us each to-go cups of cold water.

We thanked her and left her two $20 bills, asking her to give one to the cook who'd made an exception for us. Grace, pure and simple. When I'd look back at this stretch, what would stick with me—beyond Glenn not being able to enjoy the meal he'd hiked so hard to earn—was the undeserved favor offered by a restaurant worker who welcomed us in when he didn't have to.

In the gathering darkness, I found us a camping spot on a sand bar next to the North Fork Feather River. We were the only hikers around.

After Glenn crawled into his tent, I filtered him three liters of water from the river, setting his plastic bottles alongside his tent, parallel, not perpendicular, to the tent, equally spaced, to conform to his PCT *feng shui*.

"'Night, Crab Net."

He didn't respond. He was either asleep or dead, the snoring suggesting the former.

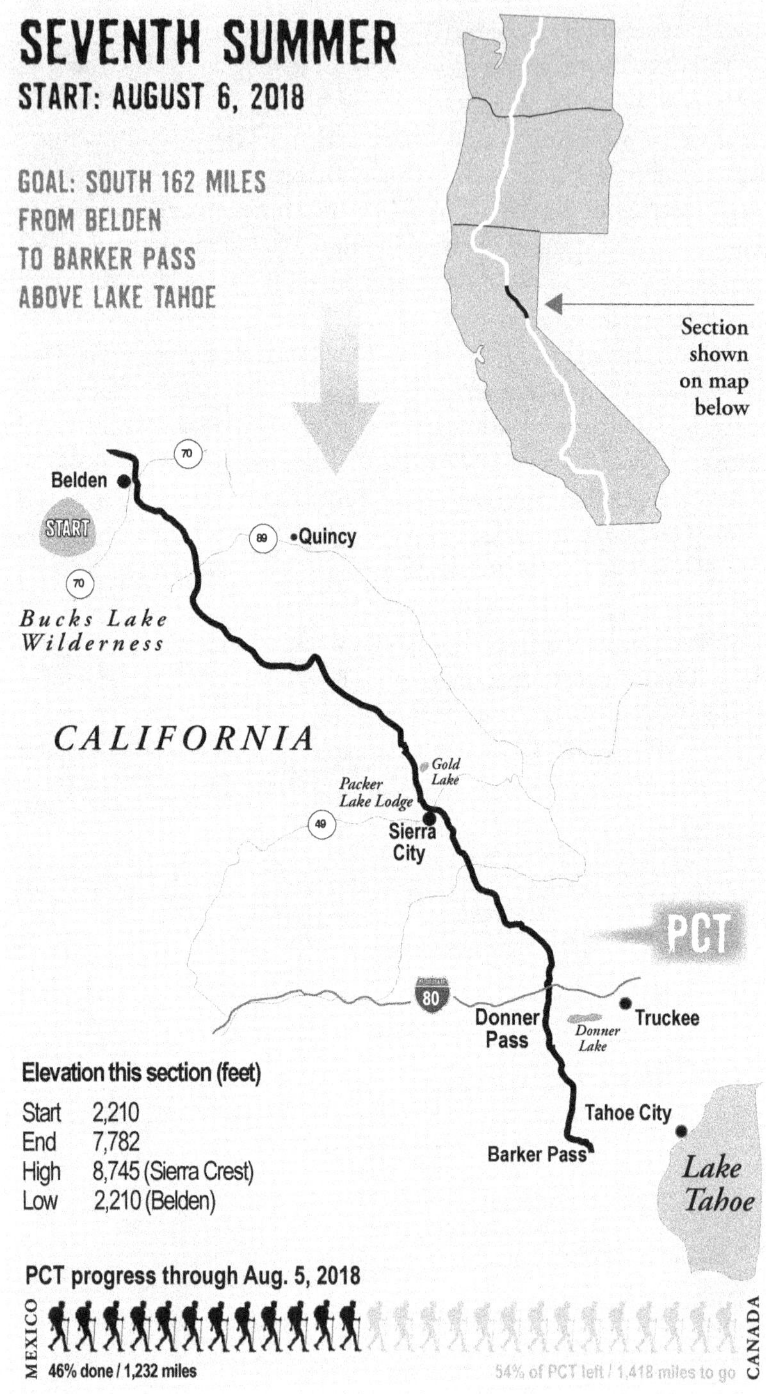
SEVENTH SUMMER
START: AUGUST 6, 2018
GOAL: SOUTH 162 MILES
FROM BELDEN
TO BARKER PASS
ABOVE LAKE TAHOE
Section shown on map below
70
Belden
START
89
Quincy
70
Bucks Lake Wilderness
CALIFORNIA
Gold Lake
Packer Lake Lodge
49
Sierra City
PCT
80
Donner Pass
Donner Lake
Truckee
Tahoe City
Barker Pass
Lake Tahoe
Elevation this section (feet)
Start 2,210
End 7,782
High 8,745 (Sierra Crest)
Low 2,210 (Belden)
PCT progress through Aug. 5, 2018
MEXICO
46% done / 1,232 miles
54% of PCT left / 1,418 miles to go
CANADA

14 BEAUTY

I had long ago decided that once you reached a certain age
the only sensible response was to act as if you would live forever
but know you might die before lunch.

—Colin Fletcher

The climb south out of the Feather River Canyon was diabolical, a long stretch of tightly bunched switchbacks, though blessedly forested and, thus, not as hot as it could have been. In 4.7 miles, we would climb 3,580 feet, or 761 feet per mile, making this one of the steepest extended stretches on the PCT.

Not that I was going to remind Glenny of that. His tank and mood were low. What he needed, I figured, was a dose of humor, and I soon inadvertently created some. We were about halfway up the mountain when I realized I had to go to the bathroom—the serious stuff. And because the switchbacks were so steep, finding even a semblance of flat ground on which to crouch over a cat hole was impossible.

With Glenn up ahead, I lined up the shot like a golfer facing a treacherous sidehill lie. Alas, I missed by a good six inches. The uncommonly firm deposit started rolling downhill toward the switchback trail below us.

"Houston, we have a problem!" I said.

"What?" said Glenn, who didn't wear his hearing aids on the trail.

"I've got a runaway turd!" I said.

He furrowed his brow and tilted his head.

"What? You've gotta rent a bird?"

"No," I said, raising my voice to a shout, "I said, 'I've … got …a … runaway … turd!' My feces have become the cannonball express! I missed my cat hole!"

He started laughing, I started laughing. When we finally stopped, I imagined a worst-case scenario.

"Once it picks up speed and pebbles, the thing's gonna be lethal. Some hiker below, when asked by search and rescue what happened, is gonna say, 'I think I got hit by a piece of flying Almond Roca!'"

By now, we were laughing uncontrollably. The humor break was just what we needed. Before we knew it, we were atop a magnificent stretch where the trail was rugged but rewarded us with a 360-degree view of trees, peaks, and canyons.

In many of those canyons, 19th-century gold miners once flocked to the Feather River and its tributaries, the prospectors helping balloon California's population from 10,000 to 265,000 in only a few years in the mid-1800s. Sure, down below, in the stretches of civilization, the world had changed immensely. But it always struck me that many of the vistas I took in now were what some pioneer saw back then. A bear print on the trail in 2018 looked just like a bear print in 1852—and we'd seen a few recently.

Occasionally, to hike the PCT was to sense yourself suspended from time, as if you didn't belong to the gold-mining days or to the iPhone days, but had transcended both. Over the years, amid the hundreds of songs that ran through my head as I hiked, one that returned with regularity was Bob Dylan's "Time Passes Slowly," including the opening stanza:

> Time passes slowly up here in the mountains
> We sit beside bridges and walk beside fountains
> Catch the wild fishes that float through the streams
> Times passes slowly when you're lost in a dream …

In some ways, the PCT was a dream. A detour from real life. A chance to embrace the fullness of nature and to test the measure of yourself against the elements and terrain.

I often felt alone on the PCT, but never felt lonely. Instead, I felt as if a guest touring a grand wilderness whose admission fee was paid for with sweat—as if everything around me, including the monarch butterflies, had been choreographed for the pleasure of hikers like me.

That night we camped high, where, taking my lightweight chair—so worth the weight—I sat on a precipice, near a lone fir above a gaping basin, and read. A moment I knew would long stay with me.

Just before dark, I crawled into my tent. Like Glenn—and most PCT hikers—I pulled everything into my tent each night except my water bottles. A few people went to the trouble to hang their food in trees, with rope, to keep bears away. However, that required just the right kind of trees at just the right time and assumed you had the energy to go through what could be a troublesome process. Reports of bears hassling backpackers were few and far between. Me? I would put my pack at the foot of the tent and place my Therm-a-Rest mattress over it. Raising your legs, I'd read, was good to allow blood to flow down from your swollen feet. It seemed to work.

IN THE DEAD of night, I was jolted awake by the sound of something rustling around just outside my tent. I hated such moments. Heart pounding. Imagination racing. Mind wondering: Squirrel? Deer? Bear? Cougar? I shined my headlamp out: just a deer chewing on bitterbrush.*

Whew. I'd be lying if I said I wasn't occasionally fearful on the PCT, notably in high-mountain lightning storms, on steep snowy slopes, and in low-elevation areas near trailheads where locals were shooting guns.** I saw no need to carry a gun—and hadn't been in a situation where I doubted that decision. Sure, I'd encountered a few strange people on the trail, but the only who really scared me was the scraggly-bearded grub looking at me in the mirror on our rare returns to civilization. *Me.*

Unlike Coast Guard Rick, however, I'll just say it: I could get rattled by noises in the night—especially if Glenn was asleep. If he was still awake I could at least commiserate with a, "Did you hear that?" And feel a bit of "safety in numbers," even small numbers. But if he was asleep, I always assumed he was immune from attack and I was the primary target, my heart pounding like a tribal drum.

Never mind that black bears almost never attack people; when hearing an animal rooting around your tent in the middle of the night, no low-attack percentage eases your mind. Nor do you feel "safe" because you're inside a tent; goodness, it's rip-stop nylon, the thickness of facial tissue. All a tent does is package you for whatever's going to eat you, as if you were a Saran-Wrapped egg salad sandwich in a vending machine.

---

* I'd begun bringing my trekking poles inside my tent because deer liked to lick the "sweat salt" on the grips.

** Most notably at Panther Creek in Washington in 2016. Could they mistake us for game? Could they see us and fire a few shots our direction "just for fun?" It was the "not knowing" that worried me most.

My middle-of-the-night fear wasn't anchored in reality—a deer munching brush six feet from my head—but in imagination. More specifically, in stories I'd read, one in particular: a *Sports Illustrated* series in the 1960s about grizzlies attacking young hikers in Glacier National Park. I'd never forgotten a line about a guy searching for a possible victim and picking up something that didn't look natural to the woods. "Then," writer Jack Olsen wrote, "he took a closer look and realized that he was holding an ear."

THE NEXT DAY, Tuesday, August 7, we planned on nineteen miles but felt so good we pushed it to twenty-five, though without experiencing the dead-to-the-bone aftereffects of the Belden marathon. Such over-achieving days soon put us fifteen miles ahead of pace. So, with Glenn's OK, I called Sally one morning and suggested we might be coming out Tuesday, August 14, instead of Wednesday, August 15. Could she and Ann pick us up then?

"No, I don't think so," she said. "We've got our schedule set. See you Wednesday, love. Stay safe!"

I knew, of course, that they could easily unbook, and rebook, their room in Reno but I didn't consider it for a nanosecond. They had been shuttling us all over the West Coast since 2011; they were forever running on "BGST"—Bob & Glenn Standard Time. If they wanted to stick with the plan, so be it.

On Thursday, August 9, we stayed in perhaps the worst spot of our seven-year journey thus far: high up on a mountain, tucked into the overhanging branches of a withered tree on the side of an abandoned dirt road.

What compensated for the poor venue was the good company: a gaggle of NoBos from all over the world who were uncommonly friendly and seemed blessed with boundless energy, though a few were low on food. Knowing we had only two days until Sierra City, where our food resupplies awaited, we offered gobs of leftover food and The Young Ones gleefully accepted.

Glenn examined a young man who'd been walking with a brace since torquing his knee the day he left the Mexican border. He'd been limping for more than 1,200 miles but seemed buoyed by Glenn's suggestion that it didn't seem serious and by me giving him a week's supply of Cinnamon Bears.

"You guys are cool," said a young woman from Switzerland who plopped down on her Z-pad, cross-legged, right in front of our tents, apparently just to chat. This never happened. "Ve have never seen brothers-in-law on zee trail!"

It was fun to be engaged by young hikers, some of whom—at least up north—seemed too hell-bent for Canada to talk much. I met two women from the Czech Republic.

"I was recently in your country!" I said, then explained how Sally and I had gone to Zdar nad Sazavou in May 2017, weirdly, to lecture at a high school. Her eyes lit up.*

It was fun being an Oregonian on the trail because I felt like an ambassador for one-fifth of the PCT. People wanted to know what it was like, and where I lived in relation to the trail.

"So, you just came from Belden?" a NoBo, asked me.

"We did."

"Did you hear about the fire near there? Total bummer. They've, like, closed the PCT at that point. And told people in town to evacuate."

"Wait," I said. "When did the fire start? We just left Monday morning."

With supercharged fingers and thumb, she navigated her iPhone.

"Article in the *Chico Enterprise-Record* says, 'Fire broke out Monday night in steep terrain west of Belden, on the north side of Highway 70.'"

"We just got out of there," I said to Glenny.

"Dodged a bullet."

YOUNG HIKERS tended to value gathering in towns along the trail to drink, eat, socialize, and relax, in that order. Some reveled in being part of "trail families," people who, after starting as solos at the border—nearly two-thirds did so—teamed up with others along the way and moved up the trail as "one," like the proverbial pig in a python.

Although I didn't begrudge them their "groupishness," I was different. I reveled in quiet interactions with nature and with people, three examples of which availed themselves to me the next day, a hot Friday, August 10, 2018.

The first, at midmorning, was seeing a lake thousands of feet below me on which I could barely make out the whiteness of a sailboat's sail; someday, I said to myself, it'd be cool to sail my boat, *At Last,* on that lake—Gold Lake, I later learned—and look up this ridge and think "I was once up there, looking down at a lone sail."

The second was a mid-day swim, eat, and read session at Deer Lake; for a guy whose life was about deadlines, it was a triumph that I could so thoroughly relax. We had the lake to ourselves.

The third was an afternoon and evening at a place whose name, Packer Lake Lodge, belied its small, cozy allure. Initially, Glenn and I were the only people there, other than the woman running the place. She was a delight, warmly welcoming us.

---

* I lectured on journalism, specifically on freedom of the press. Because their country had spent decades under the thumb of Soviet communism, I expected students to find it interesting. At the end of the day, however, the buzz was all about Sally teaching the kids how to make cheeseburgers.

The "lodge" was a simple peaked-roof log cabin with a single room not much larger than a two-car garage. A covered front porch stretched across the front, framed horizontally with wood-peeled log rails. Hanging flower baskets framed the entry way: two on the left, two on the right, as with the hummingbird feeders—one on each side. A giant wood-carved fish—a brook trout, based on the speckles—hung to one side of the porch.

As if preparing for a gala event, our host walked out with a piece of chalk in her hand and wrote on a wood-framed chalkboard:

> Tonight
>
> Kalua Pork "slider" on brioche with spicy slaw and paniolo beans.
>
> Dessert ice cream sandwiches

"Dinner is at five-thirty," she said, "but you're welcome to relax on the porch until then. Can I get a cold drink for you? Beer? Lemonade? Root beer or a float?"

I could have gone with one of each, but when Glenn ordered a root beer float, it sounded great and I followed suit. About an hour before dinner, a thirty-something PCT hiker showed up: Starburst, from New Zealand.* He tipped his hat and nodded.

"Another beautiful day on the PCT, aye mates?"

He joined us on the porch, holding a glass of beer. He was a diehard cowboy camper, a NoBo who'd been on the trail for fourteen weeks and 1,200 miles. Since the border, he had slept without a tent most nights.

"There's just something about sleeping under the stars that renews the soul," he said.

"Oh, my," I said. "Could you say that again?"

"What? Why?"

"What you just said. It was absolutely poetic—plus the Kiwi accent. I love it."

"There's just something about sleeping under the stars that renews the soul."

You could go to a lot of all-inclusive resorts—Mexico, Hawaii, the Bahamas—and never hear a fellow traveler say anything so beautiful.

"Please keep the root beers coming," I said to our host.

Starburst was fun. Short-cropped hair but a bushy beard. Passionate. Ex-military. And gut level honest—quite literally, it would turn out—about

* Not his real trail name.

an encounter he'd had with a fellow hiker.

"She was beautiful and seemed to like me," he said. "But, bugger, I blew it."

"How so?" I asked.

He took a deep pull on his beer then looked beyond the lodge, to the forest, as if seeing the scene that he was about to describe.

"One night she invites me to her camp for dinner—some sort of curry freeze-dried concoction with red and green peppers. I've been trampin' since Campo and haven't tasted anything so spicy, but I eat it to be polite, right? We spend an hour eating, sipping our filtered water, and talking. We clearly like each other. Like a good movie, it's building to a beautiful ending. Then, suddenly, my stomach starts going all fireworks on me. I suddenly realize I've got to use the long drop, so I—."

"The long drop?" I asked.

"Oh, we Kiwis use that for 'take a crap outside.' In my case, *pronto*. So, I excuse myself under the guise of going to my tent for something, grab my toilet paper and make a mad dash for the woods. I'm having grave doubts about how this is going to turn out."

"And how did it?"

"Crapped m' britches, mates, plain and simple. The rocket launched before I could get m' pants down. Stuff flying everywhere. Not pretty."

I burst out laughing, Glenn following my lead. Not quite as poetic as "sleeping under the stars to renew my soul," but I had to appreciate Starburst's candor.

Shortly after the story, almost as if on cue, our host walked down the wooden steps with a tray of food for her three diners at a picnic table. An umbrella shaded us from the sun.

"Starburst, I don't want to be presumptuous," I said, "but, if I were you, I'd go easy on the spicy slaw and paniolo beans."

He laughed. We all laughed. Sitting together, we shared trail stories until our plates were clean, stomachs full, and beverage cans empty.

At dusk, our host came down the steps with a small woven basket she held out to us like a priest offering communion. "A little something for the trail ahead," she said. In the basket were three fresh-baked chocolate chip cookies, the perfect ending to the perfect day. We thanked her, paid her, added a handsome tip, then grabbed our packs.

Before going our separate ways—Starburst north, The Oregon Boys south—we took a group shot, then said our goodbyes. Between Packer Lake Lodge, swimming at Deer Lake, and seeing the sailboat from on high, it had been an unforgetable day.

As he was setting up his tent, Glenn noticed I was not setting up mine.

"No tent tonight, Bob?"

"I've been inspired," I said. "I'm cowboy-camping."

"Hey," he said, "if you're going to be inspired by one of the two things Starburst talked about—sleeping under the stars and the, uh, other one—you chose wisely."

Then he laughed unabashedly until saddling up with Louis L'Amour to once again ride with the author into the sunset of sleep.

THEY CAME in the night: Ants. Not one. Not two. But dozens. I'd chosen unwisely, putting my tarp and blowup mattress adjacent to an old log, one of the few flat, treeless places I could find. What I hadn't realized was that it was the apparent headquarters for an ant colony. And, clearly, they'd sent only their best after me, like some sort of special rangers outfit.

At any rate, they were all over me most of the night—and I was too tired/lazy to pop up my tent to seal myself away from them. I awoke grumpy and stayed that way until later that morning meeting a couple from New Hampshire who looked five to ten years older than us.

"We did the PCT together in 1976," she said, showing me a photo of the two of them standing atop the highest point on the entire trail, Forester Pass in the High Sierra. In the picture, they were smiling large, looking young, and wearing matching red plaid shirts, as if models in an L.L. Bean ad.

"Oh, my gosh," I said. "That's amazing. And you're doing *what* now?"

"I'm trying to do the whole PCT again," he said. "She's doing certain sections with me."

I knew enough of the trail's history to know that they were pioneers deserving the utmost respect.

"Man, you were doing it the hard way. No cell phones or apps to show you where every water and resupply stop is. No frameless packs."

"Yeah, it was a far different trail back then," she said. "In Washington, we went twenty-eight days without seeing another human being."

"Are you kidding me?"

"If I complete this it would give me the Double Triple Crown," he said, meaning he would have done the PCT, Continental Divide Trail, and the Appalachian Trail—all twice.

"You two are inspirations," I said. "Thanks. I needed that."

ARRIVING IN Sierra City (pop. 205) was a milestone, even if we didn't realize it at the time: we'd now hiked 1,325 miles. In our seventh summer, we were at the halfway point in our quest to complete the 2,650-mile PCT.

I should have enjoyed Sierra City more. The atmosphere was charming, a distant relative of Sisters, Oregon's western-themed main street. The food was good—I woofed down a personal pizza—and the people nice. But a live band at a wedding a few blocks from the church yard where we slept precluded me from getting much sleep. It was nobody's fault—I like to see people having fun—but, between ants and amps, I'd gotten little sleep the last two nights.

The next morning, my grogginess was joined by a third tributary of tribulation: a blister. I felt a hot spot in the metatarsal region of my right foot, my nemesis. I'd gone so long without blister problems—two years—that I panicked. Blisters, like mosquitoes and ants, cause a disproportionate amount of annoyance for their size. I patched the hot spot with Second Skin and Kinesio Tape. No improvement.

Meanwhile, an upbeat Glenn began extolling our arrival soon at a rest area on Interstate 80 (Sacramento to Reno) that had ice cream in a vending machine—at least that was the word from the bamboo telegraph, info traded on the trail.

As my blister stabbed me with pain each step, my mood slumped from bad to worse. When, four miles from the freeway, Glenn loaded up with water from a creek, I refused.

"Bob, this stuff is great," he said. "Ice cold. Load up and we'll enjoy a great break at the rest stop. They even have picnic tables!"

"I'll wait for the rest area," I said. "I'm sure the water there is cold, too."

Nope. The rest area's water tasted like warm pond scum, which only added insult to my self-inflicted injury. The ice cream vending machine was on the fritz. And though the rest stop did, indeed, have picnic tables, they were in the blazing sun and next to a four-lane freeway whose whoosh of cars was as loud as it was relentless.

I couldn't leave that rest stop fast enough. I needed some sort of pick-me-up, some sort of Trail Magic, some sort of catalyst to jar me from my dark mood. Instead, I got Donner Pass where, in the winter of 1846-47, a group of starving pioneers whose wagon train bogged down in the snow were so desperate to survive that, after people died, resorted to cannibalism. As soul-cleansing inspiration, this wasn't quite what I had in mind.

After walking beneath I-80 through a metal culvert, I did find a few blips of hope later in the day. We learned there was a restaurant on the old Donner Pass Highway that required only about a half-mile walk off trail; we enjoyed a cheeseburger. And I got an email from my agent saying that my new book, *The Wizard of Foz: Dick Fosbury's One-Man High-Jump Revolution,* had received a great review from Booklist. But I confess: as I lay in my tent that night—we slept beneath a chairlift at Donner Ski Area—I was mildly haunted by the thought that only a few miles away, near Donner Lake, thirty-nine pioneers had died during that long-ago winter.

Don't get me wrong; I didn't hear any pioneer voices bleating in the wind, see any ghostly apparitions begging for food, or feel the cold breath of George and Jacob Donner, the leaders of the party, but it was yet another restless night, my third in a row.

What ultimately brought me out of my funk was the thought of being back with Sally in two days and the sheer beauty of the trail. On Tuesday, August 14, we trekked on the spines of nearly treeless mountains. By noon we'd caught our first glimpse of glorious Lake Tahoe, of which Mark Twain once said, "I thought it must surely be the fairest picture the whole earth affords." This was not far from where much of "Bonanza," the hit TV series of the 1960s, was filmed in the ponderosa pines. The lake stretches twenty-two miles by ten, plunging to 1,600 feet, second only to Oregon's Crater Lake (1,949 feet) in depth among those in the U.S.

Tahoe was guarded by mountains, framed by trees, and rich with obscure Olympic sports history: it was fifteen miles southwest of the lake's southern edge where Fosbury had, in 1968, won a spot on the U.S. Olympic team at a trial held at Echo Summit (elevation 7,377 feet). In a nook of the El Dorado National Forest, an all-weather track had been plopped down to replicate the 7,350-foot elevation of Mexico City. The track/forest setup was so environmentally attuned that hundred-foot evergreens reached for the sky from *within* the oval.*

In the afternoon, we made our way across the Squaw Valley Ski Resort where the 1960 Winter Olympics had been held. Here and there, gigantic, woodsy vacation homes nestled in the forest. We were on relatively smooth trails that wandered through meadows sprinkled with flowers, above which granite peaks rose majestically into the sky.

How could I remain down in such a beautiful place?

That night, as I lay in my tent, I felt the usual sense of splendor, cocooned in the darkness beneath a star-scattered sky. At times, through the rooftop netting of the tent, I'd see the red-blinking light of a jetliner 30,000 feet above me and feel the oddest sense of comfort. I'd think of hundreds of people being waited on by flight attendants and think: *I'm glad I'm the guy down here, the*

---

* The out-of-the-box idea for the track in the forest came from Bill Bowerman, the University of Oregon track and field coach and an assistant on the 1968 U.S. men's team. The athletes, some of whom had rarely been out of a city, were enthralled with Echo Summit: fresh air, blue skies, and the tallest trees they'd ever seen. "It was simply perfect," said John Radetich, a high-jumping teammate of Dick's at Oregon State. "So quiet you could only hear your heartbeat."

guy in the $295 tent, the bone-tired hiker about to fall asleep after walking twelve hours in paradise.

Nothing could impede on such tranquility, not even the two NoBo brothers we met on a water break the next day who told us about how they'd been cowboy-camping a few weeks back.

"Felt some pressure on my leg, woke up, turned on my headlamp, and—yowza—there was a rattlesnake slithering over my sleeping bag." For a guy like me—no fan of snakes—it was a chilling story.

The next morning, we arrived at Barker Pass just as Sally and Ann, with Subway sandwiches in hand, did, too—our most perfectly synchronized finish yet.

BACK HOME a few weeks later, while having Geoff cut my hair, I heard the epilogue of his story regarding Thierno and Marion: How the three of them had hiked back to Seiad Valley together on a road where a dog from a nearby house attacked Marion, and how Geoff and Thierno had fended it off. How the three of them sometimes hiked together in Oregon. And how, after Geoff called it quits in southern Washington because "the whole trail was on fire," he'd learned that the French couple had left the trail, too, and were renting a car to explore Idaho and Montana.

They invited Geoff to join them on his Harley-Davidson, and the three of them spent several days together sightseeing, eating, and drinking, before parting ways in La Grande, Oregon. Back home, Geoff found a note from Marion that she'd left in his motorcycle's saddle bag: "You are so welcome to join us in France. Please come visit."

That was Trail Magic. That was how this trail drew people together as if they were pukka shells on the same necklace. On a day hike in 1999 I ran into Laura Buhl, who introduced me to the Pacific Crest Trail. Twelve years later, I hiked Oregon and wrote a book about it, *Cascade Summer.* Geoff, a pack-a-day motorcycle dude, read it and decided to do the same but failed. The next summer he succeeded. And then he decided to do the entire trail, a journey on which he met Thierno and Marion, who, of course, invited him to France.

"You know, I've given it a lot of thought about going," he said as he trimmed around my ears.

"And?"

"And I *am*!"

"Really?"

"Yeah, me, a barber from Springfield, Oregon. I'm going to France!"

"Good for you!"

Geoff spun the chair to give me a look in the mirror. What did I see besides a guy who'd just gotten a good haircut? A hiker who had started the trail at fifty-seven and was now sixty-four. A hiker who'd hoped to get the 2,650-mile PCT done in seven summers but had just finished that seventh summer and still had 1,255 miles—nearly half the trail—to go.

"The haircut looks great as usual, Geoff."

"Thanks. So, I'm headed for France next year. What about you, my friend? What's on the PCT menu for you and Glenn in 2019?"

"The Mexican border north to Cajon Pass northeast of LA. It's time to start where the thru-hikers—the *real* hikers—start."

Geoff's eyes widened.

"All right," he said. "Goodbye trees. Hello desert! Beautiful, but tough, tough, tough. And don't even ask me about coming down Fuller Ridge after doing Mount San Jacinto."

I did not.

We capped a perfect day by shooting the breeze with a New Zealand hiker at the Packer Lake Lodge and enjoying a wonderful dinner featuring Kalua Pork.

Glenn Petersen

Top: We had Deer Lake to ourselves for lunch, swimming, and reading. That's me, arcing toward a belly flop. Above: Glenn could lighten the mood simply by being Glenn, aka The Human Tent With Legs.

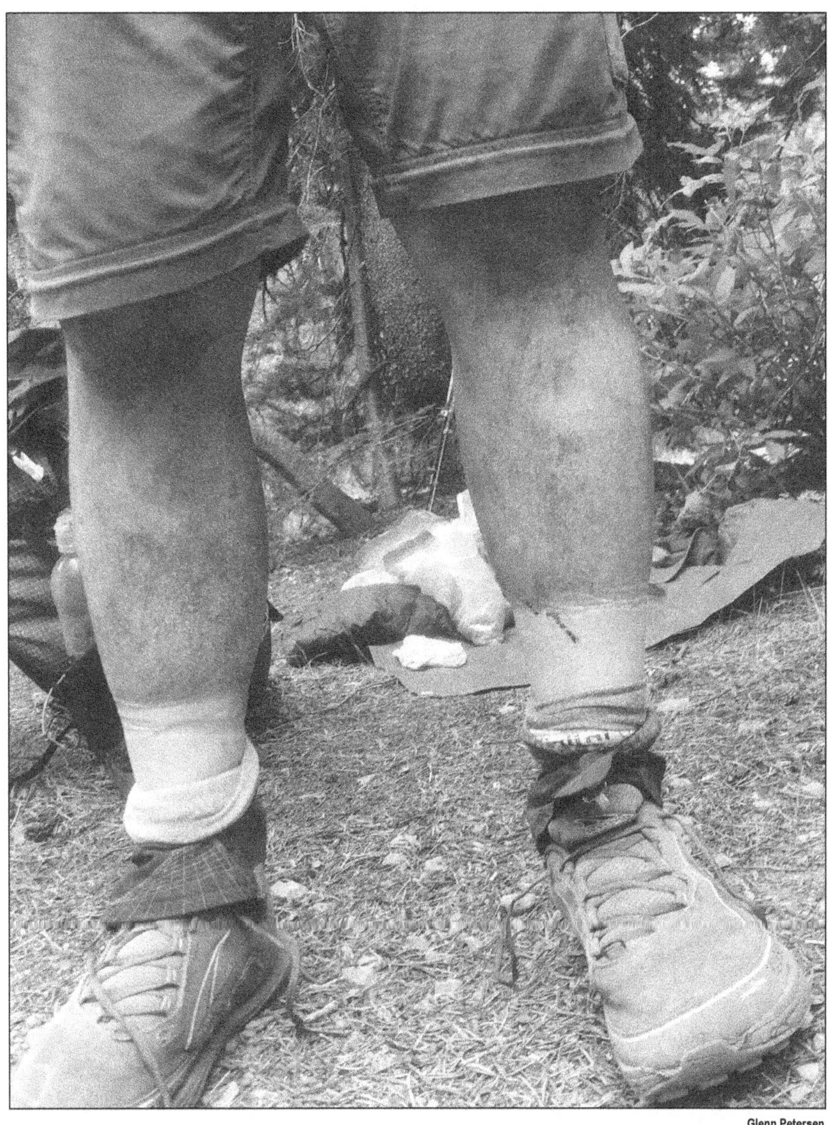

Glenn Petersen

Left page: Between Donner Pass and Barker Pass, the hiking was often above the tree line, as it was here for Glenn on Tinker Knob. Above: Imagine those legs—mine—slipping into a sleeping bag later that night. We weren't camping near water and I didn't want to waste whatever I had for a sponge bath. Ah, life on the trail.

The rain fell and as darkness swallowed the last of the day, I read for a few minutes by the light of my headlamp, thankful for extendable tent poles that once were lost but now were found—and helping me stay dry.

AGE 65

2019

NORTH FROM MEXICO & SOUTH FROM LAKE TAHOE

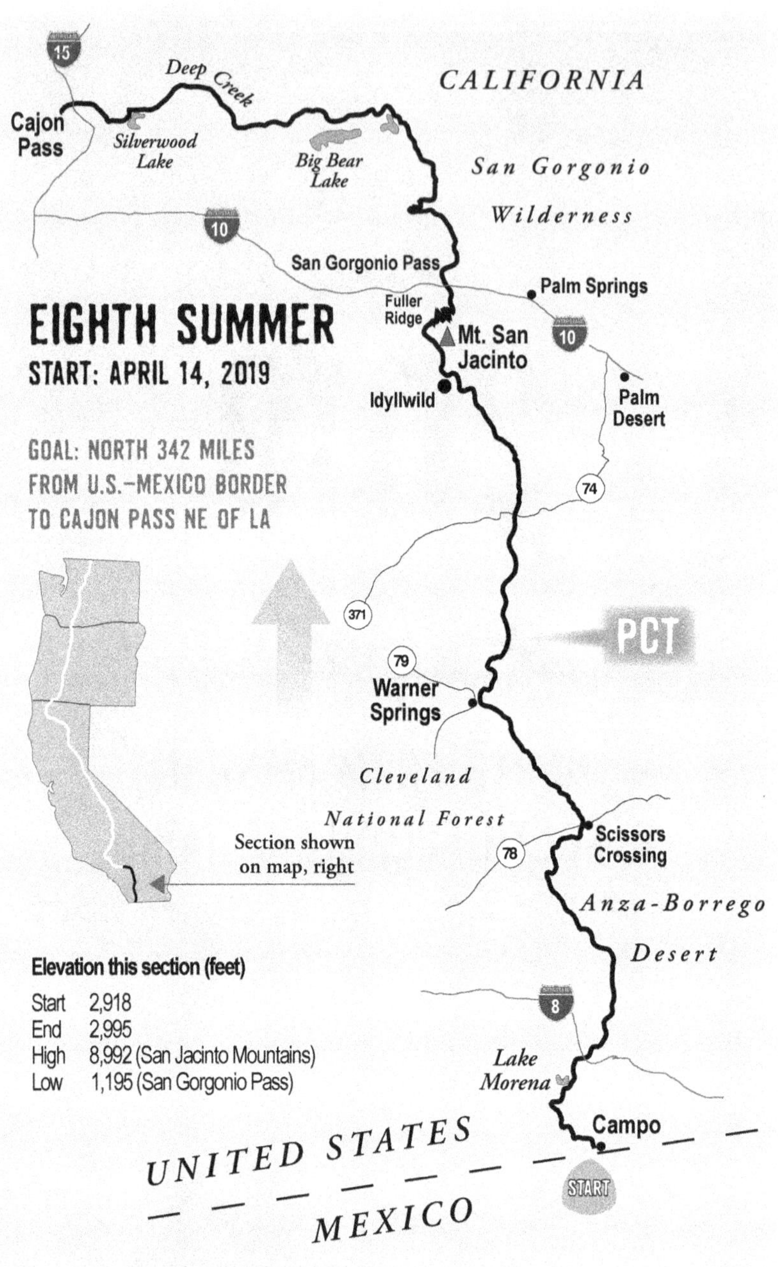

PCT progress through .... April 13, 2019

MEXICO

53% done / 1,395 miles

47% of PCT left / 1,255 miles to go

CANADA

HONOR

I'm not telling you it's going to be easy
—I'm telling you it's going to be worth it.

—Arthur L. Williams Jr.

IN THE DARKNESS, the headlights of a friend's car lit the sage-flanked road that took us just a hundred feet from the wall dividing the United States and Mexico: a forever stretch of razor wire, each of the tin sections about the width of a double-garage door and about fifteen feet high. Nonstop graffiti marred almost every section, the only recognizable word to me being "Campo," the town in which we were starting our 2019 trek.

Mike Yorkey, a friend from the San Diego suburb of Encinitas, clicked a few photos of Glenn and me standing next to, and atop, the five-pronged Southern Terminus Pacific Crest National Scenic Trail Monument.

My friendship with Mike dated back to 1974 when the two of us met at the University of Oregon's School of Journalism in Eugene. Nearly a half-century later, when I reached out for a place to spend the night before our departure, Mike was all in.

"You guys are amazing," he said as we cinched up our packs in the thirty-three-degree cold.

"Or crazy," I said. "But here we are. Thanks, Mike. Who gets up at 2:30 in the morning to haul a couple of nutzos to the U.S.-Mexico border?"

"This guy."

"Appreciate it. And please tell Nicole again how great her dinner was—and, of course, *healthy*; made us feel like visiting dignitaries."

I double-checked my new Garmin inReach Mini Explorer GPS device, which gave us two-way communication for the first time, although messages had to be short. "I've got you on my speed dial and will keep you updated on our progress. Hoping to see you at Cajon Pass, east of LA, in three weeks."

"We'll be there!" he said as doves cooed in the distance.

Our handshake became a hug, then Glenn and I were on our way.

"The irony is that Mike's about the most un-PCT person I know," I said to Glenn as we twisted our way through low brush and an occasional cactus. "Great tennis player; played for Oregon. Great writer; written well north of a hundred books."

"But not the outdoor type, huh?"

"Nope. Grew up in La Jolla. In college, he and his girlfriend went backpacking with Sally and me. Next morning, I asked how he slept. 'Not good.' 'Oh, why not?' I asked. 'The sound of that stream kept me up all night.'"

Glenn laughed. As writers, Mike and I leaned on each other for support in what could often be a lonely pursuit. But his interests were more refined than mine: pickle ball, European travel, and low-calorie, healthy cuisine among them.

"When I told him about the food I'd packed for the trip, he gulped as if I'd read a death sentence for myself."

A few minutes later, I lurched in anguish. "On, no!"

"What?" asked Glenn.

"I just realized I left my Jack Links Beef & Cheese sticks in the Yorkeys' refrigerator. When they see those packages they're gonna freak out! Might have to bring in a hazmat team!"

TWO DAYS later, in an eerie wind-whipped fog past Mount Laguna, we hiked a bit with a brother-sister team, Robert and Susan, from Germany. Like Glenn, Robert used a swath of Tyvek—more typically used as a vapor barrier in new construction—beneath his tent and the way it jutted left and right from the top of his pack made him look like a giant walking bow tie.

A satellite message arrived from Yorkey: "Found your cheese and beef sticks in the fridge. Yummy!"

"Sorry about that," I wrote back. "Some sort of cruel irony in this!"

By now, Glenn and I had noticed an interesting difference in the hikers down here compared to those up north. They were talkative, engaging, inquisitive. Of the fifty-three hikers who'd started April 14 like us, we had passed half a dozen on the first day, and none had passed us.

"It's all new to them," yelled Glenn, above the whoosh of a

ten-to-twenty-mph wind whipping rain at us. "At this point, they're not know-it-alls."

"Yeah, by the time we saw the Young Ones up north, they were Canada-crazy."

"But here," he said, "we're the experienced ones."

Another difference: water, or lack thereof. On this stretch, it wouldn't be found in creeks, streams, or lakes as on past trips, but in the ground. In springs. Troughs. Barrels. And, in particularly arid sections, in plastic jugs left by Trail Angels—we hoped.

On day four, as desert horned lizards skittered across the trail, I managed a liter of water from something called the Rodriguez Fire Tank. Hitting a rare flat stretch on the Anza Borrega Desert before Scissors Crossing, we popped up our silver, sun-reflecting umbrellas for the first time. They proved to be good for reducing heat but horrible in the wind, which blew often in these parts, making them more trouble than they were worth.

Beyond the umbrella and the inReach Explorer, my major upgrade for this trip had been a Nemo 1 Hornet one-person tent. For shoes, I'd transitioned from Altra Zero Drops to Altra TMPs. Glenn's transition this year hadn't been anything so trivial: he lost his mother.

On March 1, I had sat with him at the retirement community where Pauline, eighty-eight, lay in her final days, unresponsive; Glenn was going back through old photographs, laughing, remembering, celebrating his great relationship with her. Five days later, she passed away. The last time I'd talked to her had been in 2016 when, while doing an interview in her neighborhood, I had shown up unannounced at her doorstep just to say hello.

"Oh, so good to see you, Bob," she said. "And you're in luck: I've got fresh-baked cookies! Please, come in." It was clear where Glenn had gotten his generosity. Now, for the first time, Glenn was hitting the PCT as the proverbial "orphan." Both his parents, who'd so gamely driven us to the Elk Lake Trailhead in 2011, were gone.

ON DAY FIVE—a twenty-five miler—we worked our way north, past the PCT-famous Eagle Rock, which, yep, looks just like one, to Warner Springs. It was here, crossing a rare meadow of green grass, that we first encountered cows on the trip, which, of course, made me think of She Who Grew Up on a Farm, and loved everything bovine.* Here where, after a Woodstockian camp setup, we enjoyed a hot breakfast at a golf course restaurant

* While roughly half the PCT is in congressionally designated wilderness, about ten percent of it passes through private property whose owners allow access.

whose middle-of-nowhere location was as weird as it was welcome. And here where, after picking up a resupply box, we were reorganizing our packs outside the post office when a couple of "too-clean-to-be-hikers" guys chatted us up.

"You're doing *what*?" one asked.

"Trying to hike from Mexico to Canada," I said, "over lots of summers. You live around here?"

"Naw, just on a motorcycle trip. Where you from?"

"Eugene, Oregon."

"Really? What kind of work do you do in Eugene?"

"I was a newspaper columnist. Twenty-five years at *The Register-Guard*."

"Oh my gosh, did you know my uncle, John Schaufler?"

"Sure did. Worked in production, right? Nice guy."

The moment was a microcosm of a trail phenomenon I'd noticed over the years: regardless of where another hiker—or, this case, nonhiker—was from, if I talked to the person long enough, I usually found a connection between us: a place, a person, an interest, *something*.

Robert, twenty-four, and Susan, thirty-four, the brother-sister pair we'd seen at Mount Laguna, were from Germany and I had just signed a deal for a book about a German soldier who befriends an American soldier sixty years after their sides fought against each other in the Battle of the Bulge (*Saving My Enemy*). A hiker from Wisconsin worked for a company that built the golf courses at Bandon Dunes in Oregon where I'd played several times. Now the *Register-Guard* connection. I loved that about the trail, how it connected people who otherwise never would have met.

PCT FOOD always looked better when you'd bought it two weeks ago than when you pulled it out of your pack to eat. Over the years, I'd modified my menu a bit, replacing the morning Svenhard's Danishes with breakfast bars and, ultimately, Hostess Baby Bundts and Cinnamon Streusel Coffee Cakes. They stood up to crunching far better than Hostess Twinkies, which were tasty but squished easily. And, for dinner, I was now going heavy with packaged tuna wrapped in Mission Street Taco soft shells, with a squirt of mayo.

Glenn had bought enough packets of condiments to supply every PCT hiker for life with mustard, ketchup, and mayonnaise. Still, trail food got monotonous, meaning the promise of an actual restaurant could take on a certain promised-land allure. On Easter morning 2019, Glenn and I experienced our own personal "sunrise service" after getting up at 3 A.M. so we could catch the Paradise Valley Cafe before it closed at noon. I ordered, and ate, two complete breakfasts—a Denver omelet combo and a huge stack of French toast, every bite a wonder. Two orange juices. Hot chocolate. And a large Mountain Dew for the road. Not a breakfast of champions. No, *two* such delights.

The clientele at the cafe on Highway 74 between LA and Palm Springs was engagingly eclectic—weary-boned PCT hikers gobbling food next to stylish SoCal jet setters in black, skintight motorcycle wear.

Outsiders, I'd learned over the years, didn't know quite what to make of PCTers, some of whom self-deprecatingly referred to themselves as "hiker trash." The ones who understood them best were the owners of the restaurants and stores—and not just because hikers spent lots of money at such places and, thus, "required" respect. Instead, it was because, instead of fearing the hikers as strange and eccentric, the folks took time to listen to their stories. Gotten to know them. And asked them questions. Most realized that what these folks were undertaking—trying to hike 2,650 miles in a single spring and summer—was flat-out amazing.

THE TRAIL kept going. The wind kept blowing. At Apache Springs, below endless craggy peaks that comprise the San Jacinto Mountains, we made the most difficult water run I'd experienced—a half-mile struggle down a steep-pitched "trail" to the east. Over blowdown, under tree limbs, around rocks—just for a couple of liters of stagnant water that smelled like sulfur.

Back up at the junction, we ran into six Young Ones who'd just arrived back on the PCT after having hiked down a horrendously steep trail to a town called Idyllwild, presumably so they could drink margaritas and eat ninety-nine-cent tacos.

We wound our way around Jacinto's eastern flanks like ants on the flutes of a pie: up and down, round and round. Meanwhile, we typically found ourselves also going deep into some horseshoe-shaped indentation, then back out, conforming to the mountain's geologically eccentric shoulders.

That night, on a wind-whipped shelf, I struggled mightily just getting four pegs into my tent to hold it down. We were at 8,234 feet. Even though I fortified the pegs with football-sized rocks, I feared that my flapping tent was going to rip free and fly away, perhaps taking me with it over a cliff.

"Just imagine those six kids," I all but yelled to Glenny. "After ninety minutes to get water where we did, they must be somewhere between here and Apache Springs on a two-foot trail with a killer dropoff. Where are they going to find anyplace even remotely flat to camp?"

"Yeah," said Glenn. "And in this wind—and, in some places, having to go through snow where one misstep … ."

"Crazy."

I was fearful enough for my own safety on this night, and I was snug in a tent. But worrying about others only heightened my own fears. At such times, I found that a good catalyst for changing my mindset was humor. So, despite the howling wind, I regaled Glenn with an incident I'd experienced earlier in the day. On a portion of trail etched into an eastern flank of the San Jacintos, I'd had to go to the bathroom, the bottom-down stuff. But with the steep terrain, there was no way to get off the trail, above it, or below it.

"So, lest I end up like Starburst," I explained, "I had no choice but to dig a cat hole just to the side of the trail, fully exposed. No trees anywhere. The good news? We hadn't seen anybody since Apache Springs so at least I didn't have to worry about being interrupted."

"And the bad?"

"I hadn't had my pants back up for more than two seconds when a young woman came whipping around the bend, right at me, poles clicking, driving forward with all the grit of a Norwegian Olympic cross-county skier."

Glenn laughed. "Close call."

"You're tell me. "I mean, the stuff was buried but still steaming!"

He laughed harder.*

THE VIEW EAST from up here was spectacular, especially at night with the lights below. Long before the desert to the east became a winter wonderland for millions of snowbirds in places such as Palm Desert, Palm Springs and Laquinta—before plush golf courses moistened the arid scrub—John Muir wrote, "The view from San Jacinto is the most sublime spectacle to be found anywhere on this earth!"

But the same elevation that provided such alluring vistas also presented danger. On this day, Tuesday, April 23, the trail's upper reaches were choked with snow. Earlier, we'd experienced only a few short patches of it obscuring the trail—Glenn and I had both slapped on micro spikes, just in case, because one slip and you were gone—but late in the afternoon we found ourselves post-holing in deep stuff just below and north of the summit of 10,834-foot Mount San Jacinto.

The sun was low; light was fading. I was spent and struggling to follow any semblance of trail, worried that if we didn't get back to dirt and rock soon,

* For those wondering why I've shared four stories in this book involving solid human waste, it's because I passed on using the other six I wanted to tell. The last thing I needed was an editor telling me my book was full of crap. But, hey, it's part of the journey and in an honest telling of the tale you can't bury the truth as if it were—well, you get the idea.

darkness would spike the chances of us getting lost. And the thought of sleeping on a snowy forty-five-degree slope was not a pleasant one.

Suddenly, from behind, strode a long-legged kid—Garrett, from Colorado, we would later learn. He passed us with a friendly "hello" and tromped through the snow with a youthful bravado that I envied, his eyes obviously glued to an app that charts the trail, water, campsites, and resupply stops.*

"Follow him," I said to Glenn. "This kid looks like he knows what he's doing."

Though we'd seen only a few hikers earlier in the day, a group of us was now trudging through the steep-sloped snow, following the kid. Dusk was swallowing the light, the remnants of a sunset silhouetting the trees. Finally, as we descended just before dark, the trail transitioned from snow to patches of snow and, finally, to beloved dirt on a shelf above Fuller Ridge.

"Woo hoo!" someone yelped.

As with so many other PCT victories, however, the good news came with bad. Yes, we were safely down from what could be a dangerous mountain—a young PCT hiker from Texas would slide 600 feet to his death near Apache Peak the next summer—but we were also facing the steepest downhill stretch on the entire trail: 6,555 feet in sixteen miles, from 7,749 feet to 1,195.**

For lots of reasons, the hike down Fuller Ridge the next day proved to be deception personified. First, it was downhill every step of the way, and despite having hiked nearly 2,000 PCT miles, I was still susceptible to the folly that downhill is easy. (Tell that to my knee surgeon.) What's more, for the entire way it afforded a view of Interstate 10 (LA to Palm Springs) through San Gorgonio Pass, which created a constant, but false, sense of "almost there!" Finally, the swath of switchbacks was totally exposed—not a smidgen of shade—and offered only a trickle of water.

After four hours, I was hot, thirsty, and feeling hoodwinked by The Freeway That Would Not Get Closer, the California version of Washington's I-90 at Snoqualmie Pass. The trail kept twisting and teasing and turning downward, worming its way south into Jacinto's rock face. Our ultimate destination, Cajon Pass, of course, was north.

---

* In 2019, most hikers were relying on an app called Guthook. Using GPS, it showed you where you were in relation to the trail, identified water and camping spots, and allowed hikers to communicate with each other. It essentially replaced the Halfmile app, which had debuted in 2012 but folded in 2015. Guthook would later rebrand itself as FarOut.

** For those familiar with Central Oregon, that's 1,500 feet more than the Devils-Lake-to-South-Sister climb.

To keep my mind off such twisting torture, I had an ace up my sleeve. I'd come up with a new scheme for this trip: a preset "Question of the Day" that I planned to pull from my iPhone to kindle conversation with Glenn. When, weeks beforehand, I'd told him I planned to do this, his response was predictably *Glenn.*

"Could you give the questions to me in advance," he asked, "so I could study?"

"No, it's the spontaneity that will make it fun."

Now, on the trail, it was time to spring my secret weapon for on-trail sanity.

"OK, let's start. Best concert you ever attended?"

"Uh, haven't really been to one." *

So much for spontaneity.

AS WE POUNDED downward with mind-numbing monotony, my iPhone buzzed. By this point in our eight years of hiking, I'd disciplined myself to disconnect from the real world. Except for grabbing scores of baseball or football games played by Oregon, Oregon State, or grandkids, I ignored most email and text messages, didn't follow news, and only rarely posted a Facebook or Twitter update. I would update Ann and Sally—and, on this stretch, Yorkey—with inReach satellite messages so they could note our progress. I would, of course, read any replies they sent. But I didn't routinely check text messages.

For some reason, however, when I saw a text from Geoff, I checked it out. He loved the PCT as deeply as anyone I'd known, and when he wasn't hiking it, he was forever finding ways to reconnect to it, in this case by following my occasional updates.

"Where are you?" he asked.

"Mile 199," I texted back. "7 mi. from bottom of Fuller Ridge, assuming there is a bottom. Is there?"

No reply from a guy who had hiked this section. The day wore on. We wore out.

"The only thing tougher than doing this ridge in the heat would be doing it a month ago in the snow," I told Glenn. "I have no idea how the thru-hikers do that. Last night was tough enough."

About 5:30 P.M., we finally reached the bottom—still miles from the

---

* Even though I later learned his very own mother, Pauline, a longtime member of the Altar Guild at Bethesda Lutheran Church in Eugene, saw Elvis Presley at the University of Oregon's McArthur Court in November 1976, nine months before he died.

freeway—and collapsed in two heaps. A guy approached from the north.

"You the Oregon Boys?"

"We are," I said, not used to such inquiries.

"Your friend Geoff is waiting for you down there in his pickup."

My brow furrowed. The guy pointed to what appeared to be Geoff Tyson's white 1993 Toyota pickup about a quarter mile to the north. Who else drives a beater like that?

Are you kidding me? I looked at Glenn and shook my head. We walked down the trail to the road and there stood Geoff, holding a sack of carnita street tacos and two cups of strawberry lemonade on ice.

"Gentlemen," he said, pointing to his twenty-five-year-old pickup. "Your limo awaits. Anyone for dinner in Palm Springs? The tacos are just hors d'oeurvres."

"Geoff, what the—what are you doing here?" I asked.

"Fuller Ridge is a bitch," he said. "I remember. Thought you could use a little reward for surviving it."

He was nearly a thousand road miles from our home in Oregon.

"Hey, I had some time off and decided to revisit some of my old PCT haunts. And as long as I was down this way, I thought I'd offer The Oregon Boys a little Trail Magic. Ready?"

"Are you kidding me?" I said as we stowed our packs in back and piled in.

We chowed down at a sit-down restaurant in Palm Springs—French dip sandwich for me—and updated Geoff on our experience thus far. The dinner was as if part of a dream, the kind of scene you imagine happening on a hot, trail-weary afternoon but doesn't. Only, this one *did.*

"Thanks, man," I said in my goodbye to Geoff, who would be fast asleep in the back of his canopied pickup when we hit the trail at 5 A.M. "Meant a lot that you did that for us. I'm honored."

"My pleasure," he said.

He knew I meant it and I knew he meant it.

FORGET ISAAC NEWTON, on the PCT what goes *down* must go *up*. After descending 6,555 feet down Fuller Ridge to reach the lowest elevation on the California portion of the trail (1,195 feet), we now faced a 7,800-foot, sixty-two-mile climb from San Gorgonio Pass (I-10) to just southwest of Heartbreak Ridge. That would comprise a killer three days: counting our Fuller Ridge descent, it would mean an elevation gain and loss of 14,355 feet.

Thursday, April 25, began with us weaving up dry and rocky Whitewater Canyon. The trail loosely followed a braid of dry riverbeds, coming and going on a whim, apparently washed away by spring runoff. We'd see rock cairns that some thoughtful hikers had stacked to mark where the trail went to one side of the bed. We'd follow a vague path for a few hundred feet to the other, then lose the trail altogether.

Meanwhile, the day was heating up and shade almost impossible to find. By now, sunblock was second nature; we lubed up at sunrise and, often, again after lunch. At these elevations, we were being exposed to nearly twice as much ultraviolet radiation as someone at sea level. This stretch was technically part of the Colorado Desert—California's hottest and driest—where less than two inches of rain fall per year. During a midmorning break, we burrowed into the center of a low scrub tree for shade, almost as if we were more animal than human.

As a veteran hiker, I'd come to believe that mental weariness was more challenging than physical wear and tear. My feet could be trashed, my legs rubber, and my shoulders aching from a forty-pound pack, but if my mind was elsewhere, the hours could pass quickly. But once I lost my mind—and, yeah, that's an accurate description—I was toast.

When feeling the wheels start to wobble, I'd resort to all sorts of thoughts to recalibrate my spirit: think of my family back home, remind myself of the thousands of PCT hikers who'd trod on this very trail, and, when desperate, think about how hiking the PCT was like writing a book. To tell a story, you discipline yourself to click one key at a time to create one word, words that become a sentence, sentences that become a paragraph, paragraphs that become a chapter, chapters that become a book. *So,* I'd tell myself, *one keystroke at a time, baby.*

In theory it was wondrous, in practice less so. By late afternoon, whatever good mojo Geoff, Palm Springs, and French dips had instilled in me had vanished. The diabolical trail, oppressive heat, and second straight night with little sleep were taking their toll. By five o'clock I was ready to be done. Glenn wanted to press on.

"Three-point five to a flat space to camp," he said.

"All uphill, I imagine," I huffed, as if that was his fault.

"Pretty much, yep."

That we disagreed about when to shut down wasn't my beef with him. That he hadn't bothered to ask me how I was feeling *was.*

"You just assume I've got another three-point-five in me," I said. "Hey, next time, please *ask*. You know, I'm part of this team, too."

"Sorry. Can you make it?"

"Do I have a choice?"

We trudged on in silence. I wasn't proud of my poutiness but anyone who thinks you can hike with someone for eight summers without having a few inter-team meltdowns is naïve. They say remodeling a house is one of the most severe stressors on a marriage, largely because it requires constant decisions. Likewise, the trail requires constant decisions, the biggest of which follows every hiker like a vulture: *Walk or quit?* Given as much, is it any wonder that two brothers-in-law might experience a similar touch of friction while being together 24/7 day after day, year after year, often while hot and tired—and, yes, while constantly needing to choose this or that?

Maybe the wonder wasn't that we occasionally clashed—or at least, I think we did; Glenn's poker face may or may not have been hiding feelings suggesting he wanted to, at times, dropkick me to Mexico. Maybe the wonder was that we got along fabulously for about 99.5 percent of the time.

Finally, as dusk neared, we found a small campsite that looked as if it could fit two or three tents. We'd done the additional three-plus miles—and I'd felt every step.

"This OK?" Glenn asked.

"Fine," I huffed.

Silently, we made camp. Soon, Garrett, the Colorado kid, arrived.

"Room for one more?"

We welcomed him; he would, I figured, ease the tension. Garrett pulled out his iPhone.

"Just saw a rattler," he said, showing us a photo. I wanted to see one, too—from a safe distance. So far, no luck.

We scarfed down some food and were just about to slip into our tents when another hiker approached from the south, a guy about the age of Glenn and me. We would come to call him New Hampshire Don, a doctor doing some PCT section-hiking.* Over the next week, we'd hike with him off and on.

A few days later, Tuesday April 30, Don unpacked some emotional baggage after he and I had lagged behind Glenn.

"A few years back," he said, "I lost a son. Twenty-one. Took his own life."

"Oh, I'm so sorry, Don. I can't imagine anything more difficult."

"Thanks. It's been hard."

While initially stunned, I felt honored that he'd been willing to share; experience—and leading a few Christian men's retreats—had taught me that, as Henry David Thoreau said, "Most men live lives of quiet desperation."

I listened, and lamented, as Don told me about his son, a troubled kid who kept looking to find his niche in the world but couldn't. Over the years, between talking to hikers and reading more than a dozen first-person

* Not his real name or home state.

accounts of long-distance hikes, I'd come to realize that a good number of people out here were carrying far more than pack weight. They were carrying emotional weight, the baggage of the past.

As Don told me more about his son, I wondered if I was privileged to be hearing the heart of a man reluctant to share back home. As if out here, in the wilderness, to a stranger, he felt safer than with those he was closest to. I had two sons soon to be forty. I'd written a book about fathers and sons. I sensed he found me safe.

"What nags is always the guilt," he said. "What did I do wrong? What did *we* do wrong—my wife and I? Were we too hard on him? Not hard enough?"

I told him a little about Greg and Linda, my brother- and sister-in-law, losing a sixteen-year-old son. But I reminded myself Don didn't need my stories or advice. More than anything, what he seemed to need was simply someone to listen.

New Hampshire Don cooled quickly to our up-at-4:05-A.M. schedule, so we didn't hike together much. But just when we thought we'd seen the last of him, he would pop up while we were having lunch at Lake Silverwood or dinner somewhere else.

At Big Bear Lake, where I got my first—and last—shower of the three-week trip, the three of us grabbed an Uber and went out for heavenly pizza.

Days later, after a straight and "ledgy" hike along Deep Creek as I listened to the audio version of *Where the Crawdads Sing,* I was nestled in the meager shade of sagebrush scrub when New Hampshire Don showed up. His feet were trashed, and he'd broken a pole on that treacherous dry creek bed days ago.*

"I'm thinking of either calling it quits at Cajon Pass," he said. "Or buying poles in LA and trying to get to Kennedy Meadows."

Frankly, I felt bad for the guy. He seemed lonely. I had Glenn. Most folks out here had someone, if not lots of "someones." Who did he have?

We arrived at Cajon the next day—on the exact date we hoped to: May 2, the fourteenth birthday of Cade, our oldest grandson. My friend Mike, with whom I'd been updating our progress, was waiting for us, along with his wife, who, as owner of Nicole's Swiss Bliss, had brought us an array of samples that had my taste buds dancing the Macarena.

We'd forwarded the Yorkeys Wet Ones, fresh clothes, and plastic bags for our stinky ones. In Mike and Nichole's BMW—don't see too many of those

* I was on my seventh pair since 2011, most failing because one of the adjustable sections would no longer lock, a few because of broken tips. Poles, water filters, shoes, and socks were the four items that needed replacing most often over the years.

with Hiker Trash in them!—we dropped New Hampshire Don at an REI so he could get new poles, then bid him farewell.

Hiking the PCT was like summer camp. You'd make new friends then, boom, they were gone, the trail bringing people together and sending us on our separate ways.

Over the years, I had too often looked at other hikers as conduits of information or encouragement for *my* benefit. My short relationship with Don reminded me of my shortsightedness. Maybe, for some, I was *that* person to them. Maybe they weren't what I necessarily needed, but I was what *they* needed.

It was a humbling thought, one that reminded me that the PCT was not only making me physically stronger but broadening my horizons. Not just regarding me but my fellow travelers, some of whom needed the trail for reasons far deeper than my own.

Mike Yorkey

Starting from the Mexican border, where PCT thru-hikers begin their south-to-north journeys, was special—and dark. Shortly before 6 A.M., we had the monument to ourselves.

Top: On the Anza-Borrego Desert, the flattest stretch we'd experienced on the PCT, Glenn hiked with his heat-reflecting umbrella. Above: Mickey Mouse cacti began appearing more often the closer we got to—where else?—Disneyland.

Top: Just before Warner Springs, we stopped for the obligatory pose in front of Eagle Rock. Above: Glenn livened things up during a trailside break with a little branch guitar. Not bad for a guy who said he'd never been to a concert.

Top: The thinnest of rainbows cast an arch from the San Jacinto Mountains toward the Palm Springs/Palm Desert area to the east. Above: The snowy section where the Colorado Kid led us through.

Glenn Petersen

A third of the way down diabolical Fuller Ridge, I paused to look back at where we'd been: near the top of 10,833-foot Mount San Jacinto, roughly the elevation of Oregon's Mount Hood.

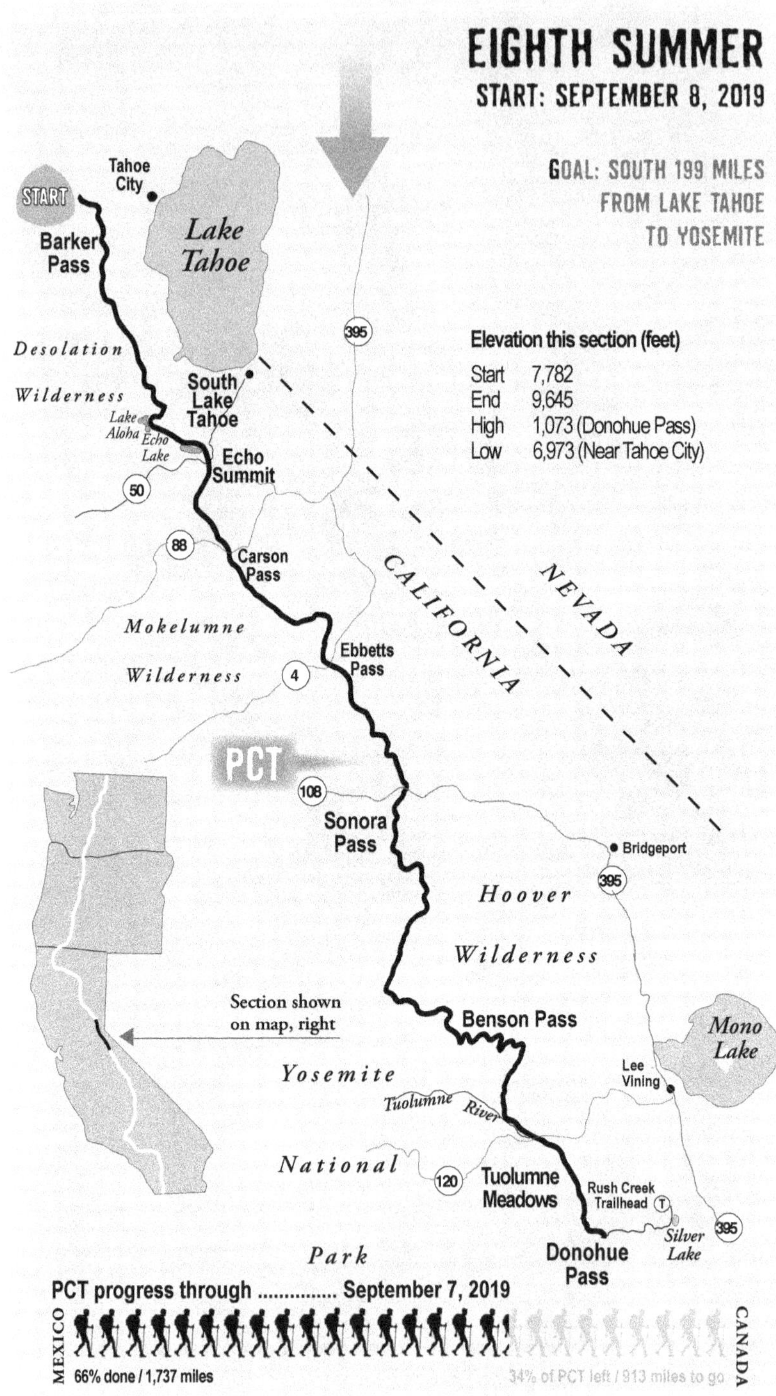
EIGHTH SUMMER
START: SEPTEMBER 8, 2019
GOAL: SOUTH 199 MILES
FROM LAKE TAHOE
TO YOSEMITE
Elevation this section (feet)
Start 7,782
End 9,645
High 1,073 (Donohue Pass)
Low 6,973 (Near Tahoe City)
START
Tahoe City
Lake Tahoe
Barker Pass
Desolation Wilderness
South Lake Tahoe
Lake Aloha
Echo Lake
Echo Summit
50
88
395
Carson Pass
CALIFORNIA
NEVADA
Mokelumne Wilderness
Ebbetts Pass
4
PCT
108
Sonora Pass
Bridgeport
Hoover Wilderness
Section shown on map, right
Benson Pass
Mono Lake
Lee Vining
Yosemite National Park
Tuolumne River
120
Tuolumne Meadows
Rush Creek Trailhead
T
Silver Lake
Donohue Pass
PCT progress through .... September 7, 2019
MEXICO
CANADA
66% done / 1,737 miles
34% of PCT left / 913 miles to go

16

HISTORY

The river was cut by the world's great flood and runs
over rocks from the basement of time.
On some of the rocks are timeless raindrops.

—Norman Maclean, *A River Runs Through It*

At Reno-Tahoe International Airport, Sammy was waiting. She and her husband, Gabe—both mid-thirties—had posted a note on a Facebook PCT page saying they were hikers from South Lake Tahoe happy to help others get to or from the trail. I happily accepted the offer. I sent her a copy of *Cascade Summer* and a $100 deposit to show we were serious; six months later, there she was, right on time after our flight from Portland.

It had been three months since we'd finished our Mexican-border-to-Cajon-Pass stretch, six weeks since we'd completed the thirty-seven-mile Oregon-border-to-Seiad-Valley stretch that we'd missed the previous year because of fire, and five days since my friend Geoff had reached Canada. Amazingly, after his failed attempt at Oregon in 2013, he'd done the whole PCT in a four-year period. What a story, the once-254-pound out-of-shape barber completing the 2,650-mile PCT. I couldn't have been prouder of him.

The way Glenn and I hiked the PCT was like a game of Yahtzee. The border-to-Seiad stretch was like getting our "ones"—a minimal-pointer, though it did include a stop at the intriguing Donomore Cabin, a buckaroo cabin for ranch hands dating back to 1935. The High Sierra, five giant passes, represented an actual Yahtzee—the best we could do: fifty points. And the

Tahoe-to-Yosemite stretch we were embarking on now was like putting the last piece in a small straight—our first three-segment summer.

I was amped for this hike. First, as beautiful as it promised to be, the Tahoe-to-Sonora-Pass stretch would represent only the warm-up band for the Beatles. Yosemite, our ultimate destination, would be breathtaking at every swivel of the head: mountains, waterfalls, meadows, a place that drew visitors from all over the world. But we'd missed it in 2014 because of fire.

Second, near South Lake Tahoe, I was hoping to camp at the very spot at Echo Summit where Fosbury, in 1968, had made a do-or-die jump in the Olympic Trials to win the third and final high-jump spot on the U.S team.

By now, my book on Fosbury, *The Wizard of Foz*, had been out for nearly a year. His story fascinated me, in part because he was a boyhood hero; I had grown up a ten-minute bike ride from Oregon State's campus in Corvallis, where Dick honed The Flop. My pals and I flopped in his pit at OSU!

The '60s were marked by violence: the Vietnam War, anti-war protests, race riots, and the assassinations of President John F. Kennedy, former Attorney General Bobby Kennedy, and civil rights leader Martin Luther King Jr. Against such heaviness, Fosbury's story was a footnote of feel-good whimsy. He literally turned his back on the establishment to invent a new style that not only propelled him to an Olympic gold medal but revolutionized the way high jumpers around the world jumped ever since.

All of which is to say that the prospect of returning to Echo Summit was fueling my second day on the trail, a twenty-mile stretch. In working on the book together, Fosbury and I, in September 2017, had gone to Echo Summit. There, Dick had shown me the exact spot where he'd jumped in the Olympic Trials forty-nine years earlier.

Now, I was going to pitch my tent there—or at least try. We were slowed by thundershowers west of Lake Aloha, which was perched dramatically on a shelf at 8,100 feet. Between donning wet-weather gear, hunkering down to wait out thunderclaps, and getting out of that gear, we'd gotten off pace.

"Sorry if I seem a bit obsessive," I told Glenn, who was probably thinking, *and this is news?* "I just really want to get that photo at Echo Summit before it gets dark. If we miss the chance tonight, we're out of luck because of our early start tomorrow. And nobody likes a flash photo."

"We'll make it, Bobby."

I liked his willingness to partner with me on this odd endeavor. We picked up the pace. Still, by the time we began hiking alongside long and luscious Echo Lake, the sun was getting low in the western sky. Between the lake and State Route 50, which transected Echo Summit en route from South Lake Tahoe to Sacramento, we faced a daunting challenge: getting over a narrow but fast-flowing creek. At several spots, I was ready to jump but Glenn overruled me. Too risky. And he was right. One slip and you could, at best, soak your sleeping bag, clothes, and tent; at worst, hurt yourself badly.

But by now I was a crazed man. The forest was getting darker by the second and we still had about a mile to go. Finally, we found a safe passage across the stream, then kicked our way down homestretch, paralleling SR 50. When we arrived at Echo Summit, now the partially treed parking lot of a winter snow park facility, we had the place to ourselves.

"Over here," I said, making my way to what would have been just inside the southern part of the north-south-facing oval, just a few hundred feet east of the PCT. "This is where Foz would have started his approach to the bar in sixty-eight. Right ... right ... here." *

I dropped my pack, feverishly dug out my tent, and started putting it up. I tossed Glenn my iPhone in the near darkness and said, "Shoot away."

"Won't go. Not enough light."

"Argh!"

"Wait. Let me try mine; it's newer."

Sure enough, his later model iPhone was able to take photos in dimmer light; he clicked a few photos so I could always be reminded that I'd slept where Fosbury had jumped—and was undoubtedly the first, and only, PCT hiker to do so. Silly? Of course. But I slept well, as you'd expect from someone who had just made history.

THE FIRST reminder that summer was ending came two mornings later, Wednesday, September 11, the latest date into the year we'd ever been on the PCT. High on a ridge, at nearly 9,000 feet, we awoke to frost on our bear vaults. My fingers were so cold I couldn't open the lid without the help of a plastic card that made it easier to unlock.**

On a midmorning break, I found cell coverage and sent Fosbury a photo of me at his spot.

"Love it!" he replied. "A first! Yeah, Bob!"

---

* See photo p. 239.

** Months before, when I'd found a YouTube segment that showed how you could take "an ordinary plastic library card" to make it easier to slide open the bear-vault lids, I'd joked to Glenn that it would never work. "Bears aren't stupid. Look for a rash of them showing up at reference desks all across America, applying for library cards under the guise that 'we love to read.' Yeah, *right*." But, hey, now that I'd successfully used such a card in a desperate situation, I was a believer.

Glenn and I descended south to Sonora Pass, where we picked up food boxes that, for $75, we'd arranged for remote delivery. The pass was different than all the others: barren but beautiful for that very reason, the topography virtually treeless. Just miles and miles of trail on long, straight stretches, notched in loose gravel.

On Saturday, September 14, a satellite message from Ann informed us that Oregon State had beaten Cal Poly 45-7 and Oregon had beaten Montana 35-3 in football. But news from a New York NoBo left us less upbeat.

"My Windy app says snow's expected to hit Benson Pass Monday afternoon," she said. "We came over it two days ago. It's really high."

Our schedule had us going over 10,125-foot Benson Pass—wait for it—Monday afternoon.

"Thanks for the heads up."

Snow had been my worst fear since we'd started the trail. It wasn't because of the Devils Peak scare a week into our Oregon leg in 2011; that turned out to be a false alarm. In fact, I think it had less to do with my own experiences than with the experiences of others, foremost among them the unnamed Yukon adventurer in Jack London's short story, "To Build a Fire," and the eight climbers who died atop Mt. Everest in Krakauer's *Into Thin Air.* Snow changed everything. It could obscure a trail, cause you to slip on a steep slope, and soak your body, clothes, and sleeping bag, putting you in danger of hypothermia.

Not that I was thinking about such things the next morning when we were breaking camp in the darkness of 4 A.M. I clipped the side buckles on my pack's hood and was giving the camp a last look with my headlamp when I realized I'd forgotten to pack my extendable tent poles. *Argh.* Rather than unpack everything, I simply used a small bungee to strap them atop my pack.

After twenty miles, we arrived at Dorothy Lake just as dusk was giving way to darkness. Wiped, we dropped our packs to drink in the beauty of a lake that spread out before us like a liquid welcome mat.

I leaned against my pack, closed my eyes, and listened to the silence—until, moments later, I jerked forward as if jolted by a nightmare. I rolled onto my knees, and started pawing in and around my pack like a madman.

"What's wrong?" Glenn asked.

"I gotta terrible feeling."

"What?"

"My tent poles—they're gone. They must have come unstrapped from the top of my back."

"You sure?"

"Yeah. I've got no idea where I lost them, but probably at that creek a mile or so back where we stopped for water."

My timing couldn't have been worse. The next night, I was likely going to be camping in snow and I had no way of erecting my tent. My mind fast-forwarded to the possible consequence of my carelessness. The bottom line wasn't discomfort—I imagined I'd need to move into Glenn's already-tight one-man tent—but *danger*. For me to be in Glenn's tent would mean our packs, which we normally kept inside our respective tents, would have to go outside, wrapped, probably, in my waterproof tent to stay dry. But in rain or snow, using such a discombobulated setup would increase the chances of us getting our clothes and sleeping bags wet. It could not only be a logistical nightmare, but, at nearly 11,000 feet, put our lives at risk.

In the fading light, a fellow SoBo headed toward us on the trail.

"Any chance you saw tent poles on the trail?" I asked. "Near that last water stop?"

"Sorry," she said.

What if a NoBo we passed saw them and picked them up? Or tossed them aside, assuming nobody was coming for them? What if I lost them five miles back—or ten?

"I've gotta run back and find them," I said to Glenn. I grabbed my headlamp.

"Whoa, wait, slow down. Take some food, water, and your pack with your sleeping bag inside—just in case."

"Tell you what, if I haven't found the poles by the time I've gotten to that creek I'll turn around. I *won't* keep going north. I'll head back here; this is where we meet. OK? You stay put. I'll come to you."

"Good idea. No farther than the creek."

"Roger."

"And you've got your cell phone and satellite phone?"

"Check."

Already weary after more than ten hours of hiking, I nevertheless started jogging toward the creek. I was soon huffing and puffing and wet with sweat.

Heavenly father, I ask that my poles would be there ...

Another SoBo headed my way.

"You see ... any ... tent poles," I said, panting, "... along the trail ... near ... last creek?"

"Nope."

"Thanks."

How could I have done this? I was a PCT veteran and I'd made a rookie mistake. I should have taken the time to put them inside my pack, vertically, where I usually stored them. But I was lazy. And now paying the price for it.

The forest darkened. Five minutes became ten; ten became fifteen. It was almost pitch black when I rounded a bend, heard the quiet trickle of a creek, and saw metal in the beam of my lamp.

Yes!

THE FIND was fortunate. As we headed up Benson Pass Monday afternoon, a sky that had been robin's-egg blue turned sinister. In less than an hour, pewter-gray clouds bullied their way in, some feathered with dark tinges clearly pregnant with precipitation. The wind picked up.

Chugging up the final miles of the 10,125-foot pass—I was slightly ahead of Glenn—I met a fellow SoBo who was roughly our age and not looking good. A tad overweight to begin with, he was bent over his poles, breathing hard.

"You OK?" I asked.

When he nodded yes instead of taking the energy to talk, sweat dripping off his nose, I wondered.

"You with some others?"

"Yeah ... coupla guys … up … ahead," he said, nodding the direction I was going.

"Got plenty of food and water? Got a tent?"

Another nod. "I'm ... OK."

"All right. Hang in there. Supposed to snow."

Twenty minutes later, as I passed two other older guys, I asked if the guy I'd seen was part of their group.

"Yeah, he's just a slacker," said one guy, laughing.

"He looked to be hurting."

I didn't mean to be a finger-wagger, but at this elevation, in mid-September, caution seemed the better part of valor. This disjointed threesome didn't strike me as PCT hikers, partly because of how out of shape the one guy was and partly because this was Yosemite Wilderness, where lots of feeder trails offered quick access to the PCT.

"As someone who nearly got hypothermia up here a few years back, I'm just saying you might want to keep an eye on him. He's pretty far back—almost a quarter-mile by now. And the forecast is for snow."

Their shoulder shrugs suggested their pride, not their hiking buddy, was the priority here. I mentally shook my head and trudged on.

My problem—or my asset—was imagination. I'd see a guy like that and imagine the story two days later on the regional section front of the *Los Angeles Times.*

> YOSEMITE (AP)—A Riverside, California, man died of hypothermia Wednesday in the Yosemite Wilderness after he became separated from two hiking companions just before an unseasonal snowstorm slammed Benson Pass … .

Enough. I'd done what I could.

I turned my mind to my own situation, whose challenge escalated when scattered raindrops became a steady downpour. Glenn and I stopped to cover our packs and throw on our rain gear.

"We don't wanna be camping up top in this," yelled Glenn above the wind and rain. "We need to get up and over this pass and find a flat place before dark."

"And before this rain turns to snow," I yelled, about five minutes before exactly that happened.

We trudged up Benson Pass, the trail now dusted in white, our elevation hitting the 10,000-foot mark.

"Glad I got tent poles," I said.

"Me, too. Woulda been cozy in one tent."

"Yeah, I don't wanna even think about that."

We reached the top and began zigzagging down the south side. As we made a quick stop for water at Wilson Creek—no fun when you're tired and cold—we started scouting for a place to sleep. The snow turned back to rain.

We'd had little experience setting up our tents in precipitation, but knew the trick was to do so without getting our sleeping bags or sleep clothes wet. If that happened, we could get chilled in a hurry, which upped the chances of hypothermia.

For now, a more pressing problem was finding a spot remotely flat enough to set up our tents. Not far from Matterhorn Canyon, I saw a nominee.

"This?" I asked, pointing to a spot.

"We can do better," said Glenn.

"How about over there?" I asked fifteen minutes later.

"Let's keep looking."

By now, our distinct styles were as embedded in our daily patterns as tent stakes pounded into hard pan. I was an "any-port-in-a-storm" guy. Glenn was a "we-can-do-better" guy. Finally, we agreed on a semi-flat spot, Glenn's decision to stop, I presumed, having less to do with me finding the perfect place than rain pounding us into a state of desperation.

With urgency, we popped up our tents, threw our packs inside, then dove in ourselves. I was exhausted, panting from ten hours of hiking and ten minutes of frantic camp setup. I blew up my mattress and rooted around for dinner in a pack that had far more empty sandwich bags than those holding food.

The inside of my tent was a mess, though in a weird way I kind of enjoyed the chaos.

"You know how you can tell when you've been on the PCT too long?"

"How?" Glenn asked.

"When you can't tell the difference between what's a garbage bag and what's a food bag. I'm afraid I'm going to eat some garbage—and find it tastes no worse than the food."

More seriously, I thought of that struggling guy I'd seen. Where was he now and how was he doing? I mentally shook my head.

The rain fell and as darkness swallowed the last of the light, I read for a few minutes by the light of my headlamp, thankful for extendable tent poles that once were lost but now were found—and helping me stay dry. I fell asleep to the sound of rain pleasantly pattering my tent only inches above my head.

THE NEXT DAY, Tuesday, September 17, the weather cleared, the terrain grew less steep, and the beauty of north Yosemite burst forth in an array of grandeur. Matterhorn Creek splashed down giant slabs of rocks, waterfalls cascaded off cliffs, and domes of pale white granite towered above the trees.

The PCT could tingle your senses in myriad ways: the obvious visual scenes through the day, but also the more subtle unseen ones: the sweet sound of water trickling in a stream that crossed the trail, the smell of pitch when you were fighting your way through blowdown, and the warmth of meadow grass while lying back for a post-lunch nap.

With my time in the High Sierra almost over, I realized that what had enchanted me most in 2014 and this year had been its water. Lakes. Streams. Creeks. Waterfalls. It had an ethereal sense to it, almost as if what you saw could not be real. Could not be that clear. Could not hammer through a rocky notch, sweep beneath an overhanging bank, or sashay through a meadow with such energy or elegance.

In Oregon, our high mountain water seemed to come tinted in blues and greens, and have a beauty all its own. But the High Sierra waters seemed translucent. No images from my camera—photos or video—could do these streams and creeks justice; nor, frankly, can these words I write now.* But I am reminded that our truest connection to an experience is not through words or images but through memory. Simply remembering something cuts out the middleman, allowing us to forever carry that moment in time forward, wherever we go. No intercessory or amplifier required.

---

* That said, I've placed a few video clips of water on the PCT on my web site at bobwelchwriter.com. See page 357 to scan a QR code.

WITH THE SAME obsession that drove us twenty-six miles in a single day to Belden, we quickened our pace in search of a cheeseburger at Tuolumne Meadows before the restaurant closed. We made it but I found the burgers disappointing. Still, it was fun hobnobbing with other hikers, eating ice cream, and camping in an actual campground with tent spots as flat as tennis courts.

On the PCT, small moments like these were cathartic: Little clusters of community reconnecting you to the idea that you weren't alone. Going to sleep that night, I could hear the occasional laughter from a fireside chat that some Ranger Rick was holding for the weekend warriors nearby, and it comforted me. Some of us were on long journeys, others on weekend getaways, but we were all one beneath the canopy of stars and trees and glacier-carved domes.

The next morning, Glenn and I enjoyed a pleasant hike in Tuolumne Meadows, a place that Muir had described as "the widest, smoothest, most serenely spacious, and in every way the most delightful pleasure park in all the High Sierra." We photographed deer (more here than I'd seen on the rest of the trail combined),* cracked jokes, and looked forward to our last night on the PCT before our Thursday, September 19 pickup by Sally and Ann at the Rush Creek Trailhead where we'd started the John Muir Trail five years before.

At Yosemite, it crossed my mind that even though I was getting older, hiking, weirdly, was getting, if not easier, *less hard*. It wasn't that I suddenly fashioned myself as Malto, the sheik-like speedster I met in 2011. Nor that I thought I'd become a PCT version of cinema's *Benjamin Button*, aging in reverse. But I was quietly pleased—if not puzzled—that hiking wasn't trashing me at the end of each day as it had in the earlier years. It wasn't that we were, over the years, decreasing our mileage; we stayed steady, averaging about eighteen miles per day, year in and year out. It was simply that eighteen *now* wasn't hurting like eighteen did *then*.

I attributed that to several reasons:

▲ Finding Altra shoes with a wide toe box that, with a few exceptions, helped me avoid blisters.

▲ Swimming. Although I prepared harder for Oregon in 2011 than for any other section, starting to swim in 2016 had done wonders for my cardiovascular system—and caused little wear and tear on my body in the process.

▲ Learning to maximize my trekking poles. Over the years, I came to

---

* Glenn and I had been surprised by the lack of wildlife we'd seen on the trail over the years: the hind end of a bear, the eyes of a mountain lion, a few dozen deer, marmots and squirrels, chipmunks, and lizards galore. But beyond that, not much.

believe that I could climb mountains as much with my arms as with my legs; I shortened my trekking poles, leaned into the slope, and drove my arms downward almost like a sprinter. I actually came to enjoy uphill more than downhill, in part because of this.

▲ Improving my on-trail organization. I used to be so tired at night my attitude was, *I'll figure it out in the morning.* But that had changed. I had found a rhythm for on-trail logistics that was fast, efficient, and good for my confidence. Now, before sleeping, my socks, gaiters, and bicycle gloves would go in a see-through plastic bag so in the fog of 4 A.M. I could easily find what I needed. My headlamp, morning meds, and breakfast snacks went in a mesh pouch that hung from the side of the tent. And, when packing my ULA Catalyst each morning—my Ohm had worn out—I'd adopted a "stuff and go" style with my sleeping bag and tent that saved time and energy. Only one person needed those items: me. If they were easily found, who cared whether they were rolled into a stuff sack that only added more weight? (The lone exception: major water crossings, in which case I'd make sure my bag was in a dry sack so it wouldn't get soaked if I fell in.)

▲ Hiking smarter. Experience helped me realize what worked and what didn't. Example: early on, I used a Camelbak hydration bladder, but found it encouraged me to drink more water than I needed—and often leaked into my pack. I ditched it for plastic bottles.

▲ Enduring years on the trail, which I'd become convinced had strengthened my body in general and my feet in particular.* My feet and trekking-pole fingers were callused, my mind more attuned to the moment.

▲ Finally, realizing that Canada was not a pipe dream but attainable. Like the proverbial horse smelling the barn, the pull of the border was starting to put zip in my step, hope in my heart, and resolve in my desire to reach it.

AS THE MORNING deepened, our moods lightened. We'd been on the PCT for eleven days and 190 miles; now, we were only twenty-six miles short of our destination. However, within half an hour, two threats arose:

One came from the sky—another storm, replete with charcoal-colored clouds that looked as if copied and pasted from Benson Pass. NoBos who'd

* In 2011, only days before we began our quest to do Oregon, I remember thinking that if I couldn't get from my car to the front door of *The Register-Guard* without feeling pain on the bottoms of both feet, how was I going to hike 456 miles on rugged trails? Now, a decade later, that pain was gone and I'd hiked nearly 2,000 miles. When I shared this with a Eugene physical therapist, Steven Robert, he surmised the trail deserved some credit. "The PCT," he said, "has become your physical therapist. Every day you hike it's strengthening your feet."

just come off 11,056-foot Donohue Pass, our last major obstacle, warned us of wicked winds up top.

The other threat came from a National Park ranger.

"May I see your permit?" she asked.

In our 2,000-plus miles, only once had we been "carded," though I wasn't worried in the least. Glenn—clearly the husband of Ann—was a master organizer; knowing him, he had the permit on his iPhone, a hard copy in his back pocket, and a backup in an easily accessible pouch of his pack.

So why was I suddenly watching him madly dig through his pack like I had done a few days earlier, trying to find my tent poles? In a few moments of fiendish searching, he had come up empty. I knew how frustrated he'd been with an online permit system so convoluted that it seemed designed to dissuade, not encourage, hikers from hiking.

"Sir, I need to see your—."

"Please, don't get me started," said Glenn, sweat staining his face. "Your system—. I spent—. Hold on, it's here somewhere."

Whoa. I hadn't seen Glenn Petersen like this since a mosquito-inspired meltdown at Jack Spring in 2011. Finally, he found the permit.

"There!" he said.

The ranger looked at the permit as if she were a cop and Glenn had been caught doing fifty-five in a school zone.

Please don't ruin our trip on our last full day by telling us we can't continue.

She folded the permit and handed it back to him.

"You're good to go," she said. "But I need to warn you: We've got some weather moving in. Snow possible. I advise you not to camp too high."

We thanked her, strapped on our packs, and headed out. We looked back to see the ranger—just doing her job, I reminded myself—pulling over another southbound hiker. She was a small, thirty-something woman in a short dress. On a leash, she was tugging—how else can I say this?—a chihuahua that had lime green booties on its feet about the size of thimbles. Since starting our PCT journey in 2011, I thought I'd seen and heard it all—from hikers carrying guitars to some weirdo camping where Fosbury had begun his approach to make the 1968 Olymp—wait, that was *me.* But I'd never seen a chihuahua with green booties hiking the PCT.

"Hard enough doing this trail alone," I told Glenn as we headed out, "but that dog is just one more moving part. Yikes. And with a storm maybe moving in."

The woman and her dog reminded me that the people walking the PCT were a variety pack of nationalities, ethnicities, looks, styles, motives, and opinions. After an hour, as we stopped in a meadow to filter water from the

Tuolumne River's Lyell Fork, the woman and her dog passed us. The sky above Donohue Pass was getting darker. It was shortly after noon. And it was 4.2 miles and 2,000 feet to the top. Two Pisgahs.

"What do you think?" I asked Glenn.

"Not looking good."

"It'll cost us a day if we don't get over the pass this afternoon," I said.

"I think we should wait."

Soon, however, we noticed the clouds beginning to break up.

"Definitely looking better," Glenn said.

We decided to head up Donohue, but be ready to turn back if things worsened in the least. We picked up our pace.

"Hey, look, there's the chihuahua up ahead," I said. "When we pass those two, I'm gonna thank that woman for inspiring us!"

Just below the timberline we met three groups of people, including a young woman who'd recently graduated from University of Oregon's School of Journalism and Communication, where I'd been an adjunct professor.

"We just saw a bear!" she said. "About a quarter mile south of here."

I looked intently as we passed that stretch, but no such luck.

The sun slipped lower in the western sky. We climbed higher on Donohue's north flank, through a rocky cauldron in which a small lake was being fed by a stream from Maclure Glacier. It was desolate, like something on a *Star Wars* planet, far, far away.

Twice on this trip, in the late afternoons when my mind started to wobble, I'd hallucinated. I once thought I saw a station wagon on a gravel road, another time a young man and woman folding a red-striped beach towel. Nope, no road, no car, no man, no woman, no towel. Other times, my weary mind would see roots or rocks or gnarled trees that looked like dragons or fish or animals, including the University of Washington Huskies' mascot, Sun Dodger. But I couldn't deny what I saw a half mile above us: The woman and her green-booted chihuahua. Tiny specks in this granite terrain above the timberline. Unbelievable. *They were light years ahead of us!*

Two hours later, at 4:45 P.M., we reached Donohue's 11,056-foot summit. No snow. Light winds. Clouds shrouded the 11,000-foot mountains to our west, including Amelia Earhart Peak, but the brooding front seemed to be overnighting there.

I was high—in elevation and in spirits. "Yeah, baby! Downhill to the trailhead!" Glenn slapped gloves with me.

Looking down before we began our descent, I saw them for the last time: far below, the woman and her chihuahua, offering me a lesson in how not to assume things about people, and dogs, you don't know.

A couple thousand feet south of Donohue Pass, as we slept, snow softened the woods, and mantled our tents, throughout the night. We awoke, my headlamp showed, to a forest blanketed in white.

"Can we even find the trail from where we're camped?" Glenn asked in the 4 A.M. darkness.

"I'll take a look. Keep an eye on my light and turn yours on so I don't get lost."

I slipped on my shoes and walked through the ankle-high fresh powder.

"Coupla three inches of snow on the trail," I said, "but with GPS I think we can find our way down."

Glenn crawled out of his tent, looked around, and concurred. We needed only eleven miles to the Rush Creek Trailhead. At this point, wild horses couldn't have stopped us—even if they'd been wearing micro spikes. The snow faded as we hiked lower. By noon, we were done with our biggest summer yet—576.7 miles, more than one-fifth of the PCT.

EN ROUTE HOME—Ann and Sally up front, Glenn and I in back—we were stunned to see how white Mount Shasta in Northern California was. Winter, a wisp of which we'd awakened to the previous morning, was coming early to the West Coast.

We exited at Yreka for food, giving me the chance to exploit some online trivia I'd picked up. "This place is home of the Yreka Bakery, which is spelled the same forward or backward," I said. "Is that amazing or what?"

We were at a McDonald's when in hobbled a middle-aged man with a backpack and poles. He had a brace on his knee and a gray and red stocking cap on his head. When I asked, he said he was a PCT hiker from Georgia.

"And you're hoping to make Canada this year?"

"That's the plan, but I've got a bum knee."

Frankly, Canada seemed like a long shot to me. It was already September 19. Most PCT hikers who complete the entire trail do so by October 1. At his pace, no way was he going to get close to Canada this season; snow was already falling, he still had a thousand miles left, and, he was talking to Doc Petersen about his ailing knee.

Then again, the lure of Canada seemed to cast the same spell on some hikers that gold once did on Yukon miners. We wished him well and returned to the car with milkshakes-to-go in our hands.

"Hey, he made sixteen hundred miles," I said to anyone in the Pilot willing to listen, meaning probably just me. "Go back to Georgia, my friend. Relax. Watch college football. Return next summer and finish the trail. Some people are just too crazed for Canada."

Glenn and I arrived home and resumed our regularly scheduled lives. In early October I emailed Garrett, the kid from Colorado who'd emerged out of nowhere to lead us through the snow near the top of Mount San Jacinto.

"Made Canada September 28!" he wrote back.

"Bravo, my friend! Way to go!"

As usual, I dreamed of the PCT each night for weeks after I returned. Every year this happened after coming home from the trail. In every dream, I was needing to hike to some destination on a tightly spun trail and being prevented from doing so by some unforeseen force that wouldn't let me move forward. It was as if, after eight years, the trail had not only worn into my feet, my joints, and my muscles, but into my very *being*.

Another phenomenon I noticed when I'd return from a PCT stretch: The Coast Range and Cascade foothills flanking the Willamette Valley would seem to have shrunk, so etched into my memory had become the towering mountains of the PCT.

On October 20, 2019, I saw an article online from Portland TV station KGW headlined:

Search crews rescue Pacific Crest Trail hiker

Who in the world, I wondered, was hiking the PCT this late in the year?

The story said his name was Robert Campbell, he was fifty, and he was from—*oh my gosh!*—Georgia. I took one look at the photo and knew this was the same guy we'd seen at McDonald's in Yreka a month ago. I called Glenn.

"Incredible," he said. "And where did they find him?"

"Hard to pinpoint exactly, but west of the Three Fingered Jack/Mount Jefferson area," I said. "Got lost. Got wet in the snow and rain. Ran out of food. Search and rescue found him at some semi-developed campground. Guess he spent a night in an outhouse. Pick your poison: freeze to death or spend a night in an outhouse."

"That guy is lucky to be alive," said Glenn.

The kicker: after telling the reporter that he probably would have died had rescuers not arrived when they did—and after crediting God for saving his life—Campbell said he planned to recover for the next couple of days then resume his hike. He hoped to make Canada before Thanksgiving.

For once, I was speechless.

Steve Murdock/City of South Lake Tahoe

Glenn Petersen

Top: The tree-studded track at Echo Summit during the 1968 Olympic Trials. The white dot shows where Fosbury began his high-jump approach. Ironically, the photo was taken from on or near the PCT, which Congress approved as a National Scenic Trail that same year. Above left: Fifty-one years later, in 2019, I set up my tent at that precise spot. Below, left: I knew the location because in 2017, while researching my book on Fosbury, he had shown me. The plaque behind us noted California having given the unique track and field site historical status.

Top: In an otherwise arid stretch, Latopie Lake lay on a shelf just south of Sonora Pass. Above: Glenn wound his way down the yawning switchbacks south of the pass, a section that would take us into the tall timber of Kennedy Canyon.

The Tuolumne River cut through the Yosemite granite with a sense of grandeur.

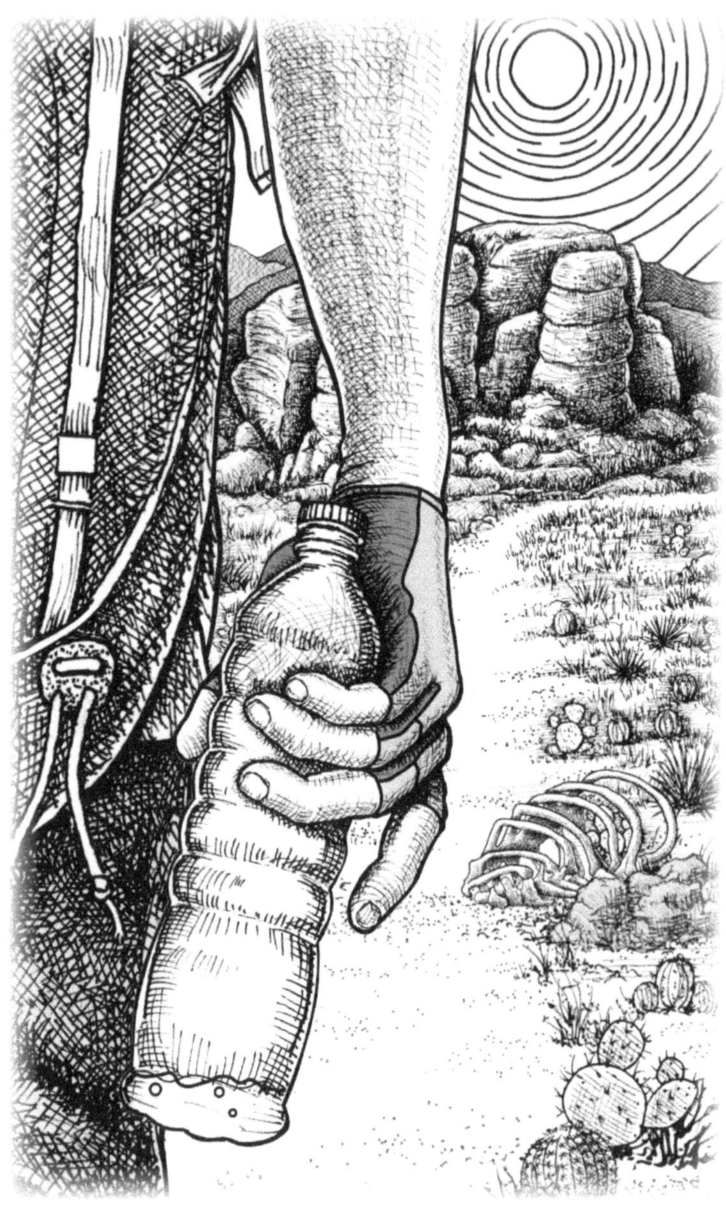

"Do not leave Cajon Pass without enough water to climb 5,000 feet and walk 22 miles," Berger and Smith warned in their book. We took them seriously. Even though our phone apps suggested there was water available at a cache five miles up the desert trail, we didn't assume that was a sure thing.

AGE 67

2021

CALIFORNIA & WASHINGTON

NINTH SUMMER

START: JUNE 14, 2021

HEAT

Delays have dangerous ends.

—Shakespeare (Henry VI, Part I)

As 2020 dawned, we had, for nearly a decade, been bouncing north and south on the Pacific Coast's mountainous spines like human pinballs. It might have appeared as if we were engaged in a pursuit with no purpose, no end game. And yet in the backs of our minds, one word, one place, one goal illuminated the method to our madness: *Canada.*

OK, so the Georgia guy wasn't the only one fixated on reaching the border; we just weren't as obsessed about it as he and some others were.

Once we'd committed to doing the entire trail in 2015, the original plan was to complete it in seven summers. Now, heading into our ninth, we had concocted a slam-bang finish representing unprecedented ambition: in 2020, two segments totaling 682 miles, the equivalent of 1.5 "Oregons." With only a quarter of the PCT left, we planned to finish with a 424-mile leg from Cajon Pass northeast of Los Angeles to Crabtree Meadow near Mount Whitney (late spring 2020) and a 258-mile crescendo from Snoqualmie Pass to the Canadian border (late summer 2020).

As the year unfolded, Glenn and I were both busy as usual. Although he was now working only at an Urgent Care instead of juggling three jobs, Glenn figured he'd spent more than a dozen hours on the Internet figuring out how to secure permits to enter Canada and hike an additional eight miles to Manning Park, where Sally and Ann could pick us up after our August finish. In late February, he was green-lighted by the Canadian government to do so. I had filed for the same permit but was still awaiting approval.

With help from family, I had recently moved my mother, Marolyn, to Eugene so we could better take care of her. Mom had been an adventurer herself, having hiked hundreds of miles of Oregon's high country and, after my father died, been part of an all-female crew on a sailboat plying the Caribbean. Though she was ninety-two, we still sailed together regularly at Fern Ridge Lake west of Eugene.

Mom had followed our PCT journey with enthusiasm, reading my columns, emailing me questions, even buying a map of the trail so she could follow our progress. I'd never forgotten calling her from the PCT in 2011 with an update when we'd reached Oregon's Santiam Pass, where our family had hiked, fished, and camped in my youth.

"Oh, Bob," she said, "your father would be so proud of you."

Now, despite mild concern about a new virus called COVID-19 that had entered the U.S. in January 2020, everything was falling into place for us to finish what we'd begun in 2011. Mom was enjoying her new digs ten minutes from our house, a retirement community on the Willamette River that broadened her social world, bolstered her support system, and allowed her to watch geese as she had so enjoyed doing from a similar perch—an apartment—above the Willamette in Corvallis.

Glenn and I had booked our flight to leave for LA April 24, 2020, to start leg one north from Cajon Pass. And, on March 6, I received my permit to enter Canada.

"Nothing stopping us now!" I texted Glenn.

Except, it turned out, a world pandemic.

FOUR DAYS AFTER I got my permit, the World Health Organization declared COVID-19 to be exactly that: a pandemic. With COVID cases and death tolls rising worldwide, events such as the NCAA and Pac-12 basketball tournaments were canceled. Mom's retirement community closed its restaurant and required people to remain in their rooms, even to eat. And the PCTA encouraged hikers to postpone or cancel their trips.

Some defied the PCTA and hit the trail anyway. Many had planned their hikes for years. Quit jobs. Made plane reservations. Organized resupply setups.

Online battles broke out between those who felt they had a right to hike the PCT and those who felt the bigger concern was safety for all.

"Many people think, 'What better place to be than in the wilderness on a remote mountain trail somewhere?'" said PCTA Director of Communication Scott Wilkinson. "But it's actually a very social undertaking. In a normal year you're hiking in waves of hundreds of other hikers. ... They often camp together. And most hikers don't carry more than a week's worth of food, so they're always going to have to come off the trail to resupply."

With no small amount of regret, Glenn and I postponed our PCT "grand finale" indefinitely.

Meanwhile, I had bigger concerns. Mom was wilting like a non-watered flower. Each day I would phone her from beneath her fourth-floor room so we could talk "face to face" but each day she was slower getting to her balcony. After getting permission to visit her, wearing a mask and gloves, I had Glenn, over the phone, ask her questions about her health.

"Bob, you need to get her to Urgent Care," he later told me.

We did so. Urgent Care recommended we take her to the emergency room, where she was admitted to the hospital, not because of COVID but because of atrial fibrillation. After five days, we brought her home to live with us—and, as it turned out, to die with us. Hospice arrived to help. Twelve days later, just after midnight on May 12, 2020, Mom peacefully passed away as I slept on a couch next to her bed. She had just turned ninety-three, having celebrated her birthday at an upscale restaurant she loved, Sabai, with Sally, me, and her great-granddaughter, Avin.

No service, of course, could be held. But having seen far too many nightly news scenes on TV of people *not* being allowed to be with their hospitalized loved ones when they died because of COVID, I felt blessed that we'd been able to be with her at the end.

GREG'S DEATH five years earlier had put my future into perspective; it reminded me how precious time was. Mom's death put my past in perspective; it reminded me how blessed I was to have had her and my father as parents, in part because of their love for the outdoors that they passed on to me.

In the fall, with COVID restrictions having relaxed, I sailed for a weekend at smoky Cultus Lake, just east of the PCT in Central Oregon, to scatter the ashes of Mom's that had not been cast to the sea at Yachats. It was at our family beach cabin where she had played on the sand since she was nine, and it was at Cultus where she had reveled in the joy of high-lakes camping.

My Cultus weekend was meaningful and miserable, a one-man celebration of an amazing life, but the memorial was marred by a pall of smoke from a wildfire that had roared down the McKenzie River Valley east of Eugene a few days earlier. From the middle of the lake, I couldn't see shore in any direction, a worrisome sensation that only further discombobulated me. Wasn't it enough that I was wearing two masks wet with tears? After I scattered Mom's ashes in the lake she so loved, I had to use my inReach GPS to find my way back to the boat launch and head for home.

That same month, Glenn and I hiked in the Wallowa Mountains, tucked in Oregon's northeast corner, partly to keep in shape and partly to experience a place we had not hiked. On our first night out, we camped at Ice Lake, where I took a photo despite low clouds obscuring the 9,832-foot Matterhorn beyond. Weeks later, I was on a phone call, mindlessly staring at a sketch my then-late-twenties father had drawn that was now framed and hanging on our dining room wall. In that moment, for the first time, I noticed the penciled words he'd written beneath it: "Ice Lake - Wallowas ... W. Welch."

I almost dropped the phone. I suddenly realized, I had stood in the same remote wilderness where my father had stood more than seventy years earlier. Most sons subconsciously spend a lifetime trying to earn the respect of their fathers and I sensed my dad—the guy whose fishing movie ended with the line about him hoping I'd find the same untamed wilderness he had—would be happy to know the wilderness and his son were alive and well.

BY SPRING 2021, COVID having abated and vaccines now in use, Glenn and I finalized plans for what we had hoped to hike in 2020, with one exception. Because of the virus, Canada was not allowing hikers through at Manning Park, so once we reached the border we would have to backtrack thirty-one miles to exit the PCT east at Harts Pass in Washington.

We would do that in August as our grand finale. For now, our bigger concern was the hot, dry desert stretch northeast of LA, starting in June: Cajon Pass to Crabtree Meadow, with a side trip up Mount Whitney.

"Some hikers consider (the climb out of Cajon) the most arduous in southern California," said *The Pacific Crest Trail.*

I asked Geoff for advice. He wrote:

> Leave Cajon Pass as early as possible; don't plan on any water until Wrightwood. Whatever you do, do *not* take the Acorn Trail down to Wrightwood. Be very careful about water planning from Tehachapi to Walker Pass. Don't plan on water at Joshua Tree Springs. It's radioactive. The first crossing at Spanish Needle Creek will be dry (milepost 669). Second crossing will be dry (669.5). But walk up the drainage forty to sixty yards and you will find a leaf spout. Do not plan on water caches being stocked. I carried six to seven liters at times.

"This sounds every bit as tough as the books make it sound," I told him.

"It's beautiful country," said Geoff. "I liked the desert. But it's brutal. Hot.

Steep. Sandy. And hardly any water."

Rob Widmer, who I'd met in 2011 when he and his wife, Barbara, turned around rather than face Devils Peak, had hiked this stretch.* "Watch out for the wind on Tehachapi Pass," he wrote. "One night I couldn't even get my tent secured in the ground."

To better understand this segment, I contacted a hiker-friendly guy in Wrightwood, Luis "Lou" Mena, whose email address I'd found on the PCT's Facebook page. He was invaluable in helping us understand what we were up against in this desert environment—a lot.

Ideally, we would have left earlier in the less-hot time of early spring, but I could not. I had a new book, *Saving My Enemy,* coming out April 27 and my publisher wanted me to commit to six weeks of radio interviews. Thus, Glenn and I had agreed on a June 14 departure, six weeks later than we'd originally planned.

I don't know about Glenn, but, in retrospect, I was whistling in the dark. Not only were we starting late in the year, but in what history would remember as the hottest June in U.S. history. The entire West Coast was sizzling. "The event is unprecedented in its timing, intensity and scope," said Washington State University climate scientist Deepti Singh.

At 1 P.M. June 14, 2021, with the temperature already ninety, Glenn and I made what would prove to be a critical mistake: instead of waiting for the relative cool of morning, we hit the trail at Cajon Pass for an afternoon climb that would take us from 3,000 to 8,250 feet in two days. We chose not to wait until the next morning to start because an afternoon leg would put us ahead of schedule and lessen the chances that we'd have to scramble at the end to make our pickup time. To be blunt, we were shortsighted.

Under the freeway and into the low scrub we hiked. The eight-lane Interstate 15 and heavy winds made me feel as if I were hiking into a giant blow dryer set on high: hot and noisy.

"Do not leave Cajon Pass without enough water to climb 5,000 feet and walk 22 miles," Berger and Smith warned in their book. We took them seriously. Even though our phone apps suggested there was water available at a cache five miles up the desert trail, we didn't assume that was a sure thing. In Oregon and Washington, we rarely took more than two liters of water on a stretch; on this day, we each took *six*—twelve pounds' worth in each pack.

From the get-go, something seemed off with Glenn. On breaks, he'd curl

---

* Rob and his brother Kurt, both Oregon State University graduates like Glenn, were, in 1984, founders of what became the regionally famous Widmer Brothers Brewery in Portland.

up in the shade of the chaparral and go to sleep. He complained of the heat—not his nature. His disposition, I started to realize, mirrored that of opening day 2015, six years before, when our brother-in-law Greg had died while Glenn and I were hiking north from the Columbia River.

Then again, trail history had taught me that a good night's sleep could do wonders to rejuvenate tired bodies. On many occasions, I could remember falling asleep while thinking I couldn't walk another step—and hiking twenty-plus miles the next day. I was hoping that would be the case here.

Amid a sea of desert scrub, we ate, Glenn only sparingly. The warning signs were there, but I rationalized that he just needed rest; we'd been up since 3 A.M. to catch our flight from Portland. At 6 P.M Glenn hit the sack. On a wooden chair near the water cache, I sat in my boxers, popped open an umbrella for shade, and read a book. I was just about to turn in when I saw something unfamiliar in my pack—a small note of encouragement from Sally that melted my heart.

It was far more comforting thinking about her than about how we'd pitched our tents directly above the 700-mile-long San Andreas Fault, catalyst for a number of major earthquakes. Alas, our trip's forthcoming tremor would not be rooted miles below the earth, but in the heat above.

"Hot but healthy," I wrote in a wishful-thinking satellite message to Sally and Ann before turning in.

I then messaged Geoff, who, when he saw the pushpin of our location on the online map I sent him would know *exactly* where we were and what we were facing. "Camping near Swartout Road," I wrote. "90 degrees. Haven't seen another hiker. Will wake at 2 A.M. and night-hike."

"Well done," he wrote back. "Good plan for tomorrow. Sleep well."

COME MORNING, exactly what I hoped would happen *did.* Glenn rebooted. We climbed high out of Lone Pine/Swartout Canyon with good bounce to our steps. The sky transitioned from dark to light blue, tinted with the slightest swath of pink. I reveled in not being part of the thick I-15 traffic we could see heading to and from Las Vegas and marveled at how the locomotives rolling through Cajon Pass looked as if part of a miniature train setup.

Then, boom: In the time it took the toe of my left shoe to ram a shark-fin rock, I was flat on my face to the accompaniment of a loud *"Aaaaargggggghhh!"*

"Bobby, you OK?" Glenn asked.

I got to my knees, then to my feet. "Yeah, only hurt my pride." My falling, it seemed, was beginning to be a *thing.*

On the PCT, I'd come to realize, you could hurt yourself in myriad ways: slipping, tripping, bushwhacking, crossing creeks, climbing rocks, getting blisters, getting stung, getting sunburned, getting water, descending loose-gravel trails, burning yourself on stoves, you name it. One hiker told me he strained his knee while crouching over a cat hole. In 2019, on Washington's Stevens Pass, a German hiker died after being hit by a falling tree.

It was a game, really, of beating the odds. And so we pressed on, hoping to do just that. With seven uphill miles under our belts—the only kind available here—we lunched late morning beneath the shade of a rare stretch of pines. All was good. The vegetation had shifted from chaparral to evergreens; the occasional shade lifted our spirits. As we continued up, however, I noticed Glenn once again laboring. His usual upbeat nature waned. Never chatty, he grew eerily quiet.

About noon, without a word, he tossed his pack aside, laid down in the middle of the trail, rolled to his back, and fell asleep.

"Glenny?" I asked, repeating his question to me earlier. "You OK?"

"Yeah. Just tired."

"Drink some water. How are you *really*?"

"Fine."

"You're not fine. Quit playing John Wayne."

Cognitively, he seemed to be slipping; how much, I wasn't sure. Seemingly in slow motion, he rolled over, sat up, and pulled out his water bottle and took a few swigs.

"Take some more," I said.

He took a few gulps. His long-sleeved shirt—don't get me going about how he insisted on long, dark sleeves and long, dark pants, even on hot days like this—was saturated with sweat, his skin pale. With his gray brimmed hat flipped up in front, he looked like an 1849 miner, older than the sixty-eight he was.

"You OK to go?"

He nodded. We had come about ten miles and had ten to reach that night's destination: Blue Ridge Campground. The plan was to get water in seven miles at a place high above the town of Wrightwood called Guffy Campground, which Glenn had earlier told me "wasn't a sure deal." By now, I'd learned that just because something said "campground" didn't mean you should expect flush toilets, running water, or even campers; sometimes it meant a few beat-up picnic tables and a creek that ran dry months ago.

I looked at my iPhone map. If we struck out at Guffy, it would be another five miles to State Route 2 (Angeles Crest Scenic Byway), where we could hitch a ride down to Wrightwood.

We headed on, me ahead, glancing back now and then to make sure Glenn was still coming. About an hour after we'd resumed hiking—about 2

P.M.—I heard it: "*Aaaaaaaaaaahhhhhhhhhhhh!*"

I turned. Glenn was flailing on the trail. Rattlesnake? Bee? I shed my pack. "What is it? What?"

"Cramp! Oh, ah! My leg. Killing me! *Ah! Ah! Ah!*"

He wriggled in pain.

"What can I do?"

"Nothing. Just … gotta —*Ah! Ah! Ah!*—work it out."

"Glenn, you're the doctor here. What do you need? How can I help you?"

He looked dazed. Here but not here. Barely talking.

"Gotta sleep."

It was about 1 P.M. I looked around. We hadn't seen another hiker since we'd left Cajon Pass the previous day. The PCT herd was hundreds of miles ahead, and stragglers, obviously, weren't braving this heat.

The situation suddenly crystallized for me: Glenn needed to get down to Wrightwood. And the only one who could get him there was me. I felt the unease of responsibility twisted with a twinge of terror.

Heavenly Father … .

I pulled out my iPhone and looked at the map. We were heading west-northwest at about 6,500 feet, just beyond Gobblers Knob. We'd need to climb another 1,700 feet up Wright Mountain just to get to a side trail that zigzagged down the height of two Empire State Buildings—2,312 feet—to the little ski community where Lou lived. The drop came in only 2.1 miles, its 1,101-feet-per-mile slope more than thirty percent steeper than the diabolic southbound escape out of the canyon at Belden, which was perhaps the steepest continual stretch on the PCT.

When I saw, on the map, the name of the connecting trail between the PCT and the town, I mentally gulped: Acorn Trail.

Wasn't that the trail Geoff warned me not to take? How could this be? How could the very trail we needed—our lifeline to water, rest, and perhaps medical attention—be the only trail Geoff had explicitly told me to avoid? Dang. Why hadn't I asked why we shouldn't take it? I needed to talk to Geoff.

"Glenny, I'm gonna walk down the trail and see if I can get some cell coverage. Be right back, OK?"

He nodded. He was on his back, in a sliver of shade, trying to sleep. I walked 100 feet forward. Nothing. Finally, I found two bars, enough to make a call. But Geoff wasn't answering. It was a Tuesday; he was likely cutting hair at the barber shop, which was only five minutes from our house.

I called Sally. "Glenn's showing signs of heat exhaustion and I need to get him to this town, but the trail to get there is one Geoff warned me not to take. I need to know why. His line is busy. Could you zip over to the shop

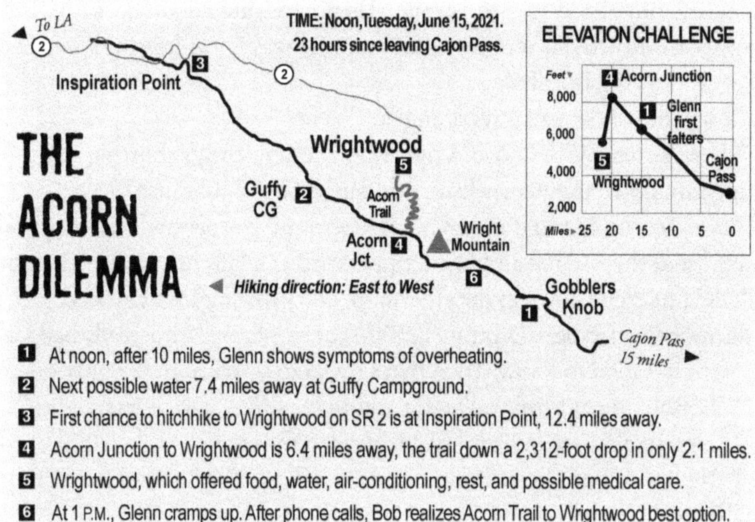

and have Geoff call me?"

"I would but I'm in Albany with Mom and Dad."

"No worries. I'll figure this out. Meanwhile, please pray. And, hey, don't tell Ann yet, OK?"

"Got it."

I returned to Glenn.

"Feel like moving on, soldier?"

"Little more sleep."

I grabbed my inReach satellite device from its front-shoulder strap and messaged Geoff. But with all these trees could I even get a satellite connection?

> We are at MP 360. Guffy 364. Iffy water. Glenn seriously dragging. Heat exhaust? … Acorn a bailout? What's trail like?

When the device warbled, meaning the message had gotten through, I sighed in relief. He wrote back immediately.

> Pretty steep for a mile or so. Then a mellow decent through neighborhood. I don't like "iffy" when it comes to water. I'd take the Acorn Trail.

Geoff's "go" signal for Acorn eased my fears, confirmed my instincts, and, frankly, made me feel not so alone in all this; I would ask him later about why he'd been so adamant that I avoid the trail. For now, I needed to get

Glenn moving. I did so—for a mile. Then he wanted another break. I took the opportunity to call Wrightwood Lou, who was camp-hosting seventy-five miles away at Big Bear Lake.

"Hey, Bob, how you guys doing?"

"Been better. We're above Wrightwood, and Glenny's shutting down. I'm taking him down the Acorn Trail. Is it dangerous? Washouts? What?"

"No, Acorn's a good trail and not dangerous if you're watching what you're doing," said the Marine and former police officer. "It's just steeper than holy hell. PCTers come down in the afternoon, party that night, then head back up in the morning facing a daunting 2,500-foot climb. Bad idea, really bad idea."

"Got it. Good to know. Then that's my plan—Acorn to Wrightwood."

"So, Bob, to confirm: you're not asking for search and rescue, right?"

"Copy that. No search and rescue needed for now."

"OK, call if I can help more. Headin' back to Wrightwood in the morning. Keep in touch."

I updated Sally, then returned to Glenn, who was still asleep.

"Hey, wake up, Crab Net."

One eye opened, then the other.

"We're taking the Acorn Trail to Wrightwood. It's just over two miles to the cutoff"—it was actually three but I lied to keep him hopeful—"then another two miles down." I didn't mention another mile from there to the motel, in a town so small (pop. 4,500) it didn't offer Uber service. "We'll get a motel, water, food, and medical attention if you need it. Sound good?"

He nodded a tepid yes.

I helped him on with his pack, then called the Canyon Creek Inn, a hole-in the-wall motel Geoff recommended, and reserved a room. We started up again, reaching the Acorn Trail Junction at 2:45 P.M. The trip down was like a mini-Fuller Ridge experience. Because the slope of Wright Mountain was almost straight down, I felt as if I could reach out and touch the peaked roofs of the houses below. But it seemed to take forever, partly because of the two dozen switchbacks and partly because Glenn required rest breaks.

We checked in to the Canyon Creek Inn just before 5 P.M., the last mile across town seeming like five.

"Drink, drink, drink," I said to Glenn in our room. "Then take a cold shower. I'm heading to the store. Whataya need?"

"Chocolate … milk … and … V-8," he rasped, his voice like that of an old man's.

"Seriously? Not Gatorade? Electrolyte drinks? Fruit? Salty stuff?"

"Nope."

At the store, I asked if Wrightwood had an Urgent Care.

"Sorry," said the young man working the register. "You'd have to go into Lancaster for that."

"Which is how far?"

"An hour—forty-five minutes without cops."

When I returned, Glenn assured me he didn't need medical attention. He phoned Ann and told her what was going on. He was moving like Tim Conway, the shuffling old man in the old "Carol Burnett" TV show. As I pulled the garbage out of my pack to throw away, Glenn crawled into one of the two double beds.

"Bobby," he said, his voice weak, "I don't know where ... we go from here."

"I do: Mile High Pizza. Pepperoni OK?"

"Sure. But I'm just so tired ... I'm afraid if I get back on the trail ... the same thing's gonna happen ... as happened today." He coughed. His voice was weak. "I thought I was in better shape."

I knew he'd done his prep work. He'd been hiking a 1,500-foot hill west of Corvallis and hitting the treadmill whenever he could, sometimes twice a day, up to two hours at a time.

"This isn't about you being out of shape, Glenn, this is about both of us being stupid. We got greedy, trying to get an extra half-day of hiking when we should have stayed in a motel and left early this morning. Glenny, we hiked 6,500 feet straight up in ninety-degree weather with a hot wind in our face. We're veterans and we made a stupid rookie mistake.

"Actually, we made another mistake: coming so late in the year. And that's a hundred percent on me. It was my book promo stuff that forced us to leave six weeks later than we originally planned, when it would have been cooler."

Glenn never was one to guilt me, even when the opportunity availed itself, and he didn't now.

"I have no confidence," he said. "I'm wondering ... if I can even go on."

"You mean, you think we should call it quits?" I asked. "Like go home?"

"Bobby, I can only speak for myself," he said. "I'm not sure that a night, or even two nights, here is going to recharge me."

Until now, I'd looked upon the Wrightwood detour as little more than a tire change during the Indianapolis 500. I now realized how this experience had not only weakened Glenn physically but shaken him mentally. Beyond our 2015 debacle when we quit after two days, since commiting to hike the entire PCT I had never doubted that we would reach Canada. Now, for the first time, I did.

"Well, we don't have to decide right now," I said. "I'm going to go grab our pizza. Let's talk when I get back."

By the time I'd ordered, walked a few blocks to get fresh fruit at a grocery store, and returned for the pizza, I'd processed everything with fast-forward speed. I felt guilty about my conclusion: I wanted to go on, even if it meant doing so alone. I knew how to follow maps, how to find water, how to rely on others when necessary. I could do this—couldn't I?

From the beginning, we'd agreed that the guy who didn't quit should feel free to continue; that's what I'd done the first year, at Glenn's insistence, after his vertigo attack. But would that be fair to Glenn?

My thinking sloshed back and forth like an angry sea. *In favor of me going it alone:* Precedent. When vertigo had slammed Glenn in 2011, he'd encouraged me to finish alone. And we weren't getting any younger; every year we postponed would make the next year's miles all the harder. *Against me going*: If I went alone and Glenn decided to get back on the trail to catch up, we'd be out of synchronization. And what about 2014, when I'd sprained my ankle in the High Sierra and Glenn had said, *You quit, I quit*?

If only I could be so selfless. I called Sally. Updated her. Asked her if she was good with me going on alone. "If you think it's safe and you think it's the right thing to do, I trust you," she said.

Back at the room, over pizza that Glenn barely touched, I floated my idea to him with the subliminal hope that he would discourage me from going ahead, which would make my decision easy. I wouldn't press on without his blessing. He talked about the heat, having to hike at night, the challenge of finding water, and the lack of other people on the trail to, say, help find water, but his bottom line was: if I needed to go on, I should feel free to do so.

"Maybe ... I could rent a car ... and help resupply you," he said.

His generosity moved me, but that idea wasn't practical. The trail rarely crossed a road. And, meanwhile, Glenny would be baking in a car with nothing to do. How fun would that be?

We fell asleep having no definite plan about where we were going from here. But, inside, I knew what I wanted to do: hike on.

AT 4 A.M. I awoke in a sweat as if the idea of going on alone had been a horrible nightmare. *What was I thinking? How crazy could I be?* Going it alone was a recipe for disaster—and a lesson in how easily our emotions can become the tail wagging the dog of common sense.

"Glenn," I said in the morning. "I rethought this. I'm *not* going on by myself. It'd be the stupidest thing I've done since, well, two days ago, leaving in ninety-degree heat."

"If that's what you want, but don't *not* go on my account."

"Hey, I appreciate that, but I've thought it over. I'm good with heading home. And if Sally knew the full context of hiking alone in this heat, she wouldn't want me out there either."

Quiet. Then, outside, a dog barked. Far away, a leaf blower cranked up.

"Hey, I have an idea," Glenn said, his voice suddenly re-energized. "Look, we both have ten more days off. What if we fly home, rest up for a few days, repack, then drive back down to Lone Pine?"

His mind had obviously been at work since he'd awakened.

"And?"

"And in the relative cool of the high mountains, get the Kennedy-Meadows-to-Crabtree-Meadow stretch done, then summit Whitney again, exit at Whitney Portal, and grab a ride back to Lone Pine. Get in some trail we need to get done, but without this blazing heat."

"Do you really think we'd have time for all that in ten days?" I asked.

"I do."

"And you think you're up for it?"

"I do. It's this heat that got me but the mountains will be cooler."

"Then let's do it," I said. "We can take my truck."

My spirits soared. The Oregon Boys would live to hike another day.

Sally, granddaughter Avin, and Mom celebrating "GG's" 93rd birthday at Eugene's Sabai restaurant two months before she passed away.

Glenn Petersen

Top: Beneath Interstate 15 at Cajon Pass, Glenn looked like we felt: as if in the tube of a giant blow dryer, loud and hot. Above: That night, directly over the San Andreas Fault, I read while in my boxers.

Above: The next day, Glenn's on-trail naps increased in frequency and duration. He was, I later learned, suffering from heat exhaustion, meaning I had to get him down the Acorn Trail to the ski town of Wrightwood. Distance from top to bottom varies from 2.1 to 2.7 miles, depending on your source.

The photo I took of Ice Lake in Oregon's Wallow Mountains in September 2020 while keeping in shape for the PCT. Glenn and I camped on the well-treed peninsula, mid-lake, to the left. Clouds obscured the Matterhorn, which, on a clearer day, would be seen in the upper right of the photo.

The scene my father, Warren, sketched in the late 1940s while attending then-Oregon State College. Note the peninsula, middle left. With a thinner cloud cover than on the day I was there, the white-faced Matterhorn was visible for him to see and draw. I was touched when I realized I'd stood on the same shore as him, though I didn't realize it at the time.

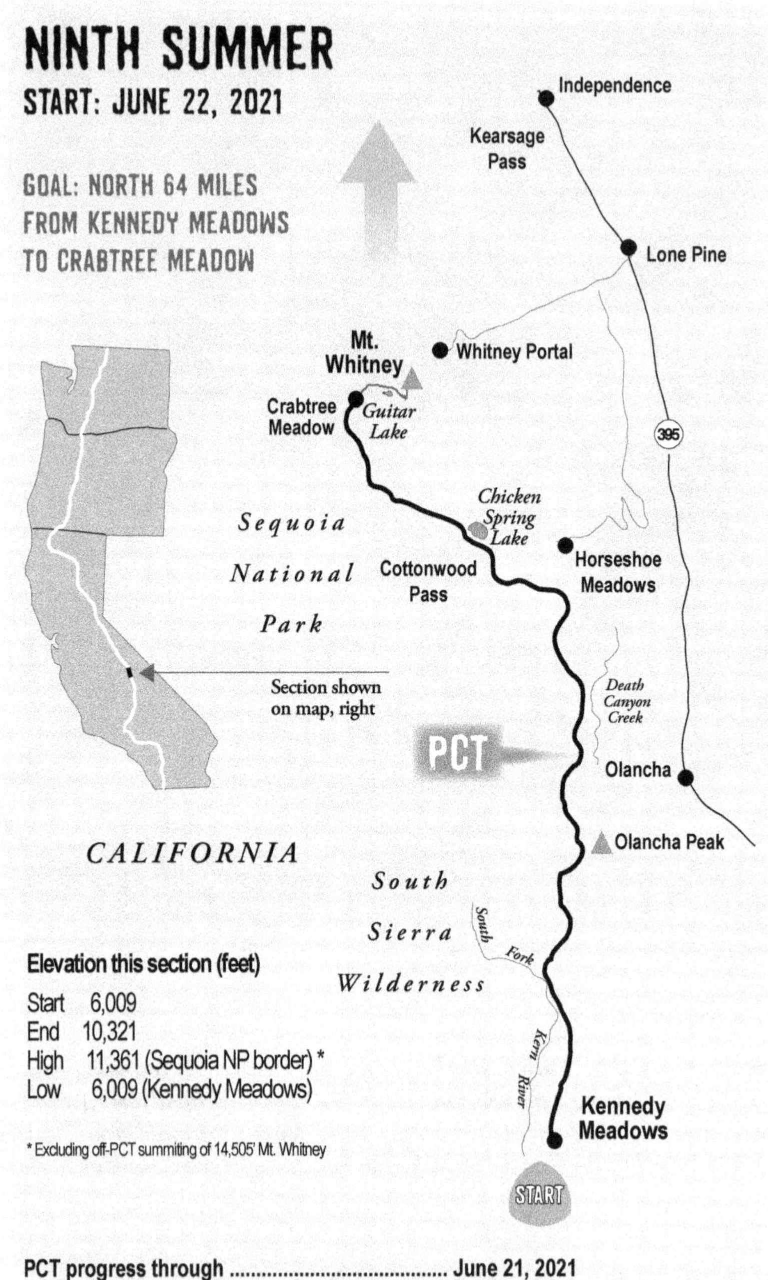

PCT progress through .... June 21, 2021

MEXICO CANADA

76% done / 2,015 miles

24% of PCT left / 635 miles to go

18

RESILIENCY

Failure is just another way to learn how to do something right.

—Marian Wright Edelman

IT WAS A QUICK turnaround. Only five days after arriving home, we piled into my 2015 Toyota pickup and began what would be a thirteen-hour, 686-mile drive to Lone Pine, California—just a few hours north of LA, where we had just been. Lone Pine was not new to us; we had started and ended our 2014 John Muir Trail stretch in the town on California Highway 395, above which the High Sierra towered.

"Did you read about the PCT hiker who died in the heat?" I asked Glenn as we merged onto 395 South near Reno, Nevada.

"Yeah, but I didn't get the details. When and where?"

"Wednesday, the day after we got home from Wrightwood," I said. "Just north of Paradise Valley Cafe, where we had breakfast that Easter morning in 2019."

"Sad."

"Yeah. Hundred degrees where she was. Ran out of water. Helicopter arrived about noon, but she had passed. Glad we're going to be at higher elevations, where it won't be so hot."

Glenn's phone buzzed.

"Sorry to hit you with this, but there's a fire at Whitney Portal," said Ann on speaker phone. "Hikers aren't being allowed to enter or exit there."

Given our wildfire history, why wasn't I surprised about Ann's call?

She read us some updates, which said hikers were still being allowed to summit the mountain from the west—our plan—but couldn't exit to Whitney Portal to the east, also our plan.

"I don't think we'll be able to summit Whitney now," said Glenn.

"Why not?"

"Because with the Portal closed, after getting to the top we would need to return west past Guitar Lake and come back south on the PCT nearly twenty miles and exit Cottonwood Pass to Horseshoe Meadow," he said. "That'll add a day to the trip. And besides the extra time, we're going to have a hard enough time fitting seven days of food in our bear canisters, much less eight."

I shook my head sideways. Whitney, of course, wasn't on the PCT; it was "an elective," not part of the core curriculum we needed to complete our course. But to me, a backpacker driving nearly 1,400 miles round trip and hiking to Crabtree Meadow without summiting Whitney was like a chocolate lover visiting Pennsylvania without touring Hershey.

I didn't say anything to Glenn, sensing he might be playing it safe because of what had happened above Wrightwood. Like the skilled gymnast who falls on a dismount for the first time, I sensed that his having to quit the previous week might have left him doubting himself. *Since I faltered once, I could falter again.* But in my mind, I still envisioned us atop that 14,505-foot mountain, firmly believing that last week was an aberration not likely to repeat—and knowing that we'd hiked longer hauls than this using bear canisters.

After a night in a motel south of Reno, we arrived in Lone Pine late morning. We hit a McDonald's for strawberry shakes—hors d'oeuvres!—before a full lunch at Bonanza, a Mexican place. While searching my pockets to pay for lunch I realized a jolting truth: As only I could do, I'd managed to lose a sandwich bag with $220 in cash at Mickey D's.

"Can I be any more stupid?"

Glenn opened his mouth to speak.

"Don't answer that. Let's go!"

We zipped back to McDonald's. Goodness, if I ever got this trail done, it wasn't going to be *because* of my perseverance but *despite* my propensity for stuff like this. Despite face-planting on the trail. Despite losing tent poles.

"Your lucky day," the manager said. "A woman found it in a booth and turned it in."

I tipped him $20 for being honest, happy she'd left contact info. I would tip her, too, thankful that there were still honest people in the world.

We soon left my pickup in a secure location recommended by Kathleen New, president of Lone Pine's Chamber of Commerce and the designated driver for The Oregon Boys to get to Kennedy Meadows, about ninety minutes southwest of Lone Pine.

Kathleen was awesome. Funny. Rough-hewn. And passionate about Lone Pine (pop. 2,104), where she'd spent most of her life. The irony was that while she reminded me of Aunt Eller from the musical *Oklahoma!*—a frontier woman who you didn't want to mess with—she didn't drive a four-wheel drive pickup but a late-model, battery-powered Prius.

We snaked our way west off Highway 395, climbing to 6,200 feet from Lone Pine's 3,727. We arrived at Kennedy Meadows, paid Kathleen $275 plus tip, thanked her, confirmed our pickup date, June 30, at Horseshoe Meadow, and checked out the general store. It and Grumpy Bears Retreat Restaurant & Tavern a mile away comprised an oasis of food, drink, and community, the only such on-trail place in the 300 miles between Tehachapi/Mojave and Muir Trail Ranch that hikers could gather. And yet the place was off the grid—so remote it ran on generators. It had no power. No land lines. And apparently few people interested in contact with the rest of the world.

IT FELT GOOD to be back on the PCT, as if with each step we were building back our confidence. Though we were starting in the afternoon, which had gotten us in trouble at Cajon Pass, it was fifteen degrees cooler, we were going only three miles, and we would be camping on a river.

Not wanting a Wrightwood repeat, Glenn had purposely designed an easier-than-usual trip, our average day just under thirteen miles, about five miles fewer than normal. He also had shed his long-sleeve/long-pants look for short sleeves and short pants, which I quietly cheered.

"How was the desert north of Wrightwood?" I asked a kid from Berkeley who'd been thru-hiking since early April.

"Hell," he said. "Night hiking. Eighteen mile carries without water. Glad we're done with that nightmare."

And I was glad I had decided against trying that section alone. The forces working against me to finish the PCT, I'd come to realize, weren't just earth, wind, and, fire, but *me*. I needed to stay smart, focused, patient, and committed—so I could overcome the other stuff. So I could get to Canada. So *we* could get to Canada.

Glenn's heat exhaustion had reminded me of something that I'd taken for granted: that one of us couldn't finish this trip alone. Like partners in the three-legged race at the company picnic, we were inextricably linked, and needed to stay all in with each other.

At our camping spot alongside the South Fork Kern River, we sent satellite greetings to Ann and my son Ryan, who share the same June 22 birthday, then breathed deep the freshness of the forest air, which reminded me a bit of Central Oregon, where Sally and I had lived in the late '70s and early '80s.

For NoBos going the distance, Kennedy Meadows was the gateway to heaven, the transition between desert dryness and High Sierra splendor: bearable temperatures; cold, clear, plentiful water; towering Sequoias; and huge granite mountains keeping watch like sentinels.

It was easy to get lost in the beauty, the ever-changing trail, the quiet *click-click-click* of trekking poles and the sound of boots hitting the trail in synchrony with the poles—*left pole, right foot / right pole, left foot*—that is, until, just south of Olancha Peak, where I heard what sounded like the rumble of thunder. Only the sky was clear and this thunder was roaring louder and *louder* and *LOUDER*. I turned around just in time to see a low-flying military jet screaming directly at me, barely above the tree line.

Whhhhoooooooooooooooooooooooooooooooooooossssssssssssssssssshhhhhhhhh!

The forest shook, driving me to my knees. The jet could not have been more than a thousand feet above the timberline. Low-flying planes were an anomaly on the PCT, but apparently because of nearby Edwards Air Force Base, I had found no stretch of the trail with more aeronautical noise than the Sierra Nevada—an irony given that it was also the wildest section.

At Death Canyon Creek, where we stopped Thursday night, June 24, to camp among the gnarled western junipers, I saw a young man soaking his feet in the water. He looked and sounded pretty beaten down. As we talked, he reminded me of the lost soul Krakauer wrote about in *Into the Wild,* Chris McCandless, a young East Coast blue blood who ultimately died in an abandoned bus in the Alaskan outback.

"Want some weed?" he asked while I was filtering water for the next day.

"No, thanks," I said. "So, where you from?"

"Bend, up in Oregon."

"And what do you do for work?"

"Firefighter.

"Good for you; I appreciate folks like you. My first job out of college was in Bend. Sports editor of *The Bulletin.*"

"No way," he said.

"That, my friend, was a long time ago. Seventeen thousand people then; 100,000 now. When we moved, in eighty-three, it was like: *Will the last person to leave please turn off the lights?* So, where you headed?"

"Canada, eventually, but I'm running out of money. Got me a job flippin' burgers at Grumpy's back at K-Meadows for a few weeks. That helped. But gettin' off at Horseshoe Meadow and gonna hitch up to Lone Pine to resupply."

I sensed he was searching for something far more than resupplies. Not supposing that the Good Samaritan vetted the guy he helped, I fished a $20 bill out of my pocket and handed it to him.

"Dinner in Lone Pine's on me. God bless you."

"Hey, appreciate that. Wishin' you and your brother [in-law] well."

Was he running from something? Did he have the proverbial "defining wound" for which the trail might be salve? I didn't know. I suspected that, in some way or the other, many arrived on the PCT with "pre-existing conditions," whether, like New Hampshire Don, their past was divulged in a conversation with a stranger or stowed deep within.

John Muir himself arrived in California at age thirty, having survived a father who thrashed him mercilessly with a switch and an industrial accident that had left him temporarily blind. In the late 1860s, from his home in Wisconsin, he tramped south and west, finally finding his beloved High Sierra—and, for the first time, peace—in what he called "the sanity and joy of wild nature."

Not, of course, that it was a panacea for all, perhaps including the young man at Death Canyon Creek.

AS WE MADE our way north, I found myself awed by the beauty of the trees in general and the bark in particular. So often on the PCT, my eyes defaulted to the far-off beauty, the mountains, basins, canyons, sky, and lakes in the distance. But now I was stopping to take close-up photos of trees: so diverse in color, texture, size, and shape.* Some bark looked like pieces in a jigsaw puzzle; some trees, especially junipers, were gnarled and twisted as if arthritic after surviving for centuries.

What a privilege, I reminded myself, to get to see this stuff. It was like being backstage at a Broadway show, seeing scenes that few got to view. Was it possible to miss this beauty while hiking the trail? Yes, I supposed, especially if you only had eyes for Canada. But, frankly, even at a fast pace with no intent of enjoying the aesthetics, a hiker would *accidentally* see more wonder on the PCT than most, with intent, would see from afar.

Early on our fourth day—Thursday, June 26—I messaged Ann on my inReach and learned that Whitney Portal was still closed by fire. But I wasn't giving up on hopes to summit, even if it meant having to hike an extra twenty miles back south to exit at Horseshoe Meadow. Ann's weather report showed

---

* We'd been on the trail so long, and technology was improving so fast, that I was on my third iPhone since we started the trail in 2011. The quality of my early photos paled in comparison with those taken on my latest device. My father the photographer would have been amazed at the iPhone camera.

little sign of rain for the next few days, which boded well for my idea. So, when Glenn and I arrived for a break at Chicken Spring Lake at 8:30 A.M., I quickly rehearsed my sales pitch and launched it.

"Glenny, according to your schedule, right here is where we should be camping *tonight*," I said. "And yet here we are, in the morning. We're already a day ahead of schedule! And we still have plenty of food left. We can do Whitney and get to the Horseshoe Meadow Trailhead on Monday as planned. And the forecast is favorable: Ann says no rain."

Glenn raised his eyebrows—considering the possibilities, but not sold—then went to the maps to crunch the numbers. Caution was one of his core values; he always defaulted to "convince me." But, to his credit, he was usually willing to *be* convinced.

"Let's do it," he said.

Whitney here we come!

On Friday, June 27, at 8:10 A.M., five days after we started, we reached the cutoff to Whitney at Crabtree Meadow, the point we'd reached hiking south from the Rush Creek Trailhead in 2014 before summiting the mountain.

"My friend, this is a red-letter day," I said. "We've now hiked everything on the PCT from Kennedy Meadows north to Snoqualmie Pass, Washington."

ON THE WAY to Guitar Lake we encountered handfuls of young PCTers returning to the trail after having reached the top of Whitney the day before. The consensus: *Beautiful, clear, but crazy windy.*

"So glad I took my sleeping bag," said a young woman. "Brutally cold."

We arrived at Guitar Lake late morning, meaning for the first time in forever, we had time on our hands. From the west, Whitney needed to be a same-day ascent; because it was all rock and vertical walls, camping was impossible. We planned to leave at 1 A.M. the next day and, as in 2014, catch a sunrise from the summit.

Only one other party was camped at the lake, far from us, at the north end, happily skinny-dipping. I napped, read, and soaked my feet in the lake. I soon heard voices—oddly, children's voices—coming from the meadow between the lake and the steep, rocky, western flank of Whitney. I soon saw a mother and father—fortyish?—and no fewer than seven children, who, I later learned, ranged in age from twelve to one.

The little ones seemed out of context at 11,000 feet in the wilderness, at a location a couple day's hike from the nearest road. My reporter's instincts kicked in. As the children and the father ate near the lake, I engaged the mother in conversation.

"I've been on the trail nine summers," I said, "and only seen a handful of children, none as young as the ones in this bunch. What's your story?"

"We've hiked sixty miles in Sequoia National Park," she said.

"Oh, my gosh."

"And we're going up Whitney now."

"Like *today* now?"

"Like right after lunch. The four oldest kids did the entire John Muir Trail last year."

"That's amazing," I said, quickly calculating the time it might take for them to summit Whitney—perhaps five to seven hours. It's five miles and 3,045 feet in elevation gain—on a trail that can be frighteningly narrow in the day, much less on a cold night with two adults trying to keep track of seven kids. This stretched my to-each-his-own default, but not far enough to question the decision—at least in an obvious fashion.

"So, you're good with coming down in the dark?"

"Oh, yeah," she said. "We have headlamps."

"Well, all right, then. Great chatting. And good luck."

Later, Glenn and I watched as the two parents organized the kids and started up Whitney, the youngest strapped to the father in a front pack.

"Part of me wants to pat them on the back, and part of me wants to contact California Children's Services," I told Glenn. "I mean, Whitney is 14,505 feet, highest point in the Lower Forty-Eight."

Glenn shook his head.

"I know. Assuming they make it, they're going to hit the top just about the time it's getting dark. That's a long steep, narrow trail to be coming down—and there's absolutely no forgiveness. One wrong step . . . ."

"Yeah," I said, "and you heard what everyone was telling us this morning—it's icy cold up there."

We finished our grub and turned in. I was asleep by 7 P.M., Glenn already having been out for an hour. I slept fitfully, worried, I think, about those kids. At 9:34 P.M. I awoke, glancing at my iPhone and thinking I'd heard the voice of a child, then rationalized it must have been part of a dream.

We rose and, headlamps on, hit the trail at 1:12 A.M. Neither of us was particularly chatty this time of morning, but Glenn seemed extra quiet as we made our way up a series of switchbacks so steep we might as well have been climbing an apartment's fire escape—in the dark.

Later, Glenn would tell me he was wondering the same thing I was: Were we going to find a shivering child lying on the side of the trail? Or the entire family hunkered down in some cave? Something worse?

We didn't see another hiker until reaching the crest-divide junction near the top, and then only a few people. When we finally reached the summit at

5:09 A.M., we were the fifth and sixth people on top. I was spent, but thanks to Glenn's suggestion that we take Diamox from day one, not feeling any affects from the elevation.

The wind was whipping at what must have been thirty to forty mph. I was wearing a down jacket, long johns, gloves, stocking cap, and a bandanna around my neck and ears—and was still cold. After taking photos of the sun rising to the east, beyond Death Valley, we hunkered down inside our sleeping bags and, as we sat and viewed the world below, powered up on food and drink for the way down.

"I'll sign us in," I said. "Then let's roll, huh?"

"Sounds good."

I opened the metal box where the sign-in book was stored outside the rock hut and added "The Oregon Boys" to the list. That's when I saw them: the names of the family we'd seen at Guitar Lake—a long list of kids and their ages. Unbelievable. They'd made it!

"Yeah, I heard them come by the lake sometime after 9 P.M.," said a fellow hiker. "A few of the kids were crying."

So, apparently, I *had* heard a child at 9:34 P.M. I was amazed that they'd made it and concerned that the parents had put these kids at considerable risk. As impressive as this feat was, to me it seemed akin to driving too fast on a snowy road: You were fine and looked downright courageous—until one little thing went wrong, then you were endangering yourself and those around you. I know, you could say the same about any hikers on the trail, including Glenn and me. But seven kids, some small, represented a lot of moving parts, a lot of potential for things to go wrong.

Oh, well. Move on, Welch.

WE CAMPED at Crabtree Meadow, celebrating our Whitney summit with a surprise I'd stuck in at the last minute: freeze-dried ice cream sandwiches that sounded better than they tasted.

Just before dark, while filtering the next day's water from Whitney Creek, Glenn looked wistfully at the Crabtree Meadow sign we'd seen two days earlier that signified our linking of our northern portion to the southern portion of the PCT. John Muir passed through here. Every one of the estimated 10,000-plus PCT hikers who made it to Canada passed through here. Now we were here.

The night was cool and clear, a few stars just starting to twinkle. Beyond the marmots and chipmunks, we had the meadow to ourselves.

"Drink it in," Glenn said, "because we'll never be here again."

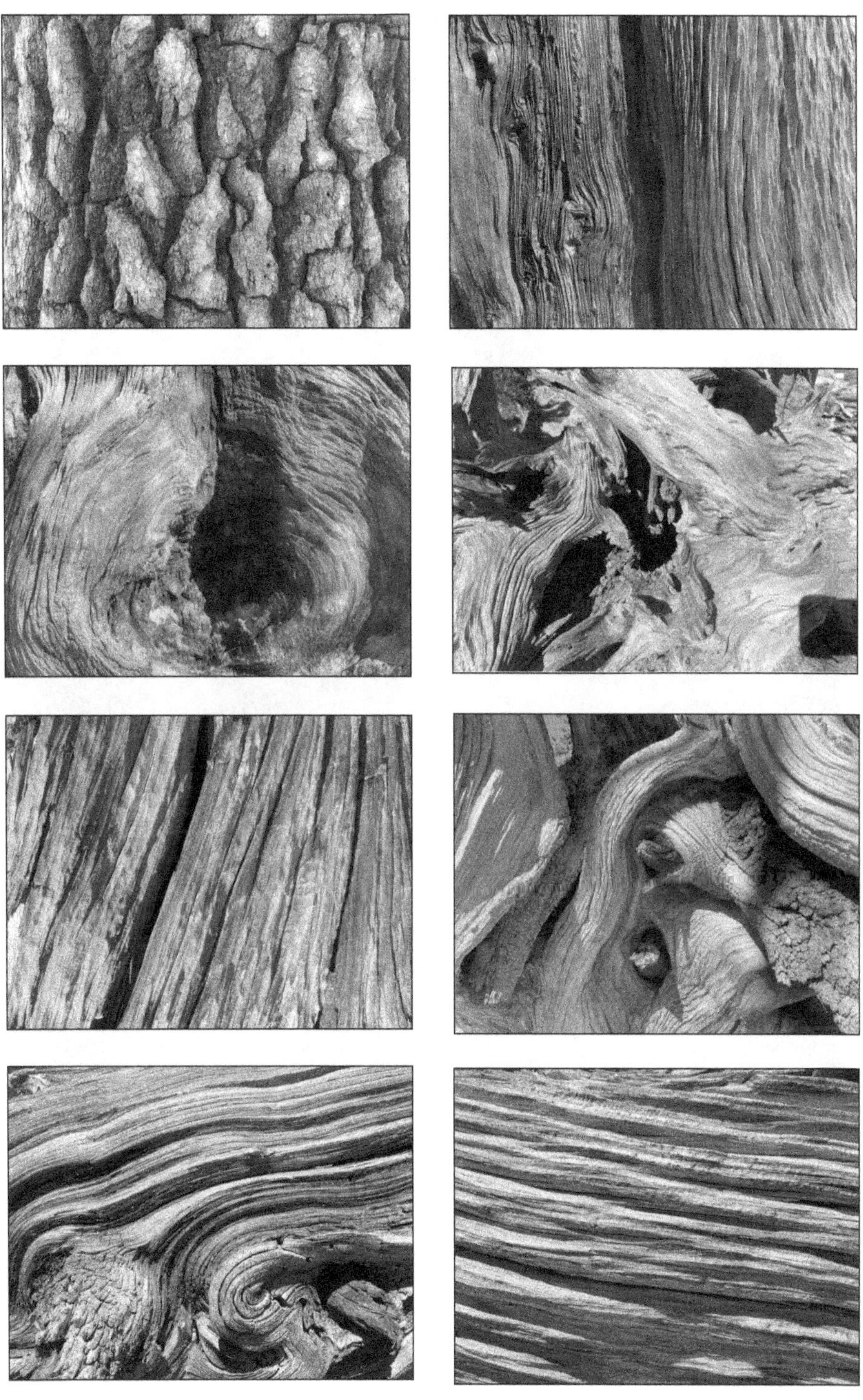

Between Kennedy Meadows and Crabtree Meadow, I was enamored by the beauty of the trees up close. Like snowflakes, no two were alike.

Whitney wasn't a technical climb; a trail went to the top. But at times that trail could be dicey, including this stretch that Glenn was carefully negotiating. The dropoff to the west was nearly 3,000 feet.

Top: The finely chiseled spires of Mount Whitney reached to the sky at first light as a fellow hiker made his way up the 14,505-foot icon. Right: Once on top, I found it beautiful—as it had been in 2014—but I was battered by a biting wind and bitter cold. Beyond me, a near-full moon was still visible to the west—barely.

Glenn Petersen

NINTH SUMMER

START: AUGUST 17, 2021

GOAL: NORTH 191 MILES
FROM SNOQUALMIE PASS
TO RAINY PASS IN WASHINGTON

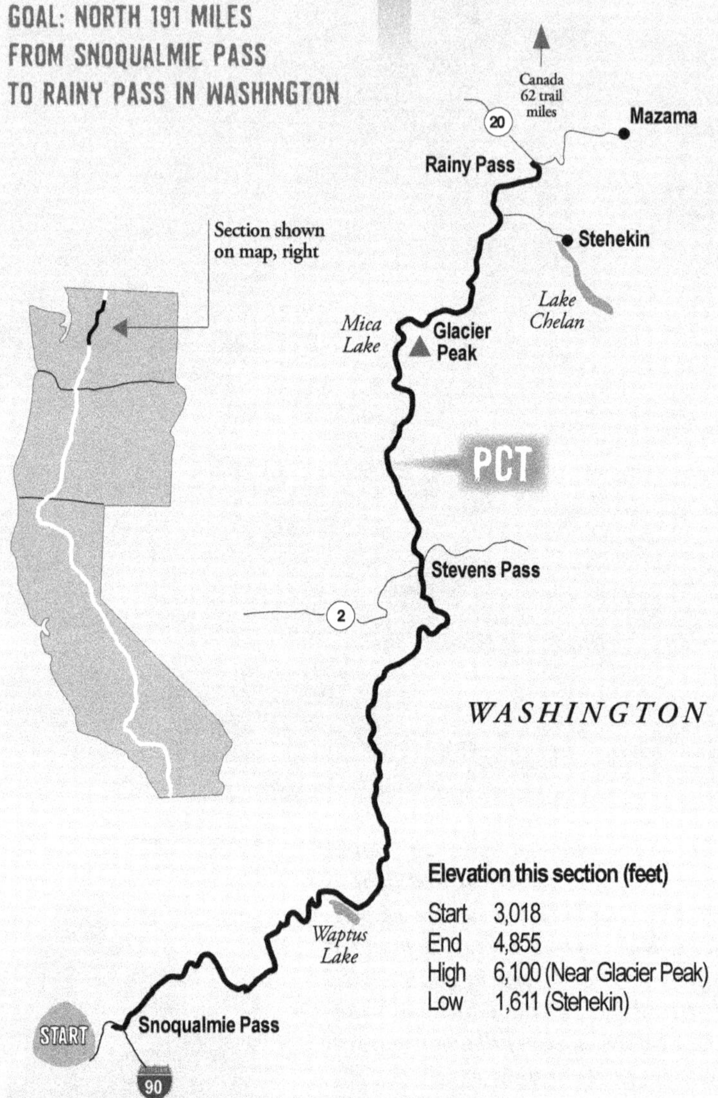

Elevation this section (feet)

Start	3,018
End	4,855
High	6,100 (Near Glacier Peak)
Low	1,611 (Stehekin)

PCT progress through .... August 16, 2021

MEXICO **78% done / 2,079 miles** 22% of PCT left / 571 miles to go CANADA

BLOWDOWN

The woods are lovely, dark, and deep,
But I have promises to keep,
And miles to go before I sleep,
And miles to go before I sleep

—Robert Frost, "Stopping by Woods on a Snowy Evening"

It was August but felt, and looked, like January. After a night at the Summit Inn, where I unveiled the Hot Dog leggings Sally had jokingly gifted me for Christmas and I planned to wear (safely beneath my Columbia detachables), Glenn and I climbed north out of Snoqualmie Pass. This was the place where, in 2016, I'd arrived from the south with the worst blisters of our journey.

In Oregon, a handful of volcanic peaks rise up from land that's otherwise gradual in slope. Washington's North Cascades are different. "While they offer tall peaks, it is the lower mountains that give the North Cascades their fierce, wild character," wrote Berger and Smith in *The Pacific Crest Trail.* Steep. Rocky. Compact. And often under a pall of wet skies, sometimes even in summer.

Bundled in rain gear and gloves—visibility was about a quarter mile—we passed though Huckleberry Saddle at about 5,000 feet. The trail was so high, rocky, narrow, and forlorn that it felt as if we'd hiked back in time, as if we were 19th-century pioneers with no idea what lay ahead of us.

"Caution Stockmen," read a weathered sign. "No Turnouts Next 4 Mi.

Packtrains Cannot Pass."

Over the years, I'd run into a dozen or so horses, a few pack trains, and, of course, the Bud Lite guy near Mount Jefferson. It could be challenging letting horses and mules get by you if you were on a trail chiseled into the side of a steep slope. I always erred on the cautious side, the mountain side, getting as far out of the way of the animals as I could. As a journalist, I'd gone on two elk-hunting trips with a handful of guys on horses and pack mules in Oregon's Blue Mountains: Ninety-five percent of the time, the animals were calm as could be. But when they got spooked, you didn't want to be anywhere near them; they were like four-legged TNT.

Suddenly, a couple of ghostly figures emerged from the mist, heading toward us as if long-lost relatives of Ichabod Crane.

"Hello," I all but yelled above the whoosh of the wind. "Where you headed?"

"Started at Stehekin and going to Bridge of the Gods," the woman said. "Wait, we're from Eugene; we used to read your column! Imagine running into you up here in a sleet storm. I'm Janet [Morrison]. This is Jeff [Kern]. Where you headed?"

I told them our plans to try to finish the PCT. They filled us in on theirs. And we went our separate ways. The next day, we ran into a mother and her early-twenties son; she'd been a nurse in Albany, and when I mentioned my brother-in-law, she said, "Oh, sure I know who Dr. Petersen is." Two days later, I would run into a guy who had gone to the same high school, Crescent Valley in Corvallis, that She Who had attended. That was the PCT, a place that, at times, made you feel you were in the middle of nowhere—and at other times made you feel right at home.

WITH THREE QUARTERS of the trail done, the original plan going into this year, 2021, had been to complete the entire PCT in one sensational summer. We would do 657 miles spread over two ambitious sections: the desert north of LA (Cajon Pass to Kennedy Meadows) in May-June, and Northern Washington (Snoqualmie Pass to Canada) in August.

Now that the desert was left undone because of our Wrightwood hiccup, we had resigned ourselves to a new plan: doing just the second part in August 2021, then finishing the desert section—and the entire trail—the following year, in May-June 2022, meaning Kennedy Meadows would be our finish line.

However, the more we thought about *not* ending in Canada, the more we chafed against the idea. It seemed anticlimactic *not* to finish at the border. So we decided to only go to Rainy Pass in 2021 and finish the whole enchilada at the Canadian border in August 2022—after getting the desert done north of LA in late spring 2022. With only sixty-two miles left, the finish would be like a pro golfer having to only tap in a six-incher to win a tourney.

But we couldn't get ahead of ourselves; we still had nearly 600 miles to go and Washington was deceptively tough. "Beauty and the beast," my friend Geoff called it. "You'll love it. But you have to earn every step you take."

Lakes. Streams. Mountains. Trees without end. But also, just past Waptus Lake, more blowdown than I'd ever seen. On day four, Thursday, August 19, I counted forty-three logs across the trail in a mile-long swath along Spinola Creek. At one jam-up, sixteen downed trees were piled in a jumble, as if a recent storm had ripped through the area and no trail crew had attempted to re-cut a path.

It was exhausting. Normally, Glenn and I averaged about two miles per hour, but on this section, it was far less than one. Over, under, and around the downed timber we struggled.

I tried to lighten the mood with humor, belting out—with my best Johnny Cash twang—"I fought the logs, and the ... logs won, I fought the logs, and the ... logs won."

The challenge would be hard enough for a thirty-something hiker carrying a twenty-five-pound pack. But Glenn and I were both nearly seventy and each carrying thirty-five-pound packs. It was a darned-if-you do/darned-if-you-don't situation. If I took off my pack to crawl—army-man style—under a log, I wasted time and energy. If I didn't take off my pack I faced, at best, having to stand up with all that weight on my aging knees, one of which had been surgically repaired, or, at worst, finding myself wedged beneath a downed tree like a giant rubber doorstop.

Senior Hiker Trapped Under
Fallen Tree, Eats Hand to Survive

By the time we broke for lunch, I'd ripped my left arm on a snag, bloodied my right knee, and nearly castrated myself on a knot.

What's more, flies and mosquitoes had emerged with gumption and gusto. Unlike many of my PCT compadres, I hadn't been terribly bothered by mosquitoes since our first year, at Freye Lake, which put me in the minority. In the PCT Survey, hikers list mosquitoes as their biggest "issue," ahead of runners-up "smoke/fire," "heat," "wind," "cold," and "snow." But now, in northern Washington, annoying insects were adding insult to literal injury, the biting horseflies the worst of the bunch.

And then there was this little matter: I couldn't taste any of my trail food or smell the subtle fragrance of the forest. After getting COVID in October 2020, I hadn't tasted or smelled anything in ten months. This *wasn't* the fun part, but I reminded myself that better times, and smoother trails, lay ahead.

THE NEXT DAY, I was on the type of trail I call a "dinosaur's neck"—steep dropoffs on both sides but not as narrow on top as a knife's edge—when I planted my foot to make a sharp turn and it happened: the nylon fabric of my right shoe ripped away from the sole, leaving my foot all but exposed. Glenn was ahead of me, far from shouting distance. I pulled over, undid the duct tape I'd wrapped around the shafts of my trekking poles for such emergencies, and taped my shoe. (Odell Lake's Mike Jones, the fishing guide who'd patched me up in 2011, would have been proud of my wrap job.)

That night we camped on the peninsula of cozy Glacier Lake, nestled beneath Surprise Mountain, which Glenn would find aptly named. I fell asleep to the soothing sound of a distant hoot owl. At 3:33 A.M. I bolted upright when hearing a rustling in Glenn's tent.

"What is it, Petersen?"

"Mouse! Chewed its way into my tent!"

I laughed at his surprise and went back to sleep while he somehow cajoled the intruder to exit.

Two hours later, we were pumped to be nearing Stevens Pass Ski Area on this Saturday morning, August 21. Not only were our packs light because we hardly had any food—I had nothing left but a few Cinnamon Bears—but we would be picking up resupply boxes.

Resupplying sounded simple, but was not. As our navigator, Glenn had to deal with an array of questions in setting up our refueling schedule: First, how many breakfasts, lunches, and dinners would we need to have sent to each stop? Was the resupply stop on the trail or far from it? If we needed a lift to it, what options were available for getting there? Shuttles? Buses? Would the place be open when we were coming through? Did they accept only U.S. Postal Service packages? UPS? Both? How much did it cost to pick up a box? Could you pay with a card? Cash? Either?

"You saw my note about having to show identification to get your box, right?" said Glenn.

"Argh! I left my driver's license at home. I *did* see your note. I just forgot my ID." Then, to lighten the moment: "Extra weight, you know."

Glenn laughed. He seldom panicked—OK, other than the wild search through his pack for our permit at Yosemite National Park. And he could, when circumstances changed, quickly improvise. Then again, so could I at times—raised, as it were, by a father who solved the problem of getting his heavy movie camera into the high lakes by building a two-ended aluminum wheelbarrow—a bicycle wheel in the middle—that he pushed from the back and his buddy, Gene, pulled from the front.

All of which is to say I had an idea. I called Sally—*yikes, I had only five percent battery left*—and asked her if she could take a photo of my driver's license and send it to me.

"At the very least," I told Glenn, "maybe the people handling the resupply boxes will give me an 'e' for effort—and hand me my food. If they don't, I'll have to hitch fifteen miles into Skykomish to buy food and hitch back, costing us at least an afternoon and throwing our whole schedule hopelessly off. Hey, brother-in-law, aren't you glad I'm your PCT hiking pal?"

Glenn smiled. But there would be more. Once at Stevens Pass, I discovered my iPhone battery was down to three percent and my backup was already dead. If my phone died, I couldn't show anyone the photo to prove the resupply box was mine.

The room at the ski area with our resupply boxes wouldn't open for fifteen minutes, so I found an outside outlet and plugged in my iPhone. A message I'd never seen before popped up: "Liquid Detected in Lightning Connector. Disconnect to allow the connector to dry. This may take several hours."

What? Several hours? How could this be happening? What was liquid doing in my lightning connector, whatever that was? And why was my phone crashing at such a critical moment?

I grabbed a backup cord, plugged it in, and felt the blessed "good vibration." *Whew.*

Later, when I was next in line at the resupply room, my nerves tightened. *Please, please, please.*

"Name?"

"Bob Welch."

"Like the Fleetwood Mac guy?" said the thirty-something guy who obviously knew a little about seventies music.

"Yeah," I said, laughing in hopes of building a relational bond that might survive anything—say, me forgetting my license.

He smiled, then went down a list, found my name, and crossed it off. He turned to a few stacks of boxes, took one, and handed it to me.

"Don't you want to see some I.D.?" I asked.

"Naw."

"Sure? I've got it—sort of."

"Naw, you're good."

It was like going to the doctor and feeling a bit disappointed that you no longer felt sick. I thanked him, high-fived Glenny, then found a picnic table and started repacking my Catalyst with the fresh supplies: food, headlamp batteries, and the important stuff, toilet paper.

"I'm Bob, of The Oregon Boys," I said to a young woman with a pierced nose who was wearing a green down coat and mustard-colored stocking cap. She was repacking at a nearby table.

"Aurora Bee," she said. "Where from?"

"Eugene, Oregon. You?"

"Southeast Alaska."

"Southeast Alaska! Hey, my son helped film and edit a movie that was filmed in Southeast Alaska—on an island across from Ketchikan. About a Native American high school basketball team that—

"Metlakatla, right?"

"Yeah, but how did you know?"

"I've seen it. *Alaskan Nets,* right? Just came out."

"Yes!"

"It's beautiful. I'm a photographer myself. Loved it!"

I immediately called Ryan and said, "I ran into a fan of yours on the PCT. Here, I'll put her on—but don't talk too long, my battery is charging." (Ah, the eye-rolling pain of having a doting father … .)

She and Ryan talked for a few minutes. Glenn and I loaded up our packs, looked around to make sure we hadn't forgotten anything, and headed north across U.S. 2.

DARK CLOUDS rumbled in the next day, Sunday, August 22, the forty-fifth wedding anniversary for Sally and me. Glenn and I put in nineteen miles and, as rain started falling, made camp, appropriately, at Sally Ann Lake.

"Happy anniversary to you and Sally," said Glenn. "From Ann and I."

"Thanks. Pretty much how I'd dreamed of spending it: inside a sleeping bag into which I just spilled half a bag of Cheetos, while it's pouring outside, 300 miles away from Sally, but only three feet from *you.*"

By morning, we couldn't see the lake a hundred feet away. The rain was not letting up.

"Decision time," said Glenn. "It's nineteen miles back to Stevens Pass. Going north, there's no off-ramp until our destination: Rainy Pass, a hundred miles away. Turn back or go ahead?"

"Go ahead," I said without hesitation. "But first, let's go back to sleep and see if the rain goes away."

"Great idea."

We moved out midmorning as the sun finally burst through—*thank you, God!*—and the marmots whistled their approval from their homes in the rocks. We hiked above *Sound of Music* slopes, through scalloped basins, and along velvety meadows abutting the White Chuck River. Beautiful country. We passed three bear hunters. Near Lake Janus, we hiked for a while with a NoBo, Crispy, a surfboard-maker from Southern California who'd lost a pole along the way.

By now, the line stuck in my head was from Crosby, Stills & Nash's song, "Wooden Ships:"

> Say can I have some of your purple berries?
> *Yes, I've been eating them for six or seven weeks now*
> *Haven't got sick once*
> Probably keep us both alive

That's not because I sensed we were on the verge of nuclear war, which the 1969 song is about, but because purple huckleberries were now lining the trail in abundance. I learned to scoop them on the run, the purple treasures as delicious as they were plentiful.

THE NEXT MORNING, Tuesday, August 24, on the lower reaches of Glacier Peak, we opened the day with a bundle of unforeseen challenges that made the PCT seem less like trail than obstacle course.

The first was perhaps the most diabolical twenty feet of the PCT I'd ever faced: up and down on the side of a forty-degree slope, over logs, under brush—all on a trail that then disappeared into a rock-bottom creek. It was like trying to navigate through the crawl space of your house during a flood—with a thirty-five-pound pack on your back.

At Kennedy Creek, the water was pounding hard, easily the most dangerous water crossing of this trip. The only way across was on a twenty-five-foot-long, two-foot-thick log. I imagined the Young Ones tiptoeing across in ten seconds, but I wasn't a Young One. I was an Old Guy with a duct-taped right shoe and a left shoe whose sole was threatening to give way, too.

I unfastened my ULA Catalyst so if I fell into the raging torrent below, the pack wouldn't pin me to the bottom like an anchor. I wrapped my legs around the log as if I were riding a horse. I then shinnied across it in five minutes that seemed like five hours, maybe six inches at a time. Later, Glenn did likewise.

I hadn't gone far when my left shoe blew apart.* Because my shoes were soaked, duct tape wouldn't work. At Pumice Creek, after we filtered water, Glenn took a look.

---

* I loved Altra shoes, but made a note to myself: Find a sturdier model for our next trip. Great fit; poor wear and tear.

"Got an idea," he said, and pulled out two strips of Velcro. He wrapped both of my shoes in a protective wrap that squeezed the sole and nylon together.

"Thanks," I said. "Feels great."

Beyond Pumice Creek, I scrambled up a steep pitch with a do-or-die dropoff to my left, about 100 feet above the rushing water. Ahead, I spotted a SoBo heading my way. The trail was narrow and there was no room to pass so, to my right—the "inside" of the trail—I backed into a clump of low-hanging branches to let the guy get by.

"Thanks, mate," he said.

Once he passed, the spring from the bent-back limbs nudged me back on the trail more forcefully than I expected. My left foot slipped off the trail, then my right. And, just like that, both legs were dangling over the edge, my fingers digging into a trail lip no thicker than a wrapping-paper tube, my toes dug into the side of the dropoff.

"Aahhhhhhh!"

As if on automatic pilot, I got a toehold into the cliff with my left shoe—or what was left of it—and swung my right leg up on the trail, almost like doing the old straddle high-jump style. The Aussie who'd passed me grabbed my pack and pulled me away from the edge, the maneuver allowing me to leverage myself safely back on the trail, albeit flat on my face. I rolled over, away from the edge, and exhaled.

"Wow, you OK, mate?" he asked.

What could I say? It wasn't even 8 A.M. and I had resorted to wearing Velcro-fortified shoes, shinnied a twenty-five-foot log over a pounding creek, and cheated death on a ledge.

"Yeah, fine. Great! Just another day on the PCT!"

LATER THAT afternoon, we came to a lake so beautiful, so deeply turquoise, so alone in the middle of nowhere that it mesmerized me. Near Glacier Peak, on a shelf below Fire Mountain, Mica Lake looked like a painting.* We had it to ourselves. I took off my pack, snacked, took photos, and just soaked in the liquid beauty, feeling honored to have briefly shared this time and place.

That night, we camped alone on Mica Lake's outlet stream, above which I availed myself of a rare treasure in these wilds: a wooden potty perched atop a knoll. No sides. No roof. Just a flip-lid wooden toilet that afforded its user a breathtaking view of mountains beyond mountains—perfect if, say,

---

* See back cover of book.

the moment required deep contemplation. Naturally, I had to experience it because I knew I would never go to the bathroom in a more beautiful setting.

We were just north of Glacier Peak, in a place so remote that it was unfathomable why the Forest Service felt such an apparatus was necessary. But this mystery paled compared to the one I would encounter the next morning.

We had zigzagged down glacier-fed Milk Creek, whose silty waters pounded fast and hard beneath a bridge that took us to the creek's east side. Amid eye-level foliage, we then did the same going up: nearly two dozen oxygen-sucking switchbacks. The payoff was a spectacular view of 10,541-foot Glacier Peak and the strangest find of my PCT experience thus far: a two-foot by six-foot strip of rusted metal—maybe a quarter-inch thick—punched every few inches with a three-inch-diameter hole, forty-two holes in all.

"What in the world is this?" I asked Glenn.

"No clue."

The only non-wooden objects we'd come across in our nine years had been rusted cables from logging operations, an occasional culvert that allowed a creek to go under the trail, and concrete footings from old fire towers.

"The only way you could get this up here would be by mule—maybe. But we're—what?—sixty miles from a trailhead. What's it for?"

Glenn shook his head. I checked my altimeter: 5,750 feet.

"Is it a casing from a jet engine that fell off a plane?" I asked.

I shrugged, snapped a photo, then dug out some beef jerky, licorice, and a Milky Way bar for a midmorning snack, leaving the mystery unsolved.

IT RAINED most of Thursday night, August 26, and early Friday morning, the day we hoped to go into one of the PCT's more iconic stops, Stehekin, on the upper reaches of fjord-like Lake Chelan. It was reachable only by the PCT from the north, boats from the south, and float planes.

I awoke in the dark, about 4 A.M., feeling slightly claustrophobic. Suddenly, the tent started spinning. I knew immediately what I was experiencing: vertigo—the same malady Glenn experienced a decade earlier near Mount Hood. Light nausea washed over me. This was not good. We were 123 miles north of real civilization, Stevens Pass, and thirty-two miles south of Rainy Pass, where Sally and Ann were to pick us up in two days—in the middle of nowhere.

I'd had vertigo only one other time in my life, in 1977, on the day Elvis Presley died, though I wasn't gleaning any cosmic meaning about the juxtaposition of the two occurrences.

I rolled to my right side; bad idea. Things got worse. I rolled onto my left. Better. When the spinning stopped, I unzipped my entryway netting and started breathing fresh air. That helped even more.

An hour later, I was hiking at normal speed, as if nothing had happened. I'd somehow avoided what could have been a serious setback, only telling Glenn about it when I was out of the woods—literally—and in the sprawling metropolis of Stehekin (pop. 95).

At High Pass Bridge over the Stehekin River, we accepted a ride into "town" from a guy and his little boy in an all-terrain vehicle, joined by three other hikers, including a doctor from North Dakota.

Unable to taste, I nevertheless enjoyed (sort of) a hot and well-textured fish and chips lunch. Emotionally, I could still get pumped to eat and even enjoy the process—to an extent. Imagining what something tasted like wasn't the real deal, but it was better than nothing.

I sat on the restaurant's outdoor deck and enjoyed the beauty. Lake Chelan was fascinating. It snaked fifty miles in length with an average width of a mile, plunging to depths of 1,419 feet, 340 feet *below* sea level at one point.

After a shuttle stop at the delightful Stehekin Pastry Company for doughnuts and a turkey and cheese sandwich that I would eat, but not taste, for dinner, we returned to the PCT.

"That's too bad about your loss of taste and smell," said Glenn. "When we get back, I'll send you some 'smell training' info that might help you. It's not quack stuff."

"Appreciate that. In the meantime, you know how ripe your tent smells about now, eleven days into a trip when you haven't showered once?"

"Yep."

"I don't smell any of that. So I've got that going for me, which is nice."

"Hey," said Glenn, "I do my best to keep my tent, sleeping bag, and body clean at all times. And I brush my teeth every third day, whether I need to or not."

WE PLANNED to spend the night at Bridge Creek Campground in North Cascades National Park. Knowing we were just a day away from our Rainy Pass pickup, my spirits felt young. My hearing? Not so much.

"A sign back there said this camp is supposed to have a circus bear," I heard Glenn say as we started popping up our tents.

Huh. Who knew? I found it odd, but I'd read somewhere about Ringling Bros. having folded. Maybe these were transplants—bears that had once performed before crowds but had been rescued and set free to roam national parks. I briefly imagined a bear balancing a beach ball on its nose.

"Interesting," I said. "A circus bear."

"What did you think I said?" asked Glenn.

"That this campground is supposed to have a circus bear."

Glenn fell to his knees, bent over in unbridled laughter.

"What?" I asked.

"The sign said this campground is supposed to have *assertive* bears."

Let the record show that on this, the last night of our two 2021 trips, we were not bothered by either type: assertive or circus.

Heading north out of Snoqualmie Pass, the weather suggested winter, not summer. It was rainy, with visibility not more than a few hundred yards, even though it was summer: August 17.

Glenn Petersen

The blowdown on the stretch north of Waptus Lake was the worst I'd seen on the PCT, at times forcing us—in this case, me—to take off packs and crawl under logs.

Glenn Petersen

Top: Shinnying across Kennedy Creek. (Note hot dog leggings.) Above: the strangest object I saw on the PCT—a two-foot by six-foot, hole-pocked strip of rusted metal in a remote area near Glacier Peak. Left: At Stevens Pass, I met a young hiker, Aurora Bee, who had seen Alaskan Nets, *a just-released movie that my son, Ryan, photographed and edited. What were the chances?*

Above: The Stehekin River pounded beneath High Bridge as we left the trail and headed for Stehekin on Lake Chelan. Right: Nature has a heart, exemplified by a rock I found measuring about six inches by six inches.

Top: A suspension bridge over Bridge Creek. Left: Huckleberries were thick in this stretch. Above: Lake Chelan, home of Stehekin.

I gently treaded water in reverent awe, looking at the endless sky, listening to the subtle splash of feet and hands, and imagining this same lake only months from now, frozen beneath snow as if I'd never been here.

AGE 68

2022

CALIFORNIA'S MOJAVE DESERT & NORTHERN WASHINGTON

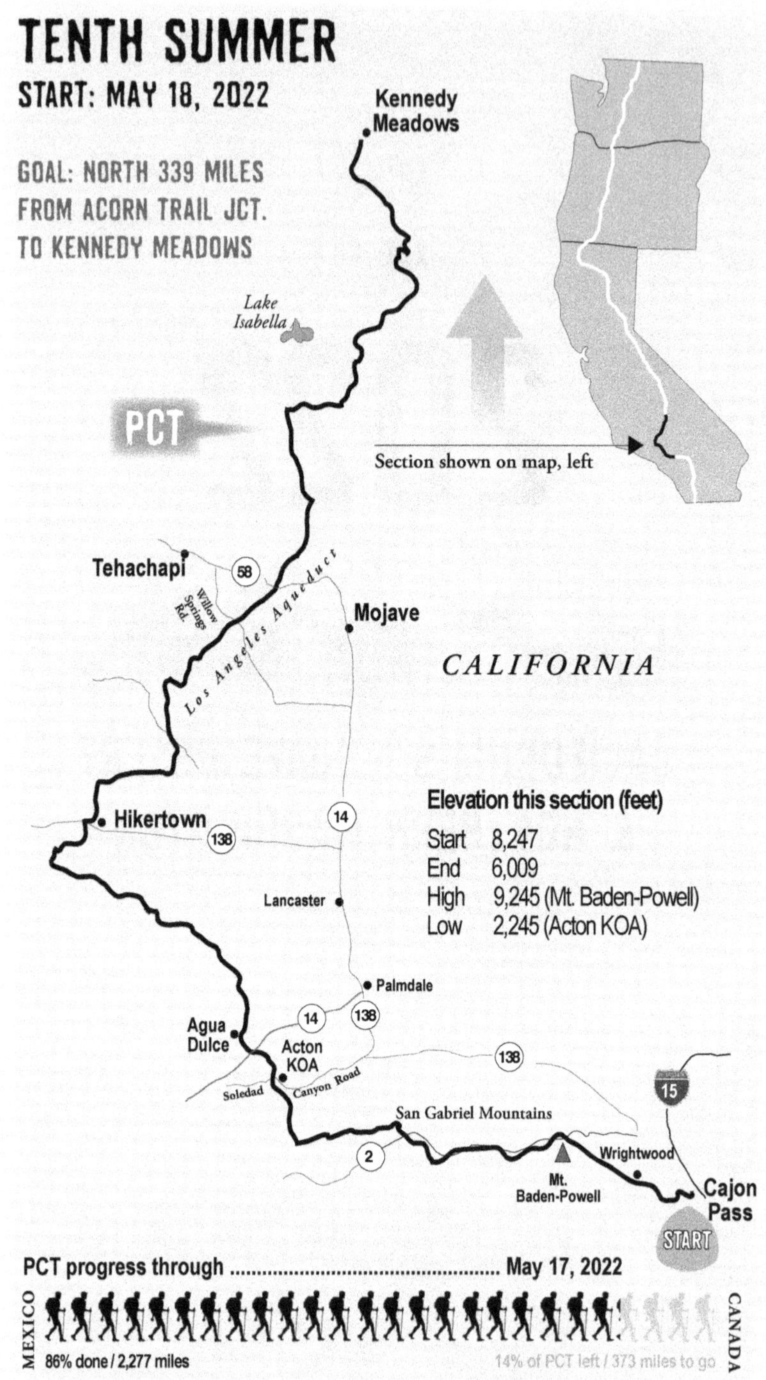
TENTH SUMMER
START: MAY 18, 2022
GOAL: NORTH 339 MILES
FROM ACORN TRAIL JCT.
TO KENNEDY MEADOWS
Kennedy Meadows
Lake Isabella
PCT
Section shown on map, left
Tehachapi
58
Willow Springs Rd.
Los Angeles Aqueduct
Mojave
CALIFORNIA
Elevation this section (feet)
Start 8,247
End 6,009
High 9,245 (Mt. Baden-Powell)
Low 2,245 (Acton KOA)
14
Hikertown
138
Lancaster
Palmdale
14
138
Agua Dulce
Acton KOA
138
Soledad
Canyon Road
15
San Gabriel Mountains
2
Wrightwood
Mt. Baden-Powell
Cajon Pass
START
PCT progress through .... May 17, 2022
MEXICO
CANADA
86% done / 2,277 miles
14% of PCT left / 373 miles to go

MOJAVE

You must do the thing you cannot do.

—Eleanor Roosevelt

A WEEK AFTER we were finally able to hold my mother's memorial service—two years, to the day, of her death in 2020 during, but not of, COVID—Glenn and I returned to try and complete the desert section north of LA: twenty-one days and 339 miles to Kennedy Meadows.

A pandemic thwarted us in 2020, heat in 2021. Now at age sixty-eight, I was hoping the third time would be the charm. *This one's for you, Mom.*

After touching down at John Wayne International, Glenn and I took an Uber to BJ's Restaurant & Brewhouse in Rancho Cucamonga to meet Wrightwood Lou for lunch. His generosity was saving us all sorts of time, money, and energy. Instead of us having to take a bus to Wrightwood and slog 2,500 feet up the Acorn Trail—a hard day's effort just to get to the starting line—Lou took us in his four-wheel-drive pickup to within a quarter mile of the Acorn cutoff on a seldom-used truck trail.

We would be starting 7,500 feet up in the San Gabriel Mountains that fans and TV viewers often see from the Rose Bowl on New Year's Day.

En route, Lou filled us in on "local knowledge," the most important of which involved a warning to be cautious while on the short walks along State Route 2. "Hug the shoulder because it's a narrow, twisting road," he said. "Thing gets beat to hell all winter and they're just now clearing it of snow, trees, limbs, and rocks."

Lou dropped us off, posed for a quick photo, and left.

"Time out?" I said to Glenn.

He looked at his Casio.

"Two-thirty-five."

"Copy that."

We were confident but not cocky. We were going nearly a month earlier in the year than in our failed 2021 attempt, so it would be less hot. The region wasn't experiencing record temperatures as it was the year before. We weren't going straight uphill for twenty-two miles. And we planned to walk only one mile the first day.

Instead, because it was only eighty degrees and we felt so good, we went nine. After last year's disastrous start, it was a massive boost to our confidence.

The next day, Thursday, May 19, we summited 9,407-foot Mount Baden Powell, named for the founder of the Boy Scouts. We were joined on the top by a tall hiker from the Czech Republic, Evo, to whom I tried to explain my 2017 trip to his country.*

As we moved north, I soon realized that we were "running with the bulls" on this section. The previous year, leaving in mid-June, we'd been far behind the PCT herd. This was different. A huge number of thru-hikers who'd left the Mexican border in late March and early April were on the same stretch we were, going the same direction. Two nights later, ours were the third and fourth tents erected in a flat, wide campground. But by the time I fell asleep, we were surrounded by more than two dozen such tents—and lots of headlamps and chatter.

At this point, about 400 miles north of the Mexican border, the thru-hikers were experienced enough to know what they were doing but not so cocky that they eschewed "talking shop." In fact, I would soon find this section the friendliest group of PCT hikers I'd encountered in my ten summers on the trail.

We met Vulture, a young man from Austria; Marie, a hard-hiking young woman from Germany; and Orange Crush, a Hood River, Oregon, man as pleasant as anyone we'd met on the trail. Glenn and I shared a lunch with OC at a rustic campground picnic table on day two. He was writing a blog as he worked his way north, and I later saw that he'd made mention of us—a definite sign of The Oregon Boys having arrived:

---

* In 2022, the year we were hiking this stretch, four in ten PCT hikers were from somewhere outside the U.S., a number that had only increased since we began hiking the trail in 2011.

> Met several Oregon hikers ... special call out to two great guys from the Eugene and Albany areas, Bob and Glenn. Really enjoyed our conversations along the hike. Hope to see more of them. They are brothers-in-law who have been working on the PCT for 11 yrs. Need to get a picture of them.

Orange Crush was enjoyable because he was as interested in our journey as we were in his, not often the case in PCT exchanges. He worked in doctor-patient software, so he and Glenn had that in common.

Friday, as we hiked a short section along SR 2, we saw a white Ford Explorer parked in a pullout. *Could it be? Yes, it was! Trail Magic!* For days, word on the trail's bamboo telegraph—greatly enhanced by iPhones and text messaging—was about Janelle, the gracious SR 2 Trail Magic Woman. As a journalist who'd taught interviewing at the University of Oregon, I naturally asked folks such as her questions.

"Was that awesome or what?" a young hiker later said to me. "Breakfast casserole!"

"Yeah," I said. "She's from Burbank, a ninety-minute drive from here, and got up at 4 A.M. to have it ready for us."

"No way. Why does she do it?

"Did part of the Appalachian Trail years ago with her daughter and was the beneficiary of some East Coast Trail Magic, so wanted to pay it forward back home."

Janelle's generosity was particularly meaningful to me because, having lost my taste and smell because of COVID and only recently gotten it back, this was the first time I'd tasted—actually *tasted*—any Trail Magic in nearly three years. After "going without" for fifteen months, about eighty percent of my taste and smell had returned.

"You see that guy from Austria?" I asked Glenn as we walked along the narrow shoulder of SR 2 before the trail resumed. "Name was Vulture."

"Think so."

"Said he was the last hiker to eat at the Cajon Pass McDonald's because it was closing for remodeling."

"Oh, gosh, there's going to be some unhappy hikers when they arrive *there*," said Glenn. "That's the first restaurant on the trail since—where?—Big Bear?"

"Sounds right. That's like seventy miles without having a—wait, what's that noise?"

A low rumble was growing louder.

"Plane, I think," said Glenn.

"Getting louder. You sure it's not a—."

Suddenly, around a bend, a Caltrans snowplow bore down at us, diesel belching. Its blade was down, apparently scraping rocks off the road. We had about two feet between the road's stripe and a wall of granite.

"G'back!" I yelled to Glenn, backing up to the granite wall and angling my arms over my head me as if getting a full-body scan at an airport TSA. Glenn did likewise. The truck roared by, the noise hammering my eardrums, the wind whipping my hat off my head, the diesel reminding me of the downside of being able to smell again. When it was gone, Glenn shook his head.

"Did he even see us?"

"I dunno," I said. "That was close."

We walked on, dazed. Like: *What just happened?*

"That was like from some Stephen King novel," I said later, once we'd gotten back on the trail. "I imagine a scene in which, at day's end, a handful of snowplow drivers are comparing notches in their dashboards."

> "How'd ya do today, Smitty?"one guy asks.
>
> "Got skunked,"' the dude answers. "Had a coupla old farts in the crosshairs but missed 'em."
>
> "One of 'em have a crab net on the back of his pack?'"
>
> "Yup."
>
> "Too bad. Them is double-pointers."

AS WE HEADED through the San Gabriels, the view below astounded me: low clouds had crept up the valleys as if frothy surf from the Pacific Ocean breaking on an Oregon Coast headland.

"Half-expect to a see a whale surface," I told Glenn.

Gradually, the trail transitioned from dirt to hard-packed white sand. The foliage shifted from pine to chaparral, sprinkled with Joshua trees and their needle-sharp spines that reminded me of the crown worn by the King Julien XIII animal in the animated movie *Madagascar* I'd seen with the grandkids.

Splashes of wildflowers flanked the trail. We were transitioning from forest to the western fringes of the Mojave Desert, even if one feature remained constant: mountains. So much for the stereotype I'd held that deserts were flat.

On Saturday, May 21, near Mount Gleason, I came across a twenty-something male hiker straight from an *Outdoor* magazine cover: Tall. Chiseled body. Picket-fence teeth. Well-groomed beard. Athletic. He was the kind of hiker who made me look at my sagging gut and think of that 1968 Mary Hopkins song: *Those were the days, my friend, we thought they'd never end . . . .*

To the side of the trail, he was arranging sticks to spell something out:

"420." Over the years, I'd seen the 500-, 1,000- and 2,000-mile markers but I was curious about why he'd chosen 420.

"The street address of my old house," he told me after I asked.

"And you're from?"

"Beaverton, Oregon, outside Portland."

"Hey, I'm from Eugene. Where'd you play college basketball?"

"How'd you know I played hoops?"

"Come on, man. You're—what?—six-two, long arms, athletic."

He laughed. "University of New Hampshire. And six-four."

"Interesting. I have a client in LA whose son plays for Boston U."

"What's his name?"

"CJ Jones."

"Are you kidding me? CJ is the best friend of one of my friends, Anthony Lucenti; I think they went to the same high school in LA, Loyola. I know CJ Jones. And so you do work for his dad?"

"No, his mom, Kirsten Jones. Helping her write a book about navigating the youth sports culture.* She was a Division I volleyball player at William & Mary."

"Crazy. So, you are—?"

"Bob of The Oregon Boys."

"Sequoia," he said, and offered a fist bump.

"Well, Sequoia, maybe we'll see you up the trail," I said with false bravado, as if I could keep pace with a guy who took one step to my three.

THE NEXT AFTERNOON—Sunday, May 22—Glenn and I were pumped to be hitting the Acton KOA, where we would get a shower, a campsite, and, if lucky, a pizza. We'd heard that even though the KOA was in the middle of nowhere, some pizza place ten miles away delivered. But when we arrived on a hill high above it, we were confused about which of two trails would get us there.

As Glenn consulted his iPhone map, Marie, the German girl, confidently swept by us—"goot afternoon," she said—and, without hesitation, headed left, away from the KOA. Glenn and I looked at each other and, without a word, followed her down a twisting trail that went far west, away from the campground, then back east, right to it.

"I've got a new trail-name for her," said Glenn. "Lois Lane. She hikes like Supergirl."

The KOA was a blend of ramshackle motor homes and trailers where

---

* *Raising Empowered Athletes,* since published by Triumph Books.

some people apparently lived, and where hikers recharged their batteries—literally and figuratively. (At such stops, any electrical outlet would be jammed with thirsty electronic devices, bellying up to the bar for rejuvenation.) A few trees provided slivers of shade. A pool awaited those brave enough to test its weirdly green waters. And a general store flanked a swath of withered-grass-turned-dirt on which half a dozen tents had popped up.

Outside the store, a PCT hiker was sitting against the building, sketching. It was, I realized, the kid from Beaverton.

"Hey, Sequoia," I said.

"Hey, good to see you again. It's Bob, right—of the Oregon Boys."

"Yep. You're obviously no dumb jock. And you're an artist to boot. Nice work!"

He laughed. I smiled and walked inside to get oriented to the camp.

"With you in a minute," said a woman with a phone in one hand and a small poodle in the other.

She set the dog down so she could take a drag on a cigarette she had parked in an ash tray, then turned her attention to the phone. "Yeah," she said. "Sheriff's here. Squad cars. Couple ambulances. They'll get it under control. OK, bye-bye." She hung up.

"What's going on?" I asked.

"Oh, just a little *situation*," she said, then swiveled her head away from me and blew out cigarette smoke. I paid for a couple of tent spots. As the woman rustled up shower towels for us, she gave me the camp's lay of the land.

"Oh, and tomorrow morning you'll probably wake to the sound of lions."

"Lions? Like African lions? Like the MGM lion?"

"Yeah, there's an animal sanctuary just beyond us."

I nodded. "OK, uh, thanks for the heads up."

In the parking lot, I noticed a handful of law-enforcement vehicles and ambulances, lights flashing. In the air, a police helicopter arrived and began circling the KOA. Around us, radios squawked. A hiker was headed my way.

"Hey," I said, extending a fist. "I'm Bob of The Oregon Boys."

"Crazy Neighbor," said the young man, completing the pump, which allowed me to notice an interesting tattoo on the inside of his arm.

"Any idea what's going on?" I asked.

"Heard a guy took his girlfriend hostage in one of the trailers and is threatening to shoot anyone who tries to come for him. Camp is in lockdown."

Welcome back to civilization—easy on the "civil."

A few minutes later, I told Glenn what I'd learned.

"Now, wait, who told you this?" he asked

"Crazy Neighbor. The hiker with the devil tattoo on his arm."

I nodded toward the guy. Glenn glanced at him, then gave me a look that said, *I might have doubted your story but if Crazy Neighbor, the guy with the devil tattoo on his arm, told you that, well, then, OK.*

Word spread that the park was, indeed, in lockdown, which might have been a first for PCT hikers in the fifty-four years of the trail's existence. Law enforcement officers stood at the entrance/exit; more were arriving. I wanted a shower, but the facility was on the other side of the park, where the "situation" was unfolding; nobody wants to take a shower in the middle of a SWAT team incident, right? So, Glenn and I set up our tents, drank great amounts of pop, and ate great amounts of potato chips.

I walked over to a sheriff deputy who didn't look busy. "Excuse me," I said. "I appreciate the seriousness of what's going on here—honest, I do. And I appreciate you guys being here. But if I were to order a pizza for delivery, would it get through? I mean, could it be handed across 'the line?'"

He smiled. "The situation is now under control. I think you'd be safe to place your pizza order."

"Copy that. And, hey, you're welcome to a few pieces if you're still around."

"Thanks," he said, smiling. "I'd better pass."

Later, when all the law enforcement types had left and the pizza arrived, I whispered to Sequoia, "We're having an Oregon Reunion at the picnic table between Glenn's tent and mine. You're invited."

"I'm there, baby! Thanks!"

The three of us tackled a thick pepperoni and sausage pizza that sent my taste buds soaring with glee. We talked about basketball, Oregon, and how we had worried about all sorts of threats on the PCT but not a law-enforcement lockdown. Finally, I could see Glenn's eyelids struggling to stay open.

It was way past his bedtime: 7:15 P.M.

GIVEN THE craziness of the Acton scene, it shouldn't have surprised me that the next morning I awakened to the sound of mating lions. You didn't have to be a zoological "Dr. Ruth" to figure out what was happening in the animal sanctuary at 4 A.M. Suffice it to say these were really happy lions.

"I'm gonna miss this place," I said to Glenny as we left, headlamps on, lions still serenading us. "It's the PCT version of the Lassen Inn."

We took a tunnel beneath the Antelope Valley Freeway (State Route 14) that connects Los Angeles to the Mojave Desert, a football field in length. We worked our way through the rust-colored Vasquez Rocks, packed together in diagonal shafts so visually intriguing that they've been a favorite for backdrops to an array of TV shows, including "Star Trek," and movies.

In the small town of Agua Dulce, we stopped for great Mexican food at a sit-down restaurant, then, in the rising afternoon heat, faced climbing 2,000 feet up toward Martindale Canyon. No shade. No downhill. No water. And lots of heat.

"No section of the PCT strikes as much dread in the hearts of hikers as this one," wrote Shawnte Salabert in *Hiking the Pacific Crest Trail: Southern California.*

I didn't want to hike a single step that afternoon. What helped me get through this stretch was being able to listen on my phone to a first-round Oregon State 6A Playoff baseball game in which my seventeen-year-old grandson was playing. His team, Sheldon High of Eugene, upset tenth-ranked Central Catholic on the road, 10-3. I'm guessing my "Go Cade! Go Irish!" yell at game's end was the first such echo across Martindale Canyon.

The heat was taking its toll, so we decided to try our first bona fide night hike, leaving at 1 A.M. after getting only a few hours of sleep. It began well and ended horribly. I enjoyed the relative cool of the night. But at first light, after about ten miles, we were dead to the bone. We popped up our tents for a couple of hours of sleep. I awoke grumpy and stayed grumpy for two days.

On Wednesday, May 25—we'd now been at it a week—we had to go nearly a mile off trail to find water. It was in the Sawmill Mountains, a place called Upper Shake, a once-developed campground that time had forgotten. It had a dirt road to it from the east, but looked as if it hadn't been visited in decades: Picnic tables with half their wood planks rotted or missing. Signs too time-distressed to read. And the coup de grâce: an outhouse that was apparently last used by Cro-Magnon Man.

Glenn had a morbid fascination with Upper Shake. I did not. While I tried to sleep in the unrelenting heat, he battled through some tall weeds to a dry creek bed and somehow found us spring water. I was grateful for the discovery, but Upper Shake gave me the creeps, like a place where you might discover partially buried remains. We were the only ones around.

Not even Glenn could sleep in this heat—and when he couldn't sleep, you knew it was hot. It was also windy; when I crawled out of my unstaked tent it rolled away like a tumbleweed.

"Let's get out of this place," I said.

Just like on Monday, I was saved by the ball—baseball. In a place where you wouldn't have bet on cell coverage, I somehow picked up Sheldon's quarterfinal game against third-ranked McMinnville High for our last few miles, which immediately took my mind off the heat and my hurts. By the time we'd made camp—next to two German men in their fifties who'd asked if they could join us—the game was in its final innings. We were up 4-3 and Cade, who seldom pitched, was brought in to relieve during a bases-loaded jam. My anxiety level spiked. But he got the last seven outs—each one an excruciating wait as I followed on the phone—to preserve the win.

"Yeah, baby!" I said, fist pumping Glenn. "All right! Semifinals Friday!"

I apologized to our two hiker friends for my hollering, explaining that the game was to me what World Cup soccer might be to them—and my grandson's team had won.

"Herzlichen Glückwunsch!"

I furrowed my brow.

"Congratulations!"

"Oh, thank you."

The two had saved vacation time for years to attempt the PCT, each going it alone. But when they met at a train station in San Diego and learned they were both heading for the trail, they joined forces.

I saw one of them two days later at a place called Hikertown, a gathering spot for hikers that's done in a miniature Old West town motif, though with more passion than thought. It was part stage set, part carnival, and part Oregon Country Fair, a hippy festival just west of my hometown of Eugene.

Said one sign: "If you're a guy and just need to pee, go find a tree."

Hikertown offered just about everything hikers might want, including a washboard for scrubbing dirty, smelly clothes. And what it lacked in shade it made up for in hospitality; the handful of people in charge worked their tails off to get hikers what they needed.

You want a pop? "Find a guy named Bob; he'll get you a pop." You want a shower? "Find a guy named Bob; he'll get you a towel." You want a haircut? "Sorry, Bob doesn't do haircuts. But someone else will give you one."

It was noon. When a cab showed up to ferry folks to a restaurant down Highway 138 for lunch, Glenn and I jumped at that chance, happily reuniting with Orange Crush, whom we hadn't seen in more than a week. Over sandwiches and chips, we agreed to meet up for a special night hike; a throng of Young Ones was heading out at 7 P.M.

Back at Hikertown, we found small bits of shade in which to rest during the afternoon. At one point, the owner of the house set me up with some soft pads in a shed. I slept a little, listened to Sheldon fall 4-3 to West Linn in the semifinals—*argh!*—and chowed down on a huge taco wrap dinner that the Hikertown people cooked for us. Finally, it was time to go, even though we hadn't been able to find Crush.

At 6 P.M., the Young Ones—Crush, maybe fifty, had dubbed them "The Yoga-lennials"—gathered for yoga to warm up. Glenn and I passed.

"My yoga," I told Glenn, "is getting up from a sitting position."

Top: Low clouds in the valleys of the San Gabriel Mountains reminded me of a foamy Pacific Ocean in Oregon. Above: On State Route 2, I was surprised by joy—in the form of breakfast casserole made by a Trail Angel named Janelle.

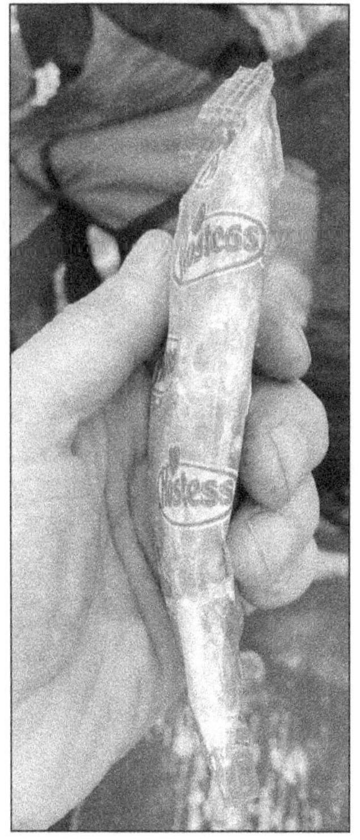

Top: Red Dragon, a spirited SoBo from Sitka, Alaska. Above: Police helicopter hovered over Acton KOA during the hostage situation. Right: Hostess Twinkies, I discovered, didn't travel well—not that I could resist packing them.

Top: Glenn hiking through the Vasquez Rocks, where many TV shows and movies have been filmed. Right: Sequoia, who somehow found the energy to sketch scenes along the way (above), enjoying pizza at the impromptu "Oregon PCT Reunion" at the Acton KOA.

Top: Hikertown was a little strange but the hospitality warm, the pop cold, and the vibe upbeat. Left: Orange Crush, who we'd met about a week earlier in the San Gabriels, checked his phone outside the schoolhouse.

TENTH SUMMER

START: MAY 27, 2022

GOAL: NORTH 193 MILES FROM HIKERTOWN TO KENNEDY MEADOWS

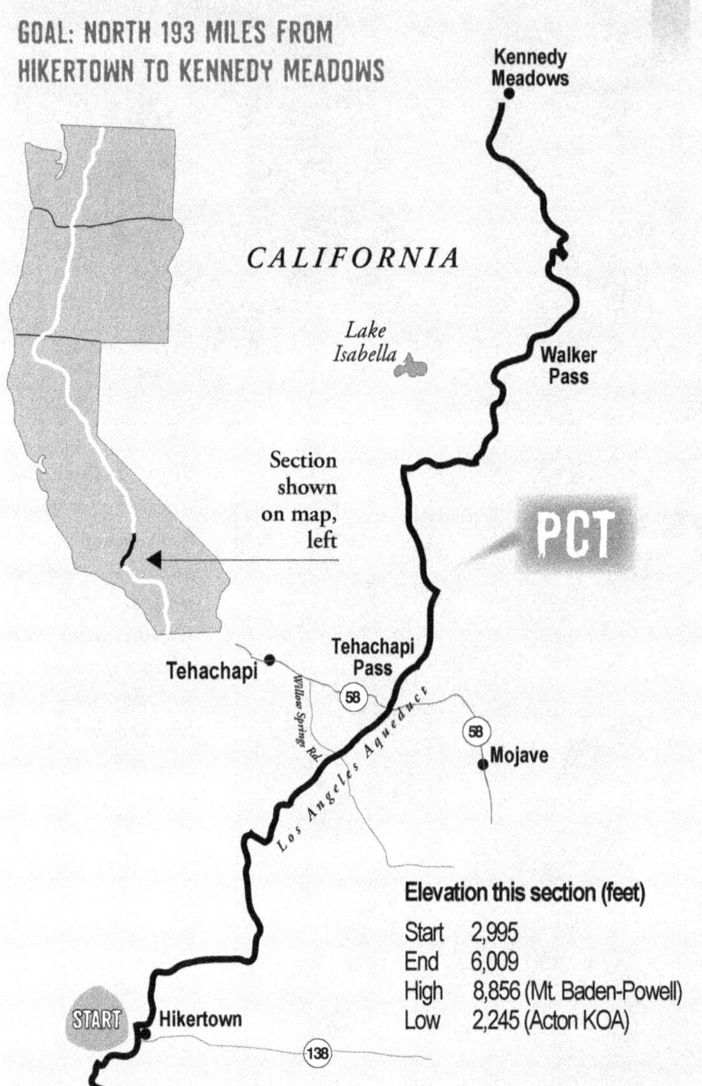

PCT progress through .... May 26, 2022

MEXICO — CANADA

92% done / 2,431 miles

8% of PCT left / 219 miles to go

21

WIND

You find out the strength of the wind by trying to walk against it, not by lying down.

—C.S. Lewis

THAT NIGHT'S HIKE was unlike any I had experienced on the PCT: part 10K fun run, part '60s hippie scene, and—in the end—part dream-turned-nightmare. As the sun slipped low on the western horizon, the Young Ones adorned themselves in glow-in-the-dark bracelets, necklaces, and the like. Though Glenn and I didn't "light up," the night felt special.

We left just before the others, paralleling the fifty-foot-wide waters of the Los Angeles Aqueduct, which were making their way from the Owens Valley northeast of Lone Pine to more than thirty-five million people and five million acres of farmland in Southern California.*

Our lead was brief; soon the pack caught us. By the time we'd taken a hard

* Though when built it was considered the largest engineering feat since Roman times and responsible for Southern California's early 1900s boom, the project had left a trail of tears. The victims included Owens Valley farmers, duped of their water by LA's water chief, William Mulholland; those who filed lawsuits and were met by Mulholland's rifle-slinging "detectives"; and 400 people who died in 1928 after an arch support dam Mulholland had built gave way and twelve billion gallons of water rushed south, leaving bodies and debris up to 200 miles away. Earlier that day, when workers had reported a crack in the dam with brown water seeping through, Mulholland had told them to "caulk it and go home."

left north, where the water now flowed underground in a twelve-foot-wide buried pipe on whose top we now trod, the Glowing Ones had passed us as if part of some psychedelic cattle drive. Soon the pipe itself disappeared underground, though the trail apparently still followed it for miles upon miles.

Into the night, and out of Antelope Valley, we pressed deeper into the darkness on an arrow-straight road rising into the foothills. The air was sticky hot. Because of the influence of the Glowing Ones' speed, we were hiking at what seemed like record pace. As if an engine running too hot for too long, my body soon began faltering, followed by my mind, or whatever was left of it.

By midnight, what had started out as a dreamlike scene—all the glow-in-the-dark colors amid the sepia-toned desert—had turned dark, period. I heard the *whoosh … whoosh … whoosh* of a giant wind turbine, the first of more than a thousand we would pass in the next week. Now, the darkness was stabbed by the not-so-friendly pulsing red lights atop the turbines, as if ambulances at an accident—which was appropriate, I suppose, because after seventeen miles of hiking at breakneck pace, I was an accident waiting to happen.

Finally, in my hazy weariness I heard Glenn mention something about Cottonwood Creek Bridge and water. Next thing I knew I was mindlessly setting up my tent in the dark, and slipping into my bag. I felt like I had in high school during a twenty-four-hour fundraising relay run, half asleep, half awake, *all* weary.

After what seemed like fifteen minutes, I felt the warmth of sunlight on my tent; it was the first time in eleven years I'd been awakened by such. It was 7 A.M. I'd gotten perhaps three hours of sleep, the effort not helped by a leaky air mattress. Hot Dog was right; nobody fixes a flat air mattress, including me. Even if I had a lake or stream to find the leak with bubbles, I didn't have the energy to unscrew the cap on the tube of glue for the patch.

So, what was the antidote to all this? Hiking, of course. We ate, watered-up, and hit the trail, the entire day spent like a couple of tiny ants winding our way through the never-ending Tehachapi Pass Wind Farm, where blades—some almost the length of football fields—slowly whirled. *Whoosh … whoosh … whoosh.* The propellers spun. The wind screamed.* The hours lagged.

I know hikers, Geoff Tyson among them, who found the desert enchanting. Not me. It wasn't without beauty; early in the morning, I'd sometimes be high up and look to the east and see the sun paint far-off hills in muted gold. But if the vistas could be beautiful, the trail itself often felt less friend than foe.

---

* With chicken-or-egg thinking, some PCT hikers insist the Tehachapi area wouldn't be so windy if someone would just turn off all the giant fans.

That night—Saturday, May 28—between Tylerhorse Canyon and Gamble Spring Canyon, we had to dry-camp high on a lofty perch where we spent nearly an hour trying to find a semi-flat spot even remotely protected from the incessant wind. Rob Widmer, a PCT friend who'd warned me about these killer winds, had not exaggerated in the least. The gusts raked the mountainside at what must have been thirty to fifty miles per hour. Putting up tents was foolhardy, if not impossible. We didn't even try.

Ever the Eagle Scout, Glenn used light rope to secure his mattress and bag to a foot-thick snag that paralleled his setup; he wasn't going to be blown away. Of course, he was asleep in minutes. Me? While in my not-secured-to-a-snag bag, I went to reposition my blowup pillow and the wind whipped it away. I last saw it pinwheeling off a cliff toward Edwards Air Force Base, fifty miles east. I got perhaps two hours of actual sleep.

THE NEXT DAY—our twelfth since we'd started—the wind did not let up. I felt like a ping-pong ball in a Powerball drawing. After three days of this, the wind was no longer a natural force but a living, breathing, enemy—dragon's breath out to defeat me, not only buffeting my body but numbing my brain.

At Willow Springs Road it was decision time. At this fork in the road, many hikers hitchhiked northwest to Tehachapi (pop. 12,939), where Glenn and I hoped to have resupply boxes awaiting us, or northeast to Mojave (pop. 4,238).* Both were seven-to-eight-mile hitches.

We'd heard that some hikers who bounced from Willow Springs to one of the two towns didn't bother returning south to resume from that spot; instead, they just headed north from State Highway 58, skipping a seven-mile PCT section that was hot, dry, and beneath wind turbines.**

We chose to stay on the PCT. Our hope was to get a ride into Tehachapi at Highway 58, even though we'd heard it was a tough hitch.

Whoosh … whoosh … whoosh. The turbines turned. The wind blew. My trekking poles clicked. My legs and feet and shoulders ached for rest. Finally,

---

* Mojave is the town where *Wild* author Cheryl Strayed spent the night before beginning her PCT adventure in 1995.

** In my earlier PCT years, I might have been bothered by hikers who skipped huge sections of the trail and later claimed to have hiked the PCT. But I'd come to believe in the "hike-your-own-hike" adage. Hiking the PCT wasn't a competition, but an experience—and each of us got to decide what that experience would be for us. By now, I'd realized that worrying about myself kept me busy enough; no need to take on the ethical choices of others, especially when those choices affected only them, not others.

Highway 58—a freeway on this stretch of it—appeared in the distance, the vehicles below so small they were barely discernible.

"Look at the overpass where cars can exit and get back on the freeway," said Glenn. "That's our only hope for a ride."

I watched it for three or four minutes. Not a single car exited or entered the freeway at that point. Hey, we were in the middle of a desert. Who'd want to get off a freeway here? There was no place to go. And since there was no place to go, who needed to get back on?

"Doesn't look real hopeful," I all but shouted over the incessant roar of the wind.

We both stared at the situation, like two astronauts stranded on the moon without a spaceship home.

"Glenny," I yelled, "I'm gonna pray that God will help us get into Tehachapi."

"Make it a good one!" he yelled back.

Horned lizards scampered across the trail. Crows squawked, the wind whipping them around as if they were black socks in a waterless washing machine. And, far below us, on a long switchback, two dots soon appeared.

"Hey, we're not alone," I told Glenny. "Couple more NoBos making their way to Highway 58 like us. Let's see if they get rides. Might give us hope."

But as we continued down, I realized something: the two people weren't NoBos like us, but SoBos, coming up the hill *toward* us. Fifteen minutes later, about three miles from the trailhead, we met Susan and Phil Dowty. Mid-fifties, perhaps. Not PCT hikers; way too clean and energetic. Locals.

"We just spent the weekend in Mammoth Lakes and were heading back to LA," said Phil. "We've always wanted to hike a portion of the PCT and so, on a whim, we just decided to pull over and hike a little section. Are you guys doing the PCT?"

"Yeah, trying to finish the whole thing after eleven years," I said.

"Oh, my gosh," said Susan. "And you're staying in Tehachapi tonight?"

"Hope to. Got reservations at the Fairfield Inn. Gonna hitch when we hit Fifty-Eight."

"No, you're not," said Phil. "You're coming with us. We'll take you to Tehachapi. You'll wait hours for a ride on Fifty-Eight."

"No, no, no, that's OK," said Glenn. "You two are on a hike."

"Honey, are you tired of hiking in the god-awful wind and heat?" Phil asked Susan.

"Sure am. Let's turn around and take these tired hikers into town."

"Well, thanks," I said. "You're an answer to prayer."

WITHIN NINETY minutes we were showered, rehydrated, and, while lying on the softest bed I've ever been on, watching Oregon State play Stanford in the Pac-12 Baseball Tournament.

The next day was the first "zero" we had taken in our nine summers on the trail—a complete day of rest.* In the morning, while Glenn slept, I walked to a nearby Big Five sporting goods store that had exactly one air mattress and one blowup pillow left. I bought them both.

At Walmart, amid a sprinkling of PCTers on similar missions, I purchased food and drink that Glenny and I needed. A Forest Service guy, seeing me walking back to the hotel with two plastic bags—think *Home Alone*—insisted on giving me a ride. "Love to help PCTers," he said. "Good luck getting to Canada. Way to go!"

Back at the room, after crunching some numbers, I told Glenn, "Two hundred and thirty miles done, one hundred and nine to go—for this leg."

We watched Tehachapi's Memorial Day Parade, ate amazing pastry at Kohnen's Country Bakery, and returned to nap.

The next morning, Tuesday, May 31, we picked up our resupplies at the post office, packed up, and took an Uber back to where we'd left off. I was carrying a record nine days of food and six liters of water, meaning a pack that was almost certainly my heaviest ever—at least forty-five pounds.

"Check it out," I said to Glenny after lifting the rusted metal registration box at the trailhead north of Highway 58.

With a felt pen, someone had written: "Cheryl Strayed was here '98." The *Wild* author may have been here in 1998, but the 1,100-mile journey she wrote about in her book started here three years earlier, in 1995. I surmised this was the work of an impostor with a history deficiency.

Strayed's book and the subsequent movie vastly increased the number of hikers on the PCT. Before her 2012 book, fewer than 200 people a year attempted a thru-hike of the trail. That doubled in 2013, shortly after her book released, and doubled again two years after the 2014 movie was released. Some blamed her for the trail getting crowded; far more considered her the patron saint of the PCT.

Me? I seldom found the trail crowded and wasn't part of the anti-Strayed faction. True, I thought, she made some poor choices after the loss of her mother—shooting up heroin and cheating incessantly on a husband who she kept reminding us was a wonderful guy—but she wrote a great book: honest, thoughtful, compelling. *Wild* was printed in more languages than I think

* The average hiker takes between fifteen and twenty "zeros"—full days off—between Mexico and Canada, PCT surveys say.

my first hiking book, *Cascade Summer,* sold *copies*, so even if sheer envy might have biased my perspective, I found it hard to blame someone for writing a best-selling book that drew more people to the trail—particularly when we all seemed OK with *us* hiking the trail, just not *them*. As writer and pioneering backpacker Colin Fletcher once quipped: "The woods are overrun, and sons of bitches like me are half the problem."

"THE MOJAVE DESERT stretch of the PCT can broil your mind, blister your feet, and turn your mouth to dust," said *The Pacific Crest* guidebook.

What we faced from Tehachapi Pass to Walker Pass was the driest portion of the entire PCT. It required lots of walking on hot, steep, sandy trails, and giant leaps of faith that good-hearted Trail Angels had left us bottled water at spots where the trail intersected a road and no natural water sources were available nearby. Said one sign: "No water at cache? Cow ponds should be reliable." And the hiker who wrote it was dead serious, leaving a detailed map about how to find such ponds. That's how desperate PCT hikers could be for water in these parts.

On Thursday, June 2, the plan was to get water at Landers Creek, about a quarter-mile off the trail to our left. This was a critical "get," one of the most important on the entire PCT. If you missed this stop, the next "for-sure" water was forty-five miles north at Walker Pass. At my hydration rate, three miles per liter, that meant carrying fifteen liters, which was impractical, if not impossible. The most I'd ever carried was six.

Granted, there were two caches along the way, but the rule of thumb was to never count on the goodness of strangers. Yes, if your app said there was water ahead, there usually was. But if there wasn't, you could be in big trouble—in the middle of nowhere.

By midafternoon, we passed a dry creek bed amid the scorching heat.

"This isn't it?" I said.

"Nope."

I kept waiting for Glenn to identify what *was* it. Landers seemed overdue. Just before an uphill portion of the trail that turned sharply from north to east, I spotted an overgrown road.

"Could this be the road to it?" I asked.

"Nope."

What did I know? We trudged on, my energy ebbing with each step.

"Hold it," Glenn said twenty minutes later. "Let me check something out." He pulled out his iPhone. "Bad news," he said.

"What?"

"We missed it."

"Missed Landers?"

"Yep."

I bit my tongue, then calmed down, accepting the fact that we'd simply need to go back a few hundred feet and water-up—that is, until Glenn, after I asked, specified how far back we had to go.

"A half mile."

I didn't say anything. Another NoBo, resting in the shade, confirmed our going too far. To be safe, we had no choice but to hike back down the grade half a mile, go a quarter mile off trail for water, return a quarter-mile to the trail, and hike another half-mile up the grade—just to get back to where we were now.

A mile in the morning, they say, feels like two in the afternoon, five in the heat. We headed back in silence. I was *not* a happy camper—and not because I believed that, as our navigator, Glenn needed to be faultless. We all make mistakes. In 2018, I was the guy who had encouraged us to hike a virtual marathon because I thought the Belden restaurant was open until 8 P.M. Nope, 7 P.M. And, now, I wasn't exactly pulling out my iPhone map and helping find Landers Creek, was I? No, what had me quietly miffed was this: Glenn couldn't just say, "Sorry about that," which would have affirmed in me the sense that my feelings actually mattered. That he'd recognized his oversight meant an extra mile for us both in the blazing heat, and he regretted his miss.

We found the water, returned to our previous spot, and grinded up the rocky, twisting trail along St. John Ridge. With each step, Glenn's unwillingness to own his mistake dug into my craw like sand in my shoe.

"You OK, Bob?" he said, apparently noticing that I hadn't spoken a word in about an hour.

"I'm fine," I lied. "I just wish you could have said—." I exhaled. "Hey, we're both tired. Let's just find a place to camp."

"There's supposed to be a cache at Kelso Valley Road," said Glenn, whose gait had gotten noticeably wobbly.

"That's—what—another three miles?"

"Something like that."

"Glenn, I don't think either of us has three miles left in us. And we have water for tonight."

"Bob, we can do it," he said with that never-say-die Lutheran resolve. "We can—."

He wobbled, tripped on a toaster-size rock, teetered as if he might recover, then fell backward on his butt, looking too tired to get up.

"Glenn, we're done for today. Finished."

I reached out my hand. He reached up with his. I pulled him up.

When you combined heat, thirst, weariness, and pride, you couldn't expect *not* to have an occasional meltdown likes this one—mine emotional, Glenn's physical. Face it, Glenn was beat. And my mind, in guidebook lingo, was "broiled." It was time to rest and reboot.

THE NEXT DAY, we exulted in the discovery of dozens of five-gallon plastic jugs of water left by Trail Angels at Kelso Valley Road.

Zigzagging up the flanks of Mayan Peak and Pinyon Mountain, I felt an exposure to the sun more intense than on any PCT leg ever. Temperatures hit triple digits. The only vegetation higher than us was the occasional Joshua tree, a stubby, poor man's palm tree in whose slender shade we sometimes took refuge on breaks. Its evergreen leaves were nearly as stout and sharp as steak knives, a lesson I occasionally learned the hard way.

That night, the wind at our camp at Bird Spring Pass rumbled like a freight train. Darkness was setting in, but I couldn't help but notice that the Young Ones were arriving, grabbing water from a Trail Angel cache, and, headlamps aglow, heading up Skinner Peak beyond.

"They're on to Canada, baby," Glenn all but yelled over the howl of the wind. "They may sleep in, but they hike late."

I hoisted my water bottle in the air. "A toast to you, Young Ones! In the words of Neil Young: *Long may you run—or, in this case, walk.*"

I scooped the contents of my Herb & Garlic Tuna Creations onto two soft shells and accidentally squeezed some mayo onto my shirt in the process. I had no idea how most hikers stayed so clean; I was always a mess.

"So, I've been thinking about who has it harder—the thru-hikers like those kids or section-hikers like us," I said as the wind whipped our tents.

"And your conclusion?" said Glenn, words muffled by a Double Stuf Oreo.

"Both. Mentally, *they* have it harder. You and I have only seventy miles and four days to Kennedy Meadows and, boom, we're done with this section. We get on an airplane and fly home, take showers, sleep in beds. They have more than 2,000 miles left. They have nearly a *hundred* more days of this left. They're not even a quarter of the way done. Mentally, that's got to wear them down. There's a reason not even half of all thru-hikers who start make it all the way. And I'd say it's as much mental as physical."

"OK, I'll buy that. What about physically?"

"*We* have it harder."

"Think so? Why?"

"Because every single day the thru-hikers hike only makes them stronger for the next day and the next. And each day, physically, it's incrementally easier because of that on-the-trail training. You've seen the folks up north; they're lean, tough, and have the legs of distance runners. Remember that kid we saw at Rockpile Lake near Mount Jeff in Oregon?"

"Yeah, Garfunkel. Austrian, right?"

"Yep. Bounded over that log like Bambi. So, yeah, like compounding interest, these guys amortize daily, building muscle and cardio so that the same effort that enabled them to do fifteen miles at the start enables them to do twenty by the High Sierra and thirty by Washington. Meanwhile, just as we start to benefit from our on-trail training, boom, we're home. You're back on the treadmill, I'm back in the pool, both of us trying desperately to stay in shape while living busy lives—and while thru-hikers are essentially training full time, *accidentally*. It's a great two-for-one for them: they get distance and conditioning each day. Back home, we get only a little conditioning!"

Only later did I realize that two other major differences separated the hiker genres, one an advantage for section-hikers, two advantages for thru-hikers.

Our advantage? Glenn and I could choose what time of the year to hike, which allowed us to, say, miss the May-June snow of the High Sierra that most thru-hikers had no choice but to navigate if they wanted to walk the whole trail in a single spring and summer.

But thru-hikers enjoy two advantages: First, what I'll call "continuity, context, and rhythm"—with themselves, each other, and the trail. Thru-hikers are like full-time teachers who know their students, the school, and the cadence of the school year. Section-hikers are like substitutes who might be teaching science at one school this week and art at a different school the next. We might be hiking north in one state in June, and south in another state in August. No continuity. No context. And no chance for long-term connection with ourselves, others, or the trail. Meanwhile, a month out, thru-hikers are "one" with all three, which makes their experience easier.

Second, expense. In doing the entire trail, it is far cheaper to thru-hike than to section-hike. In 2019, the annual PCT Survey showed the average PCT hiker spent $6,349 to hike the entire trail. By now, I had already spent nearly three times that amount—and wasn't finished. My main expense? Getting to and from trailheads: airfare, gas, motels, food, Ubers, tips, and the like. At this point, I had already traveled more than 15,000 miles getting on and off the trail *thirty-one times.* On the other hand, beyond short hitches to resupply in some town, thru-hikers needed only to get on the trail once, Mexico, and off the trail once, Canada.

None of which is to suggest that one type of hiker is better than the other, just that their experiences are far different.

BY SATURDAY, June 5, we were a day ahead of schedule and encouraged to hear Ann was able to move up our flight out of LA to Wednesday, June 8, from Thursday. In Ann and Sally, Glenn and I were blessed to have an amazing two-person support team, who, at this point, had far more important things on their minds back home: their ninety-three-year-old mother, Bonnie—our mother-in-law—who was now in hospice care.

The circle of life didn't stop for the PCT; since beginning our adventure, Sally and I had added three grandchildren and lost my mother. Glenn and Ann had welcomed all four of their grandchildren, and Glenn had lost his father and mother. Like the trail, life giveth and taketh.

At day's end, we were winding our way up a steep, well-forested trail just beyond Owens Peak and realizing nothing looked flat enough for sleep. On the PCT, darkness was akin to the music stopping in a game of musical chairs. If you didn't have a spot at that point, you were up the creek without a campsite. Which is literally what we faced on this night: Out of options, we quietly walked past a tent in a dry creek bed with hopes of cowboy-camping thirty feet beyond—until a young man popped his head out the flap.

"According to the app, there's a spot two tenths of a mile up the trail," he said. "I *highly* recommend it." He retreated back into his tent.

We left, rebuffed by the only act of out-and-out rudeness I'd experienced on the trail. His recommend "spot" turned out to be two giant fir trees on a steep slope whose backsides could barely fit a single sleeping bag. By the time we managed to get our thirty-pound packs and more-than-thirty-pound bodies up the steep slope to the trees, we were puddles of sweat.

Glenn put up his tent. I did not put up mine. Too tired. I cowboy-camped. While I was setting up, I only later realized, the lid to a Pringles tube popped off, turning my pack into an all-night diner for ants featuring pepperoni pizza crisps. The next morning, my pack was thick with the onerous insects.

We'd now been at it for nearly three weeks, a stroll in the park for thru-hikers but not for us. Our twenty nights on the trail would eclipse our previous record of eighteen (Mexico to Cajon Pass).

ON OUR LAST night of this leg, with an occasional ant still scurrying madly through my pack, we were camped high on a ridge in the Chimney Peak Wilderness when a young man from Sri Lanka came by, a Canon 35 mm camera dangling from his neck. We saw him again the next morning, at first light.

"Eagle Eye," he said.

"Bob. Together, my brother-in-law Glenn and I are The Oregon Boys."

"Pleased to meet you, Oregon Boys Bob. Where are you going?"

"Finishing at Kennedy Meadows. Then we'll have just sixty-two miles to the border to finish. Been at it eleven years. You going the whole way?"

"I hope to. My visa is good until October 10."

Eagle Eye, so named for finding a fellow hiker's iPhone, was a twenty-eight-year-old data processor who had some serious hiking experience in Nepal. I took a shine to this kid. He liked photography; I like photography. He had a light spirit, I had a light spirit—OK, until we missed a water stop.

Later, as we neared Manter Creek, Glenn said, "What impresses me about guys like Eagle Eye is how they have to do all this organizing of their food and supplies and water—with hardly knowing our country's language or geography and with no support team like you and I have in Ann and Sally."

"I know. Can you imagine you and I doing this in Sri Lanka? I'm having a hard enough time hiking a trail that's essentially in my own back yard."

We leapfrogged Eagle Eye now and then, the last time at the South Fork Kern River, where the trail began transitioning into green meadows and towering pines. Just short of the Kennedy Meadows General Store, Glenn and I had our photo taken in front of the same sign from which we'd left the summer before to head north to Crabtree Meadow, then up Mount Whitney.

"Glenny, California is officially done," I said. "Oregon is officially done. Washington will be done after four days to Canada. We've hiked all the PCT except sixty-two miles to the border."

We fist-pumped each other.

At the general store, where gas in this remote location was $8.49 a gallon, hikers in upbeat moods ate, drank, talked, drank, rested, drank, and drank.

We grabbed food and drink and enjoyed the small pleasure of sitting in chairs after 340 miles and nearly three weeks without them. Soon we heard a tittering among the Young Ones on the food deck.

"Look who's coming!" someone said, pointing out to the road.

A slow clap began, then got faster. Hootin' and hollerin'. And, finally, all-out cheers. Out on the road, headed toward the store, was Eagle Eye, trekking poles raised high, legs looking fresh, smile almost as wide as the trail itself.

"Give it up for Eagle Eye!" someone shouted and we happily did so.

WHEN A four-wheel-drive pickup pulled up to take hikers to nearby Grumpy Bears Retreat Restaurant & Tavern, we jumped aboard. Once there, we ate like rescued sailors.

Across the way, I saw Pretzel, a yoga specialist, and Triple Crown, a guy who'd already done the Appalachian Trail and Continental Divide Trail and was hoping to earn his nickname by getting to Canada. He was among the strongest hikers on the trail but, whenever we bumped into him, always accorded Glenn and me uncommon respect.

"You made it, man," said Blacksquatch (Ric Green), a former University of Florida athlete I'd talked track and field with at some water stop—and one of the few African Americans I'd seen on the trail.

It was like a reunion of sorts—and a bit like graduation for Glenn and me. That said, only a handful knew school was essentially out for us, even as their commencement in Canada, if they even made it that far, lay some three months ahead.

"Seen Orange Crush?" I asked Glenny.

"Nope."

I took the best cold shower I'd ever had. We then shot the breeze with, and camped near, a father/son team from Junction City, just northwest of Eugene, who had been regular readers of my column.

I sent Sally a final satellite message: "Best PCT trip. Ever."

In the morning, we returned to Grumpy Bears for its manhole-sized pancakes. I ate one, plus a side of eggs, hash browns, and sausage. Unbelievable. Nothing made you appreciate a hot breakfast like going weeks without one.

The mood was almost as raucous as it had been the afternoon before, when the bartender was pumping what he told me would be forty gallons of beer for the 150 PCT hikers who stopped on an average summer day.

Pretzel stopped to wish us well. Glenn talked quietly with a young woman from Bend who had some medical concerns and heard he was a doctor. Eagle Eye came to bid us farewell.

"Eagle Eye, here's my phone number. When you get to Oregon, if you need help getting around fires or anything else, you call me. Understand?"

"Yes. Thank you, Oregon Boys Bob. Good meeting you."

"Safe travels, my friend."

After my friend Mike Yorkey arrived to pick us up and take us four hours to the airport in LA, I was soon back in Eugene, pulling smelly clothes from my backpack and stowing away anything that I'd be needing for the August trip to northern Washington for the final sixty-two miles.

I had everything cleared out of the pack when out wandered something that had accompanied me thirty-five miles on the trail, 204 miles from Kennedy Meadows to John Wayne International Airport, 776 air miles from LA to Portland, and ninety miles in two cars from Portland International to Albany, then to our house in Eugene.

A single ant, with what smelled like Pringles on its breath.

South of Tehachapi, Glenn headed through among the first of more than a thousand wind turbines we would hike beneath. I wasn't a fan of the fans.

Top: In a sort of "woman at the well" scene, hikers filled up at Golden Oaks Spring. Above: The five-gallon jugs of water that awaited us on Kelso Valley Road. Right: One of the bazillion lizards that often skittered alongside us on the trail.

Between Tehachapi Pass and Walker Pass, walking past Joshua trees that offered little in the way of shade, I experienced the most intense heat I could remember on the PCT. Triple digits.

Reaching Kennedy Meadows was as blissful a moment a I'd felt on the trail. The 339-mile section ranked third behind only the Oregon and Mexico-to-Cajon-Pass stretches as our longest.

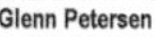

Glenn Petersen

Top: The last restaurant meal I would have on the trail—breakfast at Grumpy Bears Retreat Restaurant & Tavern—was also the best. Left: Eagle Eye, a hiker from Sri Lanka who we'd met just the previous night, rested at the general store. Above: Me with Ric Green, a former University of Florida runner who I'd talked track and field with on a water stop.

TENTH SUMMER

START AUGUST 6, 2022

Elevation this section (feet)

Start 2,591
End 4,258
High 7,126 (Above Hopkins Lake)
Low 4,258 (U.S.-Canada border)

GOAL: NORTH 62 MILES
FROM RAINY PASS
TO U.S.–CANADA BORDER

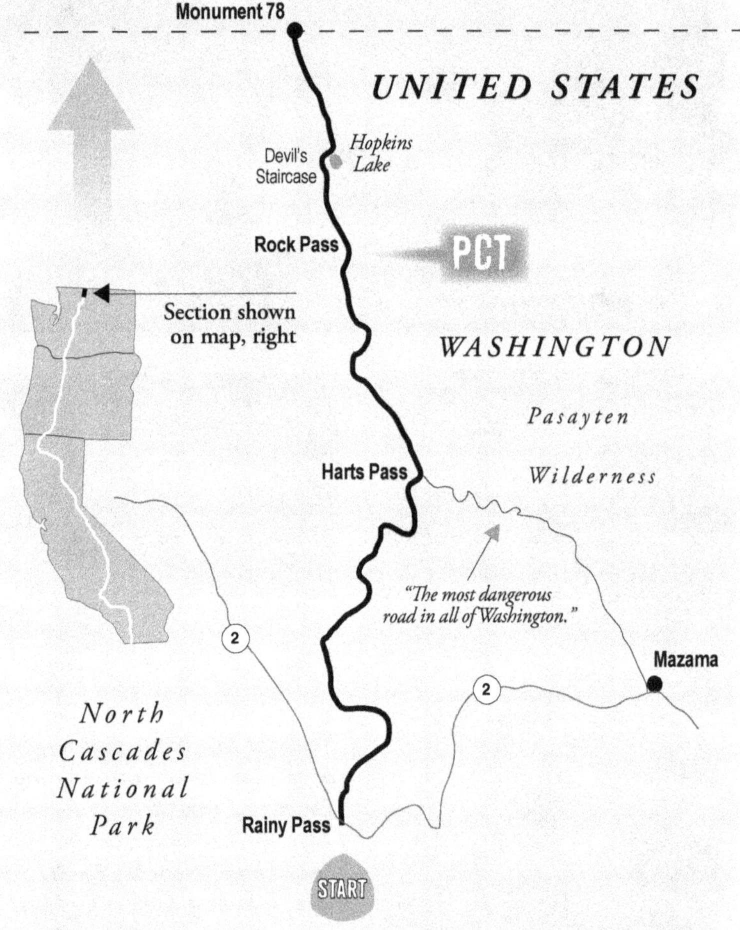

PCT progress through .... August 5, 2022

MEXICO · CANADA

98% done / 2,588 miles

2% of PCT left / 62 miles to go

22

CANADA

Old friends, old friends
Sat on their park bench like bookends
A newspaper blown through the grass
Falls on the round toes
Of the high shoes of the old friends

—Simon & Garfunkel

What I hoped would be the last trail shuttle for The Oregon Boys left Albany, Oregon, on August 6, 2022. Destination: Rainy Pass in Washington's North Cascades, sixty-two miles short of the Canadian border.

Since beginning in 2011, Glenn and I had been stopped by fire, heat, parents in failing health, and a world pandemic, but as we drove north on Interstate 5 on this Saturday morning—Ann at the wheel—I was confident this was it. Confident we would touch the border in four days to finish the 2,650-mile PCT.

It had been twelve years since our shakedown cruise; eleven since our first PCT hike; two months since our most recent hike; seven weeks since Sally and Ann's mother, Bonnie, sadly, had passed away; and six days since I had gotten a call from Eagle Eye telling me he and a few hiking friends were stymied in Shasta City, California, because of a wildfire near the trail to the north.

A fire near Etna, about forty miles south of the Oregon border, had closed the trail and he and his friends were virtually stuck. As he talked, I began imagining a solution.

"Just a minute, Eagle Eye," I said. "Hang on the line."

I went down the hall to our bedroom and leaned over She Who Slumbered in Peace.

"Morning, love," I said.

Sally groaned, whereupon I popped the question every woman longs to hear on a Saturday morning when she has no responsibilities for the weekend. "What would you think if five PCT hikers were to stay with us tonight?"

She opened one eye, then, grudgingly, the other.

"Seriously?"

I nodded.

"Sure. Fine."

That's just the way she was—adventuresome in her own way.

On what would be a 500-mile roundtrip, I picked up the five in Shasta City that afternoon and headed home. Eagle Eye rode up front with me. Though he was a humble young man, I sensed that while hiking in a country where most of his hiking friends enjoyed a certain home-field advantage, he was relishing his role as the one whose local connection had saved the day.

Once in Eugene, the seven of us sat on our back deck, sipping cold drinks and hearing about the experiences of not only Eagle Eye but of Lunch Box, of Clovis, California; Bodega, of Orlando, Florida; Pit Stop, of Tucson, Arizona; and Ghost, of Australia.

"This is heaven," said Pit Stop, leaning back in a patio chair. "Thank you two so very much."

Beyond the one near Etna, fires had closed several PCT sections, a few in Oregon. The next morning, I would ferry the group north to a trailhead near Mount Hood so they could hike to the Canadian border. By the time they'd done that, they hoped the fire danger might have eased and they could hike south through Oregon and Northern California to complete parts of the trail they'd missed.

In the morning, on our back deck, Sally served bacon, eggs, sausage, and pancakes to everybody plus a special guest, my friend Geoff Tyson, who relished the chance to talk trail with his PCT compadres.

After Lunch Box interviewed Sally and me for a PCT documentary she was making, I shuttled the five to REI, where they upgraded equipment; to Walmart, where they restocked food; to Subway, where we grabbed lunch; to the post office in Albany, where they arranged to have resupply boxes that they missed in Etna be sent to a post office in Washington; to Glenn's house a half-mile from the Albany post office, where Eagle Eye wanted to say hello to a guy he'd known for only thirty-six hours but still wanted to see; to a pharmacy in

Salem, where Pit Stop could pick up some prescription drugs; and, finally, to a trailhead on Highway 26 near Mount Hood, where they would continue their quest for Canada. My goal was a 2 P.M. dropoff. I left them at dusk.

The thirty-hour experience with them was fascinating. The Young Ones were full of energy, passionate about the trail, and humbled by the help Sally and I offered, trying to stuff gas money in my hands as I bid them farewell.

"Trail Magic!" I said, politely refusing.

And then they were gone, disappearing into the dusky woods like the Pevensie kids heading back through the closet.

"I WONDER where Eagle Eye and the gang are now," said Glenn as Ann exited Interstate 5 two hours north of Seattle and headed east toward the Cascades. "Closing in on White Pass, wouldn't you think?"

"Sounds about right," I said. "Probably doing handstands and cartwheels on The Knife's Edge about now."

A few hours later, we arrived at Rainy Pass, where we had finished up the previous August. It was Saturday. The plan was to reach Canada Wednesday morning, August 10. Though COVID restrictions had relaxed, Canada was still not allowing hikers across its border at this point because officials had no way of determining who was, and wasn't, vaccinated.

Originally, the plan had been to reach the border and push eight miles north to meet Sally and Ann at Manning Park. To get home now meant tagging the border, then hiking thirty-one miles south on the same trail we'd just taken north. Once back to Harts Pass, we then faced coming east down a twisting one-lane road that dropped 3,000 feet in only ten miles.

The Advocates, a Seattle law firm specializing in accidents and liability, called it, "Without a doubt, the most dangerous road in all of Washington." Ann, our designated driver, took one look at a YouTube video of it and said: "Nope, not driving that." We couldn't blame her.

Glenn talked of walking the road, where Sally and Ann would pick us up in the small town of Mazama. That not only sounded daunting but dangerous. Although Harts Pass wasn't on the way to anywhere else and got minimal traffic, I was holding out hope we could hitchhike.

But, first, of course, we needed to reach the border. On this final sixty-two miles we expected lots of water, lots of beauty, and lots of ups and downs. What we didn't expect was much cell coverage, which meant the only way I was going to be able to follow my ten-year-old grandson Lincoln's progress in the National 10U Babe Ruth World Series baseball tournament in Indiana was through satellite messages my daughter-in-law Deena promised to send.

As dusk neared on this Saturday, we said goodbye and hiked a relatively easy five uphill miles, finding a great, flat camping spot for our first night. Good start. Sunday went well, too, until Glenn ran out of gas midafternoon amid miles of uphill trail through seemingly unending eye-level foliage that intensified the heat by at least five degrees.

We quashed plans to camp high and improvised, nestling our tents in a grove of trees, knowing this was putting us behind schedule but remembering what had happened above Cajon Pass in 2021 when we tried to push too hard too soon. Adding insult to injury, Lincoln's Northwest All-Stars got riddled 12-1 by the hometown Indiana team in their opener.

Neither our opening day nor Linc's boded well for our respective teams. However, after a good night's sleep, Glenn's zip returned Monday—and Linc's team rebounded to win its first game.

The North Cascades, known as "America's Alps," were stunning: lots of peaks, plunging canyons, and clear, cold water. The sky was blue and the border near. Over the years, it had been one thing to think "every step is getting me closer to Canada" while, say, going south in Central California. But it was quite another to know the miles-left number had thinned to double digits—and to realize some of the peaks we were seeing were in Canada.

We were making up the miles we'd lost and feeling good. At Harts Pass, a ranger, Marianne, told us our timing was perfect.

"Snow was thick up here until just recently," she said. "Latest we've opened the ranger station that I can remember. For weeks, I kept watching hikers leave, all eager to hit the border, only to come back after hitting Rock Pass. Too much snow; didn't want to risk it. But now people are getting through."

Further north we trudged. The North Cascades were not only beautiful, but offered the highest per capita number of great names I'd seen since stepping foot on the PCT: Lake of the Pines, Blizzard Peak, Mount Frosty, Windy Joe Mountain, Three Fools Peak, and Sky Pilot Pass among them.

On Tuesday, August 9, temperatures dropped—enough, in fact, that on an afternoon break, feeling chilled, I fired up my Jetboil right on the trail and ate an early spaghetti dinner right then and there.*

"Ya gotta love freeze-dried," I told Glenny. "Look at this stamp on the package: *Best by August 2051.* Man, I'll be—what?—ninety-seven in 2051. At that point, the only way I'll be on the PCT is if they spread my ashes on it."

---

* Though I'd gone years without hot food, mainly because we were hiking in intense heat, I'd brought the Jetboil on this, our last trip for sentimental reasons. In our early years, hot foods were a staple of our dinners. And, in another tribute to the past, for breakfast I'd replaced my Hostess Baby Bundts with Svenhard's Danishes, another go-to from the early years. My favorite? The Bear Claw.

THE MOODS of other hikers were higher than I'd ever sensed them. NoBos like us were naturally pumped; it was early August and some had been on the trail since early spring, more than 120 days. Now, they were a day away from Canada. Those who'd tagged the border and were heading back to Harts Pass to exit, of course, were relishing their success.

We met a NoBo from Pennsylvania, Etiquette, and her father, Bigfoot, who had joined her for the last few sections; they were gobbling up the miles. I found an unopened eight-ounce bottle of Glenfiddich Single Malt Scotch Whiskey whose owner was likely to miss it dearly at the border. I began seeing a flurry of PCT finishers from all over: Germany, Holland, India, France, Australia, Massachusetts, and North Carolina.

"I hiked a while with a dude who did the whole trail in fifty-five days," a guy from Dallas told me. "I think it's a record." *

"Fifty-five days?" I said to Glenn. "It took me that long to figure out how to send a message on my inReach Mini."

ON TUESDAY night, we made camp at Hopkins Lake, only six miles short of the border.

"Last *official* night on the PCT," I said to Glenn as I woofed down a lemon-pepper tuna tortilla.

"Hard to believe, isn't it?"

"Eleven years, my friend," I said. "Still the trip of a lifetime?"

"You know it."

Later, I lay in my tent, looking at the star-spangled sky. Before drifting off to sleep, I thought of the Simon & Garfunkel song, "Old Friends." It laments growing old, the key line being, "How terribly strange to be seventy."

And yet the guy in the tent next to me who'd hiked 2,644 miles—and, even more impressively, had put up with *me*—was seventy. I would be seventy in eighteen months. But here we were, a morning's hike from finishing the Pacific Crest Trail. The "old friends" part rang true—our friendship was just short of fifty years—but "sitting on a park bench?" Not for The Oregon Boys.

Some perspective, I reminded myself: We hadn't found a cure for cancer or saved the earth from alien attack. We had simply walked a really long way together for more than a decade. If anything, our "senior legacy" was simply

---

* Indeed it was a record. Later, I learned that the previous day, Englishman Josh Perry had smashed the self-supported Fastest Known Time (FKT) of the PCT with a clocking of 55 days, 16 hours, and 54 minutes. He arrived at 8:56 P.M. on Monday, August 7, 2022, while Glenn and I were camping some thirty-seven miles south. He likely came past us Tuesday as we neared Hopkins Lake—even if we hadn't realized we'd brushed shoulders with greatness.

one of perseverance: We doggedly pursued a goal and, unless something went wrong in the last six miles, were going to realize that goal. As Theodore Solotaroff said about writers: their "main task is to persist." If nothing else, we had done that. Fifty-five days for one hiker, eleven years for two others. Though we'd arrived here by far different means, Josh Perry and The Oregon Boys would be bound by a common line: *They hiked the PCT.*

Would I have gotten this far alone? No, which suggested a second legacy: the power of friendship. Glenn's enthusiasm fueled mine; his commitment fueled mine; his determination fueled mine. How many times, late in the afternoon, had I felt like I could not take another step, then seen him trudging ahead of me, long pants bloused at the bottom like some World War II GI, and found the will to take another step. And another? And on and on … .

AT 4:30 A.M. WEDNESDAY, we began what we expected to be the final leg of the final leg. From the first step, a quiet excitement buzzed through me like electricity, though offset by the unfolding dread that Lincoln's team was down 2-0 in the bottom of the sixth of a seven-inning game. "This is our last chance," Deena's latest satellite message said. "Lose and we're out."

I had heard this final section was downhill, fast, and smooth. It was. But, weirdly, the closer I got to the border, the more my mind tugged me backward. Images clicked in my mind as if sequenced in a slideshow:

▲ *Click.* In 2011, the Elk Lake dinner with Cisco, Roadrunner, Sally, and Ann celebrating our first successful section completed.

▲ *Click.* In 2017, packed into the Petersen's Honda Pilot with five other hikers as we drove around a fire at the Oregon-California border, the stench ripe, our spirits high, the fellowship tight.

▲ *Click.* In 2018, the afternoon at Packer Lake Lodge when, beyond his stomach-rumbling romance story, Starburst said, "There's just something about sleeping under the stars that renews the soul."

▲ *Click.* In 2019, friend Geoff Tyson driving 2,000 miles roundtrip to take Glenn and me to dinner in Palm Springs after Fuller Ridge had filleted our souls in the heat, a gesture that said to me: *you are worthy.*

And isn't that what any of us is looking for, not only on the PCT but in life itself? To feel a sense of worth? To be seen. To *matter?*

My mind was a whirlwind of such memories: seven summers that, with a few bummers, had turned into ten incredible years of hiking the trail.

AND THEN, suddenly, there it was in an opening through the trees—the PCT's Northern Terminus, the hallowed Monument 78, *the end.* I wasn't expecting a heavenly shaft of light on it; nevertheless, my first response was how simple and understated it looked: five wooden pillars, square and rough-hewn, a fitting bookend to the similar monument on the U.S.-Mexico border.

We touched Canada at 7:20 A.M. on Wednesday, August 10, 2022, the two of us alone in the woods on an overcast day. Just us and the chipmunks and the unspoken memories of some 10,000-plus others who had, in the last half century, done the same, each of our stories unique.

It felt like an exclamation mark on a splendidly long Faulkner sentence, a sentence both convoluted and confusing and yet appropriately so given the twists and turns of a trail that did not lend itself to shortness or simplicity.

Yes, at last. Canada!

I'd heard of festive celebrations at the border: champagne, balloons, and some guy's girlfriend, in pre-COVID days, hiking eight miles south from Manning Park to greet him and his friends with a dozen Big Macs. My celebration was quiet, deep, and evolving. No whooping and hollering. No misty eyes. No lump in the throat. Just the quiet satisfaction of a possibility realized, a goal achieved, a journey ended.

"Glenny, we did it," I said, my handshake pulling him into a hug.

"Way to go, Bobby! Proud of you!"

"And me of you. Long live The Oregon Boys!"

Only when we were back home would I realize that instead of a giant emotional gushing, my reaction would be fed out like a fly fisher's line—slowly, carefully, and in tune with the one holding the rod. I would feed out more line that afternoon back at Hopkins Lake, the next morning at Rock Pass, and, in subtle ways, every day of my life since I touched the monument.

For now, we took every conceivable photo we could take, even as I reminded myself: *You don't need a photograph to authenticate an experience.* We marveled at "The Slash," a twenty-foot swath of cut timber that marks the dividing line between Canada and the U.S.* Like a mischievous schoolkid, I ventured a few steps beyond the border line. My iPhone immediately pinged me a message from my cell provider, Verizon, that said, "Welcome to Canada." And informing me that I wouldn't accrue any "additional charges while roaming." *Cool!*

I wrote in the logbook: "The Oregon Boys, after 11 years, made it. Grateful for trail makers, trail angels, and encouragement from fellow hikers—Bob & Glenn."

We ate, we drank, we marinated in the moment, then put on our packs

* It stretches 5,525 miles from Alaska to Maine—the longest international border in the world—and is deforested annually to the tune of $1.1 billion, costing the average U.S. taxpayer half a cent per year.

and headed back south, having stayed for just under an hour without seeing a soul. Along the way, I sent a satellite message to family and friends.

"Congratulations, QuackPacker!" wrote Geoff. "August 10 will be a day you will always hold dear to your heart. So happy you guys are now PCT alums!"

BACK AT Hopkins Lake for lunch, my inReach GPS device warbled. My eyes widened as I read the message from Deena in Indiana.

"Glenny!" I yelled, "Lincoln's team rallied for three runs in the last inning to win 3-2! They're still alive!"

"All right!"

While he slept, I peeled down to my skivvies in the midafternoon warmth. On my back, I frog-kicked my way near the middle of Hopkins Lake. I gently treaded water in reverent awe, looking at the endless sky, listening to the subtle splash of feet and hands, and imagining this same lake only months from now, frozen beneath snow as if I'd never been here.

If touching the border had been meaningful, this all-alone moment—just me, the lake, the mountains, the sky, and a sense of the Almighty—was even more so. I sensed relief. Joy. Completion. I sensed connection to a father who'd been gone twenty-six years but who, as Mom once suggested, would have been proud. And connection to that also-gone Mom, a woman who had still carried swim fins in her car's trunk at eighty. I felt utter privilege, humbled that my aging body had gotten me from my "let's quit" resignation on our 2010 shakedown hike to the Canadian border twelve years later.

Thank you, God, for safety, for sustenance, for a brother-in-law who walked every step with me and for another brother-in-law who came in spirit. For Ann and Sally, always there for us. And for sky, water, and enough energy, I hope, to get my broken body back to shore. Amen.

WE CAMPED that night atop Rock Pass at nearly 7,000 feet. This was the steep, loose-gravel pass that had thwarted so many NoBos from finishing just a few weeks before; I lamented their having gotten so close but having to turn back. Now, almost all the snow was gone.

I was already looking forward to the next day's nineteen miles back to Harts Pass, and perhaps a hitch to the small town of Mazama far below, where Ann and Sally would be waiting.

When a clap of thunder crackled, my instinctive reaction was fear. But as I battened down my tent for what I thought could be a long night, any worries washed away. I had a sense of peace. Indeed, the thunder shook, rattled, and rolled us for half an hour, then moved on to unhinge other PCT hikers sprinkled in the woods to the east.

In the morning, we slept in; goodness, if you couldn't justify sleeping in after hiking 2,650 miles, when could you? At 5:50 A.M., I rolled to my side, and reached for a plastic-encased Svenhard's Danish. Time to get up.

"Mmmmmm," I said to Glenn, mouth half full. "My last Svenhard's Bear Claw. What you having for breakfast?"

"The usual, Twinkies and—."

"Somebody mention bear claws?" intoned a middle-age male voice from outside my tent. In all our years on the trail, this had never happened.

I poked my head out of the rain-soaked vestibule to see a southbound hiker silhouetted against a sky reddened by the soon-to-rise sun. He seemed eager to talk, telling us, when I asked, how he had done the PCT back in 2011, gone on to complete the Continental Divide Trail, and, the previous day, reached the Canadian border to complete his second PCT thru-hike. He was fifty-six and from Colorado.

"What are you up to?" he asked.

"My brother-in-law and I reached the border yesterday, too," I said, "but, unlike you, we didn't do it all at once. We're just section hikers. Took us ten summers over an eleven-year period to get it done."

"Hey," he said, "I've been busting the chops of every section hiker I come across"—*uh, oh, maybe he was a purist who didn't consider us the real deal*—"because they say, 'We're *just* section-hikers.' I have more respect for section hikers than us thru-hikers because they might take a decade or more to finish a really long trail. Man, they've got the tenacity to get back on the trail year after year, knowing damn well how badly their feet are going hurt, how badly their whole body's gonna hurt. Thru-hikers like me just take longer vacations."

I was genuinely touched—and just audacious enough to ask if he'd be willing to say that again, on camera.

"Happy to," he said. And, as I turned on my iPhone video, he did so.*

Afterward, he asked our names.

"I'm Bob. My brother-in-law, Glenn, and I are The Oregon Boys. And you?"

"Greg 'Malto' Gressel."

"Wait," I said. "You're Malto? *The* Malto? Did you say you did the PCT in 2011?"

"Yes."

---

* The clip is on my web site, bobwelchwriter.com. To get there you scan the QR code on page 357.

"We met you near Waldo Lake!"

"Oh, yeah!"

"You're a legend!"

Malto was the Arabian sheik dude who was biting off big-mile days fueled by maltodextrin.

"So, that summer I met you, was that one of your first sections?" he asked.

"It *was* our first section—we did Oregon," I said. "Man, you're in my book, *Cascade Summer.* I mentioned running into you!"

"Someone sent me that book, this guy who was the biggest PCT blogger of 2011! And he bookmarked the page you mentioned me on!"

"What are the chances of meeting you during our first summer on the trail and on our very last morning on the PCT?" I said.

"I'm glad I heard 'bear claws,'" he said. "This is so frickin' cool! Congratulations to you two, The Oregon Boys!"

"And to you!"

AFTER ELEVEN years on the PCT, the reconnection with Malto was a final touch of Trail Magic underscoring the bonds between strangers who become friends. We were all different people from different places, different ages, and hiking the PCT for different reasons, but the trail gave us a common connection to each other that transcended it all.

"The trail is the great equalizer," my friend Geoff would later say while showing me a photo of him with his arm around a white-bearded gentlemen a few years his senior. "A blue-collar barber from Springfield, Oregon, hiked a hundred miles with Flado, a retired nuclear physicist from Slovakia."

Now, in the North Cascades, I watched as Malto walked along the ridge, turned into the woods, and headed for Harts Pass. Glenn and I soon packed up to do the same. Half an hour later—pack on, shoelaces tied, heart full—I looked out over the Rock Pass Basin to Canada, now bathed in a hint of orange sun, then exhaled.

"Time out?" I said.

Glenn looked at his Casio.

"Sixty-forty three."

"Copy that."

And with our long journey over, The Oregon Boys headed for home one final time.

Top: Between our California and Washington sections in 2022, I picked up Eagle Eye and his friends in Shasta City, California. They spent a night with us in Eugene before I took them to a trailhead near Mount Hood. Left to right: Pit Stop, of Tucson, Arizona; Ghost, of Australia; my friend Geoff Tyson, who joined us; Sally, who fixed the wonderful breakfast; Lunch Box, of Clovis, California; Bodega, of Orlando, Florida; and Eagle Eye. Above: At dawn, Glenn chugging up Glacier Pass, from which you could see mountains in Canada.

Above: Hopkins Lake, at the foot of the Devils Staircase, was where we spent our final night before reaching the border—and where I swam to celebrate reaching Canada. Photos seldom do justice to elevation drops; from this point to the lake was 2.6 switchbacking miles, taking us well over an hour. Opposite page, top: Glenn and I at the Canadian border. Lower right: Malto greeting us on our last morning on the trail—more than a decade after we'd seen him on our first leg in Oregon. What were the chances? (See page 63 for a photo of us taken in 2011.)

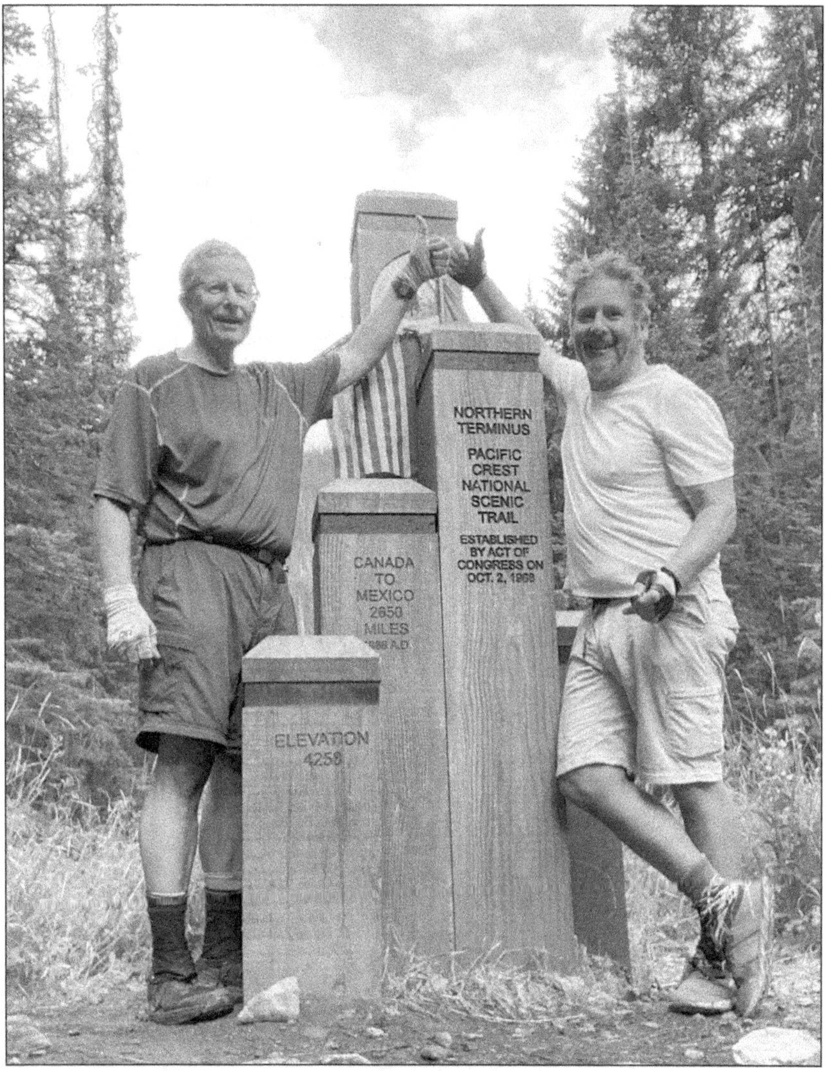
NORTHERN
TERMINUS
PACIFIC
CREST
NATIONAL
SCENIC
TRAIL
ESTABLISHED
BY ACT OF
CONGRESS ON
OCT. 2, 1968
CANADA
TO
MEXICO
2650
MILES
ELEVATION
4258

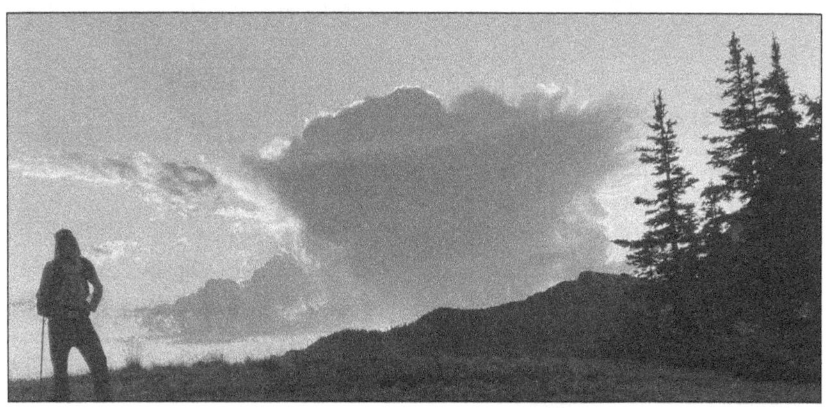

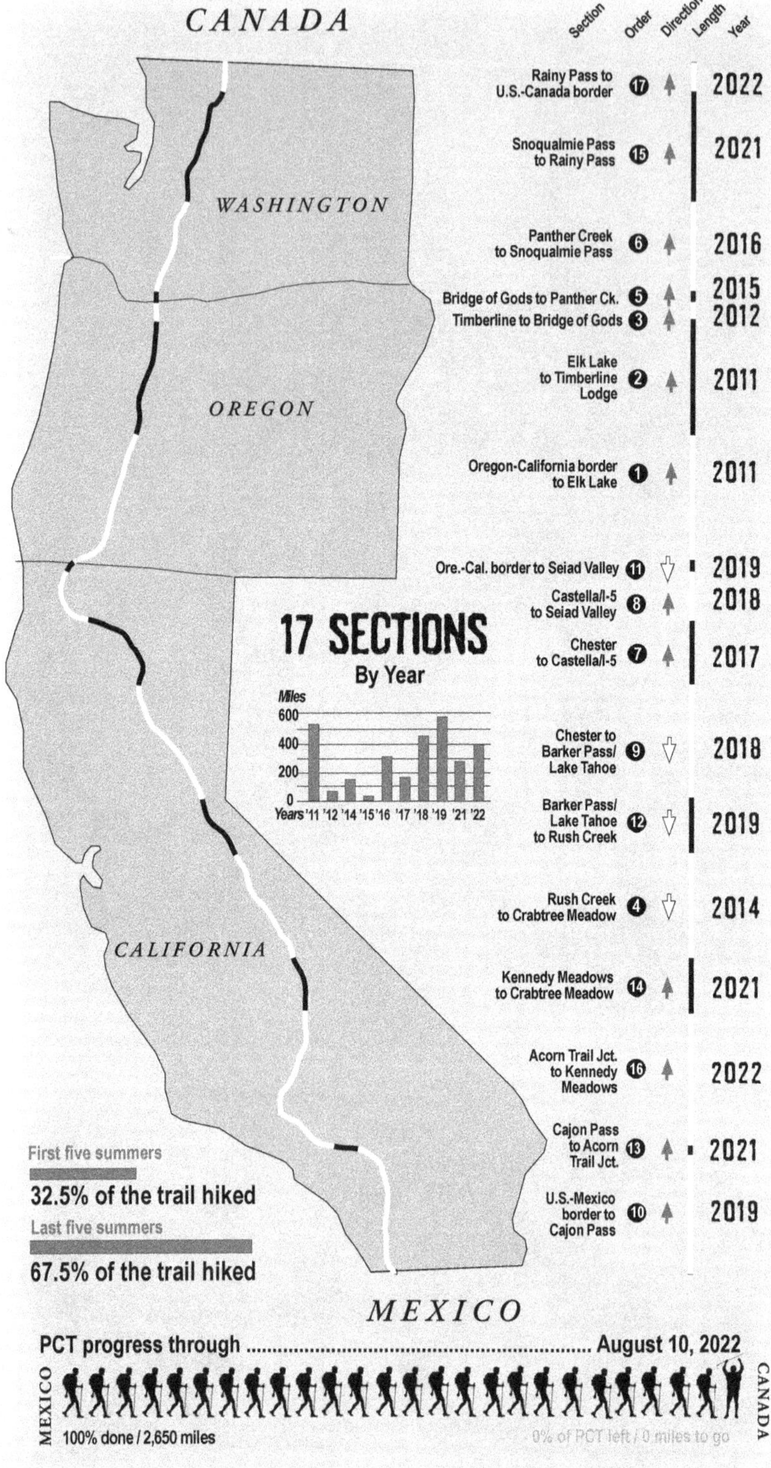
CANADA
Section
Order
Direction
Length
Year
Rainy Pass to U.S.-Canada border 17 2022
Snoqualmie Pass to Rainy Pass 15 2021
WASHINGTON
Panther Creek to Snoqualmie Pass 6 2016
Bridge of Gods to Panther Ck. 5 2015
Timberline to Bridge of Gods 3 2012
Elk Lake to Timberline Lodge 2 2011
OREGON
Oregon-California border to Elk Lake 1 2011
Ore.-Cal. border to Seiad Valley 11 2019
Castella/I-5 to Seiad Valley 8 2018
17 SECTIONS
By Year
Chester to Castella/I-5 7 2017
Miles
600
400
200
0
Years '11 '12 '14 '15 '16 '17 '18 '19 '21 '22
Chester to Barker Pass/ Lake Tahoe 9 2018
Barker Pass/ Lake Tahoe to Rush Creek 12 2019
Rush Creek to Crabtree Meadow 4 2014
CALIFORNIA
Kennedy Meadows to Crabtree Meadow 14 2021
Acorn Trail Jct. to Kennedy Meadows 16 2022
Cajon Pass to Acorn Trail Jct. 13 2021
First five summers
32.5% of the trail hiked
U.S.-Mexico border to Cajon Pass 10 2019
Last five summers
67.5% of the trail hiked
MEXICO
PCT progress through .... August 10, 2022
MEXICO
CANADA
100% done / 2,650 miles
0% of PCT left / 0 miles to go

TRAILHEAD OUT

FINAL THOUGHTS ON THE JOURNEY

It is good to have an end to journey towards;
but it is the journey that matters in the end.
—Ursula Le Guin

THAT THE moment at the border was special didn't surprise me. That I wasn't overwhelmed by it didn't either. My reaction affirmed that this had never been a crusade to reach the Canadian border but a commitment to experience a thin, twisting, enchanting trail with a good friend. This had always been about a journey, not a destination. As such, Canada had always been more "means to an end" than "end unto itself."

On hiking, Thoreau once said, "If you are ready to leave your father and mother, and brother and sister, and wife and child and friends, and never see them again … then you are ready for a walk." I was not ready to pay such a price. True, I was willing to hit pause on some things—She Who is the silent hero of my story—but often the only thing that kept me going at the end of the trail was the thought of coming home to her, to my adult sons and their wives, to my grandchildren, and to my friends.

People are relational; nature is not. People sustain us; nature does not. The ranger in *The Last Season*, Randy Morgenson, struggled with that; so, too, did Chris McCandless in Krakauer's *Into the Wild.* I love the beauty and challenge of the high mountains, but they will never replace people and God as my life's sustenance. As my old college hiking buddy Dan Roberts said: "How sad to love things that can't love you back."

Along such lines, I'm not of the opinion that the PCT magically changes people; nature is neutral. The trail has no agenda. It doesn't—*can't*— make discontent people who step on it at the Mexican border content people at the Canadian border. That said, I think people can use such an experience to hone themselves, shape themselves, and inspire themselves to change in an array of ways—physically, mentally, spiritually, you name it. But they, the people, must be the agent of change; the trail can only serve as a catalyst.

Though not in monumental ways, my PCT experience changed me. It helped me become more patient, persistent, and apt to improvise when stuck. It encouraged me to risk. It connected me to an array of people far different from me, always good for one's perspective. It splayed my shoe size from a 9½ to an 11½. And it made me less likely to ever again eat a beef and cheese stick.

I'd read books by people who had hiked the PCT and returned home to great periods of depression because it was a mountaintop experience that they could not replicate with life's less lofty routines. Me? I look for adventure in all the life trails I walk: family trails, friendship trails, spiritual trails, writing trails, sports trails, sailing trails, book trails—all such braids of experience twined in the common curiosity of wondering what's over the next pass.

REGRETS ABOUT the experience? Only one, that for this book—and, yes, I consider it an official addendum to the hike—I had to turn nearly two hundred color photos into black-and-whites. It's hard to describe the array of colors on the PCT: the sandy browns of the desert, the near-translucent waters of the High Sierra, the greens of an Oregon forest, the turquoise of Washington's Mica Lake.*

Would I have done the PCT if, in the beginning, I knew it would cost:

▲ One hundred and forty-eight days away from home?

▲ Thirty-two travel days, just getting to and from that trail, requiring 17,701 miles of going and coming?

▲ Some 180 miles of extraneous hiking miles needed to get to and from trailheads; to follow workarounds because of fire closures; to get to off-trail water and food; and to return to points that we overshot?

▲ Military Diet lunches consisting of half a cup of tuna and dry toast?

▲ An estimated $17,000 for food, equipment, travel, and the like?

▲ Pain, blisters, mosquitoes, monotony, chafing, and more than 200 squats over cat holes?

The idealistic me would argue yes, but the realistic me? I doubt it. But to be fair, if you ask that question, you must also ask another: *Would I have said*

---

* See back cover of book.

no if I had known, back then, all that I would have missed?

▲ The privilege of spending 148 days in some of the most beautiful back country on earth?

▲ The sense, from time to time, of walking on top of the world?

▲ The grace of the cook in Belden who opened the kitchen after they'd closed, just so we could have chili cheese fries?

▲ The honor of New Hampshire Don sharing about the loss of his son?

▲ The hospitality of the woman at Packer Lake Lodge?

▲ The pride of watching my friend Geoff transition from sluggard to PCT conqueror?

▲ The delight of sitting in our backyard with five young hikers, including Eagle Eye, who, when Sally asked if they wanted more of some breakfast item, always eagerly said, "Yes, please!"

▲ The bonding with a brother-in-law who not only saved my life but who taught me so much?

If I'd known what I would have missed, no way would I have passed up the trip. In fact, I now can't imagine *not* having hiked the trail.

I think of a moment soon after Glenn and I made camp at a lake that we had all to ourselves on a Friday evening. Suddenly, a twig snapped. We heard voices. Soon, the peaceful splendor was shattered by the arrival of an entire Boy Scout troop. As the Scouts got louder, I got angrier; *how dare they spoil my perfect evening!* Glenn, a former Scout, obviously had a different perspective.

"These guys are having the time of their lives," he said with a huge smile on his face. "They're going to remember this night for the rest of their lives."

His words humbled me. They broadened my perspective. Time and again, in years since, I've found myself getting aggravated by some intrusion on my time or space, then remembered that incident. Immediately, I see the experience through someone else's eyes, not mine, and it changes everything. I need to remind myself: *The trail does not belong to me. I share it with others.*

ADVENTURE comes in all shapes and sizes. It can be as active as hiking a 2,650-mile trail or as sedentary as holding a friend's hand during cancer treatments, as external as reaching out to somehow who's hurting or as internal as trying to quit an addiction. The key is a willingness, like the Pevensie kids, to walk through the closet door.

To let our imaginations stay out and play after dark. To risk. And, finally, to take that first step, not knowing where the trail will lead.

Glenn fighting the wind on Tehachapi Pass late one afternoon in June 2022.

AFTERWORD

GLENN PETERSEN

It was another great day. As usual we were up before daylight. I powered down a couple of Hostess Twinkies, and we were off. Starting in the early hours of the morning is a treat. In addition to hiking in the cool of the morning, we could get a big jump on the day's destination and enjoy the forest as it comes to life.

This day we arrived at the Canadian border shortly after 7 A.M. Wow, we made it! We celebrated! We climbed onto the border monument, took pictures, took videos, and ate snacks. The closest route to civilization was eight miles north to Manning Park in Canada. But, because of COVID, the entry into Canada remained closed.

We gathered our packs and began retracing our path thirty-one miles south to the PCT trail exit at Harts Pass in the U.S. It was a beautiful day. Hiking up and out of the Hopkins Lake Basin, we got high enough to enjoy the awesome, expansive views of Washington's North Cascades.

Near the end of the day, we arrived at a large treeless bowl with Canyon Creek far below. We switchbacked up to Rock Pass at 6,491 feet and declared this to be our campsite. Trees to our south, the bowl to our north, with clouds and thunder gathering to the west.

We had plenty of time to enjoy dinner: for me, sausage, Wheat Thins, nuts, and Oreo cookies, which had become my staples.

Dusk gathered, the temperature dropped, and it began to rain. As I climbed into my tent for one last night on the trail I was especially content.

The rain pelted my tent and the thunder boomed, but I was dry, cozy, warm and, as a bonus, I had a small paperback to read: Louis L'Amour, of course. As I fell asleep, I thought, at this moment in time: *Life couldn't be better.*

And then I thought about the two of us, Bob and me. As friends, we had experienced difficulties and joys for eleven years on the trail. I thought of the wonderful adventures we had shared.

And wondered what new adventures lay ahead for The Oregon Boys.

Ann Petersen (inset) / Sally Welch

The Oregon Boys at Portland International Airport in June 2022 after completing the desert section north of LA that had thwarted us the year before. Inset: The way we were, eleven years earlier when we started at the Oregon-California border. Why did we look so much more upbeat near the end than at the beginning?

EPILOGUE

A man is not old until regrets take the place of dreams.
—John Barrymore

Laura Buhl, the University of Oregon student who introduced me to the Pacific Crest Trail, graduated, married, hiked the 2,200-mile Appalachian Trail, and now, at fifty, is a land-use planner with the state of Oregon. She lives in Salem.

Ben and Kate, the Australians we met within moments of arriving at the Oregon-California border in 2011, were the first PCT hikers to reach Canada that year. Twelve years later, they are still together, the parents of two little boys, now seven and three. They've hiked the 3,312-mile Bicentennial Trail in Australia, sailed for six months on the East Coast of Australia (with an eighteen-month-old) and, two years ago, built an "off-grid shack" in Queensland where they home-school the boys. Kate earned her master's of education degree and works full-time; Ben stays home with the boys.

Cisco, who helped us navigate the Oregon snow in our first stretch of trail in July 2011, reached Canada later that summer. Though a leg injury forced Roadrunner to stop midway through Washington in 2011, she later finished the entire trail. The two have hiked all over the world, including five months on the Te Araroa in New Zealand (2012-13); the GR20 along the spine of the island of Corsica, in the Mediterranean (2014); partway through the Continental Divide Trail (2015); the Irish Coast to Coast Trail (2018); and hundreds of miles on the Sierra High Route, most of it above 12,000 feet.

Rob and Barb Widmer, who warned us of the dangers of Devils Peak a week into our first experience on the PCT in 2011, returned to the trail and hiked all of Oregon in 2012. Since then, Rob has completed all the PCT except for the 441-mile Walker Pass-to-Echo Summit (Lake Tahoe) stretch.

Not Phil's Dad (Richard Lee), whose Trail Magic at Tacoma Pass in Washington saved me during one of my most difficult days on the trail, is now in his fourteenth year of providing food for PCT hikers. Turns out he lives less than a mile from the house Sally and I had rented in Bellevue during the 1980s when I was a columnist for *The Journal-American.*

Luis "Lou" Mena, aka Wrightwood Lou, fell in love with hiking overseas. He and his wife, Tawna, did the 500-mile Camino Frances (Spain) in 2018, the 200-mile Portuguese Camino in 2022, and hope to do the seventy-eight-mile Camino Inglise (Spain) in 2024.

Grandson Lincoln's Northwest All-Star team finished third in the 2022 National 10U Babe Ruth World Series. An hour after Glenn and I had said goodbye to Malto on that final morning, daughter-in-law Deena's satellite message informed me that the team had won again to make the final eight out of twenty teams. Because the team's quarterfinal game the next morning would be streamed over the Internet, Glenn happily agreed to my idea of hoofing it to Harts Pass in one day instead of two. Once at the trailhead, we paid a retired Forest Service employee, Laurie Dowie, $150 to take us down Washington's "most dangerous road" to Mazama. We stayed in a hiker's hostel, the Lion's Den, that had Internet. We listened to the game the following day at 6 A.M. outside, beneath towering evergreens. With the team down 5-2, Lincoln hit a three-run triple and scored the go-ahead run himself as Northwest advanced to the final four. He was named the game's Most Valuable Player and made the tournament's All-Defensive team, making the listening experience all the sweeter.

Eagle Eye (Vinura Perera), the Sri Lankan hiker who had, with four other hikers, stayed with Sally and me, wound up stymied by fires for a second time. After parting ways, amicably, with his buddies, he hitchhiked south from Snoqualmie Pass, Washington, to Mount Hood to hike Oregon north-to-south. As more fires raged, he called it quits. Glenn and I tag-teamed to drive him from Etna, California, to Albany, Oregon (me) and from Albany to Seattle (Glenn), where he stayed with a hiker friend, resigned to giving up his dream of getting to Canada. However, after a few days of sightseeing, he got restless. As the fires abated, he returned to Snoqualmie Pass and started north, keeping me posted of his progress. With a fire near Harts Pass closing the border where Glenn and I finished, Eagle Eye bounced east and found a trail to the border. He reached Canada October 1, all alone.*

Marie, the speedster from Germany whom Glenn dubbed "Lois Lane," was deterred by fires and ended her journey at Burney Falls, California. "I hope to come back and continue at some point," she said. "At this point I just felt like I had everything I wanted my journey to be."

Sequoia (Keon Burns), the fellow Oregonian who shared pizza with Glenn and me shortly after the Acton lockdown ended, made it to Washington. But fires and the death of an uncle ended his quest for Canada. That said, the six-foot-four-inch basketball player/artist hiked 2,250 miles.

My friend Geoff Tyson hoped to do The Oregon Challenge in July 2023—hike the state's PCT portion in two weeks—but a surgery to free up his femoral artery made that impossible. Instead, he drove to Leavenworth, Washington, and spent a weekend in a friend's remote cabin going cold turkey to quit smoking. As of August 1, he hadn't had a puff. And was setting his sites on a new goal: a 2024 north-to-south hike of the PCT.

High-jumper Dick Fosbury, on whose takeoff point for the 1968 Olympic Trials at Echo Summit I camped in 2018, died on March 12, 2023, after a recurrence of lymphoma. He was seventy-six. Even though it was Mexico City that won him worldwide fame, I like to believe Foz's greatest triumph came in the pines of Echo Summit at the Trials. Down to his last jump at 7'2" in an attempt to make the third and final spot on the U.S. team, he nailed it, then cleared 7'3" on his first attempt. May we all have the courage that Fosbury had to think outside the box and to soar—even when the odds are heavily against us.

The mystery involving the heavy, rusted metal strip that I found near Glacier Peak in 2021 found a "what" answer but not a "why." In April 2023, I showed a Eugene friend steeped in aeronautics the photo and told him where I'd found it. I wondered if it could have been some casing for a jet engine that had fallen off. "No," Wally Anderson told me, "that's Marston Mat." As my eyes widened, he shared about how in World War II, in Marston, North Carolina, the U.S. developed perforated steel planking sections that interlinked to create temporary landing strips for planes. (The holes allowed for drainage.) I was convinced Anderson was right. And Glenn confirmed as much in

---

* His video documentary can be found at https://bit.ly/40CDsrf.

July2023 when, by chance, he saw samples of such mats at the Museum of Flight in Seattle.* I still have no idea what a section of Marston Mat was doing at 5,750 feet in the north Washington mountains, sixty trail miles from the nearest paved road, and in a place so rugged it would be tough landing a helicopter, much less a plane. Thus, the mystery remains unsolved.

In early September 2022, a month after Glenn and I reached the border, multiple fires in the Pasayten Wilderness near the Canadian border forced closure of the PCT at Harts Pass, meaning thru-hikers who'd reached that point couldn't complete the trail at Monument 78. It was a bitter pill for hundreds of hikers who had come so far. By spring 2023 another element emerged to vex PCT hikers: record snows in California. Bombarded with seventeen "atmospheric rivers" since October 2022, the High Sierra and other points south were buried under twice the average amount of snow as usual. By April 2023, 11,059-foot Mammoth Mountain had measured *seventy-three feet* of snow. Such mind-boggling depths spelled danger, if not impossibility, for PCT hikers trying to get over the High Sierra and across the dozens of rivers, streams, and creeks therein. By August 2023, hikers on Facebook's Class of 2023 page were reporting fewer than one in five hikers who started in Mexico had gotten through the High Sierra; most hopped forward. The record snow, combined with increased fire danger—six of the seven largest California wildfires have occurred since 2020—conspired to create a new PCT reality: the trail was arguably now more difficult to complete than at any time since at least the advent of the Halfmile app in 2012.

That said, by January 2023, Glenn was restless for more hiking. I was not. However, in writing *Seven Summers,* I found myself drawn back not to hiking per se—Glenn talked of hiking the Oregon Desert, which didn't interest me in the least—but to the PCT in particular. What, I began wondering, would Oregon look like on a north-to-south PCT trip? Glenn liked the idea, so we set an August 17, 2023 departure date for a nine-day trip to hike 123 miles of trail. The intent, at least in my eyes, was not to do the whole state in one summer, or even two or three. Instead, the intent was to take our time, hiking perhaps eight to twelve miles a day to arrive midafternoon and read, nap, cook a hot meal, watch a sunset, make s'mores, contemplate the meaning of life in the stillness of dusk, then fall asleep beneath a starry sky. Maybe even brush our teeth at some point.

---

* See photo page 350.

Ben and Kate, the Australian couple we met moments after arriving to begin our first PCT section in 2011, now "live off the grid" in Queensland with their two little boys, William, left, and Henry.

Californians Roadrunner (Baerbel Steffestun), left, and Cisco (Rich Combs) have hiked all over the world since they guided us through Oregon's snow that first year, 2011.

My friend Geoff Tyson, left, here with Flado—the retired nuclear physicist from Slovakia with whom he hiked—turned some health scares into impetus to quit smoking and commit to a north-to-south attempt of the PCT in 2024.

Ann Petersen

Top: Eagle Eye, of Sri Lanka, reached the U.S.-Canada border on October 1 to become one of the few PCT hikers in Northern Washington in late 2022 to do so—and certainly one of the last. Because of fires, he wound up reaching Canada northeast of Mazama, Washington. Above, left: Grandson Lincoln Robert Welch with the All-Defensive Team trophy he won at the National 10U Babe Ruth World Series Baseball Tournament in Indiana while I was finishing the trail in August 2022. Above, right: Nearly a year after we reached Canada, Glenn was touring the Museum of Flight in Seattle when he saw something familiar: a display featuring the same Marston Mat steel planking we'd seen near Glacier Peak. He said it was "undoubtedly" the same stuff we had seen.

ACKNOWLEDGMENTS

When I ran the Hood-to-Coast Relay from Timberline Lodge to Seaside, one person got the glory of racing to the finish line in the sand in front of hundreds of applauding onlookers. Eleven others made that possible while running in obscurity, some in the middle of the night.

It's the same with book writing. I get my name on the cover—I'm the Sand Man—but many others toiled in obscurity to make that possible. And they need to know what they've meant to me, my life, and this book. So ...

Thanks to my fellow PCT hikers,
for inspiration, information, and encouragement

Laura Buhl, who introduced me to the trail in August 1999 when we bumped into each other near Little Belknap Crater.

Craig Mayne, who, in 2010, became Mr. Miyagi to my Grasshopper.

Ben (Dyer) and Kate (Manning), Blaze, Bloodbath, the Colorado Boys, and every other hiker that first year who treated us as if we belonged.

Greg "Malto"' Gressel, who I met near Waldo Lake in 2011 and again on our final PCT morning eleven years later. His affirmation to us as section-hikers was like a sprinkle of mozzarella cheese on a fresh piece of pepperoni.

Cisco (Rich Combs) and Roadrunner (Baerbel Steffestun), who, that first year, taught us how to find the trail in the snow and who "adopted" me for three days.

The kid at Timberline Lodge in September 2011 who encouraged me to stop saying "We're *just* doing Oregon."

Rob and Barbara Widmer, who, in July 2011, warned us of the dangers of Devils Peak and who've kept in touch with me for more than a decade since.

Hot Dog, Glenn's guru-for-a-day, who warned us about the fire near the Oregon-California border, 2017, and staunchly defended foam sleeping pads.

Eagle Eye, of Sri Lanka, whose resolve to reach Canada in 2022 surpassed that of any hiker I've known.

Thierno and Marion, of France, who in 2017 came so far just to get on the PCT—and went even farther once they were on it. (I could listen to their wonderful accents forever!)

Nina and Dennis Murphy, the young Santa Cruz couple who saved us with their donation of food atop Glen Pass in 2014.

New Hampshire Don, who, in 2019, dared to share with me the hurt of losing a son.

Thanks to the Trail Angels, who, like lighthouses,
served with no sense of getting anything in return

Not Phil's Dad (Richard Lee), at Tacoma Pass in Washington, who saved me on a wet day on which I was in the dumps, 2016.

Janelle, the Burbank, California, woman who got up at 4 A.M to prepare a breakfast casserole that lifted my spirits on State Route 2 in the San Gabriel Mountains, 2022.

Wrightwood Lou (Luis "Lou" Mena), who helped us with an array of logistics and saved us a day in 2022 by driving us to the Acorn Trail Junction.

The folks who took us to, and picked us up from, trailheads: Glenn's folks, Paul and Pauline Petersen (Albany/Eugene to Elk Lake, 2011); Paul Whose Last Name I Never Got (Lone Pine to Rush Creek Trailhead, 2014); Kathleen New (Lone Pine to Kennedy Meadows and Horseshoe Meadow to Lone Pine, 2021); Sammy (Reno-Tahoe International Airport to Barker Pass, 2018); writer friend Mike Yorkey, who, beyond Sally and Ann, drove us more miles than anyone else (Encinitas, California, to Campo on the U.S.-Mexico border, 2019; Cajon Pass to John Wayne International Airport in Orange County, 2019; and Kennedy Meadows to John Wayne, 2022); Nicole Yorkey, whose amazing "last supper," hospitality, and Swiss Bliss creations given to us upon our arrival at Cajon Pass in 2019 were unforgettable; Uber driver Ehab Al Saqi (John Wayne to BJ's Restaurant & Brewhouse in Rancho Cucamonga, 2021); Phil and Susan Dowty (trailhead south of Highway 58 to Tehachapi, 2022); and Laurie Dowie for getting us down Washington's "most dangerous road," Harts Pass, in 2022 after our PCT journey was over.

Thanks to artist Don White

In December 2022, just as I started writing *Seven Summers,* I stumbled across the work of the Santiam Canyon, Oregon, artist on the Internet. I immediately imagined his drawings in my book. "I want you to capture the moments that my words and photos can't," I told him. He did so wonderfully—and with a generous and fun spirit that made working with him an absolute pleasure—and a good excuse to eat teriyaki chicken burgers at Red Robin in Albany.

Thanks to those who taught me to write,
honed my ability to write and encouraged me to write

Shirley Wirth, my fifth-grade teacher at Garfield School who, beyond my mother, was the first person to believe in me as a writer; Jim MacPherson, who honed whatever journalistic skills I had at Cheldelin Junior High and Corvallis High; Roberta Shaw, a CHS English teacher who introduced me to Hemingway and other great writers; Ed Coleman, whose Black Literature classes at the University of Oregon broadened my world, a must for writers; Jon Franklin, whose book *Writing for Story* revolutionized my writing; Keven Miller, a former *Register-Guard* editor who channeled Franklin better than anyone; Jeff Wright, who demanded excellence as my column editor at *The Register-Guard;* Dean Rea, who gave me my first job at *The Bulletin* in Bend, has mentored me for decades, and keeps on being a great journalist into his nineties; Bob Chandler, *The Bulletin* publisher who gave me much grief—"get a new dictionary, Welch!"—but also much freedom to test my skills; Arlene Bryant, my features editor at *The Journal-American* in Bellevue, Washington, who edited me like a really thorough dental hygentist; Jane Kirkpatrick, a former writing student of mine who became a historical-fiction phenom, a co-leader at my Beachside Writers Workshops, and a friend who's inspired me for decades; and, finally, the hundreds of Beachside Writers whose enthusiasm sparked my own. In particular, I honor the memory of Jeanette Bishop, who attended more Beachsiders than anyone, but who passed away while I was writing this book.

Thanks to those who kept my body going

Kathy Sherwood of Custom Orthotics, who simply would not quit in her attempt to modify my orthotics and get them right, year after year; physical therapists Brian Gesik and Ryan Wiser, who loosened up my toes before hikes; Dr. Don Jones, who did my knee surgery; Dr. Kirk Jacobson, my primary care provider; and Dr. Kraig Jacobson, Kirk's twin brother and an allergist who kept my mastocytosis in check—and blessedly held off on retiring until after I finished the PCT.

Thanks to a bunch of people who don't fit any category beyond supporting me in some critical way

Graphic designer Steve Kuhn, whose inDesign expertise saved me so many times that he and his wife, Jen, have earned a lifetime supply of Pockets of Love from Sabai in Eugene; Tom Penix, my book-layout "lifeline," for improving my designs and for encouragement galore; John Barnum, who resuscitated an old MacBook so I could retrieve 2011 PCT photos; Bob Blanchard, who, despite health challenges, edited my final draft with tender care (and the smallest sticky page markers I've ever seen an editor use!); Kelly Fenley, who added his impressive editing skills to the effort; Brent Northup, whose "proof book" feedback watered my wilting confidence; Jim Meacham, Senior Research Associate Emeritus in Geography at the University of Oregon, who painstakingly gave my amateurish maps an edit (but blame me, not him, for remaining mistakes!); Steve Hunnicut, who pinch-hit so admirably in the editing batter's box late in the game; prayer warriors Clarice Wilsey (Eugene) and Barbara Hilton (Jefferson), indefatigable in their commitment to interceding on our behalf for safe travels; my "swim team" pals Will Kerns, Adam (AquaMan) Specht, Debbie Altman, Jill Thomson, Jules DeGiulio, Ron Bellamy, Vi Peck, and 1968 Olympic bronze medalist Jack Horsley, who encouraged my aqua pursuits; mountain climber Mike Hawley, whose comeback after a fall atop Mount Thielsen defined courage for me; hiking buddies John Woodman, Jay Locey, and Dan Roberts, who shared backpacking trips with me during our early years and have remained great friends for half a century; Wally Anderson and Steven Robert, of Eugene, who supplied key nuggets of info; Jason and Ann Schar, who've shared with us road adventures, including a flat tire on the Alvord Desert, campfires, and s'mores for decades, all in the spirit of the outdoors; *Register-Guard* readers, who followed my updates from the PCT; and all who read my first book on the trail, *Cascade Summer.*

Thanks to Geoff (Doin' Stuff) Tyson, my barber and friend

After reading *Cascade Summer,* he hiked Oregon, then the entire PCT. His inspiration fueled me at times when my pursuit of Canada was flagging. And he twice read this book's rough drafts—and, oh, were they rough. But nothing can top his Trail Angel trip of 2019: driving a thousand miles to surprise Glenn and me with dinner in Palm Springs after our knee-grinding hike down Fuller Ridge. I'm still shaking my head.

Thanks to family members

My grandfather Will Adams, who overcame childhood trauma to find the freedom and beauty of the outdoors, and passed his love for camping on to my father.

My father, Warren, whose late-afternoon hikes with me from Cultus Lake to the Teddy Lakes and Muskrat Lake in the 1960s whet my interest for high-mountain trails.

My grandparents, Ben and Gayle Schumacher, who bought a beach cabin in Yachats in 1936 in whose upgrade I wrote most of this book. It's a blessing—and they're a blessing—I never take for granted.

My mother, Marolyn, who left a legacy of love and adventure, and was never happier than when flipping "Welch's egg wads" on the Coleman Stove at Cultus Lake, sailing at Fern Ridge Lake, or walking barefoot on the Yachats beach—the latter at ninety-two.

My sons, Ryan and Jason, and daughters-in-law, Susan and Deena, who inspire me with their leave-it-all-on-the-field approaches to life, and to the children they've raised with the same go-for-it spirit: Cade, Avin, Keaton, Lincoln, and McCoy.

My sister-in-law, Linda Scandrett, who allowed me the freedom to write about my relationship with her late husband Greg and reviewed that section herself, which I know was an emotional strain.

Thanks to Ann Petersen

She not only drove us, organized us, and arranged air travel for us, but edited *Seven Summers* at three stages with a tenacity unmatched in my four decades of being edited. Her commitment to this journey was invaluable.

Thanks to Glenn Petersen

For the courage to say yes in the first place, the diligence to patch my wounds, and the patience to put up with me, period. I couldn't have asked for a better partner in climb.

Thanks to Sally Jean

Nearly fifty years ago, when we married, she didn't sign up for this. And yet her encouragement fueled my entire trail experience. It was Sally who recommended Glenn as my hiking partner, who stuffed inspirational notes in my pack, who said yes to Eagle Eye and his buddies, and who inspires me daily as a quiet adventurer, lifting up those around her. From the beginning, she has been, and will always be, the best thing about coming home from the trail.

Laurie Dowie was among the dozens of people who made our trip possible. The retired U.S. Forest Service employee was fearless driving us down the white-knuckle Harts Pass road so I could follow grandson Lincoln's baseball game. At one point, she stopped to show us where, another time, she had veered to miss an oncoming vehicle and a front tire went over the edge. Instead of photographing the dramatic dropoff just beyond her, I concentrated on her. *I was intrigued by how her hair matched the color of the clouds and how she seemed to be floating amid the mountains she loved.*

APPENDIX

LINKS

Welch stuff

Scan QR code to the right or type this link—https://www.bobwelchwriter.com/about-3—into your URL window to:

▲ View color photos of the trip.

▲ Hear Bob's last-day conversation with Greg "Malto" Gressel"

▲ Hear Glenn try to scare off the mountain lion near Burney Falls.

▲ Listen to the actual sound of a mountain lion.

▲ See a little video footage of Bob and Glenn's journey.

▲ View Welch's web site: bobwelchwriter.com

Other stuff

▲ View Eagle Eye's 2022 documentary:
https://bit.ly/40CDsrf

▲ Learn about the Trailside Reader books available on the PCT:
https://pcttrailsidereader.com/

▲ Discover more about the Pacific Crest Trail Association and the PCT:
https://www.pcta.org

▲ Dive into the best site for intricate information on the trail and its flora, fauna, lakes, streams, mountains, meadows, and more:
https://www.postholer.com/databook/Pacific-Crest-Trail/1

▲ Explore the nuances of PCT hikers through Halfmile's surveys:
https://www.halfwayanywhere.com/trails/pacific-crest-trail/pct-hiker-survey-2022/

BREAKDOWN OF THE 17 SECTIONS ...

In chronological order of sections hiked

Leg No.	Yr.	Direction	State	Start Point	Date started	PCT mile
1	2011	North	Oregon	Oregon-Calif. border	July 22, 2011	1691.7
2	2011	North	Oregon	Elk Lake	Aug. 28, 2011	1952.6
3	2012	North	Oregon	Timberline Lodge	Aug. 17, 2012	2097.0
4	2014	South	California	Rush Creek Junction.	July 28, 2014	925.9
5	2015	North	Washington	Bridge of the Gods	July 18, 2015	2146.9
6	2016	North	Washington	Panther Creek	Aug. 27, 2016	2182.2
7	2017	North	California	Chester	Aug. 23, 2017	1331.3
8	2018 (1 of 2)	North	California	Castella on I-5	July 10, 2018	1500.6
9	2018 (2 of 2)	South	California	Chester	Aug. 4, 2018	1331.3
10	2019 (1 of 3)	North	California	Campo	April 14, 2019	0.0
11	2019 (2 of 3)	South	California	Oregon-Calif. border	July 28, 2019	1691.7
12	2019 (3 of 3)	South	California	Barker Pass (Tahoe)	Sept. 8, 2019	1124.8
13	2021 (1 of 3)	North	California	Cajon Pass	June 14, 2021	342.0
14	2021 (2 of 3)	North	California	Kennedy Meadows	June 22, 2021	702.2
15	2021 (3 of 3)	North	Washington	Snoqualmie Pas	Aug. 17, 2021	2393.0
16	2022	North	California	Acorn Trail Junction.	May 18, 2022	363.4
17	2022	North	Washington	Rainy Pass	Aug. 6, 2022	2591.1

... FROM START (2011) TO FINISH (2022)

Finish Point	Date finished	PCT mile	Nights this trip	Nights total	Miles/ trip	Miles/ total	% of PCT done
Elk Lake	Aug. 5, 2011	1952.6	14	14	261.6	261.6	9.9%
Timberline Lodge	Sept. 3, 2011	2097.0	7 *	21	144.4	406	15.3%
Ore.-Wash. border	Aug. 19, 2012	2146.9	2	23	49.9	455.2	17.2%
Crabtree Meadow	Aug. 9, 2014	766.3	12	35	159.6	614.8	23.2%
Panther Creek	July 20, 2015	2182.2	2	37	35.3	650.1	24.5%
Snoqualmie Pass	Sept. 7, 2016	2393.0	11	48	210.8	860.9	32.5%
Castella/I-5	Sept. 1, 2017	1500.6	9	57	169.3	1030.2	39.0%
Seiad Valley	July 19, 2018	1655.9	9	66	155.3	1187.5	44.9%
Barker Pass (Tahoe)	Aug. 15, 2018	1124.8	11	77	206.5	1395	54.6%
Cajon Pass	May 2, 2019	342.0	18	95	342.0	1737	65.5%
Seiad Valley	July 29, 2019	1655.9	1	96	35.8	1772.8	66.9%
Rush Creek Junction	Sept. 19, 2019	925.9	11	107	198.9	1993.1	74.4%
Acorn Trail Junction	June 15, 2021	363.4	1	108	21.4	2014.5	76.0%
Crabtree Meadow	June 27, 2021	766.3	5	113	64.1	2078.6	78.4%
Rainy Pass	Aug. 27, 2021	2591.1	10	123	198.1	2276.7	85.9%
Kennedy Meadows	June 7, 2022	702.2	20	143	338.8	2615.5	98.7%
Canadian border	Aug. 10, 2022	2652.6	4	147	61.5	2677	100%

* Excludes two nights I spent on the workaround after Dollar Lake fire and Glenn's vertigo.

BY THE NUMBERS

Bob's age at start: 57

At finish: 68

Glenn's age at start: 59

At finish: 70

Span of years between our "shakedown cruise" and finishing the PCT: 12

Between when we started the PCT hike and when we finished: 11

Number of summers we hiked PCT during that span: 10

Summers we initially planned on to complete the trail: 7

Miles hiked to complete the PCT: 2,650

Miles hiked to get on and off the PCT, because of missed exits, fire workarounds, reaching water sources or stores, etc.: 181

Total miles I hiked: 2,831

Total calories I burned: 740,000

Miles traveled to get to trailheads and back home: 17,701

By automobile: 12,765

By plane: 4,936

Number of days spent on the trail: 148

In months: 4.9

Elevation ascended, in feet: 489,418

Elevation descended, in feet: 448,8411

Days we walked through snow: 9

Days it rained beyond a sprinkle: 6

Percentage of those days that were in Washington: 83

In California: 17

In Oregon: 0

Number of rolls of toilet paper I used: 28

Hours Glenn and I spent together: 3,552

Hours I sensed friction between us: 12

Percentage of friction-free hours: 99.67

Showers I took while hiking the PCT: 8

Ratio of showers taken to miles hiked: 1:331

Number of motels we stayed in while hiking the trail: 3

Number of "zeros" (no hiking) days we took: 1

Neros (half days of hiking): 3

Average miles hiked per day: 17.9

Most miles hiked in a single day: 26

Fewest: 5

Average miles per hour: 2

Average number of hours hiked per day: 9.5

Total number of hours hiked: 1,406

Number of steps taken: 6 million

Average steps per day: 40,540

Number of pairs of shoes I used: 11

Number of pairs of trekking poles I used: 8

Estimated cost, including airfare, gas, motels, equipment, food, taxis, and payments/tips to drivers to get us to and from trailheads: $17,000 *

Number of resupplies we had mailed to us to pick up on trail: 16

Number of resupplies brought to us by Sally and Ann: 2

Number of resupplies at stores along the way, excluding small supplements: 0

Number of hikers from whom we mooched food: 3

Most miles hiked without resupplying: 156 (Warner Springs north to Big Bear)

Most nights on trail in one segment: 20 (Acorn Trail to Kennedy Meadows, 2021)

Fewest: 1, 2021 (Cajon Pass to Acorn Trail Junction)

Most consecutive days without crossing a road of any kind: 16 (John Muir Trail, 2014)

Number of lakes in which I swam: 9

Highest elevation of any lake in which I swam, in feet: 11,500 (Guitar, 2014)

Average weight of pack at start of a segment, in pounds: 32

Fewest hikers seen in a single day: 1 (Chester to Barker Pass, 2018)

Liters of water consumed: 882

Jack Links Original Beef & Cheese Sticks eaten: 240

Bags of one-ounce potato chips crunched: 240

Individual Dots and Cinnamon Bears gummed: 2,100

Percent of trail hiked before deciding to attempt the whole thing: 23

Photos taken: 4,977

Photos in this book: 153

Percent of photos taken that made it into the book: 3.4

Number of unique drawings done by Don White: 15

Of our 17 sections hiked, the number that occurred during PCT's unofficial Hike Nude Day, June 21: 0 (*Whew!*)

Number of forest fires that forced "redos:" 2

Number of shooting stars seen: 11

Average hours of sleep per night: 9

Percent of trail hiked the first five years: 32.5

The last five years: 67.5

Cat holes dug: 278

Percentage successfully hit: 98.5

* My share only. Doesn't include Glenn's.

BEST, WORST, ETC.

Best day: Reaching Canada, August 10, 2022.

Second-best day: (tie), reaching Elk Lake, 2011; reaching Kennedy Meadows, 2022; summiting Mount Whitney, 2014; and seeing sailboat, swimming in Deer Lake, and eating dinner at Packer Lake Lodge with Starburst, 2018.

Worst day: Death of brother-in-law, Greg Scandrett, on our first day out, July 18, 2017.

Favorite stretch of trail: Mather Pass to Forester Pass in High Sierra, California, 2014.

Least favorite: Fuller Ridge, 2019; Hat Creek Rim, California, 2017.

Easiest stretch: (tie) Warm Springs to Timothy Lake, Oregon, 2011, and Chester to Hat Creek Rim, California 2017.

Favorite Trail Magic moment: Tacoma Pass, Washington, 2016. (Not Phil's Dad, Richard Lee, behind a Coleman Stove on a dank, drizzly morning).

Scariest moment: Mountain lion's scream, eyes in dark, Burney Falls, California, 2017.

Favorite piece of gear: Trekking poles. (Helped me literally every step of the way).

Best sunrise: Sierra Buttes, California, 2018.

Best sunset: Sisters Mirror Lake, Oregon, 2011.

Funniest moment: (tie) "A circus bear in North Cascades National Park," Washington, 2021, and "Almond Roca runaway feces," Belden, California, 2018.

Strangest find: A section of "Marston Mat," used in World War II to make temporary landing strips for planes, near Glacier Peak, Washington, 2021.

Best stop: Stehekin, Washington, 2021.

Best restaurant breakfast: (tie) Grumpy Bear's Retreat Restaurant & Tavern, Kennedy Meadows, 2022, and Paradise Valley Cafe, California, 2019.

Best restaurant brunch: Timberline Lodge, Oregon, 2014.

Best restaurant dinner: Annie Creek, Mazama Village, Oregon, 2011.

Best cheeseburger: Oak Shores Grocery near Lake Morena, California, 2019.

Favorite trees: Between Chicken Spring Lake and Crabtree Meadow, California, 2021.

Favorite lake: Mica, near Glacier Peak in the North Cascades, Washington, 2021.

Favorite creek or stream: (tie) Matterhorn Creek and Evolution Creek, High Sierra, 2014.

Favorite meadow: McClure Meadow, High Sierra, California (elevation 9,638 feet), 2014.

Favorite waterfall: Tunnel Falls, Eagle Creek, Oregon, 2011.

Favorite names of geographic features on trail: Opie Dildock Pass, Deadhead Lakes, Mount Frosty, Windy Joe Mountain, Three Fools Peak, Sky Pilot Pass, Lake Sally Ann, Cloudburst Canyon, Siberian Pass, Subway Cave, Screwdriver Creek, Doddlebug Gulch, Kettlebelly Trail Junction, Popcorn Spring, Kangaroo Spring, Cigar Lake, and Zigzag River.

Favorite name of a plant found on trail: Bigelow's Sneezeweed.

Favorite trail names of hikers in our "graduating" Class of 2022: Flying Sombrero, Bad Review, Sparkle Lizard, Kansas Express, Dirty Ziplock, and Talkie Walkie.

Best campsite for ambiance: Grider Creek, south of Seiad Valley, California, 2017.

For view: Evolution Lake, California, 2014.

Coolest PCT Hiker Family I met: Left to right, Lunch Box (Jillian Hatch), of Clovis, California; Bodega (Katie Ribble), of Orlando, Florida; Ghost (Paddy Lenane), of Australia; Eagle Eye (Vinura Perera), of Sri Lanka; and Pit Stop (Madison Murdock), of Tucson, Arizona. On our trip from Shasta City, California, to a trailhead near Mount Hood, we had—in Beach Boy terms—fun, fun, fun till I threatened to take their iPhones away.

For nostalgia: Echo Summit (where Dick Fosbury jumped), California, 2018.

Best water: High Sierra and North Cascades, Washington, 2014, 2021, 2022.

Worst water: Campo to Warner Springs, Agua Dulce to Walker Pass, California, 2022.

Worst mosquitoes: Freye Lake, Oregon, 2011.

Worst flies, especially horse flies: Snoqualmie Pass to Rainy Pass, Washington, 2021.

Windiest stretch: Tehachapi Pass, California, 2022.

Place from which I had best view: Glen Pass, California, 2014. (Would have said Mount Whitney but it isn't on the PCT.)

Best quote regarding the PCT experience: "There's just something about sleeping under the stars that renews the soul." (Starburst, Packer Lake Lodge, California, 2018.)

Straightest stretch of trail: The LA Aqueduct north of Hikertown, California, 2022.

Crookedest: (tie) Opie Dildock Pass, Three Sisters Wilderness, Oregon, 2011, and Golden Staircase, High Sierra, California, 2014.

Best sign: In the window of the general store in Seiad Valley, "Please do not drive vehicles into building."

Most inspirational hiker: Eagle Eye (Vinura Perera), from Sri Lanka, 2022.

Most inspirational animal: Chihuahua wearing lime green booties, Yosemite, 2019.

BEST LOGS WE SAWED

Zzzzzzzzzzzzzzzzzzzzzzzzzzzzzzzzzzzzzzzzzzzzzzzzzzzzzzzzzzzzzzzzzzzzzzzzzzzzzzzzzzzzzzzzzzzzzzzzzzzzzzzzzzzzzzzzzzzzzzzzzzzzz.

BIBLIOGRAPHY

Beck, Steve. *Trout-Fishing the John Muir Trail.* Portland: Frank Amato, 2000.

Berger, Karen, and Daniel R. Smith. *The Pacific Crest Trail: A Hiker's Companion.* Woodstock, Vermont: The Countryman Press, 2014.

Bright, William. *California Place Names: Their Origin and Meaning.* Berkeley and Los Angeles, California: University of California Press, 1998.

Essick, Peter (photography). *The Ansel Adams Wilderness.* Washington, D.C.: National Geographic, 2014.

Go, Benedict "Gentle Ben." *Pacific Crest Trail Data Book.* Birmingham, Alabama: Wilderness Press, 2022.

Gray, William R. *The Pacific Crest Trail.* Washington, D.C.: National Geographic Society, 1975.

Hazard, Joseph T., *Pacific Crest Trails.* Seattle, Washington: Superior Publishing Company, 1946.

Hughes, Rees, and Howard Shapiro, editors. *Crossing Paths: A Pacific Crest Trailside Reader.* Seattle: Mountaineers Books, 2022.

Jardine, Ray. *The PCT Hiker's Handbook.* 1992.

Jennings, Ken. *Maphead.* New York: Scribner, 2011.

Larabee, Mark, and Barney Scout Mann, *The Pacific Crest Trail: Exploring America's Wilderness Trail.* New York: Rizzoli, 2016.

Lighter, Justin. *Trail Tested: A Thru-Hiker's Guide to Ultralight Hiking and Backpacking.* Guilford, Connecticut and Helena, Montana: Falcon Guides, 2013.

Moor, Robert. *On Trails: An Exploration.* New York: Simon & Schuster, 2016.

Muir, John. *The Mountains of California.* Berkeley, California: Ten Speed Press, 1977.

Rose, Gene. *Mount Whitney: America's Mountain,* Oakland, California: Wildrose Books, 2016.

Salabert, Shawnté. *Hiking the Pacific Crest Trail: Southern California.* Seattle, Washington: Mountaineers Books, 2019.

Schaffer, Jeffrey P., and Andy Selters. *Pacific Crest Trail: From the California Border to the Canadian Border (Oregon & Washington).* Berkeley, California: Wilderness Press, 2007.

Wenk, Elizabeth. *John Muir Trail: The Essential Guide to Hiking America's Most Famous Trail.* Berkeley, California: Wilderness Press, 2008.

BOOK CLUB QUESTIONS

1. What was the most surprising thing you learned about the Pacific Crest Trail experience and why?

2. *Seven Summers* chronicles a journey that was often painful, difficult, and, at times, defeating. Did you ever sense that Welch and his brother-in-law might have "bitten off more than they could chew" and could have had a more satisfying experience by doing fewer miles?

3. Every chapter begins with an epigram of inspiration or insight. Pick one and explain why it's particularly meaningful to you.

4. The "hike your own hike" adage runs deep on the trail. But in regard to a couple taking their seven children, ages one to twelve, to the top of 14,505-foot Mount Whitney and returning in the dark, Welch isn't so sure. Should "to-each-his-own" be unrestricted or do we have a responsibility to question people's decisions—at times to their faces?

5. Welch's struggle, he wrote, was not only against nature but against himself. Which do you think vexed him most and why?

6. If you were hiking the PCT, would you prefer to thru-hike or section-hike. Why?

7. When deciding to swim to get into better shape, Welch had to overcome some reluctance. In the end, how did he rationalize his literally taking the plunge?

8. Name one person Welch met who inspired you. Why?

9. On three occasions, Bob and Glenn's 2011 agreement to allow one person the freedom to keep hiking should the other not be able to continue came into play: two days short of the Columbia River, Oregon, 2011; Muir Trail Ranch, California, 2014; and Wrightwood, California, 2021. Were you hiking the PCT, would you have had the same agreement? Why or why not?

11. If you were to hike the PCT, who would you choose for your partner and why?

12. Welch writes of a time Boy Scouts intruded on a quiet evening at a lake, only to find that Glenn welcomed them because "they were having the time of their lives." What's the lesson here?

12. One of the favorite people Welch meets on the trail is Starburst, the

New Zealand hiker who, at Packer Lake Lodge, tells of the beauty of the stars and the embarrassment of, well, pooping his pants. Why do you think Welch found Starburst so intriguing?

13. At times, Welch prays prayers and seems to get what he asks for—the ability to hike after badly spraining an ankle just before Muir Trail Ranch, 2014, and a ride into Tehachapi when the situation seemed hopeless, 2022. What do you think? Answered prayers? Coincidences? Something else?

14. In his "Trailhead Out: Final Thoughts on the Journey," Welch says adventure "comes in all sizes and shapes. It can be as active as hiking a 2,650-mile trail or as sedentary as holding a friend's hand during cancer treatments, as external as reaching out to somehow who's hurting or as internal as trying to quit an addiction." What does he suggest is the key to making an adventure happen?

15. A sub-theme of *Seven Seasons* is age. The author and his brother-in-law are two to three times older than most other PCT hikers. Did he overplay his card by pointing out this difference throughout the book or is acknowledging the difference a healthy way to gain perspective on ourselves and others?

16. Welch writes, "People are relational; nature is not. People sustain us; nature does not." Do you sense he believes you can pursue relationships and outdoor experiences with equal passion? Do you agree with him?

17. Did the book make you want to live life more adventurously, or confirm your contentedness to live with minimal risk—and to never dig a single cat hole, literal or otherwise, your entire life?

Thanks for joining me on the journey. Though I've tried to write an accurate book, I'm sure some errors slipped through. Please feel free to email or text them to me—contact info, next page—so I can keep making the book more accurate with each printing.

ABOUT THE AUTHOR

BOB WELCH is the author of more than two dozen books, including *American Nightingale*, an Oregon Book Award finalist and featured on ABC's "Good Morning America"; *The Wizard of Foz*, Track & Field Writers of America's 2019 Book of the Year; *Saving My Enemy: How Two WWII Soldiers Fought Against Each Other and Later Forged a Friendship That Saved Their Lives;* and *Cross Purposes: One Believer's Struggle to Reconcile the Peace of Christ with the Rage of the Far Right.*

A longtime columnist at *The Register-Guard* in Eugene, he twice won the National Society of Newspaper Columnists' "Best Writing" category, once for general columns and once for humor.

Welch worked at *The Register-Guard* full-time from 1989 to 2013. He earlier worked at *The Bulletin* in Bend, Oregon (1976-1983) and *The Journal-American* in Bellevue, Washington (1983-1989).

Articles of his have appeared in numerous magazines, including *Sports Illustrated, Reader's Digest* and *Los Angeles Times.*

Welch is founder/director of the Beachside Writers Workshop and is a former adjunct professor at the University of Oregon's School of Journalism and Communication. He is a 1976 graduate of the school.

Welch speaks from coast to coast, inspiring audiences on topics related to his books.

He lives in Eugene with wife Sally.

To contact him:

Email
bobwelch@bobwelchwriter.com

Text
541-517-3936

Snail Mail
PO Box 70785
Springfield, OR 97475

Twitter
@bob_welch23

OTHER WELCH BOOKS

2012 **Cascade Summer: My Adventure on Oregon's Pacific Crest Trail"**

Welch and Petersen's 2011 quest to hike "just Oregon."

"A beautiful story ... inspirational."—Eric Blehm, author of *The Last Season,* one of *Outside* magazine's Top 10 great adventure biographies

"Masterfully captures the PCT ... marvelous."—Lewis L. McArthur, editor, *Oregon Geographic Names*

To buy: bobwelchwriter.com

2004 **American Nightingale: The Story of Frances Slanger, Forgotten Heroine of Normandy**

The life and legacy of the first nurse to die in the European WWII theater

"I recommend you enrich your life and read this touching story."—James Bradley, author, *Flags of our Fathers* and *Flyboys*

To buy: amazon.com, barnesandnoble.com, independent book stores.

2018 **The Wizard of Foz: Dick Fosbury's One-Man High-Jump Revolution**

The Medford, Oregon, and Oregon State high jumper's unlikely rise to Olympic gold with a backward style that only the wild sixties could have produced.

"Welch does magnificent justice to it all."—Kenny Moore, former *Sports Illustrated* writer and Olympic marathoner

To buy: amazon.com or independent book stores. Audio book available.

2021 **Saving My Enemy: How Two WWII Soldiers Fought Against Each Other and Later Forged a Friendship That Saved Their Lives**

Band of Brothers hero Don Malarkey finds peace in an unlikely place: a German soldier, Fritz Engelbert. Unlike any WWII story ever written.

"A quintessential tale. Once read, never to be forgotten."—Erick Jendresen, lead writer of HBO's *Band of Brothers*

To buy: amazon.com, independent book stores. Audio book available.

2021 **Cross Purposes: One Believer's Struggle to Reconcile the Peace of Christ with the Rage of the Far Right**

Welch's personal memoir of a prayer he prayed and a political uprising that rocked his world as a Christian, leading him to redefine his faith.

"A well-researched case for the incompatibility between far-right conservatism and Christianity."—Kirkus Reviews

To buy: amazon.com, or bobwelchwriter.com. Audio book available.

2024 **Wonder Year: A Little Book of Hope Amid the Madness**

Against our country's political,social, and spiritual unhinging, longtime journalist Welch takes note of the everyday wonder he sees and hears from the people in the coffee shops, ball fields, beaches, barber shops, and trails he frequents. The call is to reawaken ourselves to the inspiration in our midst—and to realize that when we, too, inspire others, we can change the world.

ABOUT THE ARTIST

DON WHITE is an award-winning artist and author who grew up in the lush Columbia River Gorge. He enjoys portraiture and landscape painting. His ink illustrations can be found in his book, *A Plymouth Pilgrim.*

As a former minister, his faith always informs his creativity. He's a fan of Northwest forests, roots rock, and maple bars. His creative heroes include author John Steinbeck and artist George Inness.

Don writes and paints from his home in Oregon's Santiam Canyon.

His art and contact information can be found at donaldwaynewhite.com

Top: In May 1974, the foursome on its first double date, backpacking on Eagle Creek: left to right, Glenn Petersen, Ann Youngberg (Petersen), Sally Youngberg (Welch), and Bob Welch. Above: The foursome forty-nine years later, August 17, 2023, on Eagle Creek before Bob and Glenn embarked on a 123-mile trip south.

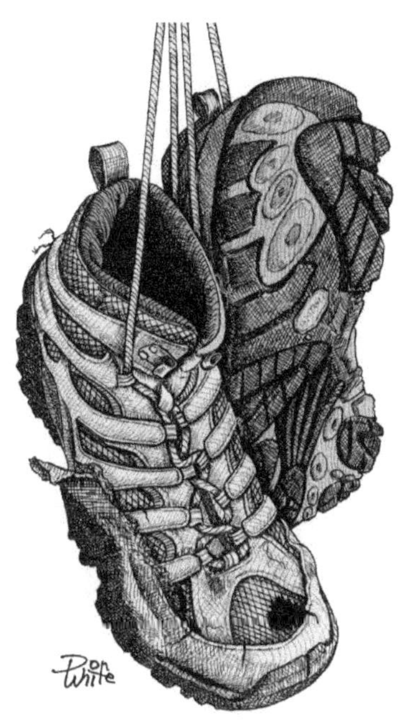

www.ingramcontent.com/pod-product-compliance
Lightning Source LLC
Chambersburg PA
CBHW022133020426
42334CB00015B/872

* 9 7 8 0 9 7 7 2 3 0 6 5 5 *